Praise for *Southern Fron*

"Inge and Piacentino's new collection, *Southern Frontier Humor*, brings forth a number of significant finds among humor writers of the Old Southwest. Just as exciting is the thoughtful introduction, couched in plain language, which shifts the focus of this collection more toward the literary aspects of the tradition, acknowledging debts to European sources and taking the authors as conscious writers rather than stodgy gentlemen-authors disparaging the lower classes. This approach makes real sense and continuity out of Southern Frontier humor as part of a larger literary stream. Several pieces from the Crockett Almanacs, including four representing women as central figures, make the point that this is literature as well as social commentary and females as well as males can show up as primary actors. This anthology is a valuable collection of the old and the new, and, helpfully, is just the right size for classroom use."

—David E. E. Sloane, author of *Mark Twain as a Literary Comedian* and *New Directions in American Humor*

"Necessarily shaped by the efforts of earlier scholars, this new anthology of humor out of the frontier South preserves the familiar names of nineteenth-century vernacular masters, even as it liberally expands the canon of what editors Inge and Piacentino beautifully argue is transgressive writing, 'the dominant strain of American humor.' *Southern Frontier Humor*, a rich repository of sketches by twenty-five hands, is a collection that reflects the varied investigative work of the past quarter-century—the tracking-down of little-known and forgotten authors in the newspaper fraternity that took its pleasure in vernacular writing, as well as interpretations of the writing by critics in assorted cultural disciplines. For teachers and students in the oncoming years, this anthology will become the most useful and reliable textual resource. Its bibliography alone, a convenience that some humor buffs might resist, guarantees that Inge and Piacentino are already the go-to guides for the twenty-first century."

—James H. Justus, author of *Fetching the Old Southwest: Humorous Writing from Longstreet to Twain*

"Throughout the volume, [the editors'] shrewd judgment and critical acumen are apparent, and the reader of this volume comes away with a balanced sense of both the range and the accomplishment of frontier humorists."

—Scott Romine, author of *The Real South: Southern Narrative in the Age of Cultural Reproduction*

"Scholars of American humor cannot fail to be intrigued and informed by this collection, which offers a new configuration of best writers from a fascinating era of our literary history. Teachers whose American literature or American studies courses include the antebellum period should consider this excellent anthology as a textbook."

—James E. Caron, author of *Mark Twain, Unsanctified Newspaper Reporter*

Southern
Frontier Humor
An Anthology

Southern
Frontier Humor
An Anthology

Edited by

M. Thomas Inge and Ed Piacentino

University of Missouri Press   Columbia and London

Copyright © 2010 by
The Curators of the University of Missouri
University of Missouri Press, Columbia, Missouri 65201
Printed and bound in the United States of America
All rights reserved
5 4 3 2 1   14 13 12 11 10

Library of Congress Cataloging-in-Publication Data

Southern frontier humor : an anthology / edited by M. Thomas Inge and Ed Piacentino.
    p. cm.
  Includes bibliographical references.
  ISBN 978-0-8262-1886-5 (pbk. : alk. paper)
  1. Southwest, Old—Literary collections. 2. American literature—Southwest, Old. 3. American wit and humor—Southwest, Old. 4. Southwest, Old—Humor. I. Inge, M. Thomas. II. Piacentino, Edward J., 1945-
  PS566.S48 2010
  810.8'0976—dc22
                    2010013725

∞™ This paper meets the requirements of the
American National Standard for Permanence of Paper
for Printed Library Materials, Z39.48, 1984.

Design and composition: Jennifer Cropp
Printing and binding: Thomson-Shore, Inc.
Typefaces: Minion, ReturnTo Earth, and Handwriting - Dakota

DEDERCATED
WIF THE SYMPERTHYS OVE THE ORTHUR,
TU THE MAN UR 'OMAN, HUEVER THEY BE,
WHAT DON'T READ THIS YERE BOOK.

—Sut Lovingood, *Yarns,* 1867

Contents

Acknowledgments	xi
Note on the Texts	xiii
Introduction: The Humor of the Old South; or, Transgression *He* Wrote	1

Augustus Baldwin Longstreet — 25
Georgia Theatrics	26
The Horse-Swap	28
The Fight	34

Solomon Franklin Smith — 43
A Tennessee Door-Keeper	44
The Consolate Widow	46
Speculation in Whiskers	47
An Unfinished Obituary	50

Charles F. M. Noland — 52
Pete Whetstone's Bear Hunt	53
Pete Whetstone's Last Frolic	54
Pete Whetstone and the Mail Boy	56

William Tappan Thompson — 57
The Major in an Embarrassing Situation	58
The Christmas Present in a Bag	62
The Runaway Match; or How the Schoolmaster Master Married a Fortune	65

George Washington Harris — 70
Sut Lovingood's Daddy, Acting Horse	71
Parson John Bullen's Lizards	75
Sut Lovingood Reports What Bob Dawson Said, After Marrying a Substitute	81
Well! Dad's Dead	85

Johnson Jones Hooper — 89
Simon Plays the "Snatch" Game — 91
Captain Suggs and Lieutenant Snipes "Court-Martial" Mrs. Haycock — 97
The Captain Attends a Camp-Meeting — 103

Joseph Glover Baldwin — 112
Simon Suggs, Jr. Esq., A Legal Biography — 113

Thomas Bangs Thorpe — 128
The Big Bear of Arkansas — 129
Letters from the Far West 2: Above the Yellow-Stone — 139
Letters from the Far West 7: Above the Head of Platte — 141
Letters from the Far West 10: Cross Timbers — 143
Letters from the Far West 12: Beyond the Cross Timbers — 146

Henry Clay Lewis — 149
A Tight Race Considerin' — 150
The Indefatigable Bear Hunter — 157
A Struggle for Life — 163

Samuel Langhorne Clemens — 171
The Celebrated Jumping Frog of Calaveras County — 172
The Story of the Old Ram — 176
Frescoes from the Past — 179

David Crockett — 191
Bear Hunting in Tennessee — 192
A Love Adventure and Uproarious Fight with a Stage Driver — 200

"*Riproarious Shemales*"
Legendary Women of the Crockett Almanacs — 202
Sal Fink, the Mississippi Screamer, How She Cooked Injuns — 203
Katy Goodgrit — 204
One of Crockett's Infant Children, Grinning Lightning at a Bear — 205
The Flower of Gum Swamp — 206

Joseph Gault — 207
A Constable Selling 'Coon Skins — 208
A Justice Commanding the Peace — 209
The Drunkard's Resurrection in His Morning Shroud — 210

James Edward Henry ———————————————————————— 212
My Man Dick   213

Hamilton C. Jones ————————————————————————— 224
Cousin Sally Dilliard   225
McAlpin's Trip to Charleston   227

William Gilmore Simms ———————————————————————— 230
Ephraim Bartlett, the Edisto Raftsman   231

Joseph M. Field ————————————————————————————— 241
A Lyncher's Own Story   242
Kicking a Yankee   247

Hardin E. Taliaferro ———————————————————————— 250
Uncle Davy Lane   251
Ride in a Peach Tree (Uncle Davy Lane)   252
The Pigeon Roost (Uncle Davy Lane)   254
Rev. Charles Gentry   255
The Origin of Whites (Rev. Charles Gentry)   256
Jonah and the Whale (Rev. Charles Gentry)   256

John S. Robb ——————————————————————————————— 258
Nettle Bottom Ball; or, Betsy Jones' Tumble in the Mush Pan 259
Fun with a "Bar." A Night Adventure on the Missouri   262

Christopher Mason Haile ——————————————————————— 268
Dear Chase   269
Pardon Jones on the Rio Grande   271

Adam Geiselhard Summer ———————————————————————— 275
Natural Angling, or Riding a Sturgeon   276

Orlando Benedict Mayer ———————————————————————— 281
The Innocent Cause, or How Snoring Broke Off a Match:
A Tale of Hog Killing Time   282

William C. Hall ————————————————————————————— 289
Mike Hooter's Bar Story   290
How Sally Hooter Got Snake-Bit: A Yazoo Sketch—No. IV   293

Francis James Robinson _____ 299
Lije Benadix 300
Old Jack C— 306

Marcus Lafayette Byrn _____ 319
Spontaneous Ebullition of a Drunkard 321
The Resurrection, or How to Take Up a Negro 323

Southern Frontier Humor: A Selected Bibliography 331

Acknowledgments

All those who have researched or written about southern humor are indebted to the groundbreaking anthology edited by William B. Dillingham and the late Hennig Cohen in 1964 for Houghton Mifflin, *Humor of the Old Southwest,* as well as its subsequent editions from the University of Georgia Press in 1975 and 1994. While Franklin J. Meine and Walter Blair had been collecting and writing about this material for over three decades, it was this anthology that largely helped define the field, sharpened the focus on the major figures, and provided critical guidance for all those scholars who followed in their footsteps. Only a few textbooks, originally created for classroom use, have had such a profound influence on criticism as practiced in its field—*Understanding Fiction* and *Understanding Poetry* by Cleanth Brooks and Robert Penn Warren come to mind. *Humor of the Old Southwest* belongs in such company.

Since the last edition appeared, a considerable body of scholarship has been published on the major figures and the place of the movement in American literary history. Additional writers who belong to the tradition have been identified, and more recent modes of criticism have been applied to their works. We have also seen the publication of a major critical statement on the subject, James H. Justus's magisterial *Fetching the Old Southwest: Humorous Writing from Longstreet to Twain,* by the University of Missouri Press in 2004. The time seems ripe to bring some fresh eyes and ideas to the subject and gather a new selection of texts.

Since Cohen and Dillingham did such a perceptive job of selecting stories and sketches the first time around, inevitably we have come up with some of the same pieces. We have, however, added some new ones and included several humorists only recently discovered. We have also included Samuel Langhorne Clemens (Mark Twain), the only major American author to contribute to and emerge from the movement. Our intention has not been to dismiss *Humor of the Old Southwest,* as it will continue to occupy its place of importance in critical history, but to continue the conversation which Cohen and Dillingham so eloquently started. We only hope to maintain the same level of discourse.

M. Thomas Inge would like to thank all of the lovers of American humor and the stories of Sut Lovingood who have encouraged and actively contributed to his research and understanding over the years. They are far too many to mention here, but each is well remembered. More specifically, gratitude is due to the administration of Randolph-Macon College for allowing him to serve as the Robert Emory Blackwell Professor of Humanities for twenty-six years now. President Robert R. Lindgren and Provost William W. Johnston kindly granted a sabbatical leave in 2008 so that the work could be finished. A Rashkind Grant awarded by the Committee on Faculty Development supported a part of the research. His research assistant, Rachelle Phillips, provided invaluable help. All of these have helped make this book possible, but finally it is Donaria who keeps everything in motion with a samba beat.

Ed Piacentino extends his gratitude and acknowledgment to High Point University, particularly Betsy Merricks and Stephanie Parsons of the reference staff of Smith Library for securing copies of some of the works featured in this anthology and Megumi Yoshioka, Mariko Ito, Ayumi Tahara, and Megumi Tanaka, English Department student assistants who helped to transcribe some of the texts. I would also like to thank Jim Kibler of the University of Georgia for biographical information on Adam G. Summer; David Estes of Loyola University of New Orleans for suggesting texts from Thomas Bangs Thorpe's "Letters from the Far West" that we have included in the anthology; Mark Keller of Middle Georgia College for responding to queries about William C. Hall; and Fritz Oehlschlaeger of Virginia Polytechnic Institute and State University for sharing insights about Joseph M. Field's "A Lyncher's Own Story." The Special Collections of Duke University Library provided a photocopy of Francis James Robinson's "Old Jack C—" for which I am deeply grateful. Finally, I wish to express special appreciation to my wife Diane for her constant love, continuous support and encouragement, and for reminding me that there is a life outside academe worth savoring.

Note on the Texts

Whenever possible, the editors have used the first available printings of the primary humorous works collected in this anthology as copy-texts As many of these works employ dialect, the editors have preserved the eccentricities of spelling, grammar, punctuation, and syntax of the originals since such corruptions often contribute to their humor. In a few instances, blatant typographical errors, probably printers' miscues, have been silently corrected and omissions emendated. We also added quotation marks in some texts to assure clarity. Following each author head note, we have identified the sources for the texts we have used.

Southern
Frontier Humor
An Anthology

Introduction

The Humor of the Old South; or, Transgression *He* Wrote

The humor of the Old South, also known as Old Southwest or frontier humor, flourished between the 1830s and 1860s, most extensively in the lower South, encompassing the rural and frontier regions of Georgia, Alabama, Louisiana, Arkansas, Mississippi, Missouri, but also, though to a lesser extent, in several states in the upper South, most notably Tennessee and North and South Carolina. Although labeled by James H. Justus, the major literary historian of this genre, as "ephemeral writing,"[1] the humor of the Old South is not actually subliterary, as has sometimes been contended. Rather, as Justus also aptly notes, the works of the Southwest humorists are "imaginative constructs— distillations of people and events observed and reconstructions of dialect and speech mannerisms overheard. . . . They are not source materials, but a literary legacy in their own right."[2]

Many antecedents and intertexts may have inspired southern frontier humor. Among the principal analogues are: William Byrd's Dividing Line histories; Ebenezer Cook's humorously satiric poem *The Sot-Weed Factor* (1708); the comic eclogues of William Henry Timrod; selections from James Kirke Paulding's *Letters from the South* (1817), which recount performative antics between a batteauxman and a wagoner, "half-horse, half-alligator" characters who attempt to out-brag one another and a tall-talish account of a rattlesnake with a large fish-like fin on his back; the widely popular stories of Washington Irving, "The Legend of Sleepy Hollow" and "Rip Van Winkle"; the folkloric Jack tales of the southern Appalachians; Rudolph Raspe's Baron Munchausen tales (initially published as *Baron Munchausen's Narrative of His Marvelous Travels and Campaigns,* 1785); Mason Locke Weems's "Awful History of Young Dred Drake" (*The Drunkard's Looking Glass,* 1812), which captures the robust energy, staged bravado, and amusing tall talk common to fight scenes on the southern frontier in the early nineteenth century; Henry Junius Nott's

"Biographical Sketch of Thomas Singularity" from *Novelettes of a Traveller* (1834), a work characterized by exaggerated and incongruous descriptions of a ludicrous nature and by the graphic and comical portrayal of the con artist; the sporting sketches found in early nineteenth-century British periodicals such as the *London Sporting Magazine* and *Bell's Life in London;* and the wide popularity of Down East humor, which also featured rustics and colloquial discourse.

Some of the defining features of the humor of the Old South are the prominence of plain folk—lower-class rustics, backwoodsmen, and other marginal types, some of whom may be disreputable–as the principal players in the action. In addition, the situations depicted tend to be outlandish and sometimes bizarre, and the folk characters are given extensive voice, speaking in a colorful vernacular discourse. Moreover, the humorists favor the dialect of the vernacular speakers over the formal English of genteel characters, the latter usually relegated to the tale's or sketch's frame and consigned to the periphery. And finally, exaggeration, sometimes carried into vulgarity and crudity, takes precedence over subtlety and innuendo, and entertainment always supersedes moral instruction.

The men (and it is not surprising that the writers were all men considering the subject matter) who wrote humorous sketches, mock letters, turf reports and tall tales featuring rustic characters and their free-wheeling ways, were not professional authors and in only a few rare cases did any of them aspire to be. Rather, they considered themselves writers by avocation. Always white and most often professionals, they worked as doctors, lawyers, judges, newspaper editors, ministers, government officials, theater managers, and actors. Yet the imaginative quality of some of their humorous pieces is not only engagingly impressive but also reflective of the socio-historical culture of the time and place. Despite their imaginative enlargements, their humorous works exhibit uniformity and as such provide, as Justus notes, a "reliable index to the social and cultural actualities of the lower South." Many scholars who have studied the humor of the Old South agree that it represents a "protorealism," delineating, "more or less faithfully, the grittier surfaces of antebellum life in the dialectal idioms heard in the margins and backwoods of the lower South."[3]

Neither is the humor of the Old South a genre rarely studied nor one that has waned significantly, even 170 years after its inception. Beginning with the pioneering scholarship of Franklin J. Meine, Walter Blair, John Q. Anderson, and Milton Rickels, and continued by their successors, including the editors of this volume and others cited here, antebellum southern humor has been given "legitimacy in the academy."[4] In *Tales of the Southwest* (1930), Meine noted that this humor was "distinctly and peculiarly Southern; and it was provincial, wholly local";[5] and seventy-four years later, John M. Grammer perceived southwestern humor as having an "ambiguous status: it is a lowborn literature that occasionally finds itself in polite company" and as being reflective of change, the "humor appear[ing] in the Southwestern narrative when wilderness disappears [and] occupy[ing], formally the *place* of wilderness: humor often becomes the lawless presence which by tugging against the civilizing imperatives of culture and morality, generates conflict in the stories."[6]

A form of comic journalism, antebellum southern humor was chiefly a newspaper event, many of the sketches, tall tales, turf reports, mock-autobiographies, almanac pieces, mock letters, and mock sermons initially published in southern newspapers such as the Milledgeville *Southern Recorder,* Augusta *State Rights Sentinel,* New Orleans *Picayune,* St. Louis *Reveille,* New Orleans *Delta,* Columbia *South Carolinian,* Lafayette *East Alabamian,* and Montgomery (Alabama) *Mail;* and in literary and sporting magazines such as the *Southern Literary Messenger,* the *Magnolia,* and *Russell's Magazine.* Due to the exchange system, many of these newspaper sketches were reprinted throughout the antebellum print world, therefore enabling an impressively widespread circulation.

But the most prominent venue for southern humor was a New York sporting weekly, the *Spirit of the Times* (1831–1861). Edited by William T. Porter, who persuaded many southern correspondents to submit their humorous pieces, the *Spirit* published and reprinted hundreds of humorous materials by known, anonymous, and pseudonymous authors, thereby providing national exposure for many amateur writers who otherwise would have remained unknown. Initially modeled on *Bell's Life in London,* a periodical that featured sketches on horse races, hunts, fishing, and the adventures of travelers, the *Spirit,* in the early years of its existence, reprinted many sketches from English sporting magazines as well as encouraged contributions on similar topics from American correspondents, hoping to appeal to the interests of gentlemen sportsmen. Writing in the February 18, 1837, issue, Porter indicated that the *Spirit* was "designed to promote the views and interests of but an infinitesimal division of those classes of society composing the great mass. . . . we are addressing ourselves to gentlemen of standing, wealth, and intelligence—the very corinthian columns of the community."[7] However, by 1856, when the circulation of the *Spirit* had increased considerably, many of the readers, Norris W. Yates has noted, "belong[ed] to a new and larger economic social class."[8]

Among the *Spirit*'s southern contributors who have been identified were: William P. Brannon, Joseph M. Field (Everpoint), Matthew E. Field (Phazma), Christopher M. Haile (Pardon Jones), William C. Hall, George Washington Harris (Mr. Free, Sugartail), Johnson Jones Hooper, Phillip B. January, George Wilkins Kendall, Henry Clay Lewis (Madison Tensas), Alexander McNutt (The Turkey Runner), Thomas Kirkman, Charles Fenton Mercer Noland (N. of Arkansas, Pete Whetstone), John S. Robb (Solitaire), Adam Geiselhard Summer, William Tappan Thompson, and Thomas Bangs Thorpe (The Bee Hunter).

Lauded as the father of the "Big Bear School" of humorous writing, Porter promoted the rough-shod brand of southern frontier comic sketches and tales, a reaction, Norris W. Yates argues, to the "bleak and crabbed aspects of New England morality, its academic garb, its rigid dogmatism and harsh judgments on human nature."[9] According to Lorne Fienberg, "the *Spirit*'s significance as a comic periodical" can be attributed to "the major writers to whom it offered first publication, and [to] the conventions of humorous writing and yarnspinning which its contributors introduced and refined over a thirty-year period."[10] In addition, Porter edited two anthologies of humorous sketches and tales collected from the *Spirit*: *The Big Bear of Arkansas and Other Sketches* (1845) and *A Quarter Race in Kentucky and Other Tales* (1846).

Some southern frontier humorists, however, who had enough sketches, tales, and letters for a collection, enjoyed increased exposure and notoriety through book publication. Those who authored or who were assisted in authoring books were: David Crockett (*A Narrative of the Life of David Crockett*, 1834, edited by Thomas Chilton); Augustus Baldwin Longstreet (*Georgia Scenes*, 1835), William Tappan Thompson (*Major Jones's Courtship*, 1844, and *The Chronicles of Pineville*, 1845), Johnson Jones Hooper (*Some Adventures of Captain Simon Suggs*, 1845); Joseph Gault (*Reports of Decisions in Justice's Courts, in the State of Georgia, from the Year of Our Lord 1820 to 1846*, 1846), Thomas Bangs Thorpe (*Mysteries of the Backwoods*, 1847); John S. Robb (*Streaks of Squatter Life and Far-West Scenes*, 1847), Joseph M. Field (*The Drama in Pokerville*, 1847), Henry Clay Lewis (*Odd Leaves from the Life of a Louisiana "Swamp Doctor,"* 1850), Joseph B. Cobb (*Mississippi Scenes; Or Sketches of Southern and Western Life*, 1851); Marcus Lafayette Byrn (*The Life and Adventures of an Arkansaw Doctor*, 1851); Joseph Glover Baldwin (*Flush Times of Alabama and Mississippi*, 1853), Francis James Robinson (*Kups of Kauphy*, 1853), Hardin Taliaferro (*Fisher's River [North Carolina] Scenes and Characters*, 1859), Kittrell J. Warren (*Ups and Downs of Wife Hunting*, 1861, and *Life and Public Services of an Army Straggler*, 1865), George Washington Harris (*Sut Lovingood: Yarns*, 1867), and Sol Smith (*Theatrical Management in the West and South for Thirty Years*, 1868).

While the sheer bulk of Old Southwest humor is extensive, interestingly the ongoing attention to this genre must be credited principally to Mark Twain, its primary American literary heir. As James M. Cox has pointed out, Twain, "whose genius was rooted in the tradition, made his way into the dominant culture and, by placating the moral sense in an absolutely disarming way, released more humor for more people than the old 'gentlemen' [newspaper humorists] would have believed possible."[11] Twain's sketches and tales, including apprenticeship pieces, "The Dandy Frightening the Squatter" and the letters of Thomas Jefferson Snodgrass, and his better-known works—"Jim Smiley and His Jumping Frog" (subsequently published under the title "The Notorious Jumping Frog of Calaveras County"), and some of the sketches from his travel book *Roughing It* (1872) such as "Jim Blaine and His Grandfather's Old Ram," "A Genuine Mexican Plug," "Buck Fanshaw's Funeral," and "A Buffalo Climbing a Tree"—all show the influence of the antebellum humorous genre. The culmination of the impact of the humor of the Old South on Twain was *Adventures of Huckleberry Finn* (1884), which includes many amusing and outlandish episodes reflecting Twain's assimilation and transformation of antebellum southern humorous materials. Some of the more memorable renditions of this earlier humorous tradition are: Pap Finn's drunken tirade against the government, the camp meeting swindle and various other deceptions of the backwoods con artists the Duke and the King, and the raftsmen's passage, originally intended for inclusion in the novel but published instead in *Life on the Mississippi* (1883). In Mark Twain's skillful hands, the materials of antebellum southern humor reached a postwar pinnacle of literary achievement.

In fact, the legacy of the humor of the Old South extended beyond Twain to some of his contemporaries. Charles Farrar Browne (Artemus Ward), David Ross Locke (Petroleum V. Nasby), Charles H. Smith (Bill Arp), and other popular literary comedians of the 1850s and 1860s who expressed their folksy humor in dialect; concocted their discourse to create amusing verbal effects through anticlimax, mixed metaphors, puns, and malapropisms; and published their pieces initially in newspapers and then as books, using letters, monologues, and anecdotes as had their southern predecessors. Also, "female local humorists" (as Kathryn McKee calls them)—Mary Noailles Murfree, Idora McClellan Moore, Sherwood Bonner, and Ruth McEnery Stuart— "reconfigured the male-dominated genre of Southwestern humor by peopling its landscapes with women ..., [thereby] authenticat[ing] the woman's real world" and "enter[ing] the world of masculine interests and narrative styles."[12] Male local colorists, too, particularly Joel Chandler Harris and Charles Waddell Chesnutt, used marginalized, dialect-speaking characters in the much same manner as Sut Lovingood and other yarn-spinning tricksters of southern backwoods humor were employed. Harris's Uncle Remus and Chesnutt's Uncle Julius successfully carry out deception both within and outside their narratives, their stories echoing some of the earmarks of their southern humorist forebears in characterization (especially the trickster figure and his victims), plot patterns, humorous exaggeration, and dialect.

While Lucinda MacKethan sees southern frontier humor as the inception of what she calls southern "resistance literature" and the men who created this genre as resisting and helping to transform the stolid norms of polite and respectable literature by "debunk[ing] notions of class privilege upon which much southern pastoral has been constructed," a better and more appropriate label for this brand of humor is transgressive.[13] By definition, transgressive means to exceed, "to pass over or go beyond." And by association and when applied to a humorous context, transgressive denotes the disruptive and chaotic, the effects of which may sometimes be extreme and bizarre. And in this transgressive context, the material of antebellum southern humor is, as James Justus notes, a "riot of conventions."[14] Such materials, Justus continues, "if they do not faithfully reflect their cultural milieu, they are assuredly refractions of it—distortions, as it were, in a cracked mirror."[15] As transgressors, southern frontier humorists challenged the high standards of antebellum romantic literature in the United States, supplanting or de-emphasizing sophisticated subject matter, genteel characterization, and stilted formal language, although some of their sketches include some of these materials. Moreover, these humorists helped to reconfigure the class, race, and gender politics that dominated antebellum American literature. As James Justus puts it, "Southwest humor is a body of writing that was born in the breakdown of hierarchical social relations and the (perceived) triumph of egalitarian ideals." [16]

As reflective of a greater democratization, the subjects the humorists featured often privileged masculine pursuits, pleasurable pastimes, and interests, some verging on the outlandish, vulgar, risqué, foolish, idiotic, and even disreputable or unlawful—all fitting under the broad umbrella of transgression. Hunting, fighting, camp meetings, roguish behavior, con artistry, horse racing, gambling, drinking and drunkenness, deception and trickery represent a major stock of the familiar fare of the humor of the Old South. In Lewis's "The Indefatigable Bear-Hunter," the one-legged hunter Mik-hoo-tah uses his wooden leg to subdue and kill a bear: "I got a fair lick! The way that bar's flesh giv in to the soft impresshuns of that leg war an honor to the mederkal perfeshun for having invented sich a weepun!"[17] The unprincipled Simon Suggs, in "Simon Gets a 'Soft Snap,'" cheats his father in a game of cards and subsequently in "The Captain Attends a Camp-Meeting" he feigns conversion and dupes the gullible people attending a revival out of their money by facetiously indicating he intends to use it for a charitable purpose. George Washington Harris's affable and roguish Sut Lovingood, an East Tennessee mountaineer, delights in preying on the foibles and vanity of authority figures as he does in "Parson John Bullen's Lizards" by releasing a bag of lizards up the preacher's pants' leg at a camp meeting, exposing his hypocritical and worldly ways. The hysterical preacher, practically naked, believing hell's serpents have possessed him, Sut graphically relates,

"lit on top ove, an' rite among the mos' pius par ove the congregashun. Ole Misses Chaneyberry sot wif her back tu the pulpit, sorter stoopin forrid. He lit a-stradil ove her long naik, a shuttin her up wif a snap, her head atwix her knees, like a shuttin up a jack-knife, an' he sot intu gittin away his levil durndest; he went in a heavy lumberin gallop, like a ole fat wagon hoss, skared at a locomotive."[18]

Horse racing (but not depicted in the expected way) is the subject of Lewis's "A Tight Race Considerin'" in which country woman Mrs. Hibbs, a "shrewd, active dame" and the "daughter of a man who had once owned a race horse,"[19] shamelessly disrobes while astride the family horse on the way to church in her enthusiasm to win a race against a circuit preacher. The sketch, one of "unplanned exhibitionism,"[20] concludes on a hilariously risqué note as the narrator, Mrs. Hibbs's son, describing the finish of the race, observes that his mother, pitched over the horse's head as it slams into the church's meeting house, flies through the window "like a lam for the sacryfise . . . mongst the mourners, leavin' her only garment flutterin' on a nail in the sash. The men shot their eyes and scrambled outen the house, an' the women gin mam so much of their close that they like to put themselves in the same fix."[21] Often featuring uninhibited characters like Mik-hoo-tah, Simon Suggs, Sut Lovingood, and Mrs. Hibbs who delight in defying or transgressing decent and respectable bounds of behavior, Lewis, Hooper, and Harris as well as many other southern frontier humorists delighted in showcasing the bizarre, extravagant, risqué, and embarrassingly unconventional.

Unrestrained exhibitionism of the sort that Sut Lovingood's trickery precipitates in the deserving Parson Bullen and that Mrs. Hibbs exhibits in Lewis's sketch occurs frequently in Old Southwest humor. This form of transgression is reflected most often in risqué or scatological references and outlandish and sometimes grotesque behavior of rustic backwoods characters who populate the tales and sketches. In William C. Hall's "How Sally Hooter Got Snake-Bit," for instance, Mike Hooter describes his daughter's exposed humiliation at a camp meeting, precipitated by her own vanity to look fashionable. In defiance of her father's objection, Sally straps a large sausage to her waist, which slides down her body as she starts dancing, making her erroneously think that something has crawled up her coat. Hall daringly converts this experience into a travesty characterized by sexual innuendo. Telling his friend John Potter to grab the supposed snake and "sling him h-llwards," to relieve his hysterical daughter, Hooter defuses an apparent dangerous moment, transforming it into a laughable one, the laughter in significant part generated by a physical comedy of errors and the implied sexual foreplay:

"Well, Potter he went and sorter felt uv him on the outside uv her coat, an' I pledge my word, he was the whappinest biggist reptile that ever scooted across er road!—I tell *you* if he warn't as big as my arm. . . . Well, when Potter diskiver that he helt the snake fast, he begin feelin' up for the reptile's tail, sorter like he didn't like to do it at fust, an' then sorter like he did. When it come to that, Sal she kinder turned red in the face and squirmed er bit, but 'twarn' no time for puttin' on quality airs then, and she stood it like er hoss. Well, Potter he kep er feelin' up, an' feelin' an' er feelin' up, sorter easy like, an' torreckly he felt somethin' in his han.' 'I've got him,' sez Potter, 'well I have, by jingo!'"[22]

Shock is likewise conveyed in southern frontier humor in the graphically grotesque renderings of bodily functions going awry. For instance, Joseph Gault in "The Drunkard's Resurrection in His Morning Shroud" features a grotesque situation of a drunkard's excessive vomiting. As Gaunt graphically observes:

I went on with W. and his son to the slaughter ground, and there lay B. He was a very red headed man, and had thrown up his late supper, stump water, and rat-tail, which made a pile as large as a quart bowl, and the jay birds, wood-peckers and old thrashers, were eating, fighting and frolicking over their early breakfast, derived from a late supper. Said W. here lies Alcohol; and laying his hand on B. said, arise Alcohol, you are not dead and are not ready to be buried yet, for you have no shroud but jay birds and wood-peckers.[23]

The boundaries of humor are similarly transgressed in Francis James Robinson's "Lije Benadix" when Lije, a low-class white, "incorrigibly lazy" and notable for having an "enormous appetite" and a "generous diet," suffers from extreme indigestion and constipation, the result of having consumed an excessive quantity of plums and cherries. In describing his symptoms, the doctor attending Lije observes: "'pulse slow and rather feeble, without fever, skin rather cooler than natural, vomiting about every half hour, ejecting a half pint of morbid secretion accumulated between the intervals of vomiting, abdomen enormously distended and as tight as a drumhead, and tongue but slightly coated.'"[24]

The grotesque in southern frontier humor sometimes extends well beyond the known boundaries for laughter, even the darker margins. Such is the case of Joseph M. Field's "A Lyncher's Own Story," a darkly comic piece about the lynching of an abolitionist who unsuccessfully tries to persuade a slave to run away. The teller, a colonel and victim of this abolitionist's scheme, reveals, apparently unintentionally, as he recounts this "little circumstance" of a lynching, that he is just as savage and passion-driven as his auditors, professed abolitionist-haters gathered in the steamboat's social hall. Though in the tale's preamble, the Colonel claims he is a calm and dispassionate gentleman and considers himself to be above barbarism, he, "as he tells the story," Cohen and Dillingham perceptively note, "hangs himself with his own rope."[25] This figurative hanging of the lyncher results from his showing that he is of the same despicable mold as his savage auditors. On one important level, "A Lyncher's Own Story" transgresses social hierarchies, undermining the apparent distinctions between the gentlemanly colonel narrator and his brutish auditors.[26] Near the end of his story, an "idea" comes into the Colonel's mind as the abolitionist slave stealer, now caught by the lynch mob, begs for his life, an "idea" to use his weight ("I am a heavy man, gentlemen") combined with that of an accomplice to bend the tree limb on which the culprit is to be hanged. In the tale's grim and sinister denouement, the Colonel's true savagery is revealed, the revelation condemning him both to his shocked and disgusted auditors and to the readers' contemptuous laughter.

"The culprit, gentlemen, took the *idea* sooner than any of the others, and his shrieks and ravings were dreadful—really dreadful! Another climbed after me, and, with the added weight, down we both came, half hid amongst the light boughs of the top, and the loose end of the rein [wrapped around his neck] was made fast in a second. *'One instant, for God's sake! I've got children!—for the sake of my soul!'*—a half-uttered scream, gentlemen, mingled with the rush of the boughs, as *we* dropped to the ground, and the nigger thief, with a jerk that *snapped his neck,* flew into the air, describing a half-circle as spanned by his halter, and swinging back to us again from the other side!"[27]

One of the most influential areas of transgression in the humor of the Old South, insofar as its impact on later American writing, is the emphasis on vernacular discourse, the colloquial-dialect speech of the plain folk that most writers in the genre privileged over highly stylized formal literary English. And it is this brand of discourse that Milton Rickels observes is the "most significant esthetic achievement" of southern frontier humor.[28] The widespread emphasis given to the voice of rustics, often uneducated in a formal sense, free-wheeling in their speech and actions, was a new and exciting development in American literature. The preeminence of dialect in antebellum southern humor represented, as James Justus has pointed out, an "impudent alternative discourse to respectable literature. It professes to be the bad boy among the Sunday schoolers, opposed to the decorous, the elegant, the genteel.... It shouts, it calls attention to itself, it celebrates lingual outlawry even at it honors the disdained and rough margins of American society."[29] Vernacular discourse was reenergizing, giving voice to marginalized characters who heretofore rarely spoke, or if they did, not in a voice authentic to their background and region of origin.

Washington Irving's "The Legend of Sleepy Hollow" (1820), the tale that inspired more individual sketches and tales of the Old Southwest humor genre than any other, manifests the ornate and polished language writers of Irving's generation typically employed in their descriptions of rustic life. In presenting his backwoodsman Brom Bones, the trickster and mischief maker who becomes the nemesis of the genteel and bookish schoolmaster Ichabod Crane, Irving does not allow Brom to speak in his own voice; rather, his omniscient narrator introduces him in consciously formal and eloquent diction:

He was broad-shouldered and double-jointed, with short curly black hair, and a bluff but not unpleasant countenance, having a mingled air of fun and arrogance. From his Herculean frame and great powers of limb he had received the nickname of BROM BONES, by which he was universally known. He was famed for great knowledge and skill in horsemanship, being as dexterous on horseback as a Tartar. He was foremost at all races and cock fights; and, with the ascendancy which bodily strength always acquires in rustic life, was the umpire in all disputes, setting his hat on one side, and giving his decisions with an air and tone that admitted of no gainsay or appeal. He was always ready for either a fight or a frolic; but had more mischief than ill-will in his composition; and with all his overbearing roughness, there was a strong dash of waggish good humor at bottom. He had three or four boon companions, who regarded him as their model, and at the head of whom he scoured the country, attending every scene of feud or merriment for miles round. In cold weather he was distinguished by a fur cap, surmounted with a flaunting fox's tail; and when the folks at a country gathering descried this well-known crest at a distance, whisking about among a squad of hard riders, they always stood by for a squall.[30]

In contrast, Sut Lovingood, the East Tennessee mountaineer created and favored by George Washington Harris, is characterized not only by his rowdy and disreputable behavior and crude and sometimes cruel trickery directed toward his deserving and hideous betters but also by his colorful, often hardly interrupted vernacular monologues that give vitality to the manner in which he describes events. In "Sut Lovingood's Daddy, Acting Horse" in the unrestrained description of his father, who foolishly assumes the function of plow horse when their family horse dies and who while plowing arouses a hornet's nest in a sassafras bush, Sut, who enjoys every moment of his dialogue, says:

"Gewhillitins! How he run: when he cum tu bushes, he'd clar the top ove em wif a squeal, gopher an' all. P'raps he tho't thar mout be anuther settilment ove ball ho'nets thar, an' hit wer sater tu go over than thru, an' quicker dun eny how. Every now an' then he'd fan the side ove his hed, fust wif wun fore laig an' then tuther, then he gin hissef a roun-handed slap what sounded like a waggin whip ontu the place whar the breech-bands tetches a hoss, a runnin all the time an' a-kerrien that ar gopher jis 'bout as fas' an' es hi frum the yeath es ever eny gopher wer kerried I'll swar."[31]

In giving the lovver-class white voice and narrative space, humorists of the Old South liberated American writing, enriching its texture with earthy dialect and hyperbolic descriptions. This form of verbal transgression, which Kenneth Cmiel calls "linguistic extravagance," began manifesting itself in the humorous writings in the 1830s and 1840s and represents the "entrance of democracy into the political imagination," the consequence being that "the concept of democracy, of rule by the people, itself implied that the language of the ruler had to adjust to the language of citizens."[32] In Mark Twain's *Adventures of Huckleberry Finn* dialect achieved a high level of literary artistry and legitimacy.

The humorists of the Old South were also transgressors in challenging some gender designators and constrictions of the time, giving white, rustic, and frontier men and women greater liberty of voice and a wider range and expanse of participation in humorous texts. Though as far as we know all these tales and sketches were written by men, sometimes the portrayal of women transcended the patriarchal perceptions of and attitudes about the female gender, particularly in regard to the defined and confined roles women should play. The popular conception of women in the antebellum period, known as the "cult of true womanhood," advocated that women should be pure, pious, submissive, silent, and humble and that they should restrict their participation to the domestic realm.[33] This image of women, embellished most frequently in heavy sentiment, was typically depicted in women's magazines, religious literature, and gift annuals of the time and served as a standard for female portraiture. Such women tended to be physically weak, dependent on men, sensitive (sometimes in excess), helpless, submissive, and suffering.[34]

One area antebellum southern humorists ridiculed in the portrayal of female characters was the notion of the angel in the household gone bad. In treating this script, the humorists portrayed women who failed to stay within the domestic bounds prescribed by nineteenth-century gender politics. Women who rebelled against such boundaries became sources of ongoing discontent and frustration to their husbands. One of the best sketches illustrating this kind of resistant woman is Augustus Baldwin Longstreet's "The Charming Creature as a Wife." Evelina Smith, the "charming creature," stands for female social propriety gone awry; her manner and behavior tantalize George, her husband, causing ongoing friction in their marriage, and in desiring to escape this frustration, George resorts to substance abuse, which leads to his self-destruction. As a wife, without domestic knowledge and training and the inclination and self-discipline to carry out orderly household management, Evelina is self-centered, flirtatious and permissive, and resistant to performing domestic duties. And as such, she is anathema to the brand of domestic harmony preferred by men and dictated by patriarchal culture of the time. Evelina, Longstreet shows, causes her husband's ruin, a pathetic man who "died the drunkard's death" through alcohol.[35]

At the other extreme is the excessively domesticated woman, the shrewish and domineering housewife who strives to keep her husband homebound and responsible, a prototype popularized in Washington Irving's "Rip Van Winkle" (1820). In American literature, it is such a figure against which men (and sometimes even adolescent boys) are solidly aligned and from which they seek relief and escape. One is reminded of the Widow Douglas, who, at the end of Twain's *The Adventures of Tom Sawyer* (1876) and again in *Adventures of Huckleberry Finn* (1884), stands for "civilization" from which Huck Finn seeks to "light out." As Gretchen Martin succinctly puts it, antebellum southern humorous tales and sketches "draw upon and develop the uniquely American desire of masculine escape."[36]

In their deconstruction of the nineteenth-century ideal of womanhood, southern humorists created a vigorous and electrifying female imaginary. In some of the anonymous sketches published between 1835 and 1856 in the Crockett Almanacs, one finds a large number of unconventionally dominant and individualized female characters, characters that Michael A. Lofaro calls "riproarious shemales," "inversion[s] of the then-current ideal of femininity, while still stressing their secondary status of women's traditional roles."[37] Lofaro also point's out that these women's "adventures and abilities are sometimes indistinguable from those of their male counterparts."[38] Characters such as Sally Ann Thunder, Lotty Ritchers, Sal Fink, Ann Whirlwind Crockett, and Thebeann Crockett exhibit traits comparable to their larger-than-life male counterparts—incredible physical strength, independence, courage, resilience, ingenuity, and capability. Other southwestern humorists would showcase similar unconventional and sometimes free-speaking women characters that transcend the narrow designations dictated by the "cult of true womanhood."

Other memorable outspoken and bold characters, through word, action, manner, and personality resist and transgress sentimentalized portraiture. Among them is Sol Smith's "The Consolate Widow," featuring an unconventional frontier woman who eschews sentimentality after her drunken husband has just been killed in a quarter-mile race when his horse runs into a building. To the widow, the real loss is not her husband but the gallon of whiskey wagered on the race. In her callously shocking response to the authorial narrator's query about her being the drunkard's wife, she curtly replies: "His throat's cut, that's all, by the 'tarnal sharp end of a log; and as for it's being *untimely,* I don't know but it's as well now as any time—*he warn't of much account, no how!*"[39]

The female trickster who resists and undercuts the patriarchal power structure and who manages to overpower the male is yet another clever, quick-witted, and independent woman that the humorists sometimes employ in playfully contesting and defying gender restraints and limitations. Sicily Burns in Harris's "Blown Up With Soda," Nettie Darling in Thompson's "The Runaway Match; or, How the Schoolmaster Married a Fortune" and Becky Wigfield in "Supposing a Case; or, The Long and Short of Rancy Cottem's Courtship," and Susy Elfins in O. B. Mayer's (Obadiah Haggis) "The Corn Cob Pipe: A Tale of the Comet of '43" represent notable examples of the female trickster type. Variations of Irving's "The Legend of Sleepy Hollow," "The Runaway Match" and "The Corn Cob Pipe," feature crafty and mischievous women who do not want to marry their suitors and who execute effective stratagems to thwart their suitors' designs. Thompson's Nettie, who is "sich a tormentin' little coquet that the boys was all afraid to court her downright yearnest,"[40] collaborates with her slave girl Silla and uses Silla to impersonate her, thereby deceiving her male suitor, Ebenezer Doolittle, a Yankee schoolmaster, into marrying her slave. Mayer's Susy collaborates with her backwoods boyfriend to undermine her father's authority regarding marriage by embarrassing and discrediting her would-be bridegroom, the schoolmaster-outsider Isom Jones.

Reconfiguration of male relationships reveals another way the southern frontier humorists challenged the strictures of gender. Masculinity and social class in the antebellum humor genre typically reflect the subversion of what Justus calls "hierarchical social relations"[41] And in this genre such hierarchies do not simply disappear; they are renegotiated and reaffirmed among men. On the southern frontier in the early nineteenth century, humorists typically interpreted and depicted masculinity, with the emphasis on individuality, physical strength and endurance, courage, boldness, cleverness, mobility, and like traits. Instead of stressing the segregation of male social classes, as Kenneth Lynn has posited, there was a bonding and commonness among men, Gretchen Martin argues, a shared understanding in matters pertaining to masculinity, such as "troublesome women, ideals of honor, and the adversarial relationship between man and nature, problems not specific to region, race, or economic definitions."[42] Through the depiction of social bonding, as shown in numerous humorous tales, men of distinct social classes "conspire in a united attack against the feminizing influences of America's more refined and polite literary productions, revitalizing the meaning of masculinity and providing an outlet for identifying and celebrating it," affording authors of the tales and their male readers "the opportunity to form a masculine community"[43] Such social interaction among men of different social and educational backgrounds can be found frequently in the genre of southern frontier humor, even among writers of patrician backgrounds and status. Such homosocial connections are established through a shared interest in male sports and manly activities such as hunting, shooting matches, fighting between men and wild animals; competitive tale swapping; drinking; and instigating and executing pranks. Longstreet's "The Shooting Match" (marksmanship contest), McNutt's "A Swim for a Deer" and Haile's "Dear Hunt" (hunting adventures); Lewis's "the Indefatigable Bear Hunter" (fight between man and beast); Simms's "Bald Head Bill Baldy" (tale swapping); Lewis's "A Tight Race Considerin'" (drinking); Harris's "Parson John

Bullen's Lizards" and "Sicily Burns's Wedding" (pranks)—all involve social interactions of plain folk characters and gentry (often the authorial narrator) on a level approaching some semblance of equality between social groups.

In "The Indefatigable Bear Hunter," for instance, there is a close homosocial bond between Dr. Madison Tensas, a frontier physician and the storyteller, and his patient, the hunter Mik-hoo-tah. In describing Mik, Tensas praises his unusual character, noting he was "one of these queer ones; gigantic in stature, uneducated, fearless of real danger, yet timorous as a child of superstitious perils," yet "beneath his rough exterior . . . ran a fiery current of high enthusiastic ambition."[44] Tensas goes on to celebrate the bear hunter's singular renown and talks fondly about the several times they have interacted. On the first occasion, Tensas recalls, he has come to see Mik to treat a wounded leg, injured in a personal encounter with a bear. It is the physician's understanding of and honesty with his patient that creates the trust between them so that the doctor can amputate Mik's leg which is beyond salvaging. Subsequently, in a "death struggle" with another bear, Mik unscrews his crude wooden prosthesis and uses it as a weapon to subdue the bear, an act that Tensas attentively listens to the hunter recount. Moreover, it becomes clear that Tensas genuinely admires Mik's courage and ingenuity, and perhaps even silently appreciates the bear hunter's enthusiastic appraisal of his accomplishment. Mik's embedded tale, his extended monologue of his encounter with the bear and his triumph with an unconventional weapon, seals his bond with Tensas and ends with an invitation to the doctor to share a drink with him, a customary act of male social bonding on the nineteenth-century southern frontier. Now considering Tensas as his friend and his desire for future bear hunts renewed, Mik feels comfortable asking the physician to make him a new prosthesis: "'Doc, les licker, it's a dry talk—when will you make me another leg? for bar-meat is not over plenty in the cabin, and I feel like tryin' another!'"[45]

Another notable social bond not only between men of different classes but also of different races is found in Hardin's Taliaferro's introductory frame to two folk sermons, "The Origin of the Whites" and "Jonah and the Whale," both of which he attributes to Charles Gentry. In Gentry, Taliaferro features an actual African American slave preacher, an affable and entertaining man whom the author knew when he was growing up in Surry County, North Carolina. Like Gentry, Taliaferro, a Baptist minister, expresses his sincere admiration for his fellow preacher, who, though a slave, is among "many good and clever negroes" he fondly remembered from his formative years. A "privileged character" and held in high esteem by his master and mistress, the Reverend Gentry did not always follow in his sermons the standard biblical interpretations; "a good deal of . . . [his theology] was quite original," Taliaferro writes.[46] While Gentry's beliefs and teachings deviate from authoritative scriptural sources, Taliaferro does not discredit or mock the preacher's transgressive folk explanations. Instead, he shows an appreciative understanding of and respect for Gentry's deviant theological views, actually defending them by expressing his vocal support:

> Naturalists have for ages been trying to account for the different forms and complexions of men. Some will have them to be of different races, not all descended from the same pair, Adam and Eve. Others contend that all have descended from the same pair, but climate and accidental causes have made the differences; hence Professor A and Professor B have their diverse theories and their disciples and admirers. When men leave the plain teachings of the Bible and go into vague speculations, one man's hypothesis is nearly as good as another's.[46]

Such toleration on Taliaferro's part is significant and bold, for it does strongly insinuate a shared bond between Gentry and himself, a connection transcending the widespread racist views of black inferiority reflective of the white antebellum racial hegemony.

Concerning the portrayal of minorities, texts in the southern frontier humorous genre have, for the most part, depicted marginalized characters, especially African Americans, in a demeaning and dehumanizing manner. In doing so, most of the writers in the genre catered to popular cultural presuppositions about race. James H. Penrod has accurately observed that antebellum southern humorists "emphasized the stereotyped traits that have prevailed in the minds of Americans for generations" and that the roles of blacks "were those of comic characters in support of the principal actors."[48]

Among these humorists, perhaps the worst offender of stereotyped portraiture of African Americans is George Washington Harris. In both "Frustrating a Funeral" and "Sut at a Negro Night Meeting," his prankster and storyteller Sut Lovingood incites fear, cruelty, pain, and pandemonium at an African American burial and camp meeting, respectively. Whereas in "Frustrating" Sut dupes and humiliates his victims by substituting a drunk black man for the deceased both to frighten the superstitious mourners and make them look like fools, in the camp meeting sketch, he employs his favorite painful prop of hornets to disrupt the gathering and make the blacks objects of ridicule. In describing the result of his ruthless prank and the chaos it creates in "Sut at a Negro Night Meeting," Sut shamelessly observes:

> "Thar wer lots ove niggers, mix'd heads an' tails in that orful straw-pile—heds, laigs, arms, feet, ainds ove bainches, bunches ove straw an' strings ove dartin ho'nets a-showin tharsefs a-top fur a moment; then sum uther things wud cum upermos'. Hit looked like forty-eight cords ove black cats a-fitin, wif turpentine a soakin in roun the roots ove all thar tails."[49]

Henry Clay Lewis, in several of the sketches in *Odd Leaves from the Life of a Louisiana Swamp Doctor,* also resorts to stereotyping African Americans, the humor deriving from the cruelty and suffering inflicted on black characters. To illustrate, in "Cupping on the Sternum," Lewis's medical apprentice Madison Tensas confesses his ignorance and demonstrates his ineptitude at the expense of a bewildered black woman when he scarificates her posterior rather than her breast area, the breast being the source of affliction, and inflicts on her unnecessary pain and distress. And in "How to Cure Fits," when all else fails in his attempt to cure an ailing black woman, presumably suffering from the "fits" (but actually feigning illness), Tensas, now a frontier doctor, uses what he calls a "new plan of treatment," the threat of throwing her off a bridge into the bayou followed by "a liberal flagellation, [which] complete[s] the cure," to enable her to return to work.[50]

Despite the prevalence of African American stereotyping in the humor of the Old South, several humorists did challenge prevalent antebellum racial hierarchies. Hardin E. Taliaferro, John S. Robb, James Edward Henry, Francis James Robinson, and even Lewis—all wrote sketches and tales resisting, contesting, and reconfiguring character portraiture influenced by biased racial attitudes and racist ideologies. Taliaferro's dialect folk sermon "Jonah and the Whale" is one of the most telling examples of transgression in African American portraiture in Old Southwest humor. In it, Taliaferro employs an embedded narrator, the Reverend Charles Gentry, an actual slave preacher from Surry County, North Carolina, whom he admired from his youth, to relate his own highly originally humorous but instructive version of the Jonah story. In giving Gentry a bold and subversive voice (Gentry actually speaks in the dialect of an untutored black), to concoct his own variation of Old Testament scripture, Taliaferro, whether consciously or not, offered an important life lesson in survival for his audience of slaves. Rather than being released from the whale's stomach by the intervention of God, as in the original biblical account, Jonah relies on his own practicality and invention, ingeniously using his sharp fingernails "ter claw and scratch the fish's paunch, 'tarmined to git out'n dar."[51] And Jonah successfully executes his escape, the whale regurgitating him and Jonah landing safely on the shore of the sea. Taliaferro unwittingly promotes racial subversion, his slave preacher given license to affirm independence, with Jonah serving as an object lesson of one who overcomes insurmountable odds and is an inspiration to the preacher's slave listeners.

Like "Jonah and the Whale," James Edward Henry's "My Man Dick" challenges the notion of white superiority, albeit within an amusing context. The title character Dick, the body servant of Tol Grinaway, is an affable rascal-prankster whose lies and underhanded actions unnerve and anger his master. In what becomes the principal pattern in the sketch, Dick's pranks and deceptive words repeatedly create embarrassing situations for his master, diminishing his social position and demonstrating his inability to manage and control his slave. Tol's ineptitude empowers Dick, allowing him to undermine the master-slave relationship, thereby subverting through his prankish transgressions the racial status quo.

The most prolific and daring exemplar in the treatment of racial transgressions in antebellum southern humor, however, and "one of the few Southern humorists to treat the black man in his fiction extensively and often without stereotype" is Henry Clay Lewis.[52] Though white and a southerner by adoption, Lewis, a Jew, may have felt socially marginalized and therefore may have shared a natural kinship with African American slaves. The author of six sketches featuring African American characters, Lewis not only employed humor centered on black suffering as we have seen previously, but also depicted humorous situations reflecting racial transgression and featuring black characters who, as Edwin T. Arnold notes, may relate to Lewis's alter ego literary persona Madison Tensas. According to Arnold, who views Lewis's alter ego within a psychological/psychoanalytic context, "each figure of blackness becomes more personal, more nearly a part of Tensas, because each is, essentially, a projection of those forces that normally lie hidden below the surface of reason but bide their time, awaiting the moment of revelation."[53] Of Lewis's works examining blackness, "The Struggle for Life" is his most perplexing, fanciful, and transgressive experiment in African American portraiture. In this harrowing sketch, Dr. Tensas encounters a black dwarf, whom he views as the "nearest resemblance to the ourang outang mixed with the devil that human eyes dwelt upon."[54] When Tensas gives the dwarf an excessive quantity of brandy, the slave becomes uncontrollably drunk and demands more, threatening Tensas and shouting at him: "D—n you, white man, I will kill you ef you don't give me more brandy!"[55] Subsequently, when Tensas refuses to comply, the dwarf physically attacks him, attempting to strangle him. Interestingly, Tensas comes to identify with his black assailant, equating blackness with the demonic elements within his own psyche. Believing that the dwarf has killed him but that he has been restored to life, smelling the odors of the burning flesh of the slave consumed by the campfire into which he has leaped, Tensas excitedly shouts: "Great God! can that disfigured half-consumed mass be my evil genius?"[56]

One other area of transgression that we need to address is unique, that is, the only migration of antebellum southern humor south of the U.S. South. To our knowledge, there is only one humorist who expanded the genre to include Mexico—Christopher Mason Haile. A native of Rhode Island and former U.S. Military Academy cadet who migrated to Louisiana in the late 1830s, Haile founded and edited a newspaper, and contributed numerous humorous epistles, principally to the New Orleans *Picayune,* under the pseudonym Pardon Jones. Between 1846 and 1848 Haile served as a special Mexican War correspondent for the *Picayune,* sending dispatches from the war front, but he also wrote humorous missives, featuring his persona Pardon Jones and the fictitious Dead Cow Brook Artillery Company composed of ragtag volunteers who were engaged in the war in Mexico. In the majority of these Mexican War letters, Haile makes fun of the behavior of these American volunteers, many of whom make fools of themselves, both through what they say and how they act. In various sketches, Pardon Jones, Haile's affable persona, accentuates the comical miscues of the bungling soldiers, including a slapstickish description of one who tries to steal a horse that he has neglected to untie, and ludicrous misadventures such as the failed attempts of a love-struck fool to romance Mexican women. In examining Americans in a cross-cultural engagement with Mexicans from a comic perspective, Haile broadened the subject matter and the geography of the humor of the Old South.

In challenging the prevalent genteel standards of antebellum culture and the conventions of literary romanticism, southern frontier humorists helped to transform the American literary landscape. They accomplished this by privileging the way of life of southern plain folk, rustics, and backwoodsmen (and women), showcasing their raw colloquial speech over Standard English and popularizing in print form the southern vernacular, thereby extending the range of American written discourse toward greater democratization. Moreover, these humorists transgressed the boundaries of race and gender in defying and sometimes undermining some of the familiar stereotypes associated with the portrayal of African Americans and women. In so doing they gave women and blacks (often slaves) more prominent and less demeaning roles and more assertive and effective voice in narratives. And in the case of the Mexican War letters of Haile's Pardon Jones, the humor of the Old South extended the territory of southern humor, carrying it beyond the familiar southern landscape and the southern provincial experience. In depicting American culture encountering that of Mexico, Haile's humorous letters demonstrated that the materials of southern humor could be successfully applied to the treatment of the intersection of two distinct cultures.

Yet it is as initiators of a transgressive strain in southern literature that the humorists of the Old Southwest had their most significant and most enduring impact. In addition to Mark Twain and his contemporaries, the legacy of antebellum southern humor has flowered in many modern and contemporary southern writers and in popular culture. In fact, the literary influence has been wide and extensive. Subjects, character types, and stylistic strategies employed first by the southern frontier humorists have been assimilated in William Faulkner, the most prominent legatee, and by many other writers who have drawn on this rich vein, notably Erskine Caldwell, Flannery O'Connor, Eudora

Welty, Woody Guthrie, Harry Crews, Guy Owen, William Price Fox, Donald Harington, Fred Chappell, Roy Blount, Jr., Mark Steadman, Barry Hannah Cormac McCarthy, Zora Neale Hurston, Ralph Ellison, Alice Walker, Ishmael Reed, and Yusef Komunyakaa. In popular culture, the influence includes the comic strips Al Capp's *Li'l Abner* and Billy De Beck's *Snuffy Smith;* both the sitcoms and films *The Beverly Hillbillies* and *The Dukes of Hazzard;* comic music videos such as Ray Stevens's "The Mississippi Revival" or pop songs like Johnny Horton's "The Battle of New Orleans"; and southern comedians Dave Gardner, Gamble Rogers, Jerry Clower, Andy Griffith, Justin Wilson, and Jeff Foxworthy. The widespread continuity between this older southern humor and the modern and contemporary varieties suggests that the tradition of Old Southwest humor not only has become but also continues to be the dominant strain of American humor. More recently and predictably, the ongoing tradition of southern frontier humor has found its way into cyberspace, a convenient and readily accessible "place for representing culture." [57] A liberal and democratic medium, the so-called "electronic frontier" (a term coined by Derek Alderman) consists of thousands of Web sites, with new ones emerging almost every day, featuring colorful rustics with narratives and jokes and cartoons about rednecks and hunting, fishing, games, drinking, religious experiences, boasting, deception, bawdry, and other subjects found in antebellum southern humor. What does all this mean? Perhaps the best answer may be found in a recent review of an essay collection exploring this legacy. In it, James Justus perceptively points out that "the great advantage of humorists has always been the company they keep," a statement that speaks volumes about the durable and far-reaching (and ongoing) influence) of the humorists of the Old South. [58]

Notes

1. James H. Justus, *Fetching the Old Southwest: Humorous Writing from Longstreet to Twain*, 6.
2. Ibid., 16.
3. James H. Justus, introduction to *The Humor of the Old South*, ed. M. Thomas Inge and Edward J. Piacentino, 3.
4. Justus, *Fetching the Old Southwest*, 575.
5. Franklin J. Meine, "Tall Tales of the Southwest," in *The Frontier Humorists: Critical Views*, ed. M. Thomas Inge, 16.
6. John M. Grammer, "Southwestern Humor," in *A Companion to Literature and Culture of the American South*, ed. Richard Gray and Owen Robinson, 371, 375.
7. Quoted in Lorne Fienberg, "*Spirit of the Times*," in *American Humor Magazines and Comic Periodicals*, ed. David E. E. Sloane, 272.
8. Norris W. Yates, *William T. Porter and the "Spirit of the Times": A Study of the Big Bear School of Humor*, 21.
9. Ibid., 5.
10. Fienberg, "*Spirit of the Times*," 273.

11. James M. Cox, "Humor of the Old Southwest," in *The Comic Imagination in American Literature* ed. Louis D. Rubin, Jr., 112.
12. Kathryn Burgess McKee, "Writing in a Different Direction: Women Writers and the Tradition of Southwestern Humor, 1875–1910," 25.
13. Lucinda MacKethan "Southwestern Humor: The Beginnings of Grit Lit." *Southern Spaces* March 1, 2004. www. southernspaces.org/content/2004 (accessed February 20, 2006).
14. Justus, *Fetching the Old Southwest*, 14.
15. Ibid., 15.
16. Ibid., 569.
17. Henry Clay Lewis, "The Indefatigable Bear Hunter," in *Odd Leaves from the Life of a Louisiana Swamp Doctor*, 175.
18. George Washington Harris, "Parson John Bullen's Lizards," in *Sut Lovingood's Yarns*, ed. M. Thomas Inge, 56.
19. Henry Clay Lewis, "A Tight Race Considerin,'" in *Odd Leaves*, 43.
20. Walter Blair, "Henry Clay Lewis," in *The Mirth of the Nation: America's Great Dialect Humor,* ed. Walter Blair and Raven McDavid, 60.
21. Lewis, "A Tight Race," 53.
22. William C. Hall, "How Sally Hooter Got Snake Bit," *Humor of the Old Southwest*, 373–74.
23. Joseph Gault, "The Drunkard's Morning Shroud," in *Joseph Gault's Fifth Edition of His Reports: Entitled A Coat of Many Colors*, 15.
24. Francis James Robinson, "Lije Benadix," in *Humor of the Old Southwest*, ed. Hennig Cohen and William B. Dillingham, 380–81.
25. Hennig Cohen and William B. Dillingham, "Introduction," *Humor of the Old Southwest*, ed. Cohen and Dillingham, xxxvii.
26. Some of the insights about the Colonel's self-damnation were shared by Fritz Oehlschlaeger in an e-mail to Ed Piacentino.
27. Joseph M. Field, "A Lyncher's Own Story," in *Old Southwest Humor from the St. Louis Reveille, 1844–1850,* ed. Fritz Oehlschlaeger, 232–32.
28. Milton Rickels, "The Grotesque Body of Southwestern Humor," *Critical Essays on American Humor,* ed. William Bedford Clark and W. Craig Turner, 155.
29. Justus, *Fetching the Old Southwest*, 14.
30. Washington Irving, "The Legend of Sleepy Hollow," in *The Heath Anthology of American Literature, Vol B, Early Nineteenth Century 1800–1860,* ed. Paul Lauter, et al., 2172–73.
31. George Washington Harris, "Sut Lovingood's Daddy, Acting Horse," in *Sut Lovingood Yarns,* 36.
32. Kenneth Cmiel, "'A Broad Fluid Language of Democracy': Discovering the American Idiom," 19–20.
33. Barbara Welter, "The Cult of True Womanhood: 1820–1860," 152.
34. Cynthia Griffin Wolff, "A Mirror for Men: Stereotypes of Women in Literature," 210–12.
35. Augustus Baldwin Longstreet, "The Charming Creature as a Wife," in *Augustus Baldwin Longstreet's Georgia Scenes Completed,* ed. David Rachels, 73.
36. Gretchen Martin, "The Prison House of Gender: Masculine Confinement and Escape in Southwest Humor," in *The Humor of the Old South*, 95–96.
37. Michael A. Lofaro, "A Taste of the Tales," *Davy Crockett's Riproarious Shemales and Sentimental Sisters: Women's Tall Tales from the Crockett Almanacs (1835–1856),* 3.
38. Michael A. Lofaro, "Riproarious Shemales: Legendary Women in the Tall Tale World of the Davy Crockett Almanacs," in *Crockett at Two Hundred: New Perspectives on the Man and the Myth,* ed. Michael A. Lofaro and Joe Cummings, 135.
39. Solomon Franklin Smith, "The Consolate Widow," *Humor of the Old Southwest.* 74.
40. William Tappan Thompson, "The Runaway Match; Or, How the Schoolmaster Married a Fortune," in *Major Jones's Courtship: Detailed, with Other Scenes, Incidents, and Ad-

ventures, in A Series of Letters By Himself. Revised and Enlarged. To Which Are Added Thirteen Humorous Sketches, 215.
  41. Justus, *Fetching the Old Southwest,* 569.
  42. Martin, "The Prison House of Gender," 87.
  43. Ibid., 88.
  44. Lewis, "The Indefatigable Bear Hunter" *Odd Leaves,*164.
  45. Ibid., 175.
  46. Hardin E. Taliaferro, *Fisher's River (North Carolina) Scenes and Characters, By "Skitt" "Who Was Raised Thar,"* 186–87.
  47. Ibid., 87.
  48. James H Penrod, "Minority Groups in Old Southern Humor," 121, 128.
  49. George Washington Harris, "Sut at a Negro Night Meeting," in *Sut Lovingood's Yarns,* 134.
  50. Henry Clay Lewis, "How to Cure Fits," *Odd Leaves,* 191.
  51. Hardin E. Taliaferro, "Jonah and the Whale," in *Fisher's River,* 191.
  52. Alan H. Rose, "Blackness in the Fantastic World of Old Southwestern Humor," in *Demonic Vision: Racial Fantasy and Southern Fiction,* 26.
  53. Edwin T. Arnold, introduction to *Odd Leaves from the Life of a Louisiana Swamp Doctor,* by Henry Clay Lewis, xxxi.
  54. Henry Clay Lewis, "The Struggle for Life," in *Odd Leaves,* 192–93.
  55. Ibid., 198.
  56. Ibid., 202.
  57. Derek H. Alderman, "Rednecks, Bluenecks, and Hickphonics : Southern Humor on the Internet," in *The Enduring Legacy of Old Southwest Humor,* ed. Ed Piacentino, 264.
  58. James H. Justus, "The Company We Keep," 141.

Works Cited

Alderman, Derek H. "Rednecks, Bluenecks, and Hickphonics: Southern Humor on the Internet." In *The Enduring Legacy of Old Southwest Humor,* edited by Ed Piacentino, 261–78. Baton Rouge: Louisiana State University Press, 2006.
Arnold, Edwin T. Introduction to *Odd Leaves from the Life of a Louisiana Swamp Doctor* by Henry Clay Lewis, xi-xlviii. Baton Rouge: Louisiana State University Press, 1997.
Blair, Walter. "Henry Clay Lewis." In *The Mirth of the Nation: America's Great Dialect Humor,* edited by Walter Blair and Raven McDavid. Minneapolis: University of Minnesota Press, 1983.
Cmiel, Kenneth. "'A Broad Fluid Language of Democracy': Discovering the American Idiom." *Journal of American History* 79.3 (1992): 913–36.
Cohen, Hennig, and William B. Dillingham. Introduction to *Humor of the Old Southwest.* 3rd ed. Edited by Cohen and Dillingham, xv-xl. Athens: University of Georgia Press, 1994.
Cox, James M. "Humor of the Old Southwest." In *The Comic Imagination in American Literature,* edited by Louis D. Rubin, Jr., 101–12. New Brunswick, NJ: Rutgers Press, 1973.
Field, Joseph M. "A Lyncher's Own Story." In *Old Southwest Humor from the* St. Louis Reveille, *1844–1850,* edited by Fritz Oehlschlaeger, 226–32. Columbia: University of Missouri Press, 1990.
Fienberg, Lorne. "*Spirit of the Times.*" In *American Humor Magazines and Comic Periodicals,* edited David E. E. Sloane, 271–78. Westport, CT: Greenwood Press, 1987.
Gault, Joseph. "The Drunkard's Resurrection in His Mourning Shroud." In *Joseph Gault's Fifth Edition of His Reports: Entitled A Coat of Many Colors,* 14–16. Americus, GA: Americus Law Book Co., 1902.

Grammer, John M. "Southwestern Humor." In *A Companion to the Literature and Culture of the American South,* edited by Richard Gray and Owen Robinson, 370–87. Oxford, UK: Blackwell Publishing, 2004.

Hall, William C. "How Sally Hooter Got Snake-Bit." In *Humor of the Old Southwest,* edited by Hennig Cohen and Richard B. Dillingham, 369–75. Athens: University of Georgia Press, 1994.

Harris, George Washington. "Frustrating a Funeral." In *Sut Lovingood's Yarns,* edited by M. Thomas Inge, 163–73. New Haven, CT: College and University Press, 1966.

——. "Parson John Bullen's Lizards." In *Sut Lovingood's Yarns,* 51–58.

——. "Sut Lovingood's Daddy, Acting Horse." In *Sut Lovingood's Yarns,* 33–38.

——. "Sut at a Negro Night Meeting," In *Sut Lovingood's Yarns,* 128–37

[Henry, James Edward]. "My Man Dick." *Southern Literary Journal* February 1837 420–29.

Inge, M. Thomas, and Edward J. Piacentino, eds. *The Humor of the Old South.* Lexington: University Press of Kentucky, 2001.

——. Introduction. *The Humor of the Old South,* edited by M. Thomas Inge and Edward J. Piacentino, 1–10. Lexington: University Press of Kentucky, 2001.

Irving, Washington. "The Legend of Sleepy Hollow." In *The Heath Anthology of American Literature, Vol B, Early Nineteenth Century 1800–1860,* edited by Paul Lauter et al. 2165–84. Boston: Houghton Mifflin, 2006.

Justus, James H. "The Company We Keep." *Studies in American Humor* 3.16 (2007): 133–41.

——. *Fetching the Old Southwest: Humorous Writing from Longstreet to Twain.* Columbia: University of Missouri Press, 2004.

Lewis, Henry Clay. "Cupping on the Sternum." In *Louisiana Swamp Doctor: The Life and Writings of Henry Clay Lewis,* edited by John Q. Anderson, 89–91. Baton Rouge: Louisiana State University Press, 1962.

——. *Odd Leaves from the Life of a Louisiana Swamp Doctor.* Baton Rouge: Louisiana State University Press, 1997.

——. "How to Cure Fits." In *Odd Leaves,* 189–91.

——. "The Indefatigable Bear Hunter." *Odd Leaves,* 164–75.

——. "A Struggle for Life." *Odd Leaves,* 92–203.

——. "A Tight Race Considerin.'" *Odd Leaves,* 42–53.

Lofaro, Michael A. "A Taste of the Tales." *Davy Crockett's Riproarious Shemales and Sentimental Sisters: Women's Tall Tales from the Crockett Almanacs (1835–1856),* edited by Michael A. Lofaro,1–4. Mechanicsburg, PA: Stackpole Books, 2001.

——. "Riproarious Shemales: Legendary Women in the Tall Tale World of the Davy Crockett Almanacs." *Crockett at Two Hundred: New Perspectives on the Man and the Myth,* edited by Michael A. Lofaro and Joe Cummings, 114–52. Knoxville: University of Tennessee Press, 1989.

Longstreet, Augustus Baldwin. "The Charming Creature as a Wife." In *Augustus Baldwin Longstreet's Georgia Scenes Completed,* edited by David Rachels, 53–73. Athens: University of Georgia Press, 1998.

McKee, Kathryn Burgess. "Writing in a Different Direction: Women Writers and the Tradition of Southwestern Humor, 1875–1910." Ph.D. diss., University of North Carolina at Chapel Hill, 1996.

MacKethan, Lucinda. "Southwestern Humor: The Beginnings of Grit Lit." *Southern Spaces,* March 1, 2004. http://www.southernspaces.org/content/2004 (accessed February 20 2006).

Martin, Gretchen. "The Prison House of Gender: Masculine Confinement and Escape in Southwest Humor." In *The Humor of the Old South,* 87–100.

Mayer, O. B. [Obadiah Haggis]. "The Corn Cob Pipe: A Tale of the Comet of '43." In *Fireside Tales: Stories of the Old Dutch Fork,* edited by James Everett Kibler, Jr., 117–31. Columbia, SC: Dutch Fork Press, 1984.

Meine, Franklin J. "Tall Tales of the Southwest." In *The Frontier Humorists: Critical Views*, edited by M. Thomas Inge, 15–31. Hamden, CT: Archon, 1975.

Penrod, James H. "Minority Groups in Old Southern Humor." *Southern Folklore Quarterly* 22 (1958): 121–28.

Piacentino, Ed, ed. *The Enduring Legacy of Old Southwest Humor*. Baton Rouge: Louisiana State University Press, 2006.

Rickles, Milton. "The Grotesque Body of Southwestern Humor." In *Critical Essays on American Humor*, edited by William Bedford Clark and W. Craig Turner, 155–66. Boston: G. K. Hall, 1984.

Robinson, Francis James. "Lije Benadix." In *Humor of the Old Southwest*, .

Rose, Alan H. "Blackness in the Fantastic World of Old Southwestern Humor." *Demonic Vision: Racial Fantasy and Southern* , 19–38. Hamden, CT: Archon, 1976.

Smith, Solomon Franklin. "The Consolate Widow." In *Humor of the Old Southwest*, 73–74.

Taliaferro, Hardin E. *Fisher's River (North Carolina) Scenes and Characters, By "Skitt," Who Was Raised Thar*," 189–92. New York: Harper & Brothers, 1859.

Thompson, William Tappan. "The Runaway Match; or, How the Schoolmaster Married a Fortune." *Major Jones's Courtship: Detailed, with Other Scenes, Incidents, and Adventures, in A Series of Letters By Himself. Revised and Enlarged. To Which Are Added Thirteen Humorous Sketches*, 214–21. New York: D. Appleton, 1872.

———. "Supposing a Case; or, The Long and Short of Rancy Cottem's Courtship." *Major Jones's Courtship*, 191–98.

Welter, Barbara. "The Cult of True Womanhood: 1820–1860." *American Quarterly* 18 (1966): 151–74.

Wolff, Cynthia Griffin. "A Mirror for Men: Stereotypes of Women in Literature." *Massachusetts Review* 13 (1972): 205–18.

Yates, Norris W. *William T. Porter and the "Spirit of the Times": A Study of the Big Bear School of Humor*. New York: Arno Press, 1977.

Augustus Baldwin Longstreet (1790-1870)

Although the larger body of humorous writing in the Old Southwest arose almost simultaneously as a groundswell in several parts of the region, the man usually nominated as the father of the movement is Augustus Baldwin Longstreet. The eldest of the major figures in years, he first began to publish his sketches in 1833 and 1834 in local Georgia newspapers, the Milledgeville *Southern Recorder* and his own paper, the Augusta *State Rights' Sentinel.* By bringing them together into a book in 1835 called *Georgia Scenes, Characters, Incidents, &c., in the First Half Century of the Republic,* he not only established most of the major themes, content, and comic strategies of the writing to follow, but called the attention of the South and the nation to the power and appeal of local narrative and regional culture. When Edgar Allan Poe reviewed the book for the March 1836 *Southern Literary Messenger,* he found himself laughing out loud more "immoderately" than he ever had over any other book. He summarized or quoted at length every single story and promised to "give it a niche in our library as a sure omen of better days for the literature of the South."

Like so many of the writers who would follow in his footsteps, however, Longstreet was accomplished in many fields of endeavor and never meant to be a litterateur. Born in 1870 in Augusta, Georgia, he attended Yale College, read law, and was admitted to the bar in 1815, but his interests led him into politics and public service. He was elected a judge, owned a newspaper, was ordained a Methodist minister, and served as president of several educational institutions—Emory College, Centenary College in Louisiana, the University of Mississippi, and South Carolina College. As a strict anti-abolitionist, he stood up against the attacks on slavery by the northern branch of his church and wrote a series of pro-slavery letters collected in 1847 as a book, *A Voice from the South.* Longstreet moved his family to Mississippi during the Civil War and watched federal troops burn his home before he retired to Georgia. He spent his latter years in Bible study and writing defenses of states' rights advocate John C. Calhoun.

Although he tried his hand at a novel and wrote a good many more sketches and tales, nothing else Longstreet did brought him the fame and attention that attended *Georgia Scenes*. He understood how educated language and ordinary speech could be brought into comic conjunction to good effect, how a sophisticated narrator could be used to gain satiric distance on rowdy and racy backwoods life, and how reality itself often provides the antic sensibility with sufficient material for engaging fiction. Longstreet created two distinct fictional voices through which he narrated his tales, Lyman Hall and Abram Baldwin, both educated but markedly different in attitude. He noted in the preface for his book that "Hall is the writer of those sketches in which men appear as the principal actors, and Baldwin of those in which women are the prominent figures." But as the careful reader learns, things are more subtle than that, with one speaker more rational and distant and the other more emotional and sensitive. All of these devices influenced not only the humorous writers to come but anticipated the realistic movement in American fiction later in the century. These are among the reasons that *Georgia Scenes* saw eleven editions published between 1835 and 1897 and several more with critical introductions in the twentieth century.

Texts: "Georgia Theatrics," "The Horse-Swap," and "The Fight," from *Georgia Scenes, Characters, Incidents, &c., in the First Half of the Century of the Republic* (Augusta, GA: State Rights Office, 1835).

Georgia Theatrics

If my memory fail me not, the 10th of June, 1809 found me, at about 11 o'clock in the forenoon, ascending a long and gentle slope in what was called "The Dark Corner" of Lincoln. I believe it took its name from the moral darkness which reigned over that portion of the county at the time of which I am speaking. If in this point of view it was but a shade darker than the rest of the county, it was inconceivably dark. If any man can name a trick or sin which had not been committed at the time of which I am speaking, in the very focus of all the county's illumination (Lincolnton), he must himself be the most inventive of the tricky, and the very Judas of sinners. Since that time, however (all humour aside), Lincoln has become a living proof "that light shineth in darkness." Could I venture to mingle the solemn with the ludicrous, even for the purposes of honourable contrast, I could adduce from this county instances of the most numerous and wonderful transitions, from vice and folly to virtue and holiness, which have ever, perhaps, been witnessed since the days of the apostolic ministry. So much, lest it should be thought by some that what I am about to relate is characteristic of the county in which it occurred.

Whatever may be said of the *moral* condition of the Dark Corner at the time just mentioned, its *natural* condition was anything but dark. It smiled in all the charms of spring; and spring borrowed a new charm from its undulating grounds, its luxuriant woodlands, its sportive streams, its vocal birds, and its blushing flowers.

Rapt with the enchantment of the season and the scenery around me, I was slowly rising the slope, when I was startled by loud, profane, and boisterous voices, which seemed to proceed from a thick covert of undergrowth about two hundred yards in the advance of me, and about one hundred to the right of my road.

"You kin, kin you?"

"Yes, I kin, and am able to do it! Boo-oo-oo! Oh, wake snakes, and walk your chalks! Brimstone and—fire! Don't hold me, Nick Stoval! The fight's made up, and let's go at it.—My soul if I don't jump down his throat, and gallop every chitterling out of him before you can say 'quit!'"

"Now, Nick, don't hold him! Jist let the wild-cat come, and I'll tame him. Ned'll see me a fair fight; won't you, Ned?"

"Oh, yes; I'll see you a fair fight, blast my old shoes if I don't."

"That's sufficient, as Tom Haynes said when he saw the elephant. Now let him come."

Thus they went on, with countless oaths interspersed, which I dare not even hint at, and with much that I could not distinctly hear.

In Mercy's name! thought I, what band of ruffians has selected this holy season and this heavenly retreat for such Pandaemonian riots! I quickened my gait, and had come nearly opposite to the thick grove whence the noise proceeded, when my eye caught indistinctly, and at intervals, through the foliage of the dwarf-oaks and hickories which intervened, glimpses of a man or men, who seemed to be in a violent struggle; and I could occasionally catch those deep-drawn, emphatic oaths which men in conflict utter when they deal blows. I dismounted, and hurried to the spot with all speed. I had overcome about half the space which separated it from me, when I saw the combatants come to the ground, and, after a short struggle, I saw the uppermost one (for I could not see the other) make a heavy plunge with both his thumbs, and at the same instant I heard a cry in the accent of keenest torture, "Enough! My eye's out!"

I was so completely horrorstruck, that I stood transfixed for a moment to the spot where the cry met me. The accomplices in the hellish deed which had been perpetrated had all fled at my approach; at least I supposed so, for they were not to be seen.

"Now, blast your corn-shucking soul," said the victor (a youth about eighteen years old) as he rose from the ground, "come cutt'n your shines 'bout me agin, next time I come to the Courthouse, will you! Get your owl-eye in agin if you can!"

At this moment he saw me for the first time. He looked excessively embarrassed, and was moving off, when I called to him, in a tone emboldened by the sacredness of my office and the iniquity of his crime, "Come back, you brute! and assist me in relieving your fellow-mortal whom you have ruined forever!"

My rudeness subdued his embarrassment in an instant; and, with a taunting curl of the nose, he replied, "You needn't kick before you're spurr'd. There a'nt nobody there, nor ha'nt been nother. I was jist seein' how I could 'a' *fout*." So saying, he bounded to his plough, which stood in the corner of the fence about fifty yards beyond the battle ground.

And, would you believe it, gentle reader! his report was true. All that I had heard and seen was nothing more nor less than a Lincoln rehearsal; in which the youth who had just left me had played all the parts of all the characters in a Courthouse fight.

I went to the ground from which he had risen, and there were the two prints of his two thumbs, plunged up to the balls in the mellow earth, about the distance of a man's eyes apart; and the ground around was broken up as if two stags had been engaged upon it. —HALL.

The Horse-Swap

During the session of the Supreme Court, in the village of——, about three weeks ago, when a number of people were collected in the principal street of the village, I observed a young man riding up and down the street, as I supposed, in a violent passion. He galloped this way, then that, and then the other; spurred his horse to one group of citizens, then to another; then dashed off at half speed, as if fleeing from danger; and, suddenly checking his horse, returned first in a pace, then in a trot, and then in a canter. While he was performing these various evolutions, he cursed, swore, whooped, screamed, and tossed himself in every attitude which man could assume on horseback. In short, he *cavorted* most magnanimously (a term which, in our tongue, expresses all that I have described, and a little more), and seemed to be setting all creation at defiance. As I like to see all that is passing, I determined to take a position a little nearer to him, and to ascertain, if possible, what it was that affected him so sensibly. Accordingly, I approached a crowd before which he had stopped for a moment, and examined it with the strictest scrutiny. But I could see nothing in it that seemed to have anything to do with the cavorter. Every man appeared to be in good humour, and all minding their own business. Not one so much as noticed the principal figure. Still he went on. After a semicolon pause, which my appearance seemed to produce (for he eyed me closely as I approached), he fetched a whoop, and swore that "he could out-swap any live man, woman, or child that ever walked these hills, or that ever straddled horseflesh since the days of old daddy Adam. Stranger," said he to me, "did you ever see the *Yallow Blossom* from Jasper?"

"No," said I, "but I have often heard of him."

"I'm the boy," continued he; "perhaps a *leetle*, jist a *leetle*, of the best man at a horse-swap that ever trod shoe-leather."

I began to feel my situation a little awkward, when I was relieved by a man somewhat advanced in years, who stepped up and began to survey the "*Yallow Blossom's*" horse with much apparent interest. This drew the rider's attention, and he turned the conversation from me to the stranger.

"Well, my old coon," said he, "do you want to swap *hosses?*"

"Why, I don't know," replied the stranger; "I believe I've a beast I'd trade with you for that one, if you like him."

"Well, fetch up your nag, my old cock; you're just the lark I wanted to get hold of. I am perhaps a *leetle,* just a *leetle,* of the best man at a horse-swap that ever stole *cracklins* out of his mammy's fat gourd. Where's your *hoss?*"

"I'll bring him presently; but I want to examine your horse a little."

"Oh! look at him," said the Blossom, alighting and hitting him a cut; "look at him. He's the best piece of *hoss*flesh in the thirteen united univarsal worlds. There's no sort o' mistake in little Bullet. He can pick up miles on his feet, and fling 'em behind him as fast as the next man's *hoss,* I don't care where he comes from. And he can keep at it as long as the sun can shine without resting."

During this harangue, little Bullet looked as if he understood it all, believed it, and was ready at any moment to verify it. He was a horse of goodly countenance, rather expressive of vigilance than fire; though an unnatural appearance of fierceness was thrown into it by the loss of his ears, which had been cropped pretty close to his head. Nature had done but little for Bullet's head and neck; but he managed, in a great measure, to hide their defects by bowing perpetually. He had obviously suffered severely for corn; but if ribs and hip bones had not disclosed the fact, *he* never would have done it; for he was in all respects as cheerful and happy as if he commanded all the corn-cribs and fodderstacks in Georgia. His height was about twelve hands; but as his shape partook somewhat of that of the giraffe, his haunches stood much lower. They were short, strait, peaked, and concave. Bullet's tail, however, made amends for all his defects. All that the artist could do to beautify it had been done; and all that horse could do to compliment the artist, Bullet did. His tail was nicked in superior style, and exhibited the line of beauty in so many directions, that it could not fail to hit the most fastidious taste in some of them. From the root it dropped into a graceful festoon; then rose in a handsome curve; then resumed its first direction; and then mounted suddenly upward like a cypress knee to a perpendicular of about two and a half inches. The whole had a careless and bewitching inclination to the right. Bullet obviously knew where his beauty lay, and took all occasions to display it to the best advantage. If a stick cracked, or if any one moved suddenly about him, or coughed, or hawked, or spoke a little louder than common, up went Bullet's tail like lightning; and if the *going up* did not please, the *coming down* must of necessity, for it was as different from the other movement as was its direction. The first was a bold and rapid flight upward, usually to an angle of forty-five degrees. In this position he kept his interesting appendage until he satisfied himself that nothing in particular was to be done; when he commenced dropping it by half inches, in second beats, then in triple time, then faster and shorter, and faster and shorter still, until it finally died away imperceptibly into its natural position. If I might compare sights to sounds, I should say its *settling* was more like the note of a locust than anything else in nature.

Either from native sprightliness of disposition, from uncontrollable activity, or from an unconquerable habit of removing flies by the stamping of the feet, Bullet never stood still; but always kept up a gentle fly-scaring movement of his limbs, which was peculiarly interesting.

"I tell you, man," proceeded the Yellow Blossom, "he's the best live hoss that ever trod the grit of Georgia. Bob Smart knows the hoss. Come here, Bob, and mount this hoss, and show Bullet's motions." Here Bullet bristled up, and looked as if he had been hunting for Bob all day long, and had just found him. Bob sprang on his back. "Boo-oo-oo!" said Bob, with a fluttering noise of the lips; and away went Bullet, as if in a quarter race, with all his beauties spread in handsome style.

"Now fetch him back," said Blossom. Bullet turned and came in pretty much as he went out.

"Now trot him by." Bullet reduced his tail to "*customary;*" sidled to right and left airily, and exhibited at least three varieties of trot in the short space of fifty yards.

"Make him pace!" Bob commenced twitching the bridle and kicking at the same time. These inconsistent movements obviously (and most naturally) disconcerted Bullet; for it was impossible for him to learn, from them, whether he was supposed to proceed or stand still. He started to trot, and was told that wouldn't do. He attempted a canter, and was checked again. He stopped, and was urged to go on. Bullet now rushed into the wide field of experiment, and struck out a gait of his own, that completely turned the tables upon his rider, and certainly deserved a patent. It seemed to have derived its elements from the jig, the minuet, and the cotillion. If it was not a pace, it certainly had *pace* in it, and no man would venture to call it anything else; so it passed off to the satisfaction of the owner.

"Walk him!" Bullet was now at home again; and he walked as if money was staked on him.

The stranger, whose name, I afterward learned, was Peter Ketch, having examined Bullet to his heart's content, ordered his son Neddy to go and bring up Kit. Neddy soon appeared upon Kit; a well-formed sorrel of the middle size, and in good order. His *tout ensemble* threw Bullet entirely in the shade, though a glance was sufficient to satisfy any one that Bullet had the decided advantage of him in point of intellect.

"Why, man," said Blossom, "do you bring such a hoss as that to trade for Bullet? Oh, I see no notion of trading."

"Ride him off, Neddy!" said Peter. Kit put off at a handsome lope.

"Trot him back!" Kit came in at a long, sweeping trot, and stopped suddenly at the crowd.

"Well," said Blossom, "let me look at him; maybe he'll do to plough."

"Examine him!" said Peter, taking hold of the bridle close to the mouth; "he's nothing but a tacky. He an't as *pretty* a horse as Bullet, I know; but he'll do. Start 'em together for a hundred and fifty *mile;* and if Kit an't twenty mile ahead of him at the coming out, any man may take Kit for nothing. But he's a monstrous mean horse, gentlemen; any man may see that. He's the scariest horse, too, you ever saw. He won't do to hunt on, no how. Stranger, will you let Neddy have your rifle to shoot off him? Lay the rifle between his ears, Neddy, and shoot at the blaze in that stump. Tell me when his head is high enough."

Ned fired, and hit the blaze; and Kit did not move a hair's breadth.

"Neddy, take a couple of sticks, and beat on that hogshead at Kit's tail."

Ned made a tremendous rattling, at which Bullet took fright, broke his bridle, and dashed off in grand style; and would have stopped all farther negotiations by going home in disgust, had not a traveler arrested him and brought him back; but Kit did not move.

"I tell you, gentlemen," continued Peter, "he's the scariest horse you ever saw. He an't as gentle as Bullet, but he won't do any harm if you watch him. Shall I put him in a cart, gig, or wagon for you, stranger? He'll cut the same capers there he does here. He's a monstrous mean horse."

During all this time Blossom was examining him with the nicest scrutiny. Having examined his frame and limbs, he now looked at his eyes.

"He's got a curious look out of his eyes," said Blossom.

"Oh yes, sir," said Peter, "just as blind as a bat. Blind horses always have clear eyes. Make a motion at his eyes, if you please, sir."

Blossom did so, and Kit threw up his head rather as if something pricked him under the chin than as if fearing a blow. Blossom repeated the experiment, and Kit jerked back in considerable astonishment.

"Stone blind, you see, gentlemen," proceeded Peter; "but he's just as good to travel of a dark night as if he had eyes."

"Blame my buttons," said Blossom, "if I like them eyes."

"No," said Peter, "nor I neither. I'd rather have 'em made of diamonds; but they'll do, if they don't show as much white as Bullet's."

"Well," said Blossom, "make a pass at me."

"No," said Peter; "you made the banter, now make your pass."

"Well, I'm never afraid to price my hosses. You must give me twenty-five dollars boot."

"Oh, certainly; say fifty, and my saddle and bridle in. Here, Neddy, my son, take away daddy's horse."

"Well," said Blossom, "I've made my pass, now you make yours."

"I'm for short talk in a horse-swap, and therefore always tell a gentleman at once what I mean to do. You must give me ten dollars."

Blossom swore absolutely, roundly, and profanely, that he would never give boot.

"Well," said Peter, "I didn't care about trading; but you cut such high shines, that I thought I'd like to back you out, and I've done it. Gentlemen, you see I've brought him to a hack."

"Come, old man," said Blossom, "I've been joking with you. I begin to think you do want to trade; therefore, give me five dollars and take Bullet. I'd rather lose ten dollars any time than not make a trade, though I hate to fling away a good hoss."

"Well," said Peter, "I'll be as clever as you are. Just put the five dollars on Bullet's back, and hand him over; it's a trade."

Blossom swore again, as roundly as before, that he would not give boot; and, said he, "Bullet wouldn't hold five dollars on his back, no how. But, as I bantered you, if you say an even swap, here's at you."

"I told you," said Peter, "I'd be as clever as you; therefore, here goes two dollars more, just for trade sake. Give me three dollars, and it's a bargain."

Blossom repeated his former assertion; and here the parties stood for a long time, and the by-standers (for many were now collected) began to taunt both parties. After some time, however, it was pretty unanimously decided that the old man had backed Blossom out.

At length Blossom swore he "never would be backed out for three dollars after bantering a man;" and, accordingly, they closed the trade.

"Now," said Blossom, as he handed Peter the three dollars, "I'm a man that, when he makes a bad trade, makes the most of it until he can make a better. I'm for no rues and after-claps."

"That's just my way," said Peter; "I never goes to law to mend my bargains."

"Ah, you're the kind of boy I love to trade with. Here's your hoss, old man. Take the saddle and bridle off him, and I'll strip yours; but lift up the blanket easy from Bullet's back, for he's a mighty tender-backed hoss."

The old man removed the saddle, but the blanket stuck fast. He attempted to raise it, and Bullet bowed himself, switched his tail, danced a little and gave signs of biting.

"Don't hurt him, old man," said Blossom, archly; "take it off easy. I am, perhaps, a leetle of the best man at a horse-swap that ever catched a coon."

Peter continued to pull at the blanket more and more roughly, and Bullet became more and more *cavortish:* insomuch that, when the blanket came off, he had reached the *kicking* point in good earnest.

The removal of the blanket disclosed a sore on Bullet's backbone that seemed to have defied all medical skill. It measured six full inches in length and four in breadth, and had as many features as Bullet had motions. My heart sickened at the sight; and I felt that the brute who had been riding him in that situation deserved the halter.

The prevailing feeling, however, was that of mirth. The laugh became loud and general at the old man's expense, and rustic witticisms were liberally bestowed upon him and his late purchase. These, Blossom continued to provoke by various remarks. He asked the old man if "he thought Bullet would let five dollars lie on his back." He declared most seriously that he had owned that horse three months, and had never discovered before that he had a sore back, "or he never should have thought of trading him," &c., &c.

The old man bore it all with the most philosophic composure. He evinced no astonishment at his late discovery, and made no replies. But his son Neddy had not disciplined his feelings quite so well. His eyes opened wider and wider from the first to the last pull of the blanket; and, when the whole sore burst upon his view, astonishment and fright seemed to contend for the mastery of his countenance. As the blanket disappeared, he stuck his hands in his breeches pockets, heaved a deep sigh, and lapsed into a profound revery, from which he was only roused by the cuts at his father. He bore them as long as he could; and, when he could contain himself no longer, he began, with a certain wildness of expression which gave a peculiar interest to what he uttered: "His back's mighty bad off; but dod drot my soul if he's put it to daddy as bad as he thinks he has, for old Kit's both blind and *deef,* I'll be dod drot if he eint."

"The devil he is," said Blossom.

"Yes dod drot my soul if he *eint.* You walk him, and see if he *eint.* His eyes don't look like it; but he'd *just as leve go agin* the house with you, or in a ditch, as any how. Now you go try him." The laugh was now turned on Blossom; and many rushed to test the fidelity of the little boy's report. A few experiments established its truth beyond controversy.

"Neddy," said the old man, "you oughtn't to try and make people discontented with their things. Stranger, don't mind what the little boy says. If you can only get Kit rid of them little failings, you'll find him all sorts of a horse. You are a *leetle* the best man at a horse-swap that I ever got hold of; but don't fool away Kit. Come, Neddy, my son, let's be moving; the stranger seems to be getting snappish." —HALL.

The Fight

In the younger days of the Republic there lived in the county of——two men, who were admitted on all hands to be the very *best men* in the county; which, in the Georgia vocabulary, means they could flog any other two men in the county. Each, through many a hard-fought battle, had acquired the mastery of his own battalion; but they lived on opposite sides of the Courthouse, and in different battalions: consequently, they were but seldom thrown together. When they met, however, they were always very friendly; indeed, at their first interview, they seemed to conceive a wonderful attachment to each other, which rather increased than diminished as they became better acquainted; so that, but for the circumstance which I am about to mention, the question, which had been a thousand times asked, "Which is the best man, Billy Stallions (Stallings) or Bob Durham?" would probably never have been answered.

Billy ruled the upper battalion, and Bob the lower. The former measured six feet and an inch in his stockings, and, without a single pound of cumbrous flesh about him, weighed a hundred and eighty. The latter was an inch shorter than his rival, and ten pounds lighter; but he was much the most active of the two. In running and jumping he had but few equals in the county; and in wrestling, not one. In other respects they were nearly equal. Both were admirable specimens of human nature in its finest form. Billy's victories had generally been achieved by the tremendous power of his blows, one of which had often proved decisive of his battles; Bob's, by his adroitness in bringing his adversary to the ground. This advantage he had never failed to gain at the onset, and, when gained, he never failed to improve it to the defeat of his adversary. These points of difference have involved the reader in a doubt as to the probable issue of a contest between them. It was not so, however, with the two battalions. Neither had the least difficulty in determining the point by the most natural and irresistible deductions *a priori;* and though, by the same course of reasoning, they arrived at directly opposite conclusions, neither felt its confidence in the least shaken by this circumstance. The upper battalion swore "that Billy only wanted one lick at him to knock his heart, liver, and lights out of him; and if he got two at him, he'd knock him into a cocked hat." The lower battalion retorted, "that he wouldn't have time to double his fist before Bob would put his head where his feet ought to be; and that, by the time he hit the ground, the meat would fly off his face so quick, that people would think it was shook off by the fall." These disputes often led to the *argumentum ad hominem,* but with such equality of success on both sides as to leave the main question just where they found it. They usually ended, however, in the common way, with a bet; and many a quart of old Jamaica (whiskey had not then supplanted rum) were staked upon the issue. Still, greatly to the annoyance of the curious, Billy and Bob continued to be good friends.

Now there happened to reside in the county just alluded to a little fellow by the name of Ransy Sniffle: a sprout of Richmond, who, in his earlier days, had fed copiously upon red clay and blackberries. This diet had given to Ransy a complexion that a corpse would have disdained to own, and an abdominal rotundity that was quite unprepossessing. Long spells of the fever and ague, too, in Ransy's youth, had conspired with clay and blackberries to throw him quite out of the order of nature. His shoulders were fleshless and elevated; his head large and flat; his neck slim and translucent; and his arms, hands, fingers, and feet were lengthened out of all proportion to the rest of his frame. His joints were large and his limbs small; and as for flesh, he could not, with propriety, be said to have any. Those parts which nature usually supplies with the most of this article—the calves of the legs, for example—presented in him the appearance of so many well-drawn blisters. His height was just five feet nothing; and his average weight in blackberry season, ninety-five. I have been thus particular in describing him, for the purpose of showing what a great matter a little fire sometimes kindleth. There was nothing on this earth which delighted Ransy so much as a fight. He never seemed fairly alive except when he was witnessing, fomenting, or talking about a fight. Then, indeed, his deep-sunken grey eye assumed something of a living fire, and his tongue acquired a volubility that bordered upon eloquence. Ransy had been kept for more than a year in the most torturing suspense as to the comparative manhood of Billy Stallings and Bob Durham. He had resorted to all his usual expedients to bring them in collision, and had entirely failed. He had faithfully reported to Bob all that had been said by the people in the upper battalion "agin him," and "he was sure Billy Stallings started it. He heard Billy say himself to Jim Brown, that he could whip him, *or any other man in his battalion;*" and this he told to Bob; adding, "Dod darn his soul, if he was a little bigger, if he'd let any man *put upon* his battalion in such a way." Bob replied, "If he (Stallings) thought so, he'd better come and try it." This Ransy carried to Billy, and delivered it with a spirit becoming his own dignity and the character of his battalion, and with a colouring well calculated to give it effect. These, and many other schemes which Ransy laid for the gratification of his curiosity, entirely failed of their object. Billy and Bob continued friends, and Ransy had begun to lapse into the most tantalizing and hopeless despair, when a circumstance occurred which led to a settlement of the long-disputed question.

It is said that a hundred gamecocks will live in perfect harmony together if you do not put a hen with them; and so it would have been with Billy and Bob, had there been no women in the world. But there were women in the world, and from them each of our heroes had taken to himself a wife. The good ladies were no strangers to the prowess of their husbands, and, strange as it may seem, they presumed a little upon it.

The two battalions had met at the Courthouse upon a regimental parade. The two champions were there, and their wives had accompanied them. Neither knew the other's lady, nor were the ladies known to each other. The exercises of the day were just over, when Mrs. Stallings and Mrs. Durham stepped simultaneously into the store of Zephaniah Atwater, from "down east."

"Have you any Turkey-red?" said Mrs. S.

"Have you any curtain calico?" said Mrs. D. at the same moment.

"Yes, ladies," said Mr. Atwater, "I have both."

"Then help me first," said Mrs. D., "for I'm in a hurry."

"I'm in as great a hurry as she is," said Mrs. S., "and I'll thank you to help me first."

"And, pray, who are you, madam?" continued the other.

"Your better, madam," was the reply.

At this moment Billy Stallings stepped in. "Come," said he, "Nancy, let's be going; it's getting late."

"I'd a been gone half an hour ago," she replied, "if it hadn't a' been for that impudent huzzy."

"Who do you call an impudent huzzy, you nasty, good-for-nothing, snaggle-toothed gaub of fat, you?" returned Mrs. D.

"Look here, woman," said Billy, "have you got a husband here? If you have, I'll *lick* him till he learns to teach you better manners, you *sassy* heifer you." At this moment something was seen to rush out of the store as if ten thousand hornets were stinging it; crying, "Take care—let me go—don't hold me—where's Bob Durham?" It was Ransy Sniffle, who had been listening in breathless delight to all that had passed.

"Yonder's Bob, setting on the Courthouse steps," cried one. "What's the matter?"

"Don't talk to me!" said Ransy. "Bob Durham, you'd better go long yonder, and take care of your wife. They're playing h—l with her there, in Zeph Atwater's store. Dod etarnally darn my soul, if any man was to talk to my wife as Bill Stallions is talking to yours, if I wouldn't drive blue blazes through him in less than no time."

Bob sprang to the store in a minute, followed by a hundred friends; for the bully of a county never wants friends.

"Bill Stallions," said Bob, as he entered, "what have you been saying to my wife?"

"Is that your wife?" inquired Billy, obviously much surprised and a little disconcerted.

"Yes, she is, and no man shall abuse her, I don't care who he is."

"Well," rejoined Billy, "it an't worth while to go over it; I've said enough for a fight: and, if you'll step out, we'll settle it!"

"Billy," said Bob, "are you a fair fight?"

"I am," said Billy. "I've heard much of your manhood, and I believe I'm a better man than you are. If you will go into a ring with me, we can soon settle the dispute."

"Choose your friends," said Bob; "make your ring, and I'll be in with mine as soon as you will."

They both stepped out, and began to strip very deliberately, each battalion gathering round its champion, except Ransy, who kept himself busy in a most honest endeavour to hear and see all that transpired in both groups at the same time. He ran from one to the other in quick succession; peeped here and listened there; talked to this one, then to that one, and then to himself; squatted under one's legs and another's arms; and, in the short interval between stripping and stepping into the ring, managed to get himself trod on by half of both battalions. But Ransy was not the only one interested upon this occasion; the most intense interest prevailed everywhere. Many were the conjectures, doubts, oaths, and imprecations uttered while the parties were preparing for the combat. All the knowing ones were consulted as to the issue, and they all agreed, to a man, in one of two opinions: either that Bob would flog Billy, or Billy would flog Bob. We must be permitted, however, to dwell for a moment upon the opinion of Squire Thomas Loggins; a man who, it was said, had never failed to predict the issue of a fight in all his life. Indeed, so unerring had he always proved in this regard, that it would have been counted the most obstinate infidelity to doubt for a moment after he had delivered himself. Squire Loggins was a man who said but little, but that little was always delivered with the most imposing solemnity of look and cadence. He always wore the aspect of profound thought, and you could not look at him without coming to the conclusion that he was elaborating truth from its most intricate combinations.

"Uncle Tommy," said Sam Reynolds, "you can tell us all about it if you will; how will the fight go?"

The question immediately drew an anxious group around the squire. He raised his teeth slowly from the head of his walking cane, on which they had been resting; pressed his lips closely and thoughtfully together; threw down his eyebrows, dropped his chin, raised his eyes to an angle of twenty-three degrees, paused about half a minute, and replied, "Sammy, watch Robert Durham close in the beginning of the fight; take care of William Stallions in the middle of it; and see who has the wind at the end." As he uttered the last member of the sentence, he looked slyly at Bob's friends, and winked very significantly; whereupon they rushed, with one accord, to tell Bob what Uncle Tommy had said. As they retired, the squire turned to Billy's friends, and said, with a smile, "Them boys think I mean that Bob will whip."

Here the other party kindled into joy, and hastened to inform Billy how Bob's friends had deceived themselves as to Uncle Tommy's opinion. In the mean time, the principals and seconds were busily employed in preparing themselves for the combat. The plan of attack and defence, the manner of improving the various turns of the conflict, "the best mode of saving wind," &c., &c., were all discussed and settled. At length Billy announced himself ready, and his crowd were seen moving to the centre of the Courthouse Square; he and his five seconds in the rear. At the same time, Bob's party moved to the same point, and in the same order. The ring was now formed, and for a moment the silence of death reigned through both battalions. It was soon interrupted, however, by the cry of "Clear the way!" from Billy's seconds; when the ring opened in the centre of the upper battalion (for the order of march had arranged the centre of the two battalions opposite sides of the circle), and Billy stepped into the ring from the east, followed by his friends. He was stripped to the trousers, and exhibited an arm, breast, and shoulders of the most tremendous portent. His step was firm, daring, and martial; and as he bore his fine form a little in advance of his friends, an involuntary burst of triumph broke from his side of the ring; and, at the same moment, an uncontrollable thrill of awe ran along the whole curve of the lower battalion.

"Look at him!" was heard from his friends; "just look at him."

"Ben, how much you ask to stand before that man two seconds?"

"Pshaw, don't talk about it! Just thinkin' about it's broke three o' my ribs a'ready!"

"What's Bob Durham going to do when Billy lets that arm loose upon him?"

"God bless your soul, he'll think thunder and lightning a mint julep to it."

"Oh, look here, men, go take Bill Stallions out o' that ring, and bring in Phil Johnson's stud horse, so that Durham may have some chance! I don't want to see the man killed right away."

These and many other like expressions, interspersed thickly with oaths of the most modern coinage, were coming from all points of the upper battalion while Bob was adjusting the girth of his pantaloons, which walking had discovered not to be exactly right. It was just fixed to his mind, his foes becoming a little noisy, and his friends a little uneasy at his delay, when Billy called out, with a smile of some meaning, "Where's the bully of the lower battalion? I'm getting tired of waiting."

"Here he is," said Bob, lighting, as it seemed, from the clouds into the ring, for he had actually bounded clear of the head of Ransy Sniffle into the circle. His descent was quite as imposing as Billy's entry, and excited the same feelings, but in opposite bosoms.

Voices of exultation now rose on his side.

"Where did he come from?"

"Why," said one of his seconds (all having just entered), "we were girting him up, about a hundred yards out yonder, when he heard Billy ask for the bully; and he fetched a leap over the Courthouse, and went out of sight; but I told them to come on, they'd find him here."

Here the lower battalion burst into a peal of laughter, mingled with a look of admiration, which seemed to denote their entire belief of what they had heard.

"Boys, widen the ring, so as to give him room to jump."

"Oh, my little flying wild-cat, hold him if you can! and, when you get him fast, hold lightning next."

"Ned, what do you think he's made of?"

"Steel springs and chicken-hawk, God bless you!"

"Gentlemen," said one of Bob's seconds, "I understand it is to be a fair fight; catch as catch can, rough and tumble: no man touch till one or the other halloos."

"That's the rule," was the reply from the other side.

"Are you ready?"

"We are ready."

"Then blaze away, my game cocks!"

At the word, Bob dashed at his antagonist at full speed; and Bill squared himself to receive him with one of his most fatal blows. Making his calculation, from Bob's velocity, of the time when he would come within striking distance, he let drive with tremendous force. But Bob's onset was obviously planned to avoid this blow; for, contrary to all expectations, he stopped short just out of arm's reach, and, before Billy could recover his balance, Bob had him "all underhold." The next second, sure enough, "found Billy's head where his feet ought to be." How it was done no one could tell; but, as if by supernatural power, both Billy's feet were thrown full half his own height in the air, and he came down with a force that seemed to shake the earth. As he struck the ground, commingled shouts, screams, and yells burst from the lower battalion, loud enough to be heard for miles. "Hurra, my little hornet!" "Save him!" "Feed him!" "Give him the Durham physic till his stomach turns!" Billy was no sooner down than Bob was on him, and landing him awful blows about the face and breast. Billy made two efforts to rise by main strength, but failed. "Lord bless you, man, don't try to get up! *Lay* still and take it! you *bleege* to have it!"

Billy now turned his face suddenly to the ground, and rose upon his hands and knees. Bob jerked up both his hands and threw him on his face. He again recovered his late position, of which Bob endeavoured to deprive him as before; but, missing one arm, he failed, and Billy rose. But he had scarcely resumed his feet before they flew up as before, and he came again to the ground. "No fight, gentlemen!" cried Bob's friends; "the man can't stand up! Bouncing feet are bad things to fight." His fall, however, was this time comparatively light; for, having thrown his right arm round Bob's neck, he carried his head down with him. This grasp, which was obstinately maintained, prevented Bob from getting on him, and they lay head to head, seeming, for a time, to do nothing. Presently they rose, as if by mutual consent; and, as they rose, a shout burst from both battalions. "Oh, my lark!" cried the east, "has he foxed you? Do you begin to feel him! He's only beginning to fight; he ain't got warm yet."

"Look yonder!" cried the west; "didn't I tell you so! He hit the ground so hard it jarred his nose off. Now ain't he a pretty man as he stands? He shall have my sister Sal just for his pretty looks. I want to get in the breed of them sort o' men, to drive ugly out of my kinfolks."

I looked, and saw that Bob had entirely lost his left ear, and a large piece of his left cheek. His right eye was a little discoloured, and the blood flowed profusely from his wounds.

Bill presented a hideous spectacle. About a third of his nose, at the lower extremity, was bit off, and his face so swelled and bruised that it was difficult to discover in it anything of the human visage, much more the fine features which he carried into the ring.

They were up only long enough for me to make the foregoing discoveries, when down they went again, precisely as before. They no sooner touched the ground than Bill relinquished his hold upon Bob's neck. In this he seemed to have forfeited the only advantage which put him upon an equality with his adversary. But the movement was soon explained. Bill wanted this arm for other purposes than defence; and he had made arrangements whereby he knew that he could make it answer these purposes; for, when they rose again, he had the middle finger of Bob's left hand in his mouth. He was now secure from Bob's annoying trips; and he began to lend his adversary tremendous blows, every one of which was hailed by a shout from his friends. "Bullets!" "*Hoss*-kicking!" "Thunder!" "That'll do for his face; now feel his short ribs, Billy!"

I now considered the contest settled. I deemed it impossible for any human being to withstand for five seconds the loss of blood which issued from Bob's ear, cheek, nose, and finger, accompanied with such blows as he was receiving. Still he maintained the conflict, and gave blow for blow with considerable effect. But the blows of each became slower and weaker after the first three or four; and it became obvious that Bill wanted the room which Bob's finger occupied for breathing. He would therefore, probably, in a short time, have let it go, had not Bob anticipated his politeness by jerking away his hand, and making him a present of the finger. He now seized Bill again, and brought him to his knees, but he recovered. He again brought him to his knees, and he again recovered.

A third effort, however, brought him down, and Bob on top of him. These efforts seemed to exhaust the little remaining strength of both; and they lay, Bill undermost and Bob across his breast, motionless, and panting for breath. After a short pause, Bob gathered his hand full of dirt and sand, and was in the act of grinding it in his adversary's eyes, when Bill cried, "ENOUGH!" Language cannot describe the scene that followed; the shouts, oaths, frantic gestures, taunts, replies, and little fights, and therefore I shall not attempt it. The champions were borne off by their seconds and washed; when many a bleeding wound and ugly bruise was discovered on each which no eye had seen before.

Many had gathered round Bob, and were in various ways congratulating and applauding him, when a voice from the centre of the circle cried out, "Boys, hush and listen to me!" It proceeded from Squire Loggins, who had made his way to Bob's side, and had gathered his face up into one of this most flattering and intelligible expressions. All were obedient to the squire's command. "Gentlemen," continued he, with a most knowing smile, "is—Sammy—Reynold—in—this—company—of—gentlemen?"

"Yes," said Sam, "here I am."

"Sammy," said the squire, winking to the company, and drawing the head of his cane to his mouth with an arch smile as he closed, "I—wish—you—to tell—cousin—Bobby—and—these—gentlemen here present—what—your—Uncle—Tommy—said—before—the—fight—began?"

"Oh! get away, Uncle Tom," said Sam, smiling (the squire winked), "you don't know nothing about *fighting*." (The squire winked again.) "All you know about is how it'll begin, how it'll go on, how it'll end; that's all. Cousin Bob, when you going to fight again, just go to the old man, and let him tell you all about it. If he can't, don't ask nobody else nothing about it, I tell you."

The squire's foresight was complimented in many ways by the by-standers; and he retired, advising "the boys to be at peace, as fighting was a bad business."

Durham and Stallings kept their beds for several weeks, and did not meet again for two months. When they met, Billy stepped up to Bob and offered his hand, saying, "Bobby, you've *licked* me in a fair fight; but you wouldn't have done it if I hadn't been in the wrong. I oughtn't to have treated your wife as I did; and I felt so through the whole fight; and it sort o' cowed me."

"Well, Billy," said Bob, "let's be friends. Once in the fight, when you had my finger in your mouth, and was pealing me in the face and breast, I was going to halloo; but I thought of Betsy and knew the house would be too hot for me if I got whipped when fighting for her, after always whipping when I fought for myself."

"Now that's what I always love to see," said a by-stander. "It's true I brought about the fight, but I wouldn't have done it if it hadn't o' been on account of *Miss* (Mrs.) Durham. But dod eternally darn my soul, if I ever could stand by and see any woman put upon, much less *Miss* Durham. If Bobby hadn't been there, I'd o' took it up myself, be darned if I wouldn't, even if I'd o' got whipped for it. But we're all friends now." The reader need hardly be told that this was Ransy Sniffle.

Thanks to the Christian religion, to schools, colleges, and benevolent associations, such scenes of barbarism and cruelty as that which I have been just describing are now of rare occurrence, though they may still occasionally be met with in some of the new counties. Wherever they prevail, they are a disgrace to that community. The peace-officers who countenance them deserve a place in the Penitentiary. —HALL.

Solomon Franklin Smith (1801-1869)

Born in Norwich, New York, the son of farmers, young Sol Smith fell in love with the theater when he was only fourteen after reading Shakespeare and seeing a dramatic performance in Albany. Before finding an opportunity to become a part of the theatrical world, he was a store clerk, a printer's apprentice, and a student of law. Finally in 1820 he made his professional debut on stage and proved to be especially adept in low comedy parts. After he met and married a singer and actress, he settled for a while in Cincinnati before he decided on a career in theatrical management. He followed opportunities in New York, St. Louis, New Orleans, and Mobile, Alabama. Partnered successfully with Noah M. Ludlow, the pair dominated the theatrical world in the South and West for nearly two decades and became noted for their fair dealings with performers. Smith became close friends with P. T. Barnum and brought to the stage some of the most popular actors of the time, such as Junius B. Booth, Charles and Ellen Kean, and Joseph Jefferson III.

Even before he retired from his theatrical career in 1853, and settled in St. Louis to practice law, Smith had already begun to publish comic sketches and tales about his adventures traveling through the Old Southwest—including Georgia, South Carolina, Louisiana, and Alabama—in the New York *Spirit of the Times* and the St. Louis *Reveille*. His first book collected these in 1845 as *Sol Smith's Theatrical Apprenticeship*, to be followed in 1854 by *Sol Smith's Theatrical Journey Work*. Just before his death, Smith combined both books into one, divided the material into five "acts," and published it as *Theatrical Management in the West and South for Thirty Years* in 1868. Known in the theater as "Old Sol" for his expert elderly comic roles, Smith brought to the printed page some of the same warmth and good humor he generated on stage with his stories about conmen, eccentrics, and unscrupulous activities. No doubt his experience as an actor gave him an edge in capturing the common character of the people he wrote about.

Texts: "A Tennessee Door-Keeper," "The Consolate Widow," "Speculation in Whiskers," and "An Unfinished Obituary," from *Theatrical Management in the West and South for Thirty Years* (New York: Harper & Brothers, 1868).

A Tennessee Door-Keeper

At Greenville, East Tennessee, we made a halt, and determined to treat the inhabitants of that beautiful village with three representations of the "legitimate drama," in a carpenter's shop, hastily, but tastefully fitted up for the occasion.

The first representation was attended by just *six people,* making the total receipts of the evening THREE DOLLARS!

My landlord, the carpenter, attributed the slim attendance to a *camp-meeting* that was in successful operation about two miles from town, and "reckoned" that if I would "hold on" until that broke up, we should have full *shops* every night.

Thus urged, we did "hold on," and our next performance was rewarded with a receipt of TWO DOLLARS AND A HALF!

I proposed to decamp next morning, but the printer of the Greenville Expositor (who was on the *free-list* as a matter of course) remonstrated against so sudden a move, urging that a *third* performance must be successful, as it was quite certain the camp-meeting would break up that morning, and the young folk would all return to their homes.

I yielded and advertised for "positively the last performance" the play of WILLIAM TELL, a favorite afterpiece, and a lot of comic songs.

At the time of beginning I was glad to find a crowded audience in waiting—the shop, work-bench and all, was literally crammed. One of the carpenter's apprentices, whom I had transformed into a citizen of Altorf for the occasion, told me that all but five or six of the people in front were *religious folks,* who had attended the camp-meeting faithfully to its conclusion.

The performance proceeded—the actors were in high spirits. Lyne bullied Governor *Gesler* with great fierceness; *Sarnem* whacked the carpenter's apprentice with a hearty good-will, while the latter was making a bow to the governor's cap, on a pole five feet and a half high—the arrow, aimed at the apple on Albert's head, flew, with remarkable exactness, into the horse-blanket held up as a target to receive it behind the scenes, and the play was received with shouts of satisfaction by the Greenvillians. The farce was honored by peal on peal of laughter, while the comic songs were doubly encored, every one of them.

The entertainment over, I observed there was a reluctance in the audience to depart—*they wanted another song.* I gave them one. Still they remained as if glued to their seats. I went before the curtain and thanked the people for their patronage, and informed them the performance had concluded. They did not move—they wanted yet *another song*. I gave them another, and again told them the entertainment of the evening was over, intimating, at the same time, that the stage-carpenter was waiting to take down the scenery. A gentleman in the gallery (the work-bench) here arose and addressed me as follows: "Mr. Sol Smith: Sir,—I have been requested to express to you the unanimous wish of this meeting that you will *prolong your season*. The liberal patronage bestowed upon you this evening must have convinced you that we *can* make something of a turn-out here, and I feel authorized to say that, if you will give us a performance to-morrow night, you will have another house *as crowded as this*."

A murmur of applause confirmed the opinion of the speaker, and I was greatly tempted to yield to their wishes; but, bethinking me of certain announcements for performances in towns farther south, I was obliged to decline the invitation of my kind auditors, and content myself with the eighty or ninety dollars which I supposed had been contributed that night to my ways and means. Finding me determined, the audience gradually dispersed, each individual casting wishful and sidelong glances toward the stage, which by this time was beginning to be dismantled.

Motioning the door-keeper to follow me into a sort of shed adjoining the theatre, I proceeded to open the ticket-box in his presence, while he sat down on a bench in the corner to wait for his wages. I found SEVEN TICKETS in the box, and, turning to the waiting doorkeeper, who was busily engaged chewing tobacco and spitting, I asked him what he had done with the rest.

"They are all *thar*," he replied, with great composure, looking intently on a beam of the shed, and rocking his right knee, which he held in his clenched hands, and raised about half way from the floor to his chin.

"All *there*—where?" was the very natural question that I next propounded.

"*In the box* whar you *told* me to put 'em," he answered, still eyeing the beam or rafter.

"I find but seven here," I remarked; "I want to know where are the tickets for the one hundred and sixty or one hundred and eighty people that were in the house to-night."

"I tell you again that they are all *thar*, sir," he answered, sturdily; "and I allow 'twon't be safe for any man to insinuate anything agin my character," he continued, releasing his knee, and taking a large quid of tobacco from a rusty steel box and ramming it into his mouth.

"I do not wish to insinuate anything against your character," I said, soothingly, "but I want to know what you have done with the tickets."

"They are *thar*," he again alleged—"every one of 'em thar; no one passed *me* without giving me a ticket, and the tickets are all *thar*."

I began to get a little pettish, and asked the tobacco-chewer to explain himself. "There were nearly two hundred people in the house," I urged.

"There war full that," he admitted.

"Well, then," I asked, finally, "where are the tickets? Will you explain this mystery?"

My friend, the tobacco-chewing door-keeper, here renewed his grasp on his raised knee, deliberately withdrew his eyes from the rafter, and fixing them, half closed, on mine, at length afforded me the desired *explanation,* thus:

"You engaged me to *keep your door;* and I performed my dooties to the best of my abilities, for which you are indebted to me three dollars, and I want my money. No person has passed me without a ticket. My char*a*cter is above suspicions, and no one must say nothin' agin it."

"My good friend," I ventured to say, "I don't wish to say any thing against—"

"No, I should think *not*—you'd *better* not," he continued, "for I'm too well known here; well, as I was a sayin', you employed me as *door-keeper*—mark the distinction—I had nothin' at all to do with the WINDERS—*and thar's where your hundred and eighty people came in,* you 'tarnal fool to leave 'em open when there was sich a crowd comin' in from camp-meetin'!"

I paid the fellow his three dollars, and next day was far on my road to Warm Springs, in the famous county of Buncombe, where they raise the largest peaches and the yellowest children in all creation.

The Consolate Widow

Between Caleba Swamp and Lime Creek, in the "Nation," we saw considerable of a crowd gathered near a drinking-house, most of them seated and smoking. We stopped to see what was the matter. It was Sunday, and there had been a quarter race for a gallon of whisky. The first thing I noticed on alighting was the singular position of one of the horses of the party. He was kneeling down and standing on his hinder feet, his head wedged in between the ends of two logs of the grocery, and was stone dead, having evidently ran directly against the building at full speed, causing the house partially to fall. About five paces from the body of the horse lay the rider, quite senseless, with a gash in his throat which might have let out a thousand lives. As I said, most of the crowd were seated and smoking.

"What is all this?" I inquired. "What is the matter here?"

"Matter?" after a while answered one in a drawling voice, giving a good spit, and refilling his mouth with a new cud. "Matter enough; there's been a quarter race."

"But how came this man and horse killed?" I asked.

"Well," answered the chewing and spitting gentleman, "the man was considerably in liquor, I reckon, and he run his hoss chuck agin the house, and that's the whole of it."

"Has a doctor been sent for?" inquired one of our party.

"I reckon there ain't much use of doctors *here*," replied another of the crowd. "Burnt brandy couldn't save either of 'em, man or hoss."

"Has this man a wife and children?" inquired I.

"No children, that I knows of," answered a female, who was sitting on the ground a short distance from the dead man, smoking composedly.

"He has a wife, then?" I remarked. "What will be her feelings when she learns the fatal termination of this most unfortunate race?"

"Yes," sighed the female, "it *was* an unfortunate race. Poor man! he lost the whisky."

"Did you happen to know his wife? Has she been informed of the untimely death of her husband?" were my next inquiries.

"Do I *know* her? Has she been informed of his death?" said the woman. "Well, I reckon you ain't acquainted about these parts. *I* am the unfortunate widder."

"*You,* madam! *You* the wife of this man who has been so untimely cut off?" I exclaimed, in astonishment.

"Yes, and what about it?" said she. "Untimely cut off? His throat's cut, that's all, by that 'tarnal sharp end of a log; and as for it's being *untimely,* I don't know but it's as well now as any time—*he warn't of much account, no how!*"

She resumed her smoking, and we resumed our journey.

Speculation in Whiskers

There lived in Macon a dandified individual whom I shall call Jenks. This individual had a tolerably favorable opinion of his personal appearance. His fingers were hooped with rings, and his shirt bosom was decked with a magnificent breastpin; coat, hat, vest, and boots were made exactly to fit; he wore kid gloves of remarkable whiteness; his hair was oiled and dressed in the latest and best style; and, to complete his killing appearance, he sported an enormous pair of *real whiskers!* Of these whiskers Jenks was as proud as a young cat is of her tail when she first discovers she has one.

I was sitting one day in a broker's office when Jenks came in to inquire the price of exchange on New York. He was invited to sit down, and a cigar was offered him. Conversation turning on the subject of buying and selling stocks, a remark was made by a gentleman present that he thought no person should sell out stock in such-and-such a bank at that time, as it *must* get better in a few days.

"I will sell *any* thing I've got, if I can make any thing on it," replied Jenks.

"Oh no," replied one, "not *any* thing; you wouldn't sell your *whiskers!*"

A loud laugh followed this chance remark. Jenks immediately answered, "I would; but who would *want* them? Any person making the purchase would lose money by the operation, I'm thinking."

"Well," I observed, "I would be willing to take the speculation, if the price could be made reasonable."

"Oh, I'll sell 'em cheap," answered Jenks, winking at the gentlemen present.

"What do you call cheap?" I inquired.

"I'll sell 'em for fifty dollars," Jenks answered, puffing forth a cloud of smoke across the counter, and repeating the wink.

"Well, that *is* cheap; and you'll sell your whiskers for fifty dollars?"

"I will."

"Both of them?"

"Both of them."

"*I'll take them!* When can I have them?"

"Any time you choose to call for them."

"Very well—they're mine. I think I shall double my money on them, at least."

I took a bill of sale as follows:

"Received of Sol. Smith *Fifty Dollars* in full for my crop of whiskers, to be worn, and taken care of by me, and delivered to him when called for.

J. Jenks"

The sum of fifty dollars was paid, and Jenks left the broker's office in high glee, flourishing five Central Bank X's, and telling all his acquaintances of the great bargain he had made in the sale of his whiskers.

The broker and his friends laughed at me for being taken in so nicely. "Never mind," said I; "let those laugh that win; I'll make a profit out of those whiskers, depend on it."

For a week after this, whenever I met Jenks, he asked me when I intended to call for my whiskers.

"I'll let you know when I want them," was always my answer. "Take good care of them—oil them occasionally; I shall call for them one of these days."

A splendid ball was to be given. I ascertained that Jenks was to be one of the managers—he being a great ladies' man (on account of his whiskers, I suppose), and it occurred to me that before the ball took place I might as well call for my whiskers.

One morning I met Jenks in a barber's shop. He was Adonising before a large mirror, and combing up my whiskers at a devil of a rate.

"Ah! there you are, old fellow," said he, speaking to my reflection through the glass. "Come for your whiskers, I suppose?"

"Oh, no hurry," I replied, as I sat down for a shave.

"Always ready, you know," he answered, giving a final tie to his cravat.

"Come to think of it," I said, musingly, as the barber began to put the lather on my face, "perhaps now would be as good a time as another; you *may* sit down and let the barber try his hand at the whiskers."

"You couldn't wait until to-morrow, could you?" he asked, hesitatingly. "There's a *ball* to-night, you know—"

"To be sure there is, and I think you ought to go with a clean face; at all events, I don't see any reason why you should expect to wear *my* whiskers to that ball, so sit down."

He rather sulkily obeyed, and in a few moments his cheeks were in a perfect foam of lather. The barber flourished his razor, and was about to commence operations, when I suddenly *changed my mind.*

"Stop, Mr. Barber," I said, "you needn't shave off those whiskers just yet." So he quickly put up his razor, while Jenks started up from the chair in something very much resembling a passion.

"This is trifling!" he exclaimed. "You have claimed your whiskers—take them."

"I believe a man has a right to do as he pleases with his own property," I remarked, and left Jenks washing his face.

At dinner that day the conversation turned upon the whisker affair. It seems the whole town had got wind of it, and Jenks could not walk the streets without the remark being continually made by the boys, "*There goes the man with old Sol's whiskers!*" And they had grown to an immense size, for he dared not trim them. In short, I became convinced Jenks was waiting very impatiently for me to assert my rights in the property. It happened that several of the party were sitting opposite me at dinner who were present when the singular bargain was made, and they all urged me to *take the whiskers* that very day, and thus compel Jenks to go to the ball whiskerless, or stay at home. I agreed with them it *was* about time to *reap my crop,* and promised that if they would all meet me at the broker's shop where the purchase had been made, I would make a call on Jenks that evening, after he had dressed for the ball. All promised to be present at the proposed *shaving operation* in the broker's office, and I sent for Jenks and the barber. On the appearance of Jenks it was evident he was much vexed at the sudden call upon him, and his vexation was certainly not lessened when he saw the broker's office was filled to overflowing by spectators anxious to behold the barbarous proceeding.

"Come, be in a hurry," he said, as he took a seat, and leaned his head against the counter for support; "I can't stay here long; several ladies are waiting for me to escort them to the ball."

"True, very true—you are one of the managers—I recollect. Mr. Barber, don't detain the gentleman; go to work at once."

The lathering was soon over, and with about three strokes of the razor, *one side of his face was deprived of its ornament.*

"Come, come," said Jenks, "push ahead; there is no time to be lost: let the gentleman have his whiskers—he is impatient."

"Not at all," I replied, coolly, "I'm in no sort of a hurry myself—and, now I think of it, as *your* time must be precious at this particular moment, several ladies being in waiting for you to escort them to the ball, I believe *I'll not take the other whisker to-night."*

A loud laugh from the by-standers, and a glance in the mirror, caused Jenks to open his eyes to the ludicrous appearance he cut with a single whisker, and he began to insist upon my taking *the whole of my property!* But all wouldn't do. I had a right to take it when I chose; *I was not obliged to take all at once,* and I *chose* to take but *half* at that particular period; indeed, I intimated to him very plainly that I was not going to be a very hard creditor, and that, if he "behaved himself," perhaps I should *never* call for the balance of what he owed me!

When Jenks became convinced I was determined not to take the remaining whisker, he began, amid the loudly-expressed mirth of the crowd, to propose terms of compromise, first offering me ten dollars, then twenty, thirty, forty—fifty! to take off the remaining whisker. I said, firmly, "My dear sir, there is no use talking; I insist on your wearing that whisker for me for a month or two."

"What will you take for the whiskers?" he at length asked. "Won't you sell them back to me?"

"Ah!" replied I, "now you begin to talk as a business-man should. Yes; I bought them on speculation; I'll sell them if I can obtain a good price."

"What is your price?"

"One hundred dollars—*must* double my money."

"Nothing less?"

"Not a farthing less—and I'm not anxious to sell even at *that* price."

"Well, I'll take them," he groaned; "there's your money; and here, barber, shave off this d—d infernal whisker in less than no time: I shall be late at the ball."

An Unfinished Obituary

I forgot to mention that about the middle of the season I had an attack of brain fever, and was cured (under Providence) by Doctor Marcy, then a young practitioner, now, I believe, Surgeon General of the United States Army, or something of the kind. He stuck to me like a brother, night and day, until the disease was conquered. I only mention this sickness of mine as introductory to a fact which I am about to relate. Before I had recovered my strength entirely, I took it into my head that change of air would do me good, and, without much preparation, took passage on a boat and journeyed to Louisville and Cincinnati, at both of which cities I learned that the player-folk had heard that I had died and been buried! How this report got out, I don't know but George Farren and George Hill, when I walked into the Louisville Hotel, took me for a ghost of myself. I *was* assuredly very pale and thin, but I soon convinced them and others that the figure they beheld was composed of flesh and blood; and when I appeared before my long-time friend and professional associate, Mrs. Fanny Drake, and convinced her that I was the veritable *living* being she had so long and so sincerely loved and esteemed, and whose untimely "taking off" she had been bewailing for at least two mortal days (so she said, but her daughter Julia, on being appealed to, did not remember any bewailing—bless the dear girl!), I was nearly crushed with her affectionate embraces. I arrived in Cincinnati just in time to "stop the press" of my old friend and brother typo, John H. Wood, who had prepared an elaborate obituary notice, a column long, of the person who is penning these lines. I shall never forget my sensations as I stood over the types which were to commemorate my many virtues. I actually shed tears upon them. I was not aware of the possession of the many shining qualities therein typified and set forth by my ardent friend. I now regret I did not take a proof copy of that able tribute to (supposed) departed worth; but I begged John to distribute the type immediately, which request he complied with, and that splendid "obituary" is lost to the world.

Charles F. M. Noland (1810-1858)

Born into an aristocratic Tidewater family in Loudon County, Virginia, in 1810, at age thirteen Charles F. M. Noland was appointed to West Point through the influence of his prominent father. His poor academic performance brought his dismissal after two years, so he followed his father to Arkansas where he studied law. He became involved in Arkansas territorial politics and questioned the integrity of the governor, whose nephew challenged him to a duel. Noland shot the young man fatally. He became a member of the bar in 1836 and would remain in politics his entire life at both local and national levels. He found the time, however, to begin writing sketches about frontier life and people and contributed his first sketch to William T. Porter's *Spirit of the Times* in 1836. His frequent submissions—over 300 were published—earned him a reputation as a major correspondent for that sporting journal. This led to an appointment as America's first reporter for the *London Sporting Magazine* in 1840.

Despite his privileged background, Noland identified with the rough and tumble lives of farmers, hunters, and pioneers in the Old Southwest territories. As engaging as his essays on horse racing and the outdoors were, it was not until he hit upon the notion of creating a major fictional spokesman, one Pete Whetstone, to speak for himself that he achieved literary distinction. Brash and assertive, Whetstone had an independent voice quite apart from the genteel voice of Noland himself. Expressing his own opinions in an authentic dialect, Whetstone took on a life of his own as his character developed over the next two decades in letters and tales contributed to *Spirit of the Times* and reprinted in humor anthologies. Noland's mastery of dialogue, characterization, narrative structure, and setting were so effective that many readers thought Whetstone was a real person rather than a fiction.

Texts: "Pete Whetstone's Bear Hunt," New York *Spirit of the Times,* March 25, 1837; "Pete Whetstone's Last Frolic," March 16, 1839; "Pete Whetstone and the Mail Boy," February 26, 1853.

Pete Whetsone's Bear Hunt

Devil's Fork of Little Red River (Ark.) Feb. 15th, 1837

Dear Mr. Editor,—Being that this is a rainy day, I thought I would write you about the bear hunt. Well, next morning after the fight with Dan Looney, I started out. I was mighty sore I tell you, for Dan had thumped me in the sides till I was as blue as indigo. I saddled my horse, got my wallet, and fetched a whoop, that started my dogs; they knew what I was after, and seemed mightily pleased. I took six with me, as good dogs as ever fought a bear. *Sharp-tooth* and *General Jackson,* if there was any difference, were a little the best. I struck for the Big Lick, where Sam Jones and Bill Stout were to meet me. I found them there—they had a good team of dogs. We had heard of great *sign* up the Dry Fork, and there we determined to go. It was about thirty miles off, and as we did not wish to fatigue our dogs, it took us until the middle of next day to reach it; we rested that evening, and put out by day-break next morning.

In about half an hour, old General raised a cry: I knew then we were good for a bear—the other dogs joined him. The track was cold; we worked with him till about ten, when they bounced him. Bill Stout was ahead, and raised the yell—such music, oh lord, and such fighting. I got the first shot; my gun made long fire, and I only slightly wounded him. At the crack of the gun the dogs gathered; he knocked two of my young dogs into the middle of next week before you could say Jack Robinson—the others kept him at bay until Bill Stout could shoot; his ball struck him too far back. He was a tremendous bear, and just lean enough to make a good fight. He made two other dogs hear it thunder, shook off the whole pack, and got into a thicket, and the next moment plunged down a steep cliff. I listened only for an instant, to hear the clear shrill note of Sharp-tooth, as he plunged in after him, and then socked the spurs into *Dry-bones,* and with Bill Stout on *Fire-tail,* and Sam Jones on *Hard-times,* dashed round the hill. We rode for our lives, for we knew that many of our dogs would suffer if we did not relieve them. When we overtook them, they had him at bay; two dead, and three crippled dogs told of the bloody fight they had had. Sam Jones fired; the wound was that time mortal. At the crack of the gun, the dogs again clamped him; with a powerful reach of his paw, he grabbed the old General, and the next moment fastened his big jaws on him; this was more than flesh and blood could stand: I sprung at him with a butcher-knife, and the first lick sent it to the handle. He loosened his jaws and Sam Jones caught the old General by the hind legs and pulled him away. I gave him one more stab, and he fell dead.

I examined the old General, and found that he was not much injured. We lost seven dogs that day, and many of the others were so badly crippled as to render it necessary for us to lay by a few days. Sam found a bee tree and I killed some fat turkies; with them, and the ribs of the old *he,* we had fine times. It has stopped raining, so I must stop for the present.

Ever yours,
Pete Whetstone

Pete Whetsone's Last Frolic

Devil's Fork of Little Red, *Jan. 9,* 1839

My dear Mr. Editor,—Since the last time I writ you, I have had all sorts of times; I took a trip away out South. Well, when I got to the Rock, I was in a big hurry to keep on, so I walked up early in the morning to Goodrich and Loomis, thinking I would rig out in a suit of their best, but they hadn't opened their store; so I steps into another, and bought me a pair of red broadcloth britches. The fellow measured me, and put up a pair that he said would fit me to a shaving. So I stuffs them into my saddle-bags, and put out South. Well, when I gets out, I was asked to a party, and I rigged myself out; but oh, lordy! my britches were big enough for the fat man what was blowed up in the steamboat. I had my gallowses up to the last notch, but it wouldn't all do, for I could have carried a grist of corn in them without stretching the cloth. I hardly knew what to do; my old britches couldn't do at all, and my new ones hung like a shirt on a beanpole. Thinks I, there is no frolic for Pete; but just right at this time in pops Major Greene. "Well," says he, "Kurnel, ain't you ready to go?" Says I, "I am thinking I won't go."—"Why?" says he. "Look at my britches," says I. Well, he commenced laughing; says he, "Them britches were made for Daniel Lambert."—"Well," says I, "Daniel Lambert is a stranger to me, but I know they are a pretty loose fit."—"Oh, never mind them," says he; "come, go, and nobody will notice them." So I went. I found lots of people, and an abundance of pretty gals. Well, there was no dancing, and the folks were all sitting round the room; so I slips in a corner, thinking I would hide my britches. Presently some gentleman asked a lady to sing; so up she gits, and he leads her to something in the corner, that looked like the nicest kind of a chest. Well, she opened the lid, and it was right chuck full of horseteeth; she just run her hand across them, and I never heard such a noise in all my life. I whispered to the next fellow to me, and asked what sort of a varmint that was? "Why, Kurnel," says he, "that is a pe-anny." Well, the young lady commenced, and I never heard such singing. I forgot my britches, and started to walk close up to the pe-anny, when I heard them tittering. "Daniel Lambert," says one—then I knew they were laughing at my britches. So I feels my dander rising, and began to get mad; I walked right up, bold as a sheep. There was a sort of a dandy looking genius standing by the pe-anny.—Says he "Now do, Miss, favor us with that delightful little ditty—my favorite—you know it." Then she commenced.

"When the Belly-aker is hearn over the sea,
I'll dance the Ronny-aker by moonlight with thee."

That is all I recollect. When she got through, up steps Maj. Greene, and introduces me to her. Says she, (and I tell you she looked pretty), "Col. Whetstone, what is your favorite?" Says I, "Suit yourself, and you suit me." And that made her laugh. Well, right at that, up steps a fellow that looked as if he had been sent for and couldn't go. Says he, "Miss, will you give me 'the last link is broken'?"—"Why," says she, "indeed, sir, I have the most wretched cold in the world."—"Why, Miss," says I, "you wouldn't call yours a bad cold if you had seen Jim Cole arter he lay out in the swamp and catched cold." "Why," says she (and lord, but she looked killing), "how bad was his cold?" "Why, Miss," says I, "he didn't quit spitting ice till the middle of August." That made her laugh. "Well," says she, "Kurnel Whetsone, that cures my cold." So she commenced—

"The last link is broken that binds you to me,
The words you have spoken is sorry to I."

Well, arter the lady was over, they all went into supper; lots of good things. I sat next to a young lady, and I heard them saying, "Miss, with your permission, I'll take a piece of the turkey," and so on. I sees a plate of nice little pickles.—"Miss, with your permission, I'll take a pickle," and she said I might do so. I reached over and dipped up one on my fork—it was small, and I put the whole of it in my mouth. Oh, lordy! but it burnt;—well, the more I chawed the worse it was. Thinks I, if I swallow, I am a burnt koon. Well, it got too hot for human nater to stand; so says I, "Miss, with your permission, I'll lay the pickle back," and I spit it out. Oh, lordy! what laughing. "Excuse me, ladies, if I have done wrong," says I, "but that pickle is too hot for the Devil's fork." Everybody seemed to take the thing in good part, but one chap; says he, "I never seed such rude behavior in all my life." At this I turns round to him; says I, "Look here, Mister, if you don't like the smell of freshbread, you had better quit the bakery." Well, I tell you, that shot up his fly-trap quicker. Arter supper the party broke up. Oh, confound the britches! I wish the fellow that made them could be fed on cloth for twelve months. Even the little boys made fun of them, for I heard one singing—

"Mister, Mister, who made your britches?
Daddy cut them out, and mammy sowed the stitches."

Ever yours,
PETE WHETSTONE

Pete Whetstone and the Mail Boy

Pete Whetstone, of Arkansas, was once travelling on horseback through the interior of the State, and called one evening to stay all night at a little log house near the road where entertainment and a post-office were kept. Two other strangers were there, and the mail rider rode up about dark. Supper being over, the mail carrier and the three gentlemen were invited into a small room furnished with a good fire and two beds, which were to accommodate the four persons for the night. The mail carrier was a little shabby, dirty, lousy-looking wretch, with whom none of the gentlemen liked the idea of sleeping. Pete Whetsone eyed him closely as he asked:

"Where do you sleep to-night, my lad?"

"I'll thleep with *you* I reckon," lisped the youth, "or with one o' them other fellars, I don't care which."

The other two gentlemen took the hint and occupied one of the beds together immediately, leaving the other bed and the confab to be enjoyed by Pete and the mail boy together as best they could. Pete and the boy both commenced hauling off their duds, and Pete getting in bed first, and wishing to get rid of sleeping with the boy, remarked very earnestly—"my friend, I'll tell you before hand, *I've got the Itch,* and you'd better not get in here with me, for the disease is *catching.*"

The boy, who was just getting in bed too, drawled out very coolly, "wal I reckon that don't make a bit o' difference,—I've had it now for nearly these theven years," and into bed he pitched along with Pete, who pitched out in as great a hurry as if he had waked up in a hornet's nest in the bed. The other two gentlemen roared, and the mail boy, who had got peaceable possession of a bed to himself, drawled out—"why you must be a thet o' darned fules,—mam and dad's got the eatch a heap wurth than I is, and they thlept in that bed last night when they was here at the quilting."

The other two strangers were now in a worse predicament than Pete had been, and bouncing from their nest like the house had been on fire, stripped, shook their clothes, put them on again, ordered their horses, and, though it was nearly ten o'clock, they all three left, and rode several miles to the next town before they slept, leaving the imperturbable mail carrier to the bliss of scratching and sleeping alone.

William Tappan Thompson (1812-1882)

Born in Ravena, Ohio, in 1812, William Tappan Thompson made his way South in seeking experience and opportunity. He worked for the *Daily Chronicle* newspaper in Philadelphia, and served as a secretary to a politician in Florida, before taking a job in 1835 with Augustus Baldwin Longstreet to help produce his newspaper in Augusta, Georgia, the *States' Rights Sentinel*. Longstreet, who had just published *Georgia Scenes,* a seminal work in southern humor, would prove of profound influence for the remainder of Thompson's career. After the *Sentinel* ceased publication, he served briefly in the campaign against the Seminoles in Florida, returned to Augusta to marry and begin a family, and began publishing a magazine, the *Family Companion and Ladies' Mirror*. While the writing that would establish his reputation as a major force in southern humor began here, he would continue through a variety of editorial positions finally to settle in 1849 as founding editor of the *Savannah Morning News*. A strong defender of slavery, Thompson joined the Confederate Army, traveled to Europe after the Civil War, and was active in the Democratic Party after 1868. He was a lover of all things southern, and it was his portrayal of the region in his comic tales and sketches that would cause him to be remembered.

Inspired by Longstreet's work, the Major Jack Downing stories by northeastern humorist Seba Smith, and the tall tales of Davy Crockett, Thompson began to publish in 1842 a series of letters set in the fictitious town of Pineville from an upper-middle-class plantation owner named Major Joseph Jones. Using native dialect and embodying a realistic portrayal of the rustic life of the times, Major Jones was a common-sense philosopher who satirized the trends of society towards excessive self-indulgence and superficial fashions. While a good deal of his work was based on incongruities of place and situation in a social context, much of his humor derives from misspelled words and malapropisms, devices Thompson borrowed from northeastern writers. Avoiding the violent and boisterous humor of the other writers of the Old Southwest, Thompson invested Major Jones with a naïve but respectable sense of propriety and a basic respect for domesticity. Beneath his rambling commentary about the way things were was a deep sense of what they should be and a faith in the moral nature of things.

The letters proved enormously popular. Sixteen of them were collected in 1843 in *Major Jones's Courtship* offered as a subscription premium to readers of Thompson's journal the *Southern Miscellany*. Subsequent expanded editions appeared, and by 1900 about thirteen editions had been published. Other collections followed the initial one, including *Chronicles of Pineville* in 1845 and *Major Jones's Sketches of Travel* in 1848, but none equaled the popular appeal of the first book.

Texts: "The Major in an Embarrassing Situation" and "The Christmas Present in a Bag," "The Runaway Match" from *Major Jones's Courtship: Detailed, with Other Scenes, Incidents, and Adventures, in A Series of Letters By Himself. Revised and Enlarged. To Which Are Added Thirteen Humorous Sketches* (New York: D. Appleton, 1872).

The Major in an Embarrassing Situation

Pineville, May 28, 1842.

To Mr. Thompson:—*Dear Sir*—Ever sense you was down to Pineville, it's been on my mind to write you a letter, but the boys lowed I'd better not, cause you mought take me off about my spellin and dictionary. But something happened to me tother night, so monstrous provoking, that I can't help tellin you about it, so you can put other young chaps on ther gard. It all come of chawing so much tobacker, and I reckon I've wished ther was no such plagy stuff, more'n five hundred times sense it happened.

You know the Stallinses lives on the plantation in the summer and goes to town in the winter. Well, Miss Mary Stallins, who you know is the darlinest gall in the county, come home tother day to see her folks. You know she's been to the Female College, down to Macon, for most a year now. Before she went, she used to be jest as plain as a old shoe, and used to go fishin and huckleberryin with us, with nothin but a calico sun-bonnet on, and was the wildest thing you ever seed. Well, I always used to have a sort of a sneakin notion after Mary Stallins, and so when she come, I brushed up, and was 'termined to have a right serious talk with her about old matters; not knowin but she mought be captivated by some of them Macon fellers.

So, shure enough, off I started, unbeknowin to anybody, and rode right over to the plantation—(you know ours is right jinin the widder Stallinses.) Well, when I got thar, I felt a little sort o' sheepish; but I soon got over that, when Miss Carline said, (but she didn't mean me to hear her,) "There, Pinny (that's

Miss Mary's nick-name, you know,) there's your bow come."

Miss Mary looked mighty sort o' redish when I shuck her hand and told her howdy; and she made a sort of stoop over and a dodge back, like the little galls does to the school-marm, and said "Good evenin, Mr. Jones," (she used to always call me jest Joe.)

"Take a chair, Joseph," said Miss Carline; and we sot down in the parlor, and I begun talkin to Miss Mary about Macon, and the long ride she had, and the bad roads, and the monstrous hot weather, and the like.

She didn't say much, but was in a mighty good humor and laughed a heap. I told her I never seed sich a change in anybody. Nor I never did. Why, she didn't look like the same gall. Good gracious! she looked so nice and trim—jest like some of them pictures what they have in APPLETON'S JOURNAL—with her hair all komed down longside of her face, as slick and shiny as a mahogany burow. When she laughed she didn't open her mouth like she used to; and she sot up straight and still in her chair, and looked so different, but so monstrous pretty! I ax'd her a heap of questions, about how she liked Macon, and the Female College, and so forth; and she told me a heap about 'em. But old Miss Stallins and Miss Carline and Miss Kesiah, all of 'em, kep all the time interruptin us, axin about mother—if she was well, and if she was gwine to the Spring church next Sunday, and what luck she had with her soap, and all sich stuff—and I do believe I told the old woman more'n twenty times that mother's old turkey-hen was settin on fourteen eggs.

Well, I wasn't to be backed out that-a-way—so I kep it a goin the best I could, till bimeby old Miss Stallins let her knitin drap three or four times, and then begun to nod.

I seed the galls lookin at oneanother and pinchin oneanother's elbows, and Miss Mary said she wondered what time it was, and said the College disciplines, or something like that, didn't low late hours. I seed how the game was gwine— but howsumever, I kep talkin to her like a cotton gin in packin time, as hard as I could clip it, till bimeby the old lady went to bed, and after a bit the galls all cleared, and left Miss Mary to herself. That was jest the thing I wanted.

Well, she sot on one side of the fire-place, and I sot on tother, so I could spit on the hath, whar there was nothin but a lighted chunk burnin to give light. Well, we talked and talked, and I know you would like to hear all we talked about, but that would be too long. When I'm very interested in any thing, or git bother'd about any thing, I can't help chawin a heap of tobacker, and then I spits uncontionable, specially if I'm talkin. Well, we sot thar and talked, and the way I spit, was larmin to the crickets! I axed Miss Mary if she had any bows down to Macon.

"Oh, yes," she said, and then she went on and named over Matthew Matix, Nat. Filosofy, Al. Gerber, Retric Stronomy, and a whole heap of fellers, that she'd been keepin company with most all her time.

"Well," ses I, "I spose they're mazin poplar with you, aint they, Miss Mary?"—for I felt mighty oneasy, and begun to spit a good deal worse.

"Yes," ses she, "they're the most interestin companions I ever had, and I am anxious to resume their pleasant society."

I tell you what, that sort o' stumped me, and I spit right slap on the chunk and made it "flicker and flare" like the mischief. It was a good thing it did, for I blushed as blue as a Ginny squash.

I turned my tobacker round in my mouth, and spit two or three times, and the old chuck kep up a most bominable fryin.

"Then I spose your gwine to forgit old acquaintances," ses I, "sense you's been to Macon, among them lawyers and doctors, is you, Miss Mary? You thinks more of them than you does of anybody else, I spose."

"Oh," ses she, "I am devoted to them—I think of them day and night!"

That was *too* much—it shot me right up, and I sot as still as could be for more'n a minute. I never felt so warm behind the ears afore in all my life. Thunder! how my blood did bile up all over me, and I felt like I could knock Matthew Matix into a grease-spot, if he'd only been thar.

Miss Mary sot with her handkercher up to her face, and I looked straight into the fire-place. The blue blazes was runnin around over the old chunk, ketchin hold here and lettin go thar, sometimes gwine most out, and then blazin up a little. I couldn't speak—I was makin up my mind for tellin her the sitewation of my hart—I was jest gwine to tell her my feelins, but my mouth was chock full of tobacker, so I had to spit—and slap it went, right on the lightwood chunk, and out *it* went, spang!

I swar, I never did feel so tuck aback in all my born days. I didn't know what to do.

"My lord, Miss Mary," ses I, "I didn't go to do it.—Jest tell me the way to the kitchen, and I'll go and git a light."

But she never said nothin, so I sot down agin, thinkin she'd gone to git one herself, for it was pitch dark, and I couldn't see my hand afore my face.

Well, I sot thar and ruminated, and waited a long time, but she didn't come; so I begun to think maybe she wasn't gone. I couldn't hear nothin, nor I couldn't see nothin; so bimeby ses I, very low, for I didn't want to wake up the family—ses I,

"Miss Mary! Miss Mary!" But nobody answered.

Thinks I, what's to be done? I tried agin.

"Miss Mary! Miss Mary!" ses I. But it was no use.

Then I heard the galls snickerin and laughin in the next room, and I begun to see how it was; Miss Mary was gone and left me thar alone.

"Whar's my hat?" ses I, pretty loud, so somebody mought tell me. But they only laughed worse.

I begun to feel about the room, and the first thing I know'd, spang! goes my head, agin the edge of the pantry dore what was standin open. The fire flew, and I couldn't help but swar a little. "D—n the dore," ses I—"whar's my hat?" But nobody said nothin, and I went gropin about in the dark, feelin round to find some way out, when I put my hand on the dore knob. All right, thinks I, as I pushed the door open quick.—Ther was a scream!—heads popped under the bed kiver quicker'n lightnin—something white fluttered by the burow, and out went the candle. I was in the galls room! But there was no time for apologisin, even if they could stopped squealin long enough to hear me. I crawfished out of that place monstrous quick, you may depend. Hadn't I went and gone and done it sure enough! I know'd my cake was all dough then, and I jest determined to git out of them digins as soon as possible, and never mind about my hat.

Well, I got through the parlor dore after rakin my shins three or four times agin the chairs, and was feelin along through the entry for the front dore; but somehow I was so flustrated that I tuck the wrong way, and bimeby kersplash I went, right over old Miss Stallinses spinnin-wheel, onto the floor! I hurt myself a good deal; but that didn't make me half so mad as to hear them confounded galls a gigglin and laughin at me.

"Oh," said one of 'em, (it was Miss Kesiah, for I knowed her voice,) "there goes mother's wheel! my lord!"

I tried to set the cussed thing up agin, but it seemed to have more'n twenty legs, and wouldn't stand up no how.—Maybe it was broke. I went out of the dore, but I hadn't more'n got down the steps, when bow! wow! wow! comes four or five infernal grate big coon-dogs, right at me. "Git out! git out! hellow, Cato! call off your dogs!" ses I, as loud as I could. But Cato was sound asleep, and if I hadn't a run back into the hall, and got out the front way as quick as I could, them devils would chawed my bones for true.

When I got to my hoss, I felt like a feller jest out of a hornet's nest; and I reckon I went home a little of the quickest.

Next mornin old Miss Stallins sent my hat by a little nigger; but I haint seed Mary Stallins sense. Now you see what comes of chawin tobacker! No more from

Your friend, till death, JOS. JONES.

P.S. I blieve Miss Mary's gone to the Female College agin. If you see her, I wish you would say a good word to her for me, and tell her I forgives her all, and I hope she will do the same by me. Don't you think I better write her a letter, and explain matters to her?

NOTABEMY.—This letter was writ to my pertickeler friend Mr. Thompson, when he was editen the Family Companion magazine, down in Macon. I had no notion of turnin author then; but when it come out with my name to it, and ther wasn't no use of denyin it, and specially as he writ me a letter beggin

I would go on and write for the Miscellany, I felt a obligation restin on me to continue my correspondence to that paper. All my other letters was writ to Mr. Thompson, in Madison. J.J.

The Christmas Present in a Bag

Pineville, December 27, 1842.

To Mr. Thompson:—*Dear Sir*—Crismus is over, and the thing is done did! You know I told you in my last letter that I was gwine to bring Miss Mary up to the chalk on Crismus. Well, I done it, slick as a whistle, though it come mighty nigh bein a serious bisness. But I'll tell you all about the whole circumstance.

The fact is, I's made my mind up more'n twenty times to jest go and come right out with the whole bisness; but whenever I got whar she was, and whenever she looked at me with her witchin eyes, and kind o' blushed at me, I always felt sort o' skeered and fainty, and all what I made up to tell her was forgot, so I couldn't think of it to save me. But you's a married man, Mr. Thompson, so I couldn't tell you nothin about popin the question, as they call it. It's a mighty grate favour to ax of a pretty gall, and to people what aint used to it, it goes monstrous hard, don't it? They say widders don't mind it no more'n nothin. But I'm makin a transgression, as the preacher ses.

Chrismus eve I put on my new suit, and shaved my face as slick as a smoothin iron, and after tea went over to old Miss Stallinses. As soon as I went into the parler whar they was all settin round the fire, Miss Carline and Miss Kesiah both laughed right out.

"There! there!" ses they, "I told you so! I know'd it would be Joseph."

"What's I done, Miss Carline?" ses I.

"You come under little sister's chicken bone, and I do believe she know'd you was comin when she put it over the dore."

"No I didn't—I didn't no such thing, now," ses Miss Mary, and her face blushed red all over.

"Oh, you needn't deny it," ses Miss Kesiah, "you belong to Joseph now, jest as sure as ther's any charm in chicken bones."

I know'd that was a first rate chance to say something, but the dear little creeter looked so sorry and kep blushin so, I couldn't say nothin zactly to the pint! so I tuck a chair and reached up and tuck down the bone and put it in my pocket.

"What are you gwine to do with that old chicken bone now, Majer?" ses Miss Mary.

"I'm gwine to keep it as long as I live," ses I, "as a Crismus present from the handsomest gall in Georgia."

When I sed that, she blushed worse and worse.

"Aint you shamed, Majer?" ses she.

"Now you ought to give *her* a Crismus gift, Joseph, to keep all *her* life," ses Miss Carline.

"Ah," ses old Miss Stallins, "when I was a gall we used to hang up our stockins—"

"Why, mother!" ses all of 'em, "to say stockins right before—"

Then I felt a little streaked too, cause they was all blushin as hard as they could.

"Highty-tity!" ses the old lady—"what monstrous 'finement to be shore! I'd like to know what harm ther is in stockins. People now-a-days is gittin so mealy-mouthed they can't call nothin by its right name, and I don't see as they's any better than the old time people was. When I was a gall like you, child, I use to hang up my stockins and git 'em full of presents."

The gals kep laughin and blushin.

"Never mind," ses Miss Mary, "Majer's got to give me a Crismus gift—won't you, Majer?"

"Oh, yes," ses I, "you know I promised you one."

"But I didn't mean *that*," ses she.

"I've got one for you, what I want you to keep all your life, but it would take a two bushel bag to hold it," ses I.

"Oh, that's the kind," ses she.

"But will you promise to keep it as long as you live?" ses I.

"Certainly I will, Majer."

—"Monstrous 'finement now-a-days—old people don't know nothin about perliteness," said old Miss Stallins, jest gwine to sleep with her nittin in her lap.

"Now you hear that, Miss Carline," ses I. "She ses she'll keep it all her life."

"Yes, I will," ses Miss Mary—"but what is it?"

"Never mind," ses I, "you hang up a bag big enough to hold it and you'll find out what it is, when you see it in the mornin."

Miss Carline winked at Miss Kesiah, and then whispered to her—then they both laughed and looked at me as mischievous as they could. They 'spicioned something.

"You'll be shore to give it to me now, if I hang up a bag," ses Miss Mary.

"And promise to keep it," ses I.

"Well, I will, cause I know that you wouldn't give me nothin that wasn't worth keepin."

They all agreed they would hang up a bag for me to put Miss Mary's Crismus present in, on the back porch, and about ten o'clock I told 'em good evenin and went home.

I sot up till mid-night, and when they was all gone to bed I went softly into the back gate, and went up to the porch, and thar, shore enough, was a great big meal-bag hangin to the jice. It was monstrous unhandy to git to it, but I was termined not to back out. So I sot some chairs on top of a bench and got hold of the rope and let myself down into the bag; but jest as I was gittin in, it swung agin the chairs, and down they went with a terrible racket; but nobody didn't wake up but Miss Stallinses old cur dog, and here he come rippin and tearin through the yard like rath, and round and round he went tryin to find what was the matter. I scrooch'd down in the bag and didn't breathe louder nor a kitten, for fear he'd find me out, and after a while he quit barkin.

The wind begun to blow bominable cold, and the old bag kep turnin round and swingin so it made me sea-sick as the mischief. I was afraid to move for fear the rope would break and let me fall, and thar I sot with my teeth rattlin like I had a ager. It seemed like it would never come daylight, and I do believe if I didn't love Miss Mary so powerful I would a froze to death; for my heart was the only spot that felt warm, and it didn't beat more'n two licks a minit, only when I thought how she would be surprised in the mornin, and then it went in a canter. Bimeby the cussed old dog come up on the porch and begun to smell about the bag, and then he barked like he thought he'd treed something. "Bow! wow! wow!" ses he. Then he'd smell agin, and try to git up to the bag. "Git out!" ses I, very low, for fear the galls mought hear me. "Bow! wow!" ses he. "Be gone! you bominable fool," ses I, and I felt all over in spots, for I spected every minit he'd nip me, and what made it worse, I didn't know whar abouts he'd take hold. "Bow! wow! wow!" Then I tried coaxin—"Come here, good feller," ses I, and whistled a little to him, but it wasn't no use. Thar he stood and kep up his everlastin whinin and barkin, all night. I couldn't tell when daylight was breakin, only by the chickens crowin, and I was monstrous glad to hear 'em, for if I'd had to stay thar one hour more, I don't believe I'd ever got out of that bag alive.

Old Miss Stallins come out fust, and as soon as she seed the bag, ses she,

"What upon yeath has Joseph went and put in that bag for Mary? I'll lay its a yearlin or some live animal, or Bruin wouldn't bark at it so."

She went in to call the galls, and I sot thar, shiverin all over so I couldn't hardly speak if I tried to—but I didn't say nothin. Bimeby they all come runnin out on the porch.

"My goodness! what is it?" ses Miss Mary.

"Oh, it's alive!" ses Miss Kesiah, "I seed it move."

"Call Cato and make him cut the rope," ses Miss Carline, "and lets see what it is. Come here, Cato, and git this bag down."

"Don't hurt it for the world," ses Miss Mary.

Cato untied the rope that was round the jice, and let the bag down easy on the floor, and I tumbled out all covered with corn meal, from head to foot.

"Goodness gracious!" ses Miss Mary, "if it aint the Majer himself!"

"Yes," ses I, "and you know you promised to keep my Crismus present as long as you lived."

The galls laughed themselves almost to death, and went to brushin off the meal as fast as they could, sayin they was gwine to hang that bag up every Crismus till they got husbands too. Miss Mary—bless her bright eyes—she blushed as beautiful as a morning-glory, and sed she'd stick to her word. She was right out of bed, and her hair wasn't komed, and her dress wasn't fix'd at all, but the way she looked pretty was real distractin. I do believe if I was froze stiff, one look at her sweet face, as she stood thar lookin down to the floor with her roguish eyes, and her bright curls fallin all over her snowy neck, would have fotched me too. I tell you what, it was worth hangin in a meal bag from one Crismus to another to feel as happy as I have ever sense.

I went home after we had the laugh out, and sot by the fire till I got thawed. In the forenoon all the Stallinses come over to our house and we had one of the greatest Crismus dinners that ever was seed in Georgia, and I don't believe a happier company ever sot down to the same table. Old Miss Stallins and mother settled the match, and talked over every thing that ever happened in ther families, and laughed at me and Mary, and cried about their dead husbands, cause they wasn't alive to see their children married.

It's all settled now, 'cept we haint sot the weddin day. I'd like to have it all over at once, but young galls always like to be engaged a while, you know, so I spose I must wait a month or so. Mary (she ses I mustn't call her Miss Mary now) has been a good deal of trouble and botheration to me; but if you could see her you wouldn't think I ought to grudge a little sufferin to git sich a sweet little wife.

You must come to the weddin if you possibly kin. I'll let you know when. No more from

Your friend, till death,   JOS. JONES.

N.B. I like to forgot to tell you about cousin Pete. He got snapt on egnog when he heard of my ingagement, and he's been as meller as hoss-apple ever sense.

The Runaway Match; or How the Schoolmaster Married a Fortune

It's about ten years ago sense the incident what I'm gwine to tell tuck place. It caused a great sensation in Pineville at the time, and had the effect to make fellers monstrous careful how they run away with other people's daughters without their consent ever sense.

Mr. Ebenezer Doolittle was the bominablest man after rich galls that ever was. He hadn't been keep-in' school in Pineville more'n six months before be had found out every gall in the settlement whose father had twenty niggers, and had courted all of 'em within a day's ride. He was rather old to be poplar with the galls, and somehow they didn't like his ways, and the way they did bluff him off was enough to discourage anybody but a Yankee schoolmaster, what wanted to git married, and hadn't many years of grace left. But it didn't seem to make no sort of difference to him. He undertook 'em by the job. He was bound to have a rich wife out of some of 'em if he failed in one case, it only made him more perseverin' in the next. His motto was—

"never say die."

Nettie Darling, as they used to call her—old Mr. Darling's daughter, what used to live out on the Runs—was about the torndownest mischief of a gall in all Georgia. Nettie was rich, and handsome and smart, and had more admirers than she could shake a stick at, but she was sich a tormentin' little coquet that the boys was all afraid to court her in downright yearnest. When Mr. Doolittle found her out he went for her like a house-a-fire. She was jest the gall for him, and he was determined to have her at the risk of his life.

Well, he laid siege to old Darling's house day and night, and when he couldn't leave his school to go and see her, he rit letters to her that was enough to throw any other gall but Nettie Darling into a fit of the highstericks to read 'em. Jest as everybody expected, after encouragin the feller long enough to make him believe he had the thing dead, she kicked him flat. But, 'shaw! he was perfectly used to that, and he was too much of a filosofer to be discouraged by such treatment, when the game was worth pursuin. He didn't lose no time, but jest brushed up and went right at her agin. Everybody was perfectly surprised to see him gwine back to old Mr. Darling's after the way he had been snubbed by Nettie, but they was a good deal more surprised and the boys was terribly allarmed, in about a month, at the headway he was makin. All at once Miss Nettie's conduct seemed changed towards him, and though her father and mother was desperately opposed to the match, anybody could see that she was beginnin to like the schoolmaster very much.

Things went on in this way for a while, till bimeby old Mr. Darling begun to git so uneasy about it, that he told Mr. Doolittle one day, that he mustn't come to his house no more; and that if he ketched him sendin any more love letters and kiss verses to his daughter by his nigger galls, he'd make one of his boys give him a alfired cowhidin.

But Mr. Doolittle didn't care for that neither. He could see Miss Nettie when she come a shopin in the stores in town, and ther was more'n one way to git a letter to her. What did he care for old Darling? His daughter was head and heart in love with him, and was jest the gall to run away with him too, if the old folks opposed the match. And as for the property, he was certain to get that when once he married the gall.

One Saturday, when ther was no school, Mr. Doolittle went to old Squire Rogers and told him he must be ready to marry a couple that night at exactly ten o'clock, at his office.

"Mum," says Doolittle. "You mustn't say a word about it to nobody, squire. The license is all ready, and the party wants to be very private."

Squire Rogers was one of the most accommodatin old cusses in the world, on sich occasions. Mrs. Rogers was a monstrous cranky, cross old woman, and nothing done the old squire so much good as to marry other people, it didn't make no odds who they was. Besides, Mr. Doolittle was a injured man and a great scholar, in his opinion, and belonged to his church.

Mr. Doolittle had arranged the whole business in first-rate order. Miss Nettie was to meet him at the end of her father's lane, disguised in a ridin dress borrowed for the occasion, when he was to take her in a close one-horse barouche, and "fly with her on the wings of love," as he said he would, to Squire Rogers' office, whar they would be united in the bands of wedlock before anybody in the village know'd anything about it. He had made arrangements at the hotel for a room, which he seed fixed up himself for the auspicious occasion, and he had rit a letter to a friend of his down in Augusty to come to Pineville the next week to take charge of his school, as he thought it mought be necessary for him to keep out of the way of old Darling for a few weeks, till the old feller could have time to cool down.

All day Mr. Doolittle was bustlin about as if he wasn't certain which eend he stood on, while the sunshine in his heart beamed from his taller-colored face in a way to let everybody know that something extraordinary was gwine to happen.

Jest after dark he mought been seen drivin out by himself in a barouche, towards old Mr. Darling's plantation. Everybody suspicioned something, and all hands was on the lookout. It was plain to see that Squire Rogers' importance was swelled up considerable with something, but nobody couldn't git a word out of him.

Mr. Doolittle didn't spare the lash after he got out of sight of town, and with strainin eyes and palpitatin heart he soon reached the place appinted to meet the object of his consumin affections.

Was she thar? No! Yes! Is it? Yes, thar she is I—the dear creetur! the skirt of her nankeen ridin dress, what fits close to her angelic form, flutterin in the breeze. She stands timidly crouchin in the corner of the fense, holdin her thick vale over her lovely face, tremblin in every jint, for fear she mought be discovered and tore away from the arms of her dear Ebenezer!

"Dearest angel," ses he, in a low voice.

"Oh, Ebenezer I" and she kind o' fell in his arms.

"Compose yourself, my love," ses he.

"Oh, if father should—"

"Don't fear, dearest creeter. My arm shall protect you," ses Doolittle.

And then he was jest gwine to put away her vale to kiss her—

"Oh!" ses she, "didn't I hear somebody comin'?"

"Eh?" ses Doolittle lookin quickly round. "Let's git in, my dear."

And with that he helped her into the barouche, and contented himself with imprintin a burnin kiss, that almost singed the kid glove on her dear little hand, as he closed the door. Then jumpin onto the front seat and seizin the lines, he drove as fast as he could to town, encouragin her all the way and swearin to her how he would love her and make her happy, and tellin her how her father and mother would forgive her when it was all over, and think jest as much of her as ever.

Pore gall! she was so terribly agitated that she couldn't do nothing but sob and cry, which made her dear Ebenezer love her the more and swear the harder.

When they got to the squire's office, and the boys, who was on the watch, seed him help her out of the barouche, everybody know'd her at once in spite of her disguise, and sich another excitement was never seed in Pineville. Some of the fellers was half out of their senses, and it was necessary to hurry the ceremony over as quick as possible for fear of bein interrupted by the row that was bruin.

"Be quick, Squire," ses Doolittle, handin' out the license, and shakin' like he had a ager—"for Miss Darling is very much agitated."

The Squire hardly waited to wipe his spectacles, and didn't take time to enjoy himself in readin the ceremony slow and solem, like he always did. The noise was gettin louder and louder out of doors, and somebody was knockin to get in.

"Oh, me!" ses Nettie, leanin on Mr. Doolittle's arm for support.

"Go on!" gasped Doolittle, pressin the almost faintin Nettie to his side, with his eyes on the Squire and his face as white as a sheet.

"Open the door, Rogers!" ses a hoarse voice outside.

But the Squire didn't hear nothin till he pronounced the last words of the ceremony, and Ebeneezer Doolittle and Nettie Darling was pronounced man and wife.

Jest then the door opened. In rushed old Mr. Darling and Bill and Sam Darling, followed by a whole heap of fellers.

The bride screamed and fell into the arms of the triumphant Doolittle.

"Take hold of her!" ses old Darling flourishin his cane over his head. "Take hold of the huzzy!"

"Standoff!" ses Doolittle, throwin himself into a real stage attitude, and supportin his faintin bride with one arm, "Stand off, old man! She is my lawful wife, and I claim the protection of the law!"

"Knock him down! Take hold of him!" hollered out half a dozen, and Bill Darling grabbed the bridegroom by the neck, while Squire Rogers jumped upon the table and called out—

"I command the peace! I command the peace, in the name of the State of Georgia!"

"She's my wife! my lawful wife!" shouted Doolittle. "I call upon the law!"

By this time the bride got over her fainting fit and raised her drooping head—the vale fell off and—oh, cruel fate! Mr. Ebeneezer Doolittle stood petrified with horror, holdin in his arms, not Miss Nettie Darling, but Miss Nettie Darling's waiting-gall, one of the blackest nigger wenches in Georgia, who at that interestin crisis, rolled her eyes upon him like two peeled onions, and throwin her arms around his neck, exclaimed—

"Shore dis is my husband, what Miss Netty done give me her own self,"

Sich a shout as the boys did raise!

"Go to the devil, you black--" screamed Doolittle, tryin to take her arms from his neck.

"Hold on to him, Silla," shouted all the fellers, "he's your husband according to the law."

Old Squire Rogers looked like he'd married his last couple, pore old man, and hadn't a word to say for himself. The boys and the young Darlings liked to laugh themselves to death, while old Mr. Darling who was mad as a hornit, was gwine to have Doolittle arrested for nigger stealin, right off.

Pore Doolittle! He made out at last to git loose from his wife, and to find the back door. He haint never been heard of in Pineville from that day to this.

George Washington Harris (1814-1869)

George Washington Harris was neither a writer by trade nor a southerner by birth. But he contributed to American literature one of its most distinctively southern comic figures in Sut Lovingood and brought the American literary vernacular to its highest level of achievement before Mark Twain. Harris was brought as a child to Knoxville, Tennessee, by his half-brother from the place of his birth in Allegheny City, Pennsylvania. He adapted to the attitudes and mores of the antebellum South with spirit and enthusiasm. He had little education in the formal sense, but he followed a wide cross-section of occupations, including metal working, serving as captain of a steamboat, farming, running a glass works and a sawmill, surveying, running for political office, serving as a postmaster, and working for the railroad. Such diverse occupations provided Harris with a rich education in life and a large reservoir of material from which to draw in his writing.

Writing was a leisure-time activity for Harris, who began as an author of political sketches for local newspapers and sporting epistles for the nationally popular New York *Spirit of the Times*. He quickly developed a facility for local color and dialect and a skill for bringing to life backwoods scenes and events on the printed page. When he contributed his first Sut Lovingood sketch to the *Spirit of the Times* on November 4, 1854, he outdistanced all the other humorists of the Old Southwest by allowing one central character to tell his stories in his own crude vernacular and by granting that character his full independence in thought and action. Mark Twain, who reviewed Harris's one book in 1867, *Sut Lovingood: Yarns*, would learn those lessons well and later put them to effective use in *Adventures of Huckleberry Finn*. Harris had collected a second set of stories but died on a return train trip to seek a publisher in 1869. He was buried in Trenton, Georgia, and the manuscript has never been found.

What makes Sut distinctive is the combination in his character of such human failings as bigotry, vulgarity, cowardice, and brutality, along with, more admirably, a steadfast opposition to hypocrisy, dishonesty, and all limitations set on personal and social freedom. Many readers find it difficult to like Sut, but few find it possible to resist his appeal, especially those who enjoy watching hypocrites exposed and those who take advantage of innocence appropriately punished. While authors and critics such as William Dean Howells and Edmund Wilson found Sut objectionable on grounds of good taste, others such as Twain, William Faulkner, Flannery O'Connor, and F. O. Matthiessen paid tribute to Harris's influence and genius. Sut's wildly funny pranks and incorrigible nature make him one of the most intriguing characters in American literary history.

Texts: "Sut Lovingood's Daddy, Acting Horse" and "Parson John Bullen's Lizards," from *Sut Lovingood: Yarns Spun by a "A Nat'ral Born Durn'd Fool, Warped and Wove for Public Wear"* (New York: Dick & Fitzgerald, 1867). "Sut Lovingood Reports What Bob Dawson Said, After Marrying a Substitute," *Chattanooga Daily American Union*, November 27 and 28, 1867. "Well! Dad's Dead," *Knoxville Daily Press and Herald*, November 15, 1868.

Sut Lovingood's Daddy, Acting Horse

"Hole that ar hoss down tu the yearth." "He's a fixin fur the heavings." "He's a spreadin his tail feathers tu fly. Look out, Laigs, if you aint ready tu go up'ards." "Wo, Shavetail." "Git a fiddil; he's tryin a jig." "Say, Long Laigs, rais'd a power ove co'n didn't yu?" "Taint co'n, hits redpepper."

These and like expressions were addressed to a queer looking, long legged, short bodied, small headed, white haired, hog eyed, funny sort of a genius, fresh from some bench-legged Jew's clothing store, mounted on "Tearpoke," a nick tailed, bow necked, long, poor, pale sorrel horse, half dandy, half devil, and enveloped in a perfect net-work of bridle, reins, crupper, martingales, straps, surcingles, and red ferreting, who reined up in front of Pat Nash's grocery, among a crowd of mountaineers full of fun, foolery, and mean whisky.

This was SUT LOVINGOOD.

"I say, you durn'd ash cats, jis' keep yer shuts on, will ye? You never seed a rale hoss till I rid up; you's p'raps stole ur owned shod rabbits ur sheep wif borrered saddils on, but when you tuck the fus' begrudgin look jis' now at this critter, name Tearpoke, yu wer injoyin a sight ove nex' tu the bes' hoss what ever shell'd nubbins ur toted jugs, an' he's es ded es a still wum, poor ole Tickytail!

"Wo! wo! Tearpoke, yu cussed infunel fidgety hide full ove hell fire, can't yu stan' still an listen while I'se a polishin yer karacter off es a mortul hoss tu these yere durned fools?"

Sut's tongue or his spurs brought Tearpoke into something like passable quietude while he continued:

"Say yu, sum ove yu growin hogs made a re-mark jis' now 'bout redpepper. I jis' wish tu say in a gineral way that eny wurds cupplin redpepper an Tearpoke together am durn'd infurnal lies."

"What killed Ticketytail, Sut?" asked an anxious inquirer after truth.

"Why nuffin, you cussed fool; he jis' died so, standin up et that. Warn't that rale casteel hoss pluck? Yu see, he froze stiff; no, not that adzactly, but starv'd fust an' froze arterards, so stiff that when dad an' me went tu lay him out an' we push'd him over, he stuck out jis' so (spreading his arms and legs), like ontu a carpenter's bainch, an' we hed tu wait ni ontu seventeen days fur 'im tu thaw afore we cud skin 'im."

"Skin 'im?" interrupted a rat-faced youth, whittling on a corn stalk, "I thot yu wanted tu lay the hoss out."

"The hell yu did! Aint skinnin the natral way ove layin out a hoss, I'd like tu no? See a yere, soney, yu tell yer mam tu hev you sot back jis' 'bout two years, fur et the rate yu'se a climbin yu stan's a pow'ful chance tu die wif yer shoes on, an' git laid hoss way, yu dus."

The rat-faced youth shut up his knife and subsided.

"Well, thar we wer—dad, an' me (counting on his fingers), an' Sall, an' Jake (fool Jake we calls 'im fur short), an' Jim, an' Phineass, an' Callimy Jane, an' Sharlottyann, an' me, an' Zodiack, an' Cashus Clay, an' Noah Dan Webster, an' the twin gals (Castur and Pollox), an' me, an' Catherin Second, an' Cleopatry Antony, an' Jane Barnum Lind, an' me, an' Benton Bullion, an' the baby what haint nam'd yet, an' me, an' the Prospect, an' mam herself, all lef in the woods alone, wifout ara hoss tu crup wif."

"Yu'se counted yerself five times, Mister Lovingood," said a tomato-nosed man in a ragged overcoat.

"Yas, ole Still-tub, that's jis the perporshun I bears in the famerly fur dam fool, leavin out Dad in course. Yu jis let me alone, an' be a thinkin ove gettin more hoops ontu yu. Yus leakin now; see thar." Ha! ha! from the crowd, and "Still-tub" went into the doggery.

"Warnt that a devil's own mess ove broth fur a 'spectabil white famerly tu be sloshin about in? I be durned ef I didn't feel sorter like stealin a hoss sumtimes, an' I speck I'd a dun hut, but the stealin streak in the Lovingoods all run tu durned fool, an' the onvartus streak all run tu laigs. Jis look down the side ove this yere hoss mos' tu the groun.' Dus you see em?

"Well we waited, an' wished, an' rested, an' plan'd, an' wished, an' waited agin, ontil ni ontu strawberry time, hopin sum stray hoss mout cum along; but dorg my cats, ef eny sich good luck ever cums wifin reach ove whar dad is, he'd so dod-dratted mean, an' lazy, an' ugly, an' savidge, an' durn fool tu kill.

"Well, one nite he lay awake till cock-crowin a-snortin, an' rollin, an' blowin, an' shuffling, an' scratchin hisself, an' a whisperin at mam a heap, an' at breckfus' I foun' out what hit ment. Says he, 'Sut, I'll tell yu what we'll du: I'll be hoss *myself,* an' pull the plow whilst yu drives me, an' then the "Ole Quilt" (he ment that fur mam) an' the brats kin plant, an' tend, ur jis let hit alone, es they darn pleze; I aint a carein.'

"So out we went tu the pawpaw thicket, an' peel'd a rite smart chance ove bark an' man an' me made geers fur dad, while he sot on the fence a-lookin at us, an' a studyin pow'rful. I arterards foun' out, he wer a-studyin how tu play the kar-acter ove a hoss puffectly.

"Well, the geers becum him mitily, an' nuffin wud du 'im but he mus hev a bridil, so I gits a umereller brace—hit's a litil forked piece ove squar wire 'bout a foot long, like a yung pitch-fork, yu no—an' twisted hit sorter intu a bridil bit snaffil shape. Dad wanted hit made kurb, es he hedn't work'd fur a good while, an' said he mout sorter feel his keepin, an' go tu ravin an' cavortin.

"When we got the bridil fix'd ontu dad, don't yu bleve he sot in tu chompin hit jis like a rale hoss, an' tried tu bite me on the arm (he allers wer a mos' complikated durned ole fool, an' mam sed so when he warnt about). I put on the geers, an' while mam wer a-tyin the belly ban,' a strainin hit pow'rful tite, he drapt ontu his hans, sed 'Whay-a-a' like a mad hoss wud, an' slung his hine laigs at mam's hed. She step'd back a littil an' wer standin wif her arms cross'd a-restin em on her stumick, an' his heel taps cum wifin a inch ove her nose. Sez she, 'Yu plays hoss better nur yu dus husban.' He jis' run backards on all fours, an' kick'd at her agin, an'—an' pawd the groun wif his fis.

"'Lead him off tu the field, Sut, afore he kicks ur bites sumbody,' sez mam. I shoulder'd the gopher plow, an' tuck hole ove the bridil. Dad leaned back sulky, till I sed cluck, cluck, wif my tongue, then he started. When we cum to the fence I let down the gap, an' hit made dad mad; he wanted tu jump hit on all fours hoss way. Oh geminy! what a durn'd ole fool kin cum tu ef he gins up tu the complaint.

"I hitch'd 'im tu the gopher, a-watchin him pow'ful clost, fur I'd see how quick he cud drap ontu his hans, an' kick, an' away we went, dad leanin forard tu his pullin, an' we made rite peart plowin, fur tu hev a green hoss, an' bark gears; he went over the sprowts an' bushes same as a rale hoss, only he traveled on two laigs. I wer mitily hope up 'bout co'n; I cud a'mos' see hit a cumin up; but thar's a heap ove whisky spilt twixt the counter an' the mouf, ef hit ain't got but two foot tu travil. 'Bout the time he wer beginin tu break sweat, we cum tu a sassafrack bush, an tu keep up his karacter es a hoss, he buljed squar intu an' thru hit, tarin down a ball ho'nets nes' ni ontu es big es a hoss's hed, an' the hole tribe kiver'd 'im es quick es yu cud kiver a sick pup wif a saddil blanket. He lit ontu his hans agin, an kick'd strait up onst, then he rar'd, an' fotch a squeal wus nur ara stud hoss in the State, an' sot in tu strait runnin away jis es natral es yu ever seed any uther skeer'd hoss du. I let go the line an' holler'd, Wo! dad, wo! but yu mout jis' es well say Woa! tu a locomotum, ur Suke cow tu a gal.

"Gewhillitins! how he run; when he cum tu bushes, he'd clar the top ove em wif a squeal, gopher an' all. P'raps he tho't thar mout be anuther settilment ove ball ho'nets thar, an' hit wer safer tu go over than thru, an' quicker dun eny how. Every now an' then he'd fan the side ove his hed, fust wif wun fore laig an' then tuther, then he'd gin hisself a roun-handed slap what soundid like a waggin whip ontu the place whar the breechbands tetches a hoss, a-runnin all the time an' a-kerrien that ar gopher jis 'bout as fas' an' es hi frum the yeath es ever eny gopher wer kerried I'll swar. When he cum tu the fence, he jis tore thru hit, bustin an' scatterin ni ontu seven panils wif lots ove broken rails. Rite yere he lef the gopher, geers, close, clevis, an' swingltress, all mix'd up an' not wuf a durn. Mos' ove his shut staid ontu the aind ove a rail, an' ni ontu a pint ove ho'nets stop'd thar a stingin all over; hits smell fool'd em. The balance on em, ni ontu a gallun, kep' on wif dad. He seem'd tu run jis adzactly as fas' es a hon'et cud fly; hit wer the titest race I ever seed, fur wun hoss tu git all the whipin. Down thru a saige field they all went, the ho'nets makin hit look like thar wer smoke roun' dad's bald hed, an' he wif nuffin on the green yeath in the way ove close about im, but the bridil, an' ni ontu a yard ove plow line sailin behine, wif a tir'd out ho'net ridin on the pint ove hit. I seed that he wer aimin fur the swimin hole in the krick, whar the bluff am over twenty five foot pupendiculer tu the warter, an' hits ni ontu ten foot deep.

"Well, tu keep up his karacter es a hoss, plum thru, when he got to the bluff he loped off, ur rather jis' kep on a runnin kerplunge intu the krick he went. I seed the warter fly plum abuv the bluff from whar I wer.

"Now rite thar, boys, he over-did the thing, ef actin hoss tu the scribe wer what he wer arter; fur thars nara hoss ever foaldid durned fool enuf tu lope over eny sich place; a cussed muel mout a dun hit, but dad warn't actin muel, tho' he orter tuck that karacter; hits adzactly sooted tu his dispersition, all but not breedin. I crept up tu the aidge, an' peep'd over. Thar wer dad's bald hed fur all the yeath like a peeled inyin, a bobbin up an' down an' around, an' the ho'nets sailin roun tuckey buzzard fashun, an' every onst in a while one, an' sum times ten, wud take a dip at dad's bald head. He kep' up a rite peart dodgin onder, sumtimes afore they hit im, an' sumtimes arterard, an' the warter wer kivered wif drownded ball ho'nets. Tu look at hit frum the top ove the bluff, hit wer pow'ful inturestin, an' sorter funny; I wer on the bluff myse'f, mine yu.

"Dad cudent see the funny part frum whar he wer, but hit seem'd tu be inturestin tu him frum the 'tenshun he wer payin to the bisness ove divin an' cussin.

"Sez I, 'Dad, ef yu's dun washin yerself, an hes drunk enuff, less go back tu our plowin, hit will soon be powful hot.' 'Hot—hell!' sez dad; 'hit am hot rite now. Don't (an onder went his hed) yer see (dip) these cussed (dip) infun—(dip) varmints arter me?' (dip) 'What,' sez I, 'them ar hoss flies thar, that's nat'ral dad; you aint raley fear'd ove them is yu?' 'Hoss flies! h—lan' (dip) durnation!' sez dad, 'theyse rale ginui—(dip) ball ho'nets, (dip) yu infunel ignurant cuss!' (dip) 'Kick em—bite em—paw em—switch em wif yure tail, dad,' sez I. 'Oh! soney, soney, (dip) how I'll sweeten yure—(dip) when these (dip) ho'nets leave yere.' 'Yu'd better du the levin yursef dad,' sez I. 'Leave yere! Sut yu d—n fool! How (dip) kin I, (dip) when they won't (dip) let me stay (dip) atop (dip) the warter even.' 'Well, dad, yu'l hev tu stay thar till nite, an' arter they goes tu roos' yu cum home. I'll hev yer feed in the troft redy; yu won't need eny curyin tu-nite, will yu?' 'I wish (dip) I may never (dip) see to-morrer, ef I (dip) don't make (dip) hame strings (dip) outer yure hide (dip) when I dus (dip) git outen yere,' sez dad. 'Better say yu wish yu may never see anuther ball ho'net, ef yu ever play hoss agin,' sez I.

"Them words toch dad tu the hart, an' I felt they mus' be my las, knowin dad's onmollified nater. I broke frum them parts, an' sorter cum over yere tu the copper mines. When I got tu the hous,' 'Whar's yer dad?' sez mam. 'Oh, he turn'd durn fool, an' run away, busted every thing all tu cussed smash, an's in the swimin hole a divin arter minners. Look out mam, he'll cum home wif a angel's temper; better sen' fur sum strong man body tu keep him frum huggin yu tu deth. 'Law sakes!' sez mam; 'I know'd he cudent act hoss fur ten minutes wifout actin infunel fool, tu save his life.'

"I staid hid out ontil nex' arternoon, an' I seed a feller a-travelin.' Sez I, 'How de do, mister? What wer agwine on at the cabin, this side the crick, when yu pass'd thar?' 'Oh, nuthin much, only a pow'ful fat man wer a lyin in the yard ontu his belly, wif no shut on, an' a 'oman wer a greasin ove his shoulders an' arms outen a gourd. A pow'ful curious, vishus, skeery lookin cuss he is tu b'shure. His head am as big es a wash pot, an' he hasent the fust sign ove an eye—jist two black slits. Is thar much small pox roun yere?' 'Small hell!' sez I, 'no sir.' 'Been much fightin in this neighborhood lately?' 'Nun wuf speakin ove,' sez I. He scratched his head—'Nur French measils?' 'Not jis clost,' sez I. 'Well, do yu know what ails that man back thar?' 'Jist gittin over a vilent attack ove dam fool,' sez I. 'Well, who is he eny how?' I ris tu my feet, an' straiched out my arm, an' sez I, 'Strainger, that man is my dad.' He looked at my laigs an' pussonel feeters a moment, an' sez he, 'Yas, dam ef he aint.'

"Now boys, I haint seed dad since, an' I dusent hev much appertite tu see im fur sum time tu cum. Less all drink! Yere's luck tu the durned old fool, an' the ho'nets too."

Parson John Bullen's Lizards

AIT ($8) DULLARS REW-ARD.
'TENSHUN BELEVERS AND KONSTABLES! KETCH 'IM! KETCH 'IM!
This kash wil be pade in korn, ur uther projuce, tu be kolected at ur about nex camp-meetin, *ur thararter,* by eny wun what ketches him, fur the karkus

ove a sartin wun SUT LOVINGOOD, dead ur alive, ur ailin, an' safely giv over tu the purtectin care ove Parson John Bullin, ur lef' well tied, at Squire Mackjunkins, fur the raisin ove the devil pussonely, an' permiskusly discumfurtin the wimen very powerful, an' skeerin ove folks generly a heap, an' bustin up a promisin, big warm meetin, an' a makin the wickid larf, an' wus, an' wus, inultin ove the passun orful.

Test, JEHU WETHERO

Sined by me,

JOHN BULLEN, the passun.

I found written copies of the above highly intelligible and vindictive proclamation, stuck up on every blacksmith shop, doggery, and store door, in the Frog Mountain Range. Its blood-thirsty spirit, its style, and above all, its chirography, interested me to the extent of taking one down from a tree for preservation.

In a few days I found Sut in a good crowd in front of Capehart's Doggery, and as he seemed to be about in good tune, I read it to him.

"Yas, George, that ar dockymint am in dead yearnist sartin. Them hard shells over thar dus want me the wus kine, powerful bad. *But,* I spect ait dullers won't fetch me, nither wud ait hundred, bekase thar's nun ove 'em fas' enuf tu ketch me, nither is thar hosses by the livin jingo! Say, George, much talk 'bout this fuss up whar yu're been?" For the sake of a joke I said yes, a great deal.

"Jis' es I 'spected, durn 'em, all git drunk, an' skeer thar fool sefs ni ontu deth, an' then lay hit ontu me, a poor innersent youf, an' es soun' a belever es they is. Lite, lite, ole feller an' let that roan ove yourn blow a litil, an' I'll 'splain this cussed misfortnit affair: hit hes ruinated my karacter es a pius pusson in the s'ciety roun' yere, an' is a spreadin faster nur meazils. When ever yu hear eny on 'em a spreadin hit, gin hit the dam lie squar, will yu? I haint dun nuffin tu one ove 'em. Hits true, I did sorter frustrate a few lizzards a littil, but they haint members, es I knows on.

"You see, las' year I went tu the big meetin at Rattlesnake Springs, an' wer a sittin in a nice shady place convarsin wif a frien' ove mine, intu the huckil berry thickit, jis' duin nuffin tu nobody an' makin no fuss, when the fust thing I remembers, I woke up frum a trance what I hed been knocked inter by a four year old hickory-stick, hilt in the paw ove old Passun Bullin, durn his alligator hide; an' he wer standin a striddil ove me, a foamin at the mouf, a-chompin his teeth—gesterin wif the hickory club—an' a-preachin tu me so you cud a-hearn him a mile, about a sartin sin gineraly, an' my wickedness pussonely; an' menshunin the name ove my frien' loud enuf tu be hearn tu the meetin 'ous. My poor innersent frien' wer dun gone an' I wer glad ove hit, fur I tho't he ment tu kill me rite whar I lay, an' I didn't want her to see me die."

"Who was she, the friend you speak of Sut?" Sut opened his eyes wide.

"Hu the devil an' durnashun tole *yu* that hit wer a she?"

"Why, you did, Sut"—

"I *didn't,* durn ef I did. Ole Bullin dun hit, an' I'll hev tu kill him yet, the cussed, infernel ole talebarer!"—

"Well, well, Sut, who was she?"

"Nun ove y-u-r-e b-i-s-n-i-s-s, durn yure littil ankshus picter! I *sees yu* a lickin ove yure lips. I *will* tell you one thing, George; that night, a neighbor gal got a all fired, overhandid stroppin frum her mam, wif a stirrup leather, an' ole Passun Bullin, hed et supper thar, an' what's wus nur all, that poor, innersent, skeer'd gal hed dun her levil bes' a cookin hit fur 'im. She begged him, a trimblin, an' a-cryin not tu tell on her. He et her cookin, he promised her he'd keep dark—an' then went strait an' tole her mam. Warnt that rale low down, wolf mean? The durnd infunel, hiperkritikal, pot-bellied, scaley-hided, whisky-wastin, stinkin ole groun'-hog. He'd a heap better a stole sum *man's* hoss; I'd a tho't more ove 'im. But I paid him plum up fur hit, an' I means tu keep a payin him, ontil one ur tuther, ove our toes pints up tu the roots ove the grass.

"Well, yere's the way I lifted that note ove han'. At the nex big meetin at Rattilsnaik—las' week hit wer—I wer on han' es solemn es a ole hat kivver on collection day. I hed my face draw'd out intu the shape an' perporshun ove a tayler's sleeve-board, pint down. I hed put on the convicted sinner so pufeckly that an'ole obsarvin she pillar ove the church sed tu a ole he pillar, es I walked up to my bainch:

"'Law sakes alive, ef thar ain't that *orful* sinner, Sut Lovingood, pearced plum thru; hu's nex?'

"Yu see, by golly, George, I *hed* tu promis the ole tub ove soap-greas tu cum an' hev myself converted, jis' tu keep him frum killin me. An' es I know'd hit wudn't interfare wif the relashun I bore tu the still housis roun' thar, I didn't keer a durn. I jis' wanted tu git *ni* ole Bullin, onst unsuspected, an' this wer the bes' way tu du hit. I tuk a seat on the side steps ove the pulpit, an' kivvered es much ove my straitch'd face es I could wif my han's, tu prove I wer in yearnis. Hit tuck powerful—fur I hearn a sorter thankful kine ove buzzin all over the congregashun. Ole Bullin hisself looked down at me, over his ole copper specks, an' hit sed jis' es plain es a look cud say hit: 'Yu am thar, ar you—durn yu, hits well fur yu that yu cum.' I tho't sorter different frum that. I tho't hit wud a been well fur *yu,* ef I hadent a-cum, but I didn't say hit just then. Thar wer a monstrus crowd in that grove, fur the weather wer fine, an' b'levers wer plenty roun' about Rattilsnaik Springs. Ole Bullin gin out, an' they sung that hyme, yu know:

"Thar will be mournin, mournin yere, an' mournin thar,
  On that dredful day tu cum."

"Thinks I, ole hoss, kin hit be possibil enybody hes tole yu what's a gwine tu happin; an' then I tho't that nobody know'd hit but me, and I wer comforted. He nex tuck hisself a tex pow'fly mixed wif brimstone, an' trim'd wif blue flames, an' then he open'd. He commenced ontu the sinners; he threaten'd 'em orful, tried tu skeer 'em wif all the wust varmints he cud think ove, an' arter a while he got ontu the idear ove Hell-sarpints, and he dwelt on it sum. He tole 'em how the ole Hell-sarpints wud sarve em if they didn't repent; how cold they'd crawl over thar nakid bodys, an' how like ontu pitch they'd stick tu 'em as they crawled; how they'd rap thar tails roun' thar naiks choking clost, poke thar tungs up thar noses, an' hiss intu thar years. This wer the way they wer to sarve men folks. Then he turned ontu the wimmen: tole 'em how they'd quile intu thar buzzims, an' how they *wud* crawl down onder thar frock-strings, no odds how tite they tied 'em, an' how sum ove the oldes' an' wus ones wud crawl up thar laigs, an' travil *onder* thar garters, no odds how tight they tied *them,* an' when the two armys ove Hell-sarpents met, then—That las' remark *fotch 'em.* Ove all the screamin, an' hollerin' an' loud cryin, I ever hearn, begun all at onst, all over the hole groun' jis' es he hollered out that word 'then.' He kep on a bellerin, but I got so busy jis' then, that I didn't listen tu him much, fur I saw that my time fur ackshun hed cum. Now yu see, George, I'd cotch seven ur eight big pot-bellied lizzards, an' hed 'em in a littil narrer bag, what I had made a-purpus. Thar tails all at the bottim, an' so crowdid fur room that they cudent turn roun'. So when he wer a-ravin ontu his tip-toes, an' a-poundin the pulpit wif his fis'—onbenowenst tu enybody, I ontied my bag ove reptiles, put the mouf ove hit onder the bottim ove his britches-laig, an' sot into pinchin thar tails. Quick es gunpowder they all tuck up his bar laig, makin a nise like squirrils a-climbin a shell-bark hickory. He stop't preachin rite in the middil ove the word 'damnation,' an' looked fur a moment like he wer a listenin fur something—sorter like a ole sow dus, when she hears yu a whistling fur the dorgs. The tarifick shape ove his feeters stopp't the shoutin an' screamin; instuntly yu cud hearn a cricket chirp. I gin a long groan, an' hilt my head a-twixt my knees. He gin hisself sum orful open-handed slaps wif fust one han' an' then tuther, about the place whar yu cut the bes' steak outen a beef. Then he'd fetch a vigrus ruff rub whar a hosses tail sprouts; then he'd stomp one foot, then tuther, then bof at onst. Then he run his han' atween his waisbun an' his shut an' reach'd way down, an' roun' wif hit; then he spread his big laigs, an' gin his back a good rattlin rub agin the pulpit, like a hog scratches hisself agin a stump, leanin tu hit pow'ful, an' twitchin, an' squirmin all over, es ef he'd slept in a dorg bed, ur ontu a pisant hill. About this time, one ove my lizzards scared an' hurt by all this poundin' an' feelin, an' scratchin, popp'd out his head frum the passun's shut collar, an' his ole brown naik, an' wer a-surveyin the crowd, when ole Bullin struck at 'im, jis' too late, fur he'd dodged back agin. The hell desarvin ole raskil's speech now cum tu 'im, an' sez he, 'Pray fur me brethren an' sisteren, fur I is a-rastilin wif the great inimy rite now!' an' his voice wer the mos' pitiful, trimblin thing I ever hearn. Sum ove the wimmen fotch a painter yell, an' a young docter, wif ramrod laigs, lean'd toward me monstrus knowin like, an' sez he, 'Clar case ove Delishus Tremenjus.' I nodded my head an' sez I, 'Yas, spechuly the tremenjus part, an' Ise feared hit haint at hits worst.' Ole Bullin's eyes wer a-stickin out like ontu two buckeyes flung agin a mud wall, an' he wer a-cuttin up more shines nor a cockroach in a hot skillet. Off went the clawhammer coat, an' he flung hit ahine 'im like he wer a-gwine intu a fight; he hed no jackid tu take off, so he unbuttond his galluses, an' vigrusly flung the ainds back over his head. He fotch his shut over-handed a durnd site faster nor I got outen my pasted one, an' then hung hit strait up in the air, like he jis' wanted hit tu keep on up furever; but hit lodged ontu a black-jack, an' I seed one ove my lizzards wif his tail up, a-racin about all over the ole dirty shut, skared too bad tu jump. Then he gin a sorter shake, an' a stompin kine ove twis,' an' he cum outer his britches. He tuck 'em by the bottim ove the laigs, an' swung 'em roun' his head a time ur two, an' then fotch 'em down cherall-up over the frunt ove the pulpit. You cud a hearn the smash a quarter ove a mile! Ni ontu fifteen shorten'd biskits, a boiled chicken, wif hits laigs crossed, a big dubbil-bladed knife, a hunk ove terbacker, a cob-pipe, sum copper ore, lots ove broken glass, a cork, a sprinkil ove whisky, a squirt, an' three lizzards flew permiskusly all over that meetin-groun', outen the upper aind ove them big flax britches. One ove the smartes' ove my lizzards lit head-fust intu the buzzim ove a fat 'oman, es big es a skin'd hoss, an' ni ontu es ugly, who sot thuty yards off, a fannin herself wif a tucky-tail. Smart tu the las,' by golly, he imejuntly commenced runnin down the centre ove her breas'-bone, an' kep on, I speck. She wer jis' boun' tu faint; an' she did hit fust rate—flung the tucky-tail up in the air, grabbed the lap ove her gown, gin hit a big histin an' fallin shake, rolled down the hill, tangled her laigs an' garters in the top ove a huckilberry bush, wif her head in the branch an' jis' lay still. She wer interestin, she wer, ontil a serious-lookin, pale-faced 'oman hung a nankeen ridin skirt over the huckilberry bush. That wer all that wer dun to'ards bringin her too, that I seed. Now ole Bullin hed nuffin left ontu 'im but a par ove heavy, low quarter'd shoes, short woolen socks, an' eel-skin garters tu keep off the cramp. His skeer hed druv him plum crazy, fur he felt roun' in the air, abuv his head, like he wer huntin sumthin in the dark, an' he beller'd out, 'Brethren, brethren, take keer ove yerselves, the Hell-sarpints *he's got me!*' When this cum out, yu cud a-hearn the screams tu Halifax. He jis' spit in his han's, an' loped over the frunt ove the pulpit *kerdiff!* He lit on top ove, an' rite amung the mos' pius part ove the congregashun. Ole Misses Chaneyberry sot wif her back tu the pulpit, sorter stoopin forrid. He lit a-stradil ove her long naik, a shuttin her up wif a snap, her head atwix her knees, like shuttin up a jack-knife, an' he sot intu gittin away his levil durndest; he went in a heavy lumberin gallop, like a ole fat wagon hoss, skared at a locomotive. When he jumpt a bainch he shook the yeath. The bonnets, an' fans clar'd the way an' jerked most ove the children wif em, an' the rest he scrunched. He open'd a purfeckly clar track tu the woods, ove every livin thing. He weighed ni ontu three hundred, hed a black stripe down his back, like ontu a ole bridil rein, an' his belly wer 'bout the size an' color ove a beef paunch, an' hit a-swingin out frum side tu side; he leand back frum hit, like a littil feller a-totin a big drum, at a muster, an' I hearn hit plum tu whar I wer. Thar wer cramp-knots on his laigs es big es walnuts, an' mottled splotches on his shins; an' takin him all over, he minded ove a durnd crazy ole elephant, pussessed ove the devil, rared up on hits hind aind, an' jis' *gittin* frum sum imijut danger ur tribulashun. He did the loudest, an' scariest, an' fussiest runnin I ever seed, tu be no faster nur hit wer, since dad tried tu outrun the ho'nets.

"Well, he disapear'd in the thicket jis' bustin—an' ove all the noises yu ever hearn, wer made thar on that camp groun'; sum wimen screamin—they wer the skeery ones; sum larfin—they wer the wicked ones; sum cryin—they were the fool ones (sorter my stripe yu know); sum tryin tu git away wif thar faces red—they wer the modest ones; sum lookin arter ole Bullin—they wer the curious ones; sum hangin clost tu thar sweethearts—they wer the sweet ones; sum on thar knees wif thar eyes shot, but facin the way the ole mud turtil wer a-runnin—they wer the 'saitful ones; sum duin nuthin—they wer the waitin ones; an' the mos' dangerus ove all ove em by a durnd long site.

"I tuck a big skeer myself arter a few rocks, an' sich like fruit, spattered ontu the pulpit ni ontu my head; an' es the Lovingoods, durn em! knows nuffin but tu run, when they gits skeerd, I jis' put out fur the swamp on the krick. As I started, a black bottil ove bald-face smashed agin a tree furninst me, arter missin the top ove my head 'bout an inch. Sum durn'd fool professor dun this, who hed more zeal nor sence; fur I say that eny man who wud waste a quart ove even mean sperrits, fur the chance ove knockin a poor ornary devil like me down wif the bottil, is a bigger fool nor ole Squire Mackmullen, an' he tried tu shoot hissef with a onloaded hoe-handle."

"Did they catch you Sut?"

"Ketch thunder! *No sir!* Jis' look at these yere laigs! Skeer me, hoss, jis' skeer me, an' then watch me while I stay in site, an' yu'll never ax that fool question agin. Why, durn it, man, that's what the ait dullers am fur.

"Ole Barbelly Bullin, es they calls 'im now, never preached ontil yesterday, an' he hadn't the fust durn'd 'oman tu hear 'im; *they hev seed too much ove 'im*. Passuns ginerly hev a pow'ful strong holt on wimen; but, hoss, I tell yu thar ain't meny ove em kin run stark nakid over an' thru a crowd ove three hundred wimen an' not injure thar karacters *sum*. Enyhow, hits a kind ove show they'd ruther see one at a time, an' pick the passun at that. His tex' wer, 'Nakid I cum intu the world, an' nakid I'm a gwine outen hit, ef I'm spard ontil then.' He sed nakidness warnt much ove a sin, purtickerly ove dark nights. That he wer a weak, frail wum ove the dus,' an' a heap more sich truck. Then he totch ontu me; sed I wer a livin proof ove the hell-desarvin nater ove man, an' that thar warnt grace enuf in the whole 'sociation tu saften my outside rind; that I wer 'a lost ball' forty years afore I wer born'd, an' the bes' thing they cud du fur the church, wer tu turn out, an' still hunt fur me ontil I wer shot. An' he never said Hell-sarpints onst in the hole preach. I b'leve, George, the durnd fools am at hit.

"Now, I wants yu tu tell ole Barbelly this fur me, ef he'll let me an' Sall alone, I'll let him alone—a-while; an' ef he don't, ef I don't lizzard him agin, I jis' wish I may be dod durnd! *Skeer him if yu ken.*

"Let's go tu the spring an' take a ho'n.

"Say George, didn't that ar Hell-sarpint sermon ove his'n, hev sumthin like a Hell-sarpint aplicashun? Hit looks sorter so tu me."

Sut Lovingood Reports What Bob Dawson Said, After Marrying a Substitute

"I asked Sut one day, why he had never married."

Becaze I ain't fond ove them kine ove inves'mints. If you has observed me clost, you never cotch me foolin with ile stock, patunt rights, lottery tickets, cheap jewelry, ur marriage licunses. Sum how, my turn runs more intu the substanshuls ove life. Whisky an' sich. In fac' I won't trade fur eny thing that I can't 'zamine, at leas' as clost es I ken a hoss.

I'l tell you another thing, George, I wish I may be substanshualy durn'd if I don't b'leve the breed ove wimmen am run out enyhow.

Hits true the hen tailors, an' sich cattil, hev invented a substitute, but hits sorter like rye for coffee—hit may look like coffee, an' smell like coffee, but durn my swaller if hit tastes like coffee, I don't keer how hot you make hit nor how much sugar you put in.

Bob Dawson, the sharpest trader I ever saw—jist out-smarted 'em all at tradin.' He bit at a substitute wonst, an' hit like tu a put him in the asylum. If you will listen tu me, I will norate in his own words as nigh as I kin the case; hit may be a warnin' tu you by golly. I know hit hes been tu me. I sleeps in a one hoss bed the ballunce ove my nights, aymen!

Sed Bob tu me. "Sut, I never mind ove gittin fool'd in a trade in my life but wonst. I wer over in Tennessee buying up stock, an' met up with es, I thought, the nicest material tu make Missis Dawson out of, I had seed. I cudent git tu 'zamine her pints much tho' for she wer as skittish as a colt, but I ballunced that by thinking that she warn't spiled in breakin, an' bein' onbroke I cud break her in tu suit mysef; thar wer sumfin tho' in her gait, an' was that made me think she had been broke to the saddle, if not in harness, an' I spisioned her too for bein' older than she claim'd, so I tried mitey hard to git to look in her mouth, but not a bit ove hit wud she hev—didn't kick nor bite, nor show vishusness, only shyness—jis' adzactly the shyness ove a three year old, what had never looked through a bridil.

"Well, she nibbled grass daintily, an' trotted roun' me circumspeckly ontil at las' I bid on her an' I be cussed if ever I closed a trade quicker in my life. Me, a fool, thinkin' I had her dog cheap.

"The weddin' cum off soon, rather onusualy soon, but you see I was expectant, an' anxious, she wer feard of a back down, or a rue bargine, an' what the devil was to hinder hit coming off soon.

"Arter we wer hitched in, an' an hour or so spent in passin round vittils—dancin—playin a peaner with dropsy in its laigs, an' a whezin ailment in its chest—pomgranatin' up an' down the porch, giglin, amung the galls, an' winkin amung the men, she whispered to me to slip off to bed, that she would foller in my footsteps in a half hour. I plead to have it a quarter. But no, she must have it a half 'jist for delicacy's sake you know dear.' We compromised at last on twenty-five minutes, arter whisperin about it ten. An' Sut, if it was to do over again I should sujes' twenty-five years, an' never fall a single dam snake. 'Jist for delicacy's sake'—the allfired old umbreller frame ove durnashun.

"I, Robert B. Dawson, the fresh married stock trader, went up them stair steps four at a bounce, an' heard old 'Squire Mankham remark, as I did so, 'That's faster than Bob will ever go up again.' Miss Squills, an old maid of the steel trap persuashun, replied, 'I wouldn't be astonished tho' to see him come down faster.' If it hadn't been for prolongin' that dismal gulf of half an hour atwixt me an' paradise, I'd a cum back and kill'd both of them. I did cuss the old 'Squire to myself, for his want ove confidence in me, an' Miss Squills for her want ove it in my wife.

"But when I went in atwix sheets that smelt ove dried rose leaves, an' found myself bouncin' on a steel spring mattras, I freely forgive him and all the ballance of the world. I could see floatin' in the air wreaths of honeysuckles, an' sich, with humminbirds flashin' among 'em, until I thought I was a hummingbird, or would be one, as soon as that doleful half hour devoted to delicacys, should drag its slow sled away.

"'Delicacy,' Sut Lovingood, there never was a durnder humbug on earth than it is, except the delicates themselves, an' their appurtinances. Oh! it's jist so.

"Well of course the half hour ainded, you know, sometime, and with it went all my confidence in old Hymen, and the left hand half of his worshippers—a whole skinfull ove hopes and expectashuns, an' leavin' me about as doubtin' a Thomas as ever you heard ove. *But* one of the durndest knowin' men you ever seed out ove Utah. When I hearn her turn the door knob, my heart was poundin' so hard that I hearn the echo again the head board. I felt like I wer floatin' atwix the mattrass and the ceilin' like Mahomet's coffin, an' the mountin' a mile off. I'd a give fifty dollars to have had a bar of railroad iron in my hands, to hold me down to the bed.

"She glode into the room like the embodiment of a Haleluigah, or a vision of unspeakable joy. She had a candle in her hand; its flame looked (to me, that is) like a boquet ove a thousand shades, an' as big as a half bushel. It was the effort ove my life to keep from snortin,' but I *didn't* snort, nor hev I yet, perhaps never will, at a substitute for a woman, I'm sure I won't.

"She set down the light, smiled towards the wooden run on the middle ove the head board, and commenced drawin' her pins, an' slingin' them right an' left as cool as if I, Robert B. Dawson, had been only anuther gall, or a bolster or sich. I was astonished to the frontiers ove elysiun, an' could almost see the rough crags of the common world.

"Says I, 'Julianner, my dear, hadent you better blow out the light? Jist for delicacy's sake, you know.'

"She replied in a firm voice, 'Robert, my true love, delicacy is one ove the fanciful atributes ove unmarried wimmen, an' jist as useless avterward, as their peaner or paint. You an' I are one now, so there must be no secrets or flummey atwix us; you will see me strip, sooner or later, and I might as well begin tonight. I hes my fate to meet, and I wont do eny useless dogin'; I'll meet my crosses like a man.'

"'But, my—my dear,' ventured I, 'hadent you better administer the comin' effulgince to me in broken doses. I—I think I can't stand—that is, I mean it will last the longer.'

"'Never mind,' said she, 'if you are afraid ove effulgences, shut your eyes,' and she stepped out ove a huge pile ove hoops, an' countless square yards ove starched muslin, standin' revealed a darn bean pole, in one layer of linnen, more like the ghost ove Jezable's mother, than Robert B. Dawson, the stock trader's bribe.

"Mister Lovingood, a cold horror swept over me like a huge wet wing.

"That self-poised, deliberate swindler, now Misses Robert B. Dawson, ontied a garter, an' drew from between her stockin,' an' her laig, the counterpart of a big dried codfish, made of muslin stuff't with something—bran suggested itself to me at the moment—and as she did so, her stocking fell limp, in a pile around her shoe mouth, and her laig looked like the pint aind ove a buggy shaft, with nearly the same crook to it, an' be d—d.

"I swallered a time or two, an I sed 'Julianner, dear, I never knew before that you had a wooden laig.'

"'Neither hev I,' she replied, rather tart-like. 'But I is ove a delicate organisation. That adjunk,' pointin' to the imitation, 'now goes with delicacy.'

"She looked at me, feelin' in her bussum the while, an' said, 'Robert, my love when I come to look at you clost, your eyes seems larger, an' rounder than I thought for, an' more bulgin—they bulge as much as these palpitators,' drawin' forth a pair ove somethings like sugar bowl leds, knobs an' all. When she flung 'em on the table, they bounced a time or two. Mister Lovingood, I was speechless, but I thought ot myself, 'I jist wish I may be d—d, with all my power ove thought, and will twice or three times, at least.'

"Deliberate-cool-slow, she stuck a thumb in each corner of her mouth, an' brought forth a full set ove bottom upper an' lower teeth, fastened together behine with a spring, an' laid *them* on the table, gapin' open an' facin' me. They looked like a saw tooth'd rat trap, ready set to ketch another dam fool.

"Said she, lookin' at me again, 'Robert, my love, I do declare, you are real pop eyed; I hope you are not habitualy so; it would be *so* disapointin' to me.' I jist had brains enough to think one word emphaticaly, an' that word was 'He—.' She, with her fore finger, bounced out one of her eyes, and put it in her mouth, while she lifted her whole head of hair, leavin' her skull, white an' glossy as a billiard ball. When she laid these down, she looked one eyed at me, an' then at the candle, a time or two as if undeterminded. I busy all the while recapitulatin.' 'False calves, false breasts, false teeth, false eye, false hair,' what next? The most horrible idear that ever burnt an blazed in the brain of man, was now fast resolving itself into its dreadful shape in mine, an' her remark, 'Don't be impatient, Robert love; I is most through,' flashed it into its fiendish maturity. Without darin' even a glance at her, I was up *out-gone;* I went down them stair steps six at a bounce in my shirt tail through that festive throng in my shirt tail out of that house, out of that lot, out of that town, in my shirt tail. States separate us now, an' I wish they were oceans."

Now George, arter hearin' that sperience ove poor Bob Dawson's, I puts hit to you, as a man ove gumshun, if I orter add another word only to forewarn you not tu menshun marryin' tu me agin, unless you wants that durn'd shriveled little snout ove your'n scabb'd. Ketch me rockin' cradles, or totin meal home for a palpitityator toter, or buyin' stockin's for a par ove bran bags, or givin' an 'oman a legal right tu bite me, with teeth made out ove delf. *No sir,* I'd marry the figgerhead ove a steamboat first. I jis' can't sit still, an' think 'bout thar menyfold shams an' traps an' gewolly-tockery, speshuly the palpitityators. Why don't you believe, that even Ratsnes' hes got her a par, a homemade par.

"Who the dickens is Ratsnest, Sut?"

Why sister Sall, an' be durnd to you, she saw'd a round dry gourd in two, a gourd as big as my head, an' then made a hole in the middil ove each half, an' stuff'd in white oak acorns, butt first, an' dad shave me if she dident hist the whole contrapshun intu her buzzim. I wish I may be dam if you cudent see the buldge ove the acorns across a field. Then she went on a rale turkey gobbler strut to church, a leanin' back from 'em like a littil boy totin a big drum. She looked like a dairy, by geminy. I sware I jist wanted tu kill the dam-fool, that's what ail'd me.

My stars, George, 'spose an' 'oman *wer* tu stock a par ove palpitityators ontu me, what has no more stimulus in em than the buffers over a freight car, on a cold frosty night; wudent I be in a devil ove a fix, say? Why dam if I hadent rather swim the Tennessee with a powerful interprizin fourteen foot alligator arter me when the mush ice is runnin. I jist woudent be half as feard tu face an' 'oman with a peck measure ove sanke in her buzzum, as a palpititytator toter. Now jis' answer me one questin; what in the thunder an durnashun do you recon the comein generashun ove babies am to do for milk? That's what's a pesterin'me. Oh, the devil! I wont think about it any more—le'ss go to sleep—George—George, say, George, am you awake?

"Yes, partly."

Well then lesson tu my las' words. If ever I inerjuces, insinuates, or socks ary one ove these paws in atwix the silk callicker or gingham an' the bustez ove one ove the tother sort ove cats, onless I hes had a purfeckly fur sight afore han,' I jis' wish hit may get bit off at the wrist.

No, by giminy hoss, *that* appertite's dead, an' the ballance of 'em scept for sperrits ara sinkin fas,' thanks to the hen-tailors, an' dam fools.

"The galls am all a made up show,
For fools delusion given,
With pads above, an' hoops below,
An' gizzards cold as mountain snow
Thars not one soun' in seven."

Dident I sing that verse in a way tu bring tears intu the eyes ove a brick kiln? Say.

Well! Dad's Dead

Thar never wer a man yet, so mean, but what some time, or other, done at least one good thing. Now, my Dad put off doin his good thing for an awful long time, but at last he did hit, like a white man. He died, by golly! Perfeckly squar—strait out, an' for keep. Aint you glad? Don't be fear'd to say so on my account, boys, for hit's so reasonable. Mam declar's that Gineril Washington never did a better thing in his whole life. She only grumbles that he dident ketch the idear twenty years sooner, for then, she mout "a done sumthin." But no, he hilt on, jist to spite her, ontil she broke off her last tooth, crackin' a corn bread crust, an' then he immegintly went. Why, the very las' reques' he ever made ove her wer to "let him look in her mouth." Good people, an' passuns, make a heap ove fuss over what they call the onnatralness ove folks toward the sick. Now, hits all a dad-rabbited lie, for the neighbors acted jist as natral to dad as could be. Nara durn'd one ove 'em ever come a nigh the old cuss, to fool 'im into believin' that he stood a chance to live, or even that they wanted him to stay a minit longer than he wer obleeged to, by givin him sups of warter, fannin' off the flies—axin him if he wer hongry, or any other meddlesome interfarances with nater—not them. I tell you, boys, if ever a man did git a fair launch, every way, into the river sticks, that man wer my dad; he went on time to a seccon,' an' no body a holdin on to his coattail. They acted natral clean thru, too, for when he wer a kickin' his last kicks, old Muddleg's wife come to the fence an' call'd mam out, to know if she cudent spar the frock she had on, in pay for sixty cents that dad owed her husban,' for three drinks ove "hoss botts." "That she thought mam mout afford to run in her petticoattail a while, as the weather wer good, an' hit bein' black, would pass for fust rate mournin." Hit's a wonder that las' idear hadent cotch mam, for she's great on style an' bein' in fashun, but hit dident; hit did git her back up tho' for she jist bleated like an old ewe, an' jump'd the fence to her. An' don't you believe! Mam kicked her bustle clean off ove her, the passun, an' his wife a ridin' apast at that. Her nose bled, an' mam cried, an sich a snortin' as they had. The las' words dad ever spoke, wer, "which whip'd?" I meant to tell 'im that mam had nearly turned the old crane inside out with her foot, but he cud hear nothin' then for the roar ove the river.

Well, as I wer saying, the neighbors acted natral, an' that's the right way—do as you wants to, by golly! Dad shave the hipocracy ove fixin' a dead man away nice, arter lettin' him starve. Many, many a time, has people spent enough in plantin' a corpse, that if they had ever a loan'd the half ove hit to the mortul a livin,' hit would a put off a funeral. But then the cuss wudent a went, when his time had come. Thars the devil ove hit—flustratin' doctrines so bad, you know.

Well, when dad got cool, an' stiff enuff to handle, we cudent raise ara coffin, without diggin' one up, an' totein' hit a long mile. We had an old accoutrement box, hit's true, but then mam wanted hit to ketch rain water in. So, we just sot in, an' made a regular mummy out ove him, by sowin' him up, body an' soul, in an old, black bed spraid. Who knows, boys, but what he'l git dug up, some three thousan' years arter this, an' be sot up in a glass case, for a King Pharaoo, an' a devil ove a fuss raised, about the bed spraid bein' a royal mantle? Aint that a future for a Lovingood, arter him actin' hoss, an' bein' daddy to sich a varminty fixin' as me? But thar's plenty durn'd fools, ready to do hit for him, if they only happen to find him. Arter we got done, I swar that I wondered to see how much like a rich man's iron corpse case he look'd, an' hit sorter made me proud, hit did. I look'd roun,' an' thar stood sister Sall, a blubberin,' I ax'd her what wer the matter, for the gal 'stonish'd me. Sed she, "Sowin' on that bed spraid 'minds me so much ove the time he made me sow him up in a raw hide, when he opened his dorg school. Boo! hoo! hoo!" I told her to shet right up least he mout hear her, an' want to go at hit agin, an' then we'd loose all our trouble, besides hit's bein' so disap'intin' to mam, for she had comb'd her har an' flour'd her face.

I know'd whar Old Stump Snodgrasses' steers wer a grazin,' with the yoke on. So I goes an' gits 'em, an' hitch'd on to a big shingle sled, what somebody had left on the chestnut ridge, an' we loaded dad up. Mam an' the childer wer strung along on each side, a holdin' on by the standards. "Now," sez mam, a fixin' on her sun bonnet, "hit's the rule to go *slow.*" I sot in front an' was driver, an' a feelin' come over me, like I think a durn'd, starvin,' one-hoss lawyer mus' a had, when he fust foun' hissef Captain ove Company A, at the beginnin' ove the war. I'd a cuss'd a man in a minit, but fortinatly for any man, he warnt about just then. So, when I promised mam that I would "go slow," I did hit, with dignerty and 'sponsibility. I'd liked durn'd well to a hearn *any*body venter to order me to go fast, or to go at all, for that matter. I meant to make the most out ove that persession, an' my persition in hit, you understan'.

Now, durn'd fool like, in my big strut, I never tho't wonst about the smell ove the corpse a skeerin' the steers—hit always does, you know. So, jist as soon as they cotch the first whiff ove hit, they snorted—bawl'd—histed their tails up strait, an' with one mind, run away, hoss fashion. I be dam, if they dident git from thar, like they tho't that dad wud be too late for the boat. When I look'd up in the air at the wavin' tails, with the tassels hangin' the wrong way, I tho't ove the plumes ove a hearse, an' their bellerin' minded me ove the brass horns, blowin' some ove the Dead March in Saul; an' dad shave me, if I dident feel proud agin. Thar was *some* style about us, if we wer nothin' but Lovingoods. Hit's strange, I know, but I swar the tho't come over me ove the time dad acted hoss, an' instid ove hollerin "Wo, Buck!" I bawled "Wo, dad!" jist as I had done fifteen years before, in the saidge field, an' it seem'd to me I cud hear ho'nets a hummin' somehow.

You orter a seed that old sled waltz, an' dad an' the rest ove 'em bounce, him a buttin' the childer off, one side an' then t'other. Mam sez, "Consarnd him, he's at his old tricks agin. Roll 'im overboard." But, dadrabbit me, if I hadent a died fust; I meant to steer them cattil *thru* the graveyard anyhow, jist for the name ove the thing. So, I jist sot a foot against each steer's bar sturn, for a purchase, clampin' the roots ove thar histed tails atwix' my big toes an' the nex' ones, an' I froze fast to the ropes with both han's. One aind ove my back-bone (an' I scasely know which aind) wud bounce from the sled floor, fur enuff to almost skin my snout on the yoke. Then I'd balance back agin on the ropes, ontil I'd meet the sled somewhar in the air, on hits jumps—yere I'd come, over-handed, for the yoke agin. Dad shame me, if I dident think hit would jar my heart out at the top ove my head. To a look'd at me, you'd a thought I wer a tryin' to butt the oxe's brains out, but I warnt. My toes hilt like vices, an' I kept on a freezin' to the ropes; an' jist sich a game ove over-handed, high see-saw, you never seed—sorter like a walkin'-beam steamboat, you know. You see, I hilt on in the hope that mam wud hev sence enuff to roll 'im overboard, herself, somewhar nigh the hole, but she wer entirely too busy a fendin' off his butts to think ove anything. I generley look'd over my shoulder, as I'd be a balancin' back, toward that cussed, hard sled, to form some idear how hard the next lick wud be onto my lacerated sturn, an' to see how the rest ove 'em wer a makin' hit. When I seed his head take mam a rale goat butt in the ribs, thinks, I, "now we'l hear from her." Arter gruntin' a time or two, an' makin' a face like a burnt saddle seat, she sed, "I'd like to know when the devil *will* go out ove *him*." An' then she cried, dryin' her tears on the tail ove her bonnet. I wer right glad to see her show some feelin' for the old hoss, now he had started to be gone so long.

When we struck the aidge ove the graveyard, I look'd back agin, an' foun' mysef alone with dad. Mam war left behine, about a hundred yards, tryin' her levil best to git out ove the jaws ove a tall, forked stump, that had her fast by the waist. I never did see jist sich a glimmer ove arms and laigs a reachin' for ground. I tho't about an alligator, an' my chances for bein' a full orphan, an' how flustrated mam must be.

I found that the dad rabbited steers wer aimin' to run plum astradle ove the grave. So, I tho't I'd improve the occasion, to save some liftin'. Jist as the sled flew over hit, with a slider on each side, I turned roun'—sot my foot agin dad's head, an' done jist *so*. Hit shot him out, like an arrow, an' he chug'd in, as plum and strait as 'oman lays a baby in the cradle. Bomp: I never hearn sich a jolt; he wer yearnist dead, or that fall wud a sot him to kicken.' One thing I sorter hated; he fell with his head to the east, an' I'm feared that will make him a little late a risen'. But, by golly! I cudent help hit, for we come in from the west, an' the dad burn'd steers, wer jist a flyin'. Thar's one little comfort in hit tho'—he'l rise with his back to the danger, an' I'l bet he hooves it frum thar. I made my lope from the vehikil, as soon as I could, but had to light on my head among prickly pars, an' slate. When I got the stickers pull'd out ove my eye leds, the steers wer out ove sight, gone glimmerin'. But I dident care, for I consider'd the procession over, any how. That night, when we wer all hunker'd round the hearth, sayin' nothin,' an' waitin for the taters to roast, mam, she spoke up—"oughtent we to a scratch'd in a little dirt on him, say?" "No need, mam," sed Sall, "hits loose yeath, an' will soon cave in enuff." "But, I want to plant a 'simmon sprout at his head," sed mam, "on account ove the puckery taste he has left in my mouth. Law sakes alive! Haint hit so pervokin, that we never ken do anything like eny body else? Did you notice, how yer dad kerried on as we wer sleddin' him along?" "An' us a tryin' our best to be sorry, an' solemn," added Sall. "An' then them steers, too," mam went on to say. "Blast thar flecked souls! Did you *ever* see the like?" "Well! well!" sez I, "never mind, mam; charms broke at last." "Hand me the fat goard. I wants to grease atwix my toes, dad shave thar rough tails."

Now, boys, say what you will about hit, thar's one thing you all must admit. That considerin' the family gittin' hit up, it wer a allfired, expidishus, imitation ove a funerel.

Johnson Jones Hooper (1815-1862)

Born in Wilmington, N.C., in 1815, Johnson Jones Hooper would move to the first tier of the South's antebellum humorists as the creator of Simon Suggs, one of the most famous con artists and rapscallions in American literature. In 1835 after his father had experienced a series of financial setbacks, Hooper moved to Alabama to join his brother who practiced law there. This proved to be a propitious migration for young Hooper, a chance to launch himself professionally in a new country teeming with opportunity, a place where his talents and developing interests could be applied in a number of different directions over the years: lawyer, census taker, politician, and secretary of the Provisional Congress of the Confederacy, and most significantly newspaperman and author of humorous sketches.

In December 1842 or early 1843, Hooper became the editor of the pro-Whig weekly LaFayette *East Alabamian,* where he published his first humorous sketch in August 1843, "Taking the Census in Alabama," under the byline "By a Chicken Man of 1840." Based on his experience as a census taker in Tallapoosa County, this sketch was subsequently reprinted in William T. Porter's New York sporting paper, the *Spirit of the Times,* and in Hooper's first and most famous humorous collection, *Some Adventures of Captain Simon Suggs, Late of the Tallapoosa Volunteers,* a book that in 1845 Porter recommended to Carey and Hart of Philadelphia for publication. It would go through eleven editions between 1845 and 1856. Porter became Hooper's most enthusiastic promoter, published over 50 of his stories and sporting sketches in the *Spirit,* and included one of Hooper's Simon Suggs sketches in his popular anthology *The Big Bear of Arkansas, and Other Sketches* (1845).

In 1844, Hooper published in the *East Alabamian* the first of his sketches featuring Simon Suggs, a conscienceless backwoods rogue-trickster whose ethical code the author describes as resting "snugly in his favourite aphorism—'IT IS GOOD TO BE SHIFTY IN A NEW COUNTRY'—which means that it is right and proper that one should live as merrily and as comfortably as possible at the expense of others." Hooper's *Some Adventures of Captain Simon Suggs*, which Porter hyperbolically touted in the *Spirit* as the "best half dollars worth of genuine humor, ever enclosed between two covers," takes the form of a bogus campaign biography, perhaps a satire of several campaign biographers who heralded Andrew Jackson's military and political actions. Hooper admitted too that Suggs's was inspired by Bird H. Young, a Tallapoosa County resident who, in his youth, had been well known for his rowdy behavior, practical jokes, and gambling. A picaresque novel of twelve chapters, which chronicle Suggs experiences and scrapes from age seventeen to fifty, the book has a unity lacking in most other collections of antebellum southern humor. A sly opportunist who was taught by his father to disdain book learning, Suggs says that it "spiles a man ef he's got mother-wit, and ef he aint got that, it don't do him no good"—an aphorism he would use to his personal benefit in preying on the weaknesses of others. Many of his victims are ignorant, vain, and greedy and consequently no better than he and therefore deserving of Suggs's deception and duplicity.

Hooper would subsequently edit several other Alabama newspapers and author or edit several additional books—*A Ride with Old Kit Kuncker, and Other Sketches, and Scenes of Alabama* (1849), and *The Widow Rugby's Husband, A Night at the Ugly Man's, and Other Tales of Alabama* (1851) among them. During the 1850s, Hooper was active politically, first promoting the Know-Nothing Party, then with the increase in abolitionist activity in the North, supporting sectionalism and states' rights, and finally being elected secretary of the Provisional Confederate Congress.

Called by British novelist William Makepeace Thackeray the "most promising writer of his day," Johnson Jones Hooper, except for George Washington Harris, the creator of Sut Lovingood, was the best humorist the Old South produced. His character Simon Suggs, whom Hooper came to regard as a liability and hindrance to his aspirations in public life, left a rich legacy to later southern literature, providing the probable source for the Duke's swindling of a camp meeting congregation in chapter 20 of Mark Twain's *Adventures of Huckleberry Finn* and a likely prototype for later southern scoundrels and con artists such as Faulkner's Flem Snopes, Flannery O'Connor's bogus Bible salesman in "Good Country People," and Guy Owen's Mordecai Jones in *The Ballad of the Flim-Flam Man* (1965).

Texts: "Simon Plays the 'Snatch' Game," "Captain Suggs and Lieutenant Snipes 'Court-Martial' Mrs. Haycock," and "The Captain Attends a Camp-Meeting," *Some Adventures of Captain Simon Suggs, Late of the Tallapoosa Volunteers; Together with "Taking the Census" and Other Alabama Sketches* (Philadelphia: Carey & Hart, 1845).

Simon Plays the "Snatch" Game

It is not often that the living worthy furnishes a theme for the biographer's pen. The pious task of commemorating the acts, and depicting the character of the great or good, is generally and properly deferred until they are past blushing, or swearing—constrained to a decorous behaviour by the folds of their cerements. Were it otherwise, who could estimate the pangs of wounded modesty which would result! Who could say how keen would be the mortification, or how crimson the cheek of Grocer Tibbetts, for instance, should we present him to the world in all the resplendent glory of his public and private virtues!—dragging him, as it were, from the bosom of retirement and Mrs. Tibbetts, to hold him up before the full gaze of "the community," with all his qualities, characteristics, and peculiarities written on a large label and pasted to his forehead! Wouldn't Mr. Tibbetts almost die of bashfulness? And wouldn't Mrs. Tibbetts tell all her neighbours, that she would just as soon they had put Mr. Tibbetts in the stocks, if it were not for the concomitant little boys and rotten eggs? Certainly: and Mrs. Tabitha Tibbetts in making such a remark, would be impelled by a principle which exists in a majority of human minds—a principle which makes the idea revolting, that every body should know all about us in our life-times, notwithstanding our characters may present something better even than a fair average of virtue and talent.

But "there is no rule without an exception," and notwithstanding that it is both unusual and improper, generally, to publish biographies of remarkable personages during their lives, for the reason already explained, as well as because such histories must, of necessity, be incomplete and require *post mortem* additions—notwithstanding all this, we say, there are cases and persons, in which and to whom, the general rule cannot be considered to apply. Take, by way of illustration, the case of a candidate for office—for the Presidency we'll say. His life, up to the time when his reluctant acquiescence in the wishes of his friends was wrung from him, by the stern demands of a self-immolating patriotism, MUST be written. It is an absolute, political necessity. His enemies *will* know enough to attack; his friends *must* know enough to defend.—Thus Jackson, Van Buren, Clay, and Polk have each a biography published while they live. Nay, the thing has been carried further; and in the first of each "Life" there is found what is termed a "counterfeit presentment" of the subject of the pages which follow. And so, not only are the moral and intellectual endowments of the candidate heralded to the world of voters; but an attempt is made to create an idea of his *physique*. By this means, all the country has in its mind's eye, an image of a little gentleman with a round, oily face—sleek, bald pate, delicate whiskers, and foxy smile, which they call Martin Van Buren; and future generations of naughty children who will persist in sitting up when they should be a-bed, will be frightened to their cribs by the lithograph of "Major General Andrew Jackson," which their mammas will declare to be a faithful representation of the Evil One—an atrocious slander, by the bye, on the potent, and comparatively well-favoured, prince of the infernal world.

What we have said in the preceding paragraphs was intended to prepare the minds of our readers for the reception of the fact, that we have not undertaken to furnish for their amusement and instruction, in this and the chapters which shall come after, a few incidents—for we are by far too modest to attempt a connected memoir—in the life of CAPTAIN SIMON SUGGS, OF TALLAPOOSA, without the profoundest meditation on the propriety of doing so ere the Captain has been "gathered to his fathers." No! no! we have chewed the cud of this matter, until we flatter ourself all its juices have been expressed; and the result is that, as Captain Simon Suggs thinks it "more than probable" he shall "come before the people of Tallapoosa" in the course of a year or two, he is, in our opinion, clearly "within the line of safe precedents," and bound in *honor* to furnish the Suggs party with such information respecting himself, as will enable them to vindicate his character whenever and wherever it may be attacked by the ruthless and polluted tongues of Captain Simon Suggs' enemies. And in order that our hero should not appear before his fellow citizens under circumstances less advantageous than those which mark the introduction to the public of other distinguished individuals, we have, at the outlay of much trouble and expense, obtained the services of an artist competent to delineate his countenance, so that all who have never yet seen the Captain may be able to recognize him immediately whenever it shall be their good fortune to be inducted into his presence. His autograph,—which was only produced unblotted and in orthographical correctness, after three several efforts, "from a rest," on the counter of Bill Griffin's confectionary—we have presented with a view to humor the whim of those who fancy they can read character in a signature. All such, we suspect, would pronounce the Captain *rugged, stubborn, and austere* in his disposition; whereas in fact, he is *smooth, even-tempered, and facile!*

In aid of the portrait, however, it is necessary we should add a verbal description, in order to perfect the reader's conceptions of the Captain.

Beginning then, at our friend Simon's intellectual extremity:—His head is somewhat large, and thinly covered with coarse, silver-white hair, a single lock of which lies close and smooth down the middle of a forehead which is thus divided into a couple of very acute triangles, the base of each of which is an eyebrow, lightly defined, and seeming to owe its scantiness to the depilatory assistance of a pair of tweezers. Beneath these almost shrubless cliffs, a pair of eyes with light-grey pupils and variegated whites, dance and twinkle in an aqueous humor which is constantly distilling from the corners. Lids without lashes complete the optical apparatus of Captain Suggs; and the edges of these, always of a sanguineous hue, glow with a reduplicated brilliancy whenever the Captain has remained a week or so in town, or elsewhere in the immediate vicinity of any of those citizens whom the county court has vested with the important privilege of vending "spirituous liquors in less quantities than one quart." The nose we find in the neighbourhood of these eyes, is long and low, with an extremity of singular acuteness, overhanging the subjacent mouth. Across the middle, which is slightly raised, the skin is drawn with exceeding tightness, as if to contrast with the loose and wrinkled abundance supplied to the throat and chin. But the mouth of Captain Simon Suggs is his great feature, and measures about four inches horizontally. An ever-present sneer—not all malice, however—draws down the corners, from which radiate many small wrinkles that always testify to the Captain's love of the "filthy weed." A sharp chin monopolizes our friend's bristly, iron-gray beard. All these facial beauties are supported by a long and skinny, but muscular neck, which is inserted after the ordinary fashion in the upper part of a frame, lithe, long, and sinewy, and clad in Kentucky jeans, a trifle worn. Add to all this, that our friend is about fifty years old, and seems to indurate as he advances in years, and our readers will have as accurate an idea of the personal appearance of Captain Simon Suggs, late of the Tallapoosa Volunteers, as we are able to give them.

The moral and intellectual qualities which, with the physical proportions we have endeavoured to portray, make up the entire entity of Captain Suggs, may be readily described. His whole ethical system lies snugly in his favourite aphorism—"IT IS GOOD TO BE SHIFTY IN A NEW COUNTRY"—which means that it is right and proper that one should live as merrily and as comfortably as possible at the expense of others; and the practicability of this in particular instances, the Captain's whole life has been a long series of the most convincing illustrations. But notwithstanding this fundamental principle of Captain Suggs' philosophy, it were uncandid not to say that his actions often indicate the most benevolent emotions; and there are well-authenticated instances within our knowledge, wherein he has divided with a needy friend, the five or ten dollar bill which his consummate address had enabled him to obtain from some luckless individual, without the rendition of any sort of equivalent, excepting only solemnly reiterated promises to repay within two hours at farthest. To this amiable trait, and his riotous good-fellowship, the Captain is indebted for his great popularity among a certain class of his fellow citizens—that is, the class composed of the individuals with whom he divides the bank bills, and holds his wild nocturnal revelries.

The shifty Captain Suggs is a miracle of shrewdness. He possesses, in an eminent degree, that tact which enables man to detect the *soft spots* in his fellow, and to assimilate himself to whatever company he may fall in with. Besides, he has a quick, ready wit, which has extricated him from many an unpleasant predicament, and which makes him whenever he chooses to be so—and that is always—very companionable. In short, nature gave the Captain the precise intellectual outfit most to be desired by a man of his propensities. She sent him into the world a sort of he-Pallas, ready to cope with his kind, from his infancy, in all the arts by which men "*get along*" in the world; if she made him, in respect to his moral conformation, a beast of prey, she did not refine the cruelty by denying him the fangs and the claws.

But it is high time we were beginning to record some of those specimens of the worthy Captain's ingenuity, which entitle him to the epithet "*Shifty.*" We shall therefore relate the earliest characteristic anecdote which we have been able to obtain; and we present it to our readers with assurances that it has come to our knowledge in such a way as to leave upon our mind not "a shadow of doubt" of its perfect genuineness. It will serve, if no other purpose, at least to illustrate the precocious development of Captain Suggs' peculiar talent.

Until Simon entered his seventeenth year, he lived with his father, an old "hard shell" Baptist preacher; who, though very pious and remarkably austere, was very avaricious. The old man reared his boys—or endeavoured to do so—according to the strictest requisitions of the moral law. But he lived, at the time to which we refer, in Middle Georgia, which was then newly settled; and Simon, whose wits from the time he was a "shirt-tail boy," were always too sharp for his father's, contrived to contract all the coarse vices incident to such a region. He stole his mother's roosters to fight them at Bob Smith's grocery, and his father's plough-horses to enter them in "quarter" matches at the same place. He pitched dollars with Bob Smith himself, and could "beat him into doll rags" whenever it came to a measurement. To crown his accomplishments, Simon was tip-top at the game of "old sledge," which was the fashionable game of that era; and was early initiated in the mysteries of "stocking the papers." The vicious habits of Simon were, of course, a sore trouble to his father, Elder Jedediah. He reasoned, he counselled, he remonstrated, and he lashed—but Simon was an incorrigible, irreclaimable devil. One day the simple-minded old man returned rather unexpectedly to the field where he had left Simon and Ben and a negro boy named Bill, at work. Ben was still following his plough, but Simon and Bill were in a fence corner very earnestly engaged at "seven up." Of course the game was instantly suspended, as soon as they spied the old man sixty or seventy yards off, striding towards them.

It was evidently a "gone case" with Simon and Bill; but our hero determined to make the best of it. Putting the cards into one pocket, he coolly picked up the small coins which constituted the stake, and fobbed them in the other, remarking, "Well, Bill, this game's blocked; we'd as well quit."

"But, mass Simon," remarked the boy, "half dat money's mine. An't you gwine to lemme hab 'em?"

"Oh, never mind the money, Bill; the old man's going to take the bark off both of us—and besides, with the hand I helt when we quit, I should 'a beat you and won it all any way."

"Well, but mass Simon, we nebber finish de game, and de rule—"

"Go to an orful h—l with your rule," said the impatient Simon—"don't you see daddy's right down upon us, with an armful of hickories? I tell you I helt nothin' but trumps, and could 'a beat the horns off of a billygoat. Don't that satisfy you? Somehow or another you're d—d hard to please!" About this time a thought struck Simon, and in a low tone—for by this time the Reverend Jedediah was close at hand—he continued, "But maybe daddy don't know, *right down sure,* what we've been doin.' Let's try him with a lie—twon't hurt, no way—let's tell him we've been playin' mumble-peg."

Bill was perforce compelled to submit to this inequitable adjustment of his claim to a share of the stakes; and of course agreed to swear to the game of mumble-peg. All this was settled and a peg driven into the ground, slyly and hurriedly, between Simon's legs as he sat on the ground, just as the old man reached the spot. He carried under his left arm, several neatly trimmed sprouts of formidable length, while in his left hand he held one which he was intently engaged in divesting of its superfluous twigs.

"Soho! youngsters!—*you* in the fence corner, and the *crap* in the grass; what saith the Scriptur'. Simon? 'Go to the ant, thou sluggard,' and so forth and so on. What in the round creation of the yeath have you and that nigger been a-doin'?"

Bill shook with fear, but Simon was cool as a cucumber, and answered his father to the effect that they had been wasting a little time in the game of mumble-peg.

"Mumble-peg! mumble-peg!" repeated old Mr. Suggs, "what's that?"

Simon explained the process of *rooting* for the peg; how the operator got upon his knees, keeping his arms stiff by his sides, leaned forward and extracted the peg with his teeth.

"So you git *upon your knees,* do you, to pull up that nasty little stick! You'd better git upon 'em to ask mercy for your sinful souls and for a dyin' world. But let's see one o' you git the peg up now."

The first impulse of our hero was to volunteer to gratify the curiosity of his worthy sire, but a glance at the old man's countenance changed his "notion," and he remarked that "Bill was a long ways the best hand." Bill who did not deem Simon's modesty an omen very favourable to himself, was inclined to reciprocate compliments with his young master; but a gesture of impatience from the old man set him instantly upon his knees; and, bending forward, he essayed to lay hold with his teeth of the peg, which Simon, just at that moment, very wickedly pushed a half inch further down. Just as the breeches and hide of the boy were stretched to the uttermost, old Mr. Suggs brought down his longest hickory, with both hands, upon the precise spot where the tension was greatest. With a loud yell, Bill plunged forward, upsetting Simon, and rolled in the grass; rubbing the castigated part with fearful energy. Simon, though overthrown, was unhurt; and he was mentally complimenting himself upon the sagacity which had prevented his illustrating the game of mumble-peg for the paternal amusement, when his attention was arrested by the old man's stooping to pick up something—what is it?—a card upon which Simon had been sitting, and which, therefore, had not gone with the rest of the pack into his pocket. The simple Mr. Suggs had only a vague idea of the pasteboard abomination called *cards*; and though he decidedly inclined to the opinion that this was one, he was by no means certain of the fact. Had Simon known this he would certainly have escaped; but he did not. His father assuming the look of extreme sapiency which is always worn by the interrogator who does not desire or expect to increase his knowledge by his questions, asked—

"What's this, Simon?"

"The Jack-a-dimunts," promptly responded Simon, who gave up all as lost after this *faux pas*.

"What was it doin' down thar Simon, my sonny?" continued Mr. Suggs, in an ironically affectionate tone of voice.

"I had it under my leg, thar, to make it on Bill, the first time it come trumps," was the ready reply.

"What's trumps?" asked Mr. Suggs, with a view of arriving at the import of the word.

"Nothin' a'n't trumps *now*," said Simon, who misapprehended his father's meaning—"but *clubs* was, when you come along and busted up the game."

A part of this answer was Greek to the Reverend Mr. Suggs, but a portion of it was full of meaning. They had then, most unquestionably, been "throwing" cards, the scoundrels! the "oudacious" little hellions!

"To the 'mulberry' with both o ye, in a hurry," said the old man sternly. But the lads were not disposed to be in a "hurry," for "the mulberry" was the scene of all formal punishment administered during work hours in the field. Simon followed his father, however, but made, as he went along, all manner of "faces" at the old man's back; gesticulated as if he were going to strike him between the shoulders with his fists, and kicking at him so as almost to touch his coat tail with his shoe. In this style they walked on to the mulberry tree, in whose shade Simon's brother Ben was resting. Of what transpired there, we shall speak in the next chapter.

Captain Suggs and Lieutenant Snipes "Court-Martial" Mrs. Haycock

Great was the commotion at Fort Suggs on the morning next after the occurrence of the events related in the last chapter. At FORT SUGGS we say—for so had the Captain christened "Taylor's store" and the enclosure thereof. Nor let any one reprehend him for so doing. It was but the exhibition of a vanity, which, if not laudable, at least finds its sufficient excuse in a custom that has prevailed, "time out of mind." Had not Romulus his Rome? Did not the pugnacious son of Philip call his Egyptian military settlement Alexandria? And—to descend to later times and to cases more directly in point—is there not a Fort Gaines in Georgia, and a Fort Jessup in Florida? Who then shall carp, when we say that Captain Simon Suggs bestowed *his* name upon the spot straightened by his wisdom, and protected by his valour!

Great then, we repeat, was the commotion at FORT SUGGS on the morning in question. The fact had become generally known—how could it be otherwise with thirty women in the immediate vicinity!—that Mrs. Haycock was to be "court-martialed" on that morning; and the commotion was the consequence. The widow herself was suffering great mental disquietude on this subject, in addition to considerable physical discomfort occasioned by the fall and rough handling of the previous night. Under such circumstances, it could hardly be expected that her woes would fail to find utterance. And it would have been equally unreasonable to suppose that her fellow gossips would restrain the natural propensity of the sex. Let the reader then, imagine—if he be not nervous—all the uproar and din which three dozen women can make under the most exciting circumstances, and he will have some faint conception of the commotion at Fort Suggs on the morning of the trial.

It was at an early hour; in fact—speaking according to the chronometrical standard in use at Fort Suggs—not more than "fust-drink time;" when Captain Suggs took Lieutenant Snipes aside to consult with him in regard to some of the details of preparation for the court-martial.

"Snipes," said the Captain, as he seated himself a-straddle of the fence, and saw his lieutenant safely adjusted in a like position—"Snipes, as sure's you're born, thar's a diffikilty about this here court-martial. Now I want you to tell me *how* we're to hold a *drumhead* court-martial *when we aint got a drum!*"

Lieutenant Snipes looked very much puzzled, and in fact he *was* exceedingly puzzled, and he considered the matter for several moments, but could see no way by which the "diffikilty" might be surmounted. At length, he remarked,

"It *does* look aukerd, Capting!"

"Yes. You see when these here court-martials is jumped up all of a sudden, like this, they're to be one of the drum-head sort—that's when I've *allers* hearn. Well now, supposin' we was to hold one *without the drum,* and heng or shoot that everlastin' old she-devil; *would* the law jestify us in doin' so? Sometimes I sorter think it would, and then agin it looks sorter jubous. What's *your* apinion, Lewtenant?"

"That's it—what you jist said," replied Lieutenant Snipes, deferentially.

"Good!" said the captain—"lewtenants ought allers to think jist as ther captings do. It's a good sign."

"It's what *I've* allers done, and what I allers *expects* to do," replied Snipes.

"Well, well!" remarked Suggs, whose chief object was to impress Snipes with the idea that the widow's life was in actual danger—and through his lieutenant, create that impression upon Mrs. Haycock herself, and all the rest—"Well, well, *don't* you believe that ef I was to git a bar'l, or somethin' else pretty nigh *like* a drum, and hold the court-martial by that—don't you believe *that* would justify us ef any thing was brought up herearter, supposin' we was to condemn the old woman to deth?"

"Belikes it would," said Snipes.

"I *know* it would!" said Suggs emphatically.

"*I* know so too!" remarked the lieutenant, with increased confidence.

"Well, now, all *that's* settled," said the Captain, with an air of satisfaction—"the next thing is, how are we agwine to put her to death?"

"Why, we aint *tried* her yit!" said Snipes.

"To be sure! to be sure! I'd forget that!—but you know thar's no way to git round condemnin' of her—is thar?"

"No way as *I see!*"

"It's a painful duty, Lewtenant! a very painful duty, Lewtenant Snipes; and very distressin'. But the rules of war is very strict, you know!"

"*Very* strict," said Snipes.

"And officers must do ther duty, come what may."

"They're *ableeged* to," said the lieutenant.

"Ah! well!" remarked Captain Suggs with considerable emotion, "it'll be time enough to fix how we shall execute the old critter at the trial. You think the bar'l will do?"

"Jist as good as any thing," replied Snipes—"a bar'l and a drum's sorter alike, any way."

"Well, you'd better go and fix up as well as you kin, and the natur' of the case will admit. Officers oughter dress as well as they kin at sich times, ef no other. I must go and bresh up, myself." And with that, the consultation between Captain Suggs and Lieutenant Snipes, ended; the former going off to put himself a little more in military trim; while the latter industriously employed himself in disseminating the result of the conference.

It was with extreme difficulty that the Captain arranged his costume to his own satisfaction, and made it befitting so solemn and impressive an occasion. After a great deal of trouble however, he did contrive to cut a somewhat military figure. With a sword he was already "indifferently well" provided; having found one—rusty and without a scabbard—somewhere about the premises. This he buckled on, or rather tied to his side with buckskin strings. He wore at the time, the identical blue jeans frock-coat which has since become so familiar to the people of Tallapoosa—it was then new, but on this there were, of course, no epaulettes. Long time did Captain Suggs employ himself in devising expedients to supply the deficiency. At length he hit it. His wife had a large crimson pin-cushion, and this he fastened upon his left shoulder, having first caused some white cotton fringe to be attached to the outward edge. In lieu of crimson sash, he fastened around his waist a bright-red silk handkerchief, with only a few white spots on it. And this was an admirable substitute, except that it was almost too short to tie before, and exhibited no inconsiderable portion of itself in a triangle behind. The chapeau now alone remained to be managed. This was easily done. Two sides of the brim of his capacious beaver were stitched to the body of the hat, and at the fastening on the left side, Mrs. Suggs sewed a cockade of red ferreting, nearly as big as the bottom of a saucer. Thus imposingly habited—and having first stuffed the legs of his pantaloons into the tops of a very antique pair of boots—Captain Simon Suggs went forth.

At the upper end of the enclosure, and standing near an empty whiskey barrel, was Lieutenant Snipes. He had not been so successful as the Captain in the matter of his toilette. Around his black wool hat was pasted, or stitched, a piece of deep purple gilt paper, such as is often found upon bolts of linen. Upon this was represented a battle between a lion and a unicorn; and in a scroll above were certain letters, which as Lieutenant Snipes himself remarked, "did'nt spell nothing"—at least, nothing that he could comprehend. In his hand was the handle of a hoe, armed at one extremity with a rusty bayonet—the only weapon of its kind, at that moment, to be found in the whole garrison of Fort Suggs. Equipped thus, and provided with a dirty sheet of paper, a portable inkstand, (containing poke-berry juice,) and the stump of a pen—all of which were upon the head of the barrel—the doughty Lieutenant awaited the moment when it should please Captain Suggs to arraign the prisoner and proceed with the trial.

"Tallapoosy Vollantares, parade here!" thundered Captain Suggs, as he walked up to the barrel.

Very soon the "component parts" of the "Vollantares" were grouped about their Captain.

"Form in a straight line!" squealed Lieutenant Snipes.

The company took the form of a half-moon!

Captain Suggs now ordered Mrs. Haycock to be brought out; whereupon Snipes went into the backroom of the store, and directly appeared again, leading the widow—who limped considerably, and howled like a full pack of wolves—by the hand. The Captain, however, by a judicious threat of instant decapitation, reduced the noise to a series of mere sobbings.

"Hadn't we better fix some way to have some music," said Suggs, "and march round the house once, before we perceed with the trial?"

Lieutenant Snipes suggested that there was no drum or fife, as the Captain knew, on the premises but that "uncle Billy Allen" was an excellent drummer, and Joe Nalls a first-rate performer on the fife, and that perhaps those individuals might, for the nonce, be induced to make vocal imitations of their respective instruments, and with their hands "go through the motions" indispensible to their proper effect. Captain Suggs immediately spoke to those gentlemen, and they "kindly consented" to serve, on the very equitable condition of receiving a "drink" each, as soon as the affair was over.

The "vollantares" were now formed in double files, and between the two columns Mrs. Haycock, supported by a female friend on each side, was placed.

"Music to the front!" shouted Suggs; and the order was promptly obeyed.

"Company! March!"

"Dub—dub—dub-a-dub-a-dub," went "uncle Billy Allen," inclining dangerously from the perpendicular, in order to support properly, a non-existent drum!

"Phee-ee-phee-fee," whistled Mr. Nalls, as his fingers played rapidly upon the holes of his imaginary fife!

And the company marched, as it was ordered. Suggs, of course, headed the array, walking backwards in order to inspect its movements; while Snipes, with his bayonet, walked alongside and kept a sharp eye on the prisoner. Thus they marched slowly around the enclosure, and returned to the spot whence they started.

"Halt! Form a round ring all round the drum!" ordered the Captain, pointing to the barrel.

The "vollantares" arranged themselves so as to describe, not exactly a mathematical circle, but a figure slightly approximating thereto, with the Captain, Lieutenant Snipes, and the widow, in the centre.

"Betsy Haycock," said Captain Suggs, "you're fotch up here accordin' to the rigelations of drumhead court-martial, for infringin' on the rules of war, by crossin' of the lines agin orders; and that too, when the fort was onder martial law. Ef you've got any thing to say agin havin' your life tuk, less hear it."

Poor Mrs. Haycock became livid; her eyes dilated, and all her features assumed that sudden sharpness which mortal terror often produces. Trembling in all her joints, and with pallid lips, she gasped,

"Mercy! mercy! Captain Suggs! For God's sake don't kill me—oh don't ef you please! I only went for my tobakker—for the love of the Lord *don't* murder me! Have mercy—I'll never—no never—as long—"

"It aint *me*," said the Captain interrupting her; "it aint *me* that's a-gwine to kill you; it's the *Rules of War*. The rules of war is mighty strict—aint they, Lewtenant Snipes?"

"*Powerful* strict!" said Snipes.

"You've 'fessed the crime," continued Suggs, "and ef me and the Lewtenant wanted to let you off ever so bad, the rules of war would lay us liable ef we was to. But come, Lewtenant Snipes," he added, addressing that person, "the prisoner has made her acknowledgements; take your pen and ink, and let's go and see what's to be done about it."

The Lieutenant took up his writing materials, and the couple retired to a corner of the fence, where they seated themselves upon the ground. Directly Snipes was seen to write; and then he picked up his pen and ink again, and they returned.

"What—what—what's it?" chokingly inquired the widow, as they re-assumed their positions at the barrel.

"Read out the judg*ment*," said Suggs with immense solemnity.

Snipes read what he had written in the fence-corner, as follows:

"Whares, Besty Haycock were brought up afore us, bein' charged with infringin' the rules of war by crossin' the lines agin orders, and Fort Suggs bein' under martial law at the time, and likewise ecknowledgd she was gilty, Tharfore we have tried her eccordin to said rules of war, and condems her to be baggonetted to deth in one hour from this time, witness our hands and seals."

A paleness, more ghastly than that of death, come over the widow's face as she heard the sentence. Falling to the earth, she grovelled at the feet of Captain Suggs.

"Save me—pity—help! for God's sake! Oh don't kill me Captain Suggs!—beg for me, Mr. Snipes. Oh, you won't—I know you won't murder me! You're jest in fun!—aint you? You couldn't have the *heart* to kill a poor woman creetur like me!"—and then she added in a hoarse whisper—"I'll humbler myself to you, Captain Suggs! I'll git down on my very knees, and kiss your shoe! Don't take my life away with that—" she didn't finish the sentence, but shuddered all over, as she thought of Snipes' rusty bayonet.

"Oh! Jimminny Crimminny! what a cussed old fool!" exclaimed a voice from the fence-corner, outside, which was instantly recognized as belonging to Yellow-legs—"he darsent no more kill you, 'an he dar to fight an Injun!"

The widow looked up, but took no comfort from the words. Captain Suggs, highly indignant, seized a large stone and projected it with Titan-like force, at the dirt-eater; but it struck the fence. Yellow-legs, not at all alarmed, turned his back to Suggs, and made a gesture expressive of the highest degree of contempt, and then bounded off.

"Lewtenant, perpar' for execution!" said the Captain, as he returned to the barrel.

Mrs. Haycock renewed her lamentations and entreaties.

"I wish," said Suggs, in a fit of mental abstraction, but soliloquizing *aloud;* "thar *was* some way to save her. But ef I was to let her off with a *fine,* I might be layin' myself liable to be tried for my own life."

"Oh yes! Captain Suggs, I'll pay any fine you'll put on me—I'll give up all the money I've got, ef you'll jest let me off—do now, dear Captain—"

"Hey? What? Have *I* been talkin' out loud?" inquired Suggs, starting with a disconcerted look from his reverie.

"Yes, yes!" answered the widow with great earnestness; "you said ef I'd pay a fine, you'd spar my life—didn't you now, *dear, good* Captain Suggs?"

"Ef I did, I oughent to 'a done it. I don't think I'd be jestified ef I was to let you off. The rules of war would hold me 'countable ef I did—don't you think they would, Lewtenant?"

"*Mighty* apt!" said Snipes, as he sharpened the end of his rusty bayonet on a fragment of rock, by way of preparing for the execution of the widow.

Mrs. Haycock adjured Captain Suggs by his affection for his own offspring, to impose a fine, instead of "makin' her poor fatherless children, orfins!" Tears came into Suggs' eyes at this appeal, and the sternness of the officer was lost in the sensibility of the man.

"Don't you think, Lewtenant," he asked, "bein' as it's a *woman*—a *widder* woman too—the rules of war wouldn't be as severe on us for lettin' of her off, *purvidin'* she paid a reasonable fine?"

"They wouldn't be severe at all!" replied Snipes.

"Well, well, widder! Bein' as it's you—a perticlar friend and close neighbor—and bein' *as* you're a widder, and on the 'count of my feelins for Billy Haycock, which was your husband afore he died, I s'pose I'll have to run the resk. But it's a orful 'sponsibility I'm a takin, jist for friend*ship,* widder—"

Mrs. Haycock interrupted him with a torrent of thanks and benedictions.

"Thar aint *many,*" continued Suggs, "I'd take sich a 'sponsibility for: I may be a-runnin of *my own neck* into a halter!"

"The Lord in Heaven purvent your ever sufferin' bekase you've tuk pity on a poor widder like me!" was the grateful woman's ejaculation.

"Hows'ever," added Suggs, "to shorten the matter, jist pay down twenty-five dollars, and I'll pardon you ef I *do* git into a scrape about it—I never *could* bar to see a woman suffer! it strikes me right *here!*" and the Captain placed his hand upon his breast in a most impressive manner.

The joyful Mrs. Haycock immediately untied a key from her girdle, and handing it to one of her friends, sent her into the store, with directions "to sarch low down, in the left hand corner before of her chist," and bring a certain stocking she would find there filled with coin. This was speedily done, and the amount of the fine handed to Captain Suggs.

"This here money," he remarked as he received it, "I want you all to onderstand, aint *my* money. No! no! I have to keep it here"—sliding it into his pockets—"ontwell I git *my* orders about it. It's the *government's* money, and *I* darsent spend a cent of it—do I, Lewtenant?"

"No more'n you dar to put your head in a blazin' log-pile!" answered the Lieutenant.

A whistling—just such as always implies that somebody, in the immediate neighbourhood of the whistler, *lies tremendously*—was heard at this moment, and Suggs looking around, saw Yellow-legs in his old corner, dealing a supposititious hand of cards to an imaginary antagonist—as if he would thereby intimate that Captain Simon Suggs would embezzle the public money, or at any rate, hazard its loss at cards.

"Charge baggonets on that cussed, pumkin-faced whelp of the devil!" roared the Captain in the phrensy of the moment; and Lieutenant Snipes dashed at Yellow-legs with his rusty weapon, which he plunged through a crack of the fence! Before the gallant Snipes, however, could recover from the impetus of his attack and withdraw the bayonet, the dirt-eater had pulled it off the hoe-handle, and fixing it on a dry corn-stalk, bore it aloft upon his shoulder most contumaciously, under the very nose of Captain Suggs!

****

The reader will please suppose fifteen minutes to have elapsed, and Captain Suggs and his Lieutenant to be behind the store chimney, in private conversation.

"Lewtenant Snipes!" said Suggs, "I look upon you as a high-minded, honubble officer, and a honor to the Tallapoosy Vollantares. I like to see a man do his duty like you done *yourn!* Here, take *that!*"—handing him one of Mrs. Haycock's dollars—"Simon Suggs never forgits his friends—NEVER! His motter is allers, *Fust his country,* and *then* his *friends!*"

"Capting Suggs"—was the Lieutenant's reply, as he made a minute examination of the Mexican coin in his hand—"I've said it *behind back,* and I'll say it *face;* you're a *gentleman* from the top of your head to the end of your big-toe nail! Less go in and liquor; damn expenses!"

The Captain Attends a Camp-Meeting

Captain Suggs found himself as poor at the conclusion of the Creek war, as he had been at its commencement. Although no "arbitrary," "despotic," "corrupt," and "unprincipled" judge had fined him a thousand dollars for his proclamation of martial law at Fort Suggs, or the enforcement of its rules in the case of Mrs. Haycock; yet somehow—the thing is alike inexplicable to him and to us—the money which he had contrived, by various shifts to obtain, melted away and was gone for ever. To a man like the Captain, of intense domestic affections, this state of destitution was most distressing. "He could stand it himself—didn't care a d—n for it, no way," he observed, "but the old woman and the children; *that* bothered him!"

As he sat one day, ruminating upon the unpleasant condition of his "financial concerns," Mrs. Suggs informed him that "the sugar and coffee was nigh about out," and that there were not "a dozen j'ints and middlins, *all put together,* in the smoke-house." Suggs bounced up on the instant, exclaiming, "D—n it! *somebody* must suffer!" But whether this remark was intended to convey the idea that he and his family were about to experience the want of the necessaries of life; or that some other, as yet unknown individual should "suffer" to prevent that prospective exigency, must be left to the commentators, if perchance any of that ingenious class of persons should hereafter see proper to write notes for this history. It is enough for us that we give all the facts in this connection, so that ignorance of the subsequent conduct of Captain Suggs may not lead to an erroneous judgment in respect to his words.

Having uttered the exclamation we have repeated—and perhaps, hurriedly walked once or twice across the room—Captain Suggs drew on his famous old green-blanket overcoat, and ordered his horse, and within five minutes was on his way to a camp-meeting, then in full blast on Sandy creek, twenty miles distant, where he hoped to find amusement, at least. When he arrived there, he found the hollow square of the encampment filled with people, listening to the midday sermon and its dozen accompanying "exhortations." A half-dozen preachers were dispensing the word; the one in the pulpit, a meek-faced old man, of great simplicity and benevolence. His voice was weak and cracked, notwithstanding which, however, he contrived to make himself heard occasionally, above the din of the exhorting, the singing, and the shouting which were going on around him. The rest were talking to and fro, (engaged in the other exercises we have indicated,) among the "mourners"—a host of whom occupied the seat set apart for their especial use—or made personal appeals to the mere spectators. The excitement was intense. Men and women rolled about on the ground, or lay sobbing or shouting in promiscuous heaps. More than all, the negroes sang and screamed and prayed. Several, under the influence of what is technically called "the jerks," were plunging and pitching about with convulsive energy. The great object of all seemed to be, to see who could make the greatest noise—

"And each—for madness ruled the hour—
Would try his own expressive power."

"Bless my poor old soul!" screamed the preacher in the pulpit; "ef yonder aint a squad in that corner that we aint got one outen yet! It'll never do"—raising his voice—"you must come outen that! Brother Fant fetch up that youngster in the blue coat! I see the Lord's a-workin' upon him! Fetch him along—glory—yes!—hold to him!"

"Keep the thing warm!" roared a sensual seeming man, of stout mould and florid countenance, who was exhorting among a bevy of young women, upon whom he was lavishing caresses. "Keep the thing warm, breethring!—come to the Lord, honey!" he added, as he vigorously hugged one of the damsels he sought to save.

"Oh, I've got him!" said another in exulting tones, as he led up a gawky youth among the mourners—"I've got him—he tried to git off, but—ha! Lord!"—shaking his head as much as to say, it took a smart fellow to escape him—"ha! Lord!"—and he wiped the perspiration from his face with one hand, and with the other, patted his neophyte on the shoulder—"he couldn't do it! No! Then he tried to argy wi' me—but bless the Lord!—he couldn't do that nother! Ha! Lord! I tuk him, fust in the Old Testament—bless the Lord!—and I argyed him all thro' Kings—then I throwed him into Proverbs.—and from that, here we had it up and down, kleer down to the New Testament, and then I begun to see it work him!—then we got into Matthy, and from Matthy right straight along to Acts; and *thar* I throwed him! Y-e-s L-o-r-d!"—assuming the nasal twang and high pitch which are, in some parts, considered the perfection of rhetorical art—"Y-e-s L-o-r-d! and h-e-r-e- he is! Now g-i-t down thar," addressing the subject, "and s-e-e ef the L-o-r-d won't do somethin' f-o-r you!" Having thus deposited his charge among the mourners, he started out, summarily to convert another soul!

"Gl-o-*ree!*" yelled a huge, greasy negro woman, as in a fit of the jerks, she threw herself convulsively from her feet, and fell "like a thousand of brick," across a diminutive old man in a little round hat, who was squeaking consolation to one of the mourners.

"Good Lord, have mercy!" ejaculated the little man earnestly and unaffectedly, as he strove to crawl from under the sable mass which was crushing him.

In another part of the square a dozen old women were singing. They were in a state of absolute extasy, as their shrill pipes gave forth,

"I rode on the sky,
Quite ondestified I,
And the moon it was under my feet!"

Near these last, stood a delicate woman in that hysterical condition in which the nerves are incontrollable, and which is vulgarly—and almost blasphemously—termed the "holy laugh." A hideous grin distorted her mouth, and was accompanied with a maniac's chuckle; while every muscle and nerve of her face twitched and jerked in horrible spasms.

Amid all this confusion and excitement Suggs stood unmoved. He viewed the whole affair as a grand deception—a sort of "opposition line" running against his own, and looked on with a sort of professional jealousy. Sometimes he would mutter running comments upon what passed before him.

"Well now," said he, as he observed the full-faced brother who was "officiating" among the women, "that ere feller takes *my* eye!—thar he's been this half-hour, a-figurin amongst them galls, and's never said the fust word to nobody else. Wonder what's the reason these here preachers never hugs up the old, ugly women? Never seed one do it in my life—the sperrit never moves 'em that way! It's nater tho'; and the women, *they* never flocks round one o' the old dried-up breethring—bet two to one old splinter-legs thar,"—nodding at one of the ministers—"won't git a chance to say turkey to a good-lookin gall to-day! Well! who blames 'em? Nater will be nater, all the world over; and I judge ef I was a preacher, I should save the purtiest souls fust, myself!"

While the Captain was in the middle of this conversation with himself, he caught the attention of the preacher in the pulpit, who inferring from an indescribable something about his appearance that he was a person of some consequence, immediately determined to add him at once to the church if it could be done; and to that end began a vigorous, direct personal attack.

"Breethring," he exclaimed, "I see yonder a man that's a sinner; I *know* he's a sinner! Thar he stands," pointing at Simon, "a missubble old crittur, with his head a-blossomin for the grave! A few more short years, and d-o-w-n he'll go to perdition, lessen the Lord have mer-cy on him! Come up here, you old hoary-headed sinner, a-n-d git down upon your knees, a-n-d put up your cry for the Lord to snatch you from the bottomless pit! You're ripe for the devil—you're b-o-u-n-d for hell, and the Lord only knows what'll become on you!"

"D—n it," thought Suggs, "*ef* I only had you down in the krick swamp for a minit or so, *I'd* show you who's *old! I'd* alter your tune sudden, you sassy, 'saitful old rascal!" But he judiciously held his tongue and gave no utterance to the thought.

The attention of many having been directed to the Captain by the preacher's remarks, he was soon surrounded by numerous well-meaning, and doubtless very pious persons, each one of whom seemed bent on the application of his own particular recipe for the salvation of souls. For a long time the Captain stood silent, or answered the incessant stream of exhortation only with a sneer; but at length, his countenance began to give token of inward emotion. First his eye-lids twitched—then his upper lip quivered—next a transparent drop formed on one of his eye-lashes, and a similar one on the tip of his nose—and, at last, a sudden bursting of air from nose and mouth, told that Captain Suggs was overpowered by his emotions. At the moment of the explosion, he made a feint as if to rush from the crowd, but he was in experienced hands, who well knew that the battle was more than half won.

"Hold to him!" said one—"it's a-workin in him as strong as a Dick horse!"

"Pour it into him," said another, "it'll all come right directly!"

"That's the way I love to see 'em do," observed a third; "when you begin to draw the water from their eyes, taint gwine to be long afore you'll have 'em on their knees!"

And so they clung to the Captain manfully, and half dragged, half led him to the mourner's bench; by which he threw himself down, altogether unmannered, and bathed in tears. Great was the rejoicing of the brethren, as they sang, shouted, and prayed around him—for by this time it had come to be generally known that the "convicted" old man was Captain Simon Suggs, the very "chief of sinners" in all that region.

The Captain remained grovelling in the dust during the usual time, and gave vent to even more than the requisite number of sobs, and groans, and heart-piercing cries. At length, when the proper time had arrived, he bounced up, and with a face radiant with joy, commenced a series of vaultings and tumblings, which "laid in the shade" all previous performances of the sort at that camp-meeting. The brethren were in extasies at this demonstrative evidence of completion of the work; and whenever Suggs shouted "Gloree!" at the top of his lungs, every one of them shouted it back, until the woods rang with echoes.

The effervescence having partially subsided, Suggs was put upon his pins to relate his experience, which he did somewhat in this style—first brushing the tear-drops from his eyes, and giving the end of his nose a preparatory wring with his fingers, to free it of the superabundant moisture:

"Friends," he said, "it don't take long to curry a short horse, accordin' to the old sayin,' and I'll give you the perticklers of the way I was 'brought to a knowledge'"—here the Captain wiped his eyes, brushed the tip of his nose and snuffled a little—"in less'n no time."

"Praise the Lord!" ejaculated a bystander.

"You see I come here full o' romancin' and devilment, and jist to make game of all the purceedins. Well, sure enough, I done so for some time, and was a-thinkin how I should play some trick—"

"Dear soul alive! *don't* he talk sweet!" cried an old lady in black silk—"Whar's John Dobbs? You Sukey!" screaming at a negro woman on the other side of the square—"ef you don't hunt up your mass John in a minute, and have him here to listen to his 'sperience, I'll tuck you up when I git home and give you a hundred and fifty lashes, madam!—see ef I don't! Blessed Lord!"—referring again to the Captain's relation—"aint it a *precious* 'scource!"

"I was jist a-thinkin' how I should play some trick to turn it all into redecule, when they began to come round me and talk. Long at fust I didn't mind it, but arter a little that brother"—pointing to the reverend gentlemen who had so successfully carried the unbeliever through the Old and New Testaments, and who Simon was convinced was the "big dog of the tanyard"—"that brother spoke a word that struck me kleen to the heart, and run all over me, like fire in dry grass—"

"I-I-I can bring 'em!" cried the preacher alluded to, in a tone of exultation—"Lord thou knows ef thy servant can't stir 'em up, nobody else needn't try—but the glory aint mine! I'm a poor worrum of the dust," he added, with ill-managed affectation.

"And so from that I felt somethin' a-pullin' me inside—"

"Grace! grace! nothin' but grace!" exclaimed one; meaning that "grace" had been operating in the Captain's gastric region.

"And then," continued Suggs, "I wanted to git off, but they hilt me, and bimeby I felt so missuble, I had to go yonder"—pointing to the mourners' seat—"and when I lay down thar it got wuss and wuss, and 'peared like somethin' was a-mashin' down on my back—"

"That was his load o' sin," said one of the brethren—"never mind, it'll tumble off presently, see ef it don't!" and he shook his head professionally and knowingly.

"And it kept a-gittin heavier and heavier, ontell it looked like it might be a four year old steer, or a big pine log, or somethin' of that sort—"

"Glory to my soul," shouted Mrs. Dobbs, "it's the sweetest talk I *ever* hearn! You Sukey! aint you got John yit? never mind, my lady, *I'll* settle wi' you!" Sukey quailed before the finger which her mistress shook at her.

"And arter awhile," Suggs went on, "'peared like I fell into a trance, like, and I seed—"

"Now we'll git the good on it!" cried one of the sanctified.

"And I seed the biggest, longest, rip-roarenest, blackest, scaliest—" Captain Suggs paused, wiped his brow, and ejaculated "Ah, L-o-r-d!" so as to give full time for curiosity to become impatience to know what he saw.

"*Sarpent!* warn't it?" asked one of the preachers.

"No, not a serpent," replied Suggs, blowing his nose.

"Do tell us *what* it war, soul alive!—whar *is* John?" said Mrs. Dobbs.

"Allegator!" said the Captain.

"Alligator!" repeated every woman present, and screamed for very life.

Mrs. Dobb's nerves were so shaken by the announcement, that after repeating the horrible word, she screamed to Sukey, "you Sukey, I say, you Su-u-ke-e-y! ef you let John come a-nigh this way, whar the dreadful alliga—shaw! what am I thinkin' 'bout? 'Twarn't nothin' but a vishin!"

"Well," said the Captain in continuation, "the allegator kept a-comin' and a-comin' to'ards me, with his great long jaws a-gapin' open like a ten-foot pair o' tailors' shears—"

"Oh! oh! oh! Lord! gracious above!" cried the women.

"SATAN!" was the laconic ejaculation of the oldest preacher present, who thus informed the congregation that it was the devil which had attacked Suggs in the shape of an alligator.

"And then I concluded the jig was up, 'thout I could block his game some way; for I seed his idee was to snap off my head—"

The women screamed again.

"So I fixed myself jist like I was perfectly willin' for him to take my head, and rather he'd do it as not"—here the women shuddered perceptibly—"and so I hilt my head straight out"—the Captain illustrated by elongating his neck—"and when he come up and was a gwine to *shet down* on it, I jist pitched in a big rock which choked him to death, and that minit I felt the weight slide off, and I had the best feelins—sorter like you'll have from *good* sperrits—any body ever had!"

"Didn't I *tell* you so? Didn't I *tell* you so?" asked the brother who had predicted the off-tumbling of the load of sin. "Ha, Lord! fool *who!* I've been *all* along thar!—yes, *all along thar!* and I know every inch of the way jist as good as I do the road home!"—and then he turned round and round, and looked at all, to receive a silent tribute to his superior penetration.

Captain Suggs was now the "lion of the day." Nobody could pray so well, or exhort so movingly, as "brother Suggs." Nor did his natural modesty prevent the proper performance of appropriate exercises. With the reverend Bela Bugg (him to whom, under providence, he ascribed his conversion,) he was a most especial favourite. They walked, sang, and prayed together for hours.

"Come, come up; thar's room for all!" cried brother Bugg, in his evening exhortation. "Come to the 'seat,' and ef you wont pray yourselves, let *me* pray for you!"

"Yes!" said Simon, by way of assisting his friend; "it's a game that all can win at! Ante up! ante up, boys—friends I mean—don't back out!"

"Thar aint a sinner here," said Bugg, "no matter ef his soul's black as a nigger, but what thar's room for him!"

"No matter what sort of a hand you've got," added Simon in the fulness of his benevolence; "take stock! Here am *I*, the wickedest and blindest of sinners—has spent my whole life in the sarvice of the devil—has now come in on *narry pair* and won a *pile!*" and the Captain's face beamed with holy pleasure.

"D-o-n-'t be afeard!" cried the preacher; "come along! the meanest won't be turned away! humble yourselves and come!"

"No!" said Simon, still indulging in his favourite style of metaphor; "the bluff game aint played here! No runnin' of a body off! Every body holds four aces, and when you bet, you win!"

And thus the Captain continued, until the services were concluded, to assist in adding to the number at the mourners' seat; and up to the hour of retiring, he exhibited such enthusiasm in the cause, that he was unanimously voted to be the most efficient addition the church had made during that meeting.

The next morning, when the preacher of the day first entered the pulpit, he announced that "brother Simon Suggs," mourning over his past iniquities, and desirous of going to work in the cause as speedily as possible, would take up a collection to found a church in his own neighbourhood, at which he hoped to make himself useful as soon as he could prepare himself for the ministry, which the preacher didn't doubt, would be in a very few weeks, as brother Suggs was "a man of mighty good judgment, and of *a great discorse*." The funds were to be collected by "brother Suggs," and held in trust by brother Bela Bugg, who was the financial officer of the circuit, until some arrangement could be made to build a suitable house.

"Yes, breethring," said the Captain, rising to his feet; "I want to start a little 'sociation close to me, and I want you all to help. I'm mighty poor myself, as poor as any of you—don't leave breethring"—observing that several of the well-to-do were about to go off—"don't leave; ef you aint able to afford any thing, jist give us your blessin' and it'll all be the same!"

This insinuation did the business, and the sensitive individuals re-seated themselves.

"It's mighty little of this world's goods I've got," resumed Suggs, pulling off his hat and holding it before him; "but I'll bury *that* in the cause any how," and he deposited his last five-dollar bill in the hat.

There was a murmur of approbation at the Captain's liberality throughout the assembly.

Suggs now commenced collecting, and very prudently attacked first the gentlemen who had shown a disposition to escape. These, to exculpate themselves from any thing like poverty, contributed handsomely.

"Look here, breethring," said the Captain, displaying the bank-notes thus received, "brother Snooks has drapt a five wi' me, and brother Snodgrass a ten! In course 'taint expected that you *that aint as well off as them*, will give *as much*; let every one give *accordin'* to ther means."

This was another chain-shot that raked as it went! "Who so low" as not to be able to contribute as much as Snooks and Snodgrass?

"Here's all the *small* money I've got about me," said a burly old fellow, ostentatiously handing to Suggs, over the heads of a half dozen, a ten dollar bill.

"That's what I call maganimus!" exclaimed the Captain; "that's the way *every* rich man ought to do!"

These examples were followed, more or less closely, by almost all present, for Simon had excited the pride of purse of the congregation, and a very handsome sum was collected in a very short time.

The reverend Mr. Bugg, as soon as he observed that our hero had obtained all that was to be had at that time, went to him and inquired what amount had been collected. The Captain replied that it was still uncounted, but that it couldn't be much under a hundred.

"Well, brother Suggs, you'd better count it and turn it over to me now. I'm goin' to leave presently."

"No!" said Suggs—"can't do it!"

"Why?—what's the matter?" inquired Bugg.

"It's got to be *prayed over,* fust!" said Simon, a heavenly smile illuminating his whole face.

"Well," replied Bugg, "less go one side and do it!"

"No!" said Simon, solemnly.

Mr. Bugg gave him a look of inquiry.

"You see that krick swamp?" asked Suggs—"I'm gwine down in *thar*, and I'd gwine to lay this money down *so*"—showing how he would place it on the ground—"and I'm gwine to git on these here knees"—slapping the right one—"and I'm *n-e-v-e-r* gwine to quit the grit I feel ontell it's got the blessin'! And nobody aint got to be thar but me!"

Mr. Bugg greatly admired the Captain's fervent piety, and bidding him God-speed, turned off.

Captain Suggs "struck for" the swamp sure enough, where his horse was already hitched. "Ef them fellers aint done to a cracklin," he muttered to himself as he mounted, "*I'*ll never bet on two pair agin! They're peart at the snap game, theyselves; but they're badly lewed this hitch! Well! Live and let live is a good old motter, and it's my sentiments adzactly!" And giving the spur to his horse, off he cantered.

---

* The reader is requested to bear in mind, that the scenes described in this chapter are not now to be witnessed. Eight or ten years ago, all classes of population of the Creek country were very different from what they are now. Of course, no disrespect is intended to any denomination of Christians. We believe that camp-meetings are not peculiar to any church, though most usual in the Methodist—a denomination whose respectability in Alabama is attested by the fact, that very many of its worthy clergymen and lay members, hold honourable and profitable offices in the gift of the state legislature; of which, indeed, almost a controlling portion are themselves Methodists.

Joseph Glover Baldwin (1815-1864)

One of the best educated humorists of the Old Southwest may have been Virginia-born Joseph Glover Baldwin, who attended Staunton Academy where he studied Latin and read English and American literature. After leaving school, he read law and by the age of twenty was a practicing attorney. A failed romance caused him to leave Virginia to seek his fortune in Alabama and Mississippi, where he quickly encountered all the violence, chicanery, and lawlessness that would constitute the material for the frontier humorist and keep him busy in the legal profession. He married in 1839, prospered, started a family, and ran for Congress unsuccessfully. Restless despite his success, he followed the lure of the open and wild territories further west in California. He repeated his success in San Francisco, served as a member of the California Supreme Court, and considered a run for the U. S. Senate. As a conservative, a slave-owner, and a supporter of states' rights, he sympathized with the Confederacy during the Civil War but did not live to see the conflict concluded.

Baldwin began to write and publish sketches in 1853 in the *Southern Literary Messenger,* mostly about notable personalities he met, the practice of law in the backwoods, and memoirs of comic events. The seventeen published pieces were combined with nine new ones to form a book, *Flush Times of Alabama and Mississippi,* issued to considerable popular success that same year. It would see ten editions before the end of the century. A reviewer in a newspaper in Richmond, Virginia, found Baldwin's book comparable or even superior to the work of Herman Melville.

Adopting the mode of the British essayists, Baldwin depended less on dialect and dialogue, as used primarily by many of the other humorists, and recounted his tales with the skill of an educated raconteur, amused by the oddities and absurdities of frontier life. It was the personal essay as practiced by Washington Irving that inspired Baldwin, and his writing is richly informed by allusions to Shakespeare, Samuel Johnson, Lord Byron, and other British authors, as well as Latin and the specialized language of law. He would also try his hand at a collection of political biographies in *Party Leaders* in 1855 and begin work on

"Flush Times in California," which he did not live to complete. Fortunately *Flush Times of Alabama and Mississippi* represented his best and most memorable writing and earned a place for him as a major figure among his contemporary humorists.

Texts: "Simon Suggs, Jr., Esq., A Legal Biography" from *The Flush Times of Alabama and Mississippi: A Series of Sketches* (New York: D. Appleton, 1853).

Simon Suggs, Jr., Esq.
A Legal Biography

Correspondence
Office of the Jurist-Maker,
City of Got-him, Nov. 18, 1852

COL. SIMON SUGGS, JR.

My Dear Sir,—Having established, at great expense, and from motives purely patriotic and disinterested, a monthly periodical for the purpose of supplying a desideratum in American Literature, namely, the commemoration and perpetuation of the names, characters, and personal and professional traits and histories of American lawyers and jurists, I have taken the liberty of soliciting *your* consent to be made the subject of one of the memoirs, which shall adorn the columns of this Journal. This suggestion is made from my knowledge, shared by the intelligence of the whole country, of your distinguished standing and merits in our noble profession; and it is seconded by the wishes and requests of many of the most prominent gentlemen in public and private life, who have the honor of your acquaintance.

The advantages of a work of this sort, in its more public and general bearing, are so *patent*, that it would be useless for me to refer to them. The effect of the publication upon the fame of the individual commemorated is, if not equally apparent, at least, equally decided. The fame of an American lawyer, like that of an actor, though sufficiently marked and cognizable within the region of his practice, and by the witnesses of his performances, is nevertheless, for the want of an organ for its national dissemination, or of an enduring memorial for its preservation, apt to be ephemeral, or, at most, to survive among succeeding generations, only in the form of unauthentic and vague traditions. What do we know of Henry or of Grundy as lawyers, except that they were eloquent and successful advocates? But what they did was to acquire reputation, and, of course, the true value of it, is left to conjecture; or, as in the case of the former, especially, to posthumous invention or embellishment.

It was the observation of the great Pinkney, that the lawyer's distinction was preferable to all others, since it was impossible to acquire in our profession, a false or fraudulent reputation. How true this aphorism is, the pages of this L.w M . . . . . . e will abundantly illustrate.

The value, and, indeed, the fact of distinction, consists in its uncommonness. In a whole nation of giants, the Welsh monster in Barnum's Museum would be undistinguished. Therefore, *we*—excuse the editorial plural—strive to collect the histories only of the most eminent of the profession in several States; the aggregate of whom reaches some two or three hundred names. You have undoubtedly seen some of the numbers of our work, which will better illustrate our plan, and the mode of its past, as well as the intended mode of its future, execution.

It would be affectation, my dear sir, to deny that what mainly consoles us under a sense of the hazardous nature of such an enterprise to our *personal* features—pardon the pun, if you please—and amidst the anxieties of so laborious an undertaking, is the expectation, that, through our labors, the reputation of distinguished men of the country, constituting its moral treasure, may be preserved for the admiration and direction of mankind, not for a day, but for all time. And it has occurred to me, that such true merit as yours might find a motive for your enrolment among the known sages and profound intellects of the land, not less in the natural desire of a just perpetuation of renown, than in the patriotism which desires the improvement of the race of lawyers who are to come after you, and the adding to the accredited standards of public taste and professional attainment and genius.

We know from experience, that the characteristic difference of the profession, in many instances, shrinks from the seeming, though falsely seeming, indelicacy of an egotistical parade of one's own talents and accomplishments, and from walking into a niche of the Pantheon of American genius we have opened, and over the entrance to which, "FOR THE GREAT" is inscribed. But the facility with which this difficulty has been surmounted by some, of whose success we had reason to entertain apprehensions, adds but further evidence of the capacity which the noble profession of the law gives for the most arduous exploits. Besides, sir, although the facts are expected to be furnished by the subject, yet the first person is but seldom used in the memoir—some complaisant friend, or some friend's name being employed as editor of the work; the subject sometimes, indeed, having nothing to do except to revise it and transmit it to this office.

You may remember, my dear Colonel, the exclamatory line of the poet—

    ——————"How hard is it to climb
The steep where fame's proud temple shines afar."

And so it used to be: but in this wonderfully progressive age it is no longer so. It is the pride of your humble correspondent to have constructed a plan, by means of his Journal, whereby a gentleman of genius may, with the assistance of a single friend, or even without it, wind himself, up from the vale below, as by a windlass, up to the very cupola of the temple.

May we rely upon your sending us the necessary papers, viz., a sketch of your life, genius, exploits, successes, accomplishments, virtues, family antecedents, personal pulchritudes, professional habitudes, and whatever else you may deem interesting. You can see from former numbers of our work, that nothing will be irrelevant or out of place. The sketch may be from ten to sixty pages in length.

Please send also a good daguerreotype likeness of yourself, from which an engraving may be executed, to accompany the sketch. *The daguerreotype had better be taken with reference to the engraving to accompany the memoir*—the hair combed or brushed from the brow, so as to show a high forehead—the expression meditative—a book in the hand, &c.

Hoping soon to hear favorably from you, I am, with great respect and esteem,

THE EDITOR.

P.S. It is possible that sketches of one or two distinguished gentlemen, not lawyers, may be given. If there is any exception of class made, we hope to be able to give you a sketch and engraving of the enterprising Mr. Barnum.

RACKINSACK, Dec. 1, 1852.

TO MR. EDITOR.

Dear Sir—I got your letter dated 18 Nov., asking me to send you my life and karackter for your Journal. Im obleeged to you for your perlite say so, and so forth. I got a friend to rite it—my own ritin being mostly perfeshunal. He done it—but he rites such a cussed bad hand I cant rede it: I reckon its all korrect tho.'

As to my doggerrytype I cant send it there aint my doggerytype man about here now. There never was but won, and he tried his mershine on Jemmy O. a lawyer here, and Jem was so mortal ugly it bust his mershine all to pieces trying to git him down, and liked to killed the man that ingineered the works.

You can take father's picter on Jonce Hooper's book—take off the bend in the back, and about twenty years of age off en it and make it a leetle likelier and it'll suit me but dress it up gentele in store close.

Respectfully till death,
SIMON SUGGS, JR.

P.S.—I rite from here where I am winding up my fust wife's estate which theyve filed a bill in chancery.   S. S. Jr.

CITY OF GOT-HIM, Dec. 11, 1852
COL. SIMON SUGGS, JR.

My Dear Sir—The very interesting sketch of your life requested by us, reached here accompanied by your favor of the 1st inst., for which please receive our thanks.

We were very much pleased with the sketch, and think it throws light on a new phase of character, and supplies a desideratum in the branch of literature we are engaged in—the description of a lawyer distinguished in the outdoor labors of the profession, and directing great energies to the preparation of proof.

We fear, however, the suggestion you made of the use of the engraving of your distinguished father will not avail; as the author, Mr. Hooper, has copyrighted his work, and we should be exposing ourselves to a prosecution by trespassing on his patent. Besides, the execution of such a work by no better standard, would not be creditable either to our artist, yourself, or our Journal. We hope you will conclude to send on your daguerreotype to be appended to the lively and instructive sketch you furnish; and we entertain no doubt that the contemplated publication will redound greatly to your honor, and establish yours among the classical names of the American bar.

With profound respect, &c.,
THE EDITOR.

P.S.—Our delicacy caused us to omit, in our former letter, to mention what we suppose was generally understood, viz., the fact that the cost to us of preparing engravings, &c., &c., for the sketches or memoirs, is one hundred and fifty dollars, which sum it is expected, of course, the gentleman who is perpetuated in our work, will forward to us before the insertion of his biography. We merely allude to this trifling circumstance, lest, in the pressure of important business and engagements with which your mind is charged, it might be forgotten.

Again, very truly, &c.,
ED. JURIST-MAKER.

RACKINSACK, Dec. 25, 1852.

Dear Mr. Editor—In your p. s. which seems to be the creem of your correspondents you say I can't get in your book without paying one hundred and fifty dollars—pretty tall entrants fee! I suppose though children and niggers half price—I believe I will pass. I'll enter a nolly prossy q. O-n-e-h-u-n-d-r-e-d dollars and fifty better! Je-whelli-kens!

I just begin to see the pint of many things which was very vague and ondefinit before. Put Barnum in first—one hundred and fifty dollars!

That's the consideratum you talk of is it.

    I REMAIN   Respy
                                                    SIMON SUGGS, JR.

Therefore wont go in.

P.S.—Suppose you rite to the old man!! May be he'd go in with BARNUM!!! May be he'd like to take TWO chances? HE'S young—never seen MUCH!! Lives in a new country!!! AINT SMART!! I SAY a hundred and fifty dollars!!!

SIMON SUGGS, JR., ESQ.,
OF
RACKINSACK—ARKANSAW.

This distinguished lawyer, unlike, the majority of those favored subjects of the biographical issue, whom a patriotic ambition to add to the moral treasures of the country, has prevailed on, over the instincts of a native and professional modesty, to supply subjects for the pens and pencils of their friends, was not quite, either in a literal or a metaphorical sense, a self-made man. He had ancestors. They were, moreover, men of distinction; and, on the father's side, in the first and second degrees of ascent, known to fame. The father of this distinguished barrister was, and, happily, is Capt. Simon Suggs, of the Tallapoosa volunteers, and celebrated not less for his financial skill and abilities, than for his martial exploits. His grandfather, the Rev. Jedediah Suggs, was a noted divine of the Anti-Missionary or Hardshell Baptist persuasion in Georgia. For further information respecting these celebrities, the ignorant reader—the well-informed already know them—is referred to the work of Johnson Hooper, Esq., one of the most authentic of modern biographers.

The question of the propagability of moral and intellectual qualities is a somewhat mooted point, into the metaphysics of which we do not propose to enter; but that there are instances of moral and intellectual as well as physical likenesses in families, is an undisputed fact, of which the subject of this memoir is a new and striking illustration.

In the month of July, Anno Domini, 1810, on the ever memorable fourth day of the month, in the county of Carroll, and State of Georgia, Simon Suggs, Jr., first saw the light, mingling the first noise he made in the world with the patriotic explosions and rejoicings going on in honor of the day. We have endeavored in vain to ascertain, whether the auspicious period of the birth of young Simon was a matter of accident, or of human calculation, and sharp foresight, for which his immediate ancestor on the paternal side was so eminently distinguished; but, beyond a knowing wink, and a characteristic laudation of his ability to accomplish wonderful things, and to keep the run of the cards, on the part of the veteran captain, we have obtained no reliable information on this interesting subject. It is something, however, to be remarked upon, that the natal day of his country and of Simon were the same.

Very early in life, our hero—for Peace hath her victories, and, of course, her heroes, as well as war—gave a promise of the hereditary genius of the Suggs's; but as the incidents in proof of this rest on the authority, merely, of family tradition, we shall not violate the sanctity of the domestic fireside, by relating them. In the ninth year of his age he was sent to the public school in the neighborhood. Here he displayed that rare vivacity and enterprise, and that shrewdness and invention, which subsequently distinguished his riper age. Like his father, his study was less of books than of men. Indeed, it required a considerable expenditure of birch, and much wear and tear of patience, to overcome his constitutional aversion to letters sufficiently to enable him to master the alphabet. Not that he was too lazy to learn; on the contrary, it was his extreme industry in other and more congenial pursuits that stood in the way of the sedentary business of instruction. It was not difficult to see that the mantle of the Captain had fallen upon his favorite son; at any rate, the breeches in which young Simon's lower proportions were encased, bore a wonderful resemblance to the old cloak that the Captain had sported on so many occasions.

Simon's course at school was marked by many of the traits which distinguished him in after life; so true is the aphorism which the great Englishman enounced, that the boy is father to the man. His genius was eminently commercial, and he was by no means deficient in practical arithmetic. This peculiar turn of mind displayed itself in his barterings for the small wares of schoolboy merchandise—tops, apples, and marbles, sometimes rising to the dignity of a pen-knife. In these exercises of infantile enterprise, it was observable that Simon always got the advantage in the trade; and in that sense of charity which conceals defects, he may be said to have always displayed that virtue to a considerable degree. The same love of enterprise early led him into games of hazard, such as push-pin marbles, chuck-a-luck, heads and tails, and other like boyish pastimes, in which his ingenuity was rewarded by marked success. The vivacious and eager spirit of this gifted urchin sometimes evolved and put in practice, even in the presence of the master, expedients of such sort as served to enliven the proverbial monotony of scholastic confinement and study: such, for example, were the traps set for the unwary and heedless scholar, made by thrusting a string through the eye of a needle and passing it through holes in the school bench—one end of the string being attached to the machinist's leg, and so fixed, that by pulling the string, the needle would protrude through the further hole and into the person of the urchin sitting over it, to the great divertisement of the spectators of this innocent pastime. The holes being filled with soft putty, the needle was easily replaced, and the point concealed, so that when the outcry of the victim was heard, Simon was diligently perusing his book, and the only consequence was a dismissal of the complaint, and the amercement of the complainant by the master, *pro falso clamore.* Beginning to be a little more boldly enterprising, the usual fortune of those who "conquer or excel mankind" befell our hero, and he was made the scape-goat of the school; all vagrant offences that could not be proved against any one else being visited upon him; a summary procedure, which, as Simon remarked, brought down genius to the level of blundering mediocrity, and made of no avail the most ingenious arts of deception and concealment. The master of the old field school was one of the regular faculty, who had great faith in the old medicine for the eradication of moral diseases—the cutaneous tonic, as he called it—and repelled, with great scorn, the modern quackeries of kind encouragement and moral suasion. Accordingly, the flagellations and cuffings which Simon received, were such and so many as to give him a high opinion of the powers of endurance, the recuperative energies, and the immense vitality of the human system. Simon tried, on one occasion, the experiment of fits; but Dominie Dobbs was inexorable; and as the fainting posture only exposed to the Dominie new and fresher points of attack, Simon was fain to unroll his eyes, draw up again his lower jaw, and come to. Simon, remarking in his moralizing way upon the virtue of perseverance, has been heard to declare that he "lost that game" by being unable to keep from scratching during a space of three minutes and a half; which he would have accomplished, but for the Dominie's touching him on the raw, caused by riding a race bare-backed the Sunday before. "Upon what slender threads hang the greatest events!" Doubtless these experiences of young Suggs were not without effect upon so observing and sagacious an intellect. To them we may trace that strong republican bias and those fervid expressions in favor of Democratic principles, which, all through life, and in the ranks of whatever party he might be found, he ever exhibited and made; and probably to the unfeeling, and sometimes unjust inflictions of Dominie Dobbs, was he indebted for his devotion to that principle of criminal justice he so pertinaciously upheld, which requires full proof of guilt before it awards punishment.

 We must pass over a few years in the life of Simon, who continued at school, growing in size and wisdom; and not more instructed by what he learned there, than by the valuable information which his reverend father gave him in the shape of his sage counsels and sharp experiences of the world and its ways and wiles. An event occurred in Simon's fifteenth year, which dissolved the tie that bound him to his rustic *Alma Mater,* the only institution of letters which can boast of his connection with it. Dominie Dobbs, one Friday evening, shortly after the close of the labors of the scholastic week, was quietly taking from a handkerchief in which he had placed it, a flask of powder; as he pressed the knot of the handkerchief, *it* pressed upon the slide of the flask, which as it revolved, bore upon a lucifer match that ignited the powder; the explosion tore the handkerchief to pieces, and also one ear and three fingers of the Dominie's right hand—those fingers that had wielded the birch upon young Simon with such effect. Suspicion fell on Simon, notwithstanding he was the first boy to leave the school that evening. This suspicion derived some corroboration from other facts; but the evidence was wholly circumstantial. No positive proof whatever connected Simon with this remarkable accident; but the characteristic prudence of the elder Suggs suggested the expediency of Simon's leaving for a time a part of the country where character was held in so little esteem. Accordingly the influence of his father procured for Simon a situation in the neighboring county of Randolph, in the State of Alabama, near the gold mines, as clerk or assistant in a store for retailing spirituous liquors, which the owner, one Dixon Tripes, had set up for refreshment of the public, without troubling the County Court for a license. Here Simon was early initiated into a knowledge of men, in such situations as to present their characters nearly naked to the eye. The neighbors were in the habit of assembling at the grocery, almost every day, in considerable numbers, urged thereto by the attractions of the society, and the beverage there abounding; and games of various sorts added to the charms of conversation and social intercourse. It was the general rendezvous of the fast young gentlemen for ten miles around; and horse-racing, shooting-matches, quoit-pitching, cock-fighting, and card-playing filled up the vacant hours between drinks.

In such choice society it may well be supposed that so sprightly a temper and so inquisitive a mind as Simon's found congenial and delightful employment; and it was not long before his acquirements ranked him among the foremost in that select and spirited community. Although good at all the games mentioned, card-playing constituted his favorite amusement, not less for the excitement it afforded him, than for the rare opportunity it gave him of studying the human character.

The skill he attained in measuring distances, was equal to that displayed in his youth, by his venerated father, insomuch that in any disputed question in pitching or shooting, to allow him to measure was to give him the match; while his proficiency "in arranging the papers"—vulgarly called stocking a pack— was nearly equal to sleight of hand. Having been appointed judge of a quarter race on one occasion, he decided in favor of one of the parties by three inches and a half; and such was the sense of the winner of Simon's judicial expertness and impartiality, that immediately after the decision was made, he took Simon behind the grocery and divided the purse with him. By means of the accumulation of his wonderful industry, Simon went forth with a somewhat heterogeneous assortment of plunder, to set up a traffic on his own account: naturally desiring a wider theatre, which he found in the city of Columbus in his native State. He returned to the paternal roof with an increased store of goods and experience from his sojourn in Alabama. Among other property, he brought with him a small race mare, which excited the acquisitiveness of his father, who, desiring an easier mode of acquisition than by purchase, proposed to stake a horse he had (the same he had swapped for, on the road to Montgomery, with the land speculator,) against Simon's mare, upon the issue of a game of *seven up*. Since the game of chess between Mr. Jefferson and the French Minister, which lasted three years, perhaps there never has been a more closely contested match than that between these keen, sagacious and practised sportsmen. It was played with all advantages; all the lights of science were shed upon that game. The old gentleman had the advantage of experience—the young of genius: it was the old fogy against young America. For a long time the result was dubious; as if Dame Fortune was unable or unwilling to decide between her favorites. The game stood *six and six,* and young Simon had the deal. Just as the deal commenced, after one of the most brilliant shuffles the senior had ever made, Simon carelessly laid down his tortoise-shell snuff-box on the table; and the father, affecting *nonchalance,* and inclining his head towards the box, in order to peep under as the cards were being dealt, took a pinch of snuff; the titillating restorative was strongly adulterated with cayenne pepper; the old fogy was compelled to sneeze; and just as he recovered from the concussion, the first object that met his eye was a Jack turning in Simon's hand. A struggle seemed to be going on in the old man's breast between a feeling of pride in his son and a sense of his individual loss. It soon ceased, however. The father congratulated his son upon his success, and swore that he was wasting his genius in a retail business of "shykeenry" when nature had designed him for the bar.

To follow Simon through the eventful and checkered scenes of his nascent manhood, would be to enlarge this sketch to a volume. We must be content to state briefly, that such was the proficiency he made in the polite accomplishments of the day, and such the reputation he acquired in all those arts which win success in legal practice, when thereto energetically applied, that many sagacious men predicted that *the law would yet elevate Simon to a prominent place in the public view.* In his twenty-first year, Simon, starting out with a single mare to trade in horses in the adjoining State of Alabama, returned, such was his success, with a drove of six horses and a mule, and among them the very mare he started with. These, with the exception of the mare, he converted into money; he had found her invincible in all trials of speed, and determined to keep her. Trying his fortune once more in Alabama, where he had been so eminently successful, Simon went to the city of Wetumpka, where he found the races about coming off. As his mare had too much reputation to get bets upon her, an ingenious idea struck Simon—it was to take bets, through an agent, *against* her, in favor of a long-legged horse, entered for the races. It was very plain to see that Simon's mare was bound to win if he let her. He backed his own mare openly, and got some trifling bets on her; and his agent was fortunate enough to pick up a green-looking Georgia sucker, who bet with him the full amount left of Simon's "pile." The stakes were deposited in due form to the amount of some two thousand dollars. Simon was to ride his own mare—wild Kate, as he called her—and he had determined to hold her back, so that the other horse should win. But the Georgian, having by accident overheard the conversation between Simon and his agent, before the race, cut the reins of Simon's bridle nearly through, but in so ingenious a manner, that the incision did not appear. The race came off as it had been arranged; and as Simon was carefully holding back his emulous filly, at the same time giving her whip and spur, as though he would have her do her best, the bridle broke under the strain; and the mare, released from check, flew to and past the goal like the wind, some three hundred yards ahead of the horse, upon the success of which Simon had "piled" up so largely.

A shout of laughter like that which pursued Mazeppa, arose from the crowd (to whom the Georgian had communicated the facts), as Simon swept by, the involuntary winner of the race; and in that laugh, Simon heard the announcement of the discovery of his ingenious contrivance. He did not return.

Old Simon, when he heard of this counter-mine, fell into paroxysms of grief, which could not find consolation in less than a quart of red-eye. Heart-stricken, the old patriarch exclaimed—"Oh! Simon! my son Simon! to be overcome in that way!—a Suggs to be humbugged! His own Jack to be taken outen his hand and turned on him! Oh! that I should ha' lived to see this day!"

Proceeding to Montgomery, Simon found an opening on the thither side of a faro table; and having disposed of the race mare for three hundred dollars, banked on this capital, but with small success. Mr. Suggs' opinion of the people of Montgomery was not high; they were fashioned on a very diminutive scale, he used to say, and degraded the national amusement, by wagers, which an enterprising boy would scorn to hazard at push-pin. One Sam Boggs, a young lawyer "of that ilk," having been cleaned out of his entire stake of ten dollars, wished to continue the game on credit, and Simon gratified him, taking his law license in pawn for two dollars and a half; which pawn the aforesaid Samuel failed to redeem. Our prudent and careful adventurer filed away the sheepskin, thinking that sometime or other, he might be able to put it to good use.

The losses Simon had met with, and the unpromising prospects of gentlemen who lived on their wits, now that the hard times had set in, produced an awakening influence upon his conscience. He determined to abandon the nomadic life he had led, and to settle himself down to some regular business. He had long felt a call to the law, and he now resolved to "locate," and apply himself to the duties of that learned profession. Simon was not long in deciding upon a location. The spirited manner in which the State of Arkansas had repudiated a public debt of some five hundred thousand dollars gave him a favorable opinion of that people as a community of litigants, while the accounts which came teeming from that bright land, of murders and felonies innumerable, suggested the value of the criminal practice. He wended his way into that State, nor did he tarry until he reached the neighborhood of Fort Smith, a promising border town in the very *Ultima Thule of civilization,* such as it was, just on the confines of the Choctaw nation. It was in this region, in the village of Rackensack, that he put up his sign, and offered himself for practice. I shall not attempt to describe the population. It is indescribable. I shall only say that the Indians and half-breeds across the border complained of it mightily.

The motive for Simon's seeking so remote a location was that he might get in advance of his reputation—being laudably ambitious to acquire forensic distinction, he wished his fame as a lawyer to be independent of all extraneous and adventitious assistance. His first act in the practice was under the statute of *Jeo Fails.* It consisted of an amendment of the license he had got from Boggs, as before related; which amendment, was ingeniously effected by a careful erasure of the name of that gentleman, and the insertion of his own in the place of it. Having accomplished this feat, he presented it to the court, then in session, and was duly admitted an attorney and counsellor at law and solicitor in chancery.

There is a tone and spirit of morality attaching to the profession of the law so elevating and pervasive in its influence, as to work an almost instantaneous reformation in the character and habits of its disciples. If this be not so, it was certainly a most singular coincidence that, just at the time of his adoption of this vocation, Simon abandoned the favorite pastimes of his youth, and the irregularities of his earlier years. Indeed, he has been heard to declare that any lawyer, fulfilling conscientiously the duties of his profession, will find enough to employ all his resources of art, stratagem and dexterity, without resorting to other and more equivocal methods for their exercise.

It was not long before Simon's genius began to find occasions and opportunities of exhibition. When he first came to the bar, there were but seven suits on the docket, two of those being appeals from a justice's court. In the course of six months, so indefatigable was he in instructing clients, as to their rights, the number of suits grew to forty. Simon—or as he is now called—*Colonel* Suggs, determined on winning a reputation in a most effective branch of practice—one that he shrewdly perceived was too much neglected by the profession—the branch of preparing cases *out of court* for trial. While other lawyers were busy in getting up the law of their cases, the Colonel was no less busy in getting up the facts of his.

One of the most successful of Col. Suggs' efforts was in behalf of his landlady, in whom he felt a warm and decided interest. She had been living for many years in ignorant contentedness, with an indolent, easy natured man, her husband, who was not managing her separate estate, consisting of a plantation and about twenty negroes, and some town property, with much thrift. The lady was buxom and gay; and the union of the couple was unblessed with children. By the most insinuating manners, Col. Suggs at length succeeded in opening the lady's eyes to a true sense of her hapless condition, and the danger in which her property was placed, from the improvident habits of her spouse; and, having ingeniously deceived the unsuspecting husband into some suspicious appearances, which were duly observed by a witness or two provided for the purpose, he soon prevailed upon his fair hostess to file a bill of divorce; which she readily procured under the Colonel's auspices. Under the pretense of protecting her property from the claims of her husband's creditors, the Colonel was kind enough to take a conveyance of it to himself; and, shortly afterwards, the fair libellant; by which means he secured himself from those distracting cares which beset the young legal practitioner, who stands in immediate need of the wherewithal.

Col. Suggs' prospects now greatly improved, and he saw before him an extended field of usefulness. The whole community felt the effects of his activity. Long dormant claims came to light; and rights, of the very existence of which suitors were not before aware, were brought into practical assertion. From restlessness and inactivity, the population became excited, inquisitive and intelligent, as to the laws of their country; and the ruinous effects of servile acquiescence in wrong and oppression, were averted.

The fault of lawyers in preparing their cases was too generally a dilatoriness of movement, which sometimes deferred until it was too late, the creating of the proper impression upon the minds of the jury. This was not the fault of Col. Suggs; he always took time by the forelock. Instead of waiting to create prejudices in the minds of the jury, until they were in the box, or deferring until then the arts of persuasion, he waited upon them before they were empanelled; and he always succeeded better at that time, as they had not then received an improper bias from the testimony. In a case of any importance, he always managed to have his friends in the court room, so that when any of the jurors were challenged, he might have their places filled by good men and true; and, although this increased his expenses considerably, by a large annual bill at the grocery, he never regretted any expense, either of time, labor, or money, necessary to success in his business. Such was his zeal for his clients!

He was in the habit, too, of free correspondence with the opposite party, which enabled him at once to conduct his case with better advantage, and to supply any omissions or chasms in the proof: and so far did he carry the habit of testifying in his own cases, that his clients were always assured that in employing him, they were procuring counsel and witness at the same time, and by the same retainer. By a very easy process, he secured a large debt barred by the statue of limitations, and completely circumvented a fraudulent defendant who was about to avail himself of that mendacious defence. He ante-dated the writ, and thus brought the case clear of the statute.

One of the most harassing annoyances that were inflicted upon the emigrant community around him, was the revival of old claims contracted in the State from which they came, and which the Shylocks holding them, although they well knew that the pretended debtors had, expressly in consideration of getting rid of them, put themselves to the pains of exile and to the losses and discomforts of leaving their old homes and settling in a new country, in fraudulent violation of this object, were ruinously seeking to enforce, even to the deprivation of the property of the citizen. In one instance, a cashier of a bank in Alabama brought on claims against some of the best citizens of the country, to a large amount, and instituted suits on them. Col. Suggs was retained to defend them. The cashier, a venerable-looking old gentleman, who had extorted promises of payment, or at least had heard from the debtors promises of payment, which their necessitous circumstances had extorted, but to which he well knew they did not attach much importance, was waiting to become a witness against them. Col. Suggs so concerted operations, as to have some half-dozen of the most worthless of the population follow the old gentleman about whenever he went out of doors, and to be seen with him on various occasions; and busying himself in circulating through the community, divers reports disparaging the reputation of the witness, got the cases ready for trial. It was agreed that *one* verdict should settle all the cases. The defendant pleaded the statute of limitations; and to do away with the effect of it, the plaintiff offered the cashier as a witness. Not a single question was asked on a cross-examination; but a smile of derision, which was accompanied by a foreordained titter behind the bar, was visible on the faces of Simon and his client, as he testified. The defendant then offered a dozen or more witnesses, who, much to the surprise of the venerable cashier, discredited him; and the jury, without leaving the box, found a verdict for the defendant. The cashier was about moving for a new trial, when, it being intimated to him that a warrant was about to be issued for his apprehension on a charge of perjury, he concluded not to see the result of such a process, and indignantly left the country.

The criminal practice, especially, fascinated the regards and engaged the attention of Col. Suggs, as a department of his profession and energies. He soon became acquainted with all the arts and contrivances by which public justice is circumvented. Indictments that could not be quashed, were sometimes mysteriously out of the way; and the clerk had occasion to reproach his carelessness in not filing them in the proper places, when, some days after cases had been dismissed for the want of them, they were discovered by him in some old file, or among the executions. He was requested, or rather he volunteered in one capital case, to draw a recognizance for a committing magistrate, as he (Suggs) was idly looking on, not being concerned in the trial, and so felicitously did he happen to introduce the negative particle in the condition of the bond, that he bound the defendant, under a heavy penalty, "*not*" to appear at court and answer to the charge; which appearance, doubtless, much against his will, and merely to save his sureties, the defendant proceeded faithfully not to make.

Col. Suggs also extricated a client and his sureties from a forfeited recognizance, by having the defaulting defendant's obituary notice somewhat prematurely inserted in the newspapers; the solicitor, seeing which, discontinued proceedings; for which service, the deceased, immediately after the adjournment of court, returned to the officer his personal acknowledgments: "not that," as he expressed it, "it mattered any thing to him personally, but because it *would have aggravated the feelings* of his friends he had left behind him, to of let the thing rip arter he was defunck."

The most difficult case Col. Suggs ever had to manage, was to extricate a client from jail, after sentence of death had been passed upon him. But difficulties, so far from discouraging him, only had the effect of stimulating his energies. He procured the aid of a young physician in the premises—the prisoner was suddenly taken ill—the physician pronounced the disease small pox. The wife of the prisoner, with true womanly devotion, attended on him. The prisoner, after a few days, was reported dead, and the doctor gave out that it would be dangerous to approach the corpse. A coffin was brought into the jail, and the wife was put into it by the physician—she being enveloped in her husband's clothes. The coffin was put in a cart and driven off—the husband, habited in the woman's apparel, following after, mourning piteously, until, getting out of the village, he disappeared in the thicket, where he found a horse prepared for him. The wife obstinately refused to be buried in the husband's place when she got to the grave; but the mistake was discovered too late for the recapture of the prisoner.

The tact and address of Col. Suggs opposed such obstacles to the enforcement of the criminal law in that part of the country, that, following the example of the English government, when Irish patriotism begins to create annoyances, the State naturally felt anxious to engage his services in its behalf. Accordingly, at the meeting of the Arkansas legislature, at its session of 184—, so soon as the matter of the killing a member on the floor of the house, by the speaker, with a Bowie knife, was disposed of by a resolution of mild censure, for imprudent precipitancy, Simon Suggs, Jr., Esquire, was elected solicitor for the Rackensack district. Col. Suggs brought to the discharge of the duties of his office energies as unimpaired and vigorous as in the days of his first practice; and entered upon it with a mind free from the vexations of domestic cares, having procured a divorce from his wife on the ground of infidelity, but magnanimously giving her one of the negroes, and a horse, saddle and bridle.

The business of the State now flourished beyond all precedent. Indictments multiplied: and though many of them were not tried—the solicitor discovering, after the finding of them, as he honestly confessed to the court, that the evidence would not support them: yet, the Colonel could well say, with an eminent English barrister, that if he tried fewer cases in court, he settled more cases out of court than any other counsel.

The marriage of Col. Suggs, some three years after his appointment of solicitor, with the lovely and accomplished Che-wee-na-tubbe, daughter of a distinguished prophet and warrior, and head-man of the neighboring territory of the Choctaw Indians, induced his removal into that beautiful and improving country. His talents and connections at once raised him to the councils of that interesting people; and he received the appointment of agent for the settlement of claims on the part of that tribe, and particular individuals of it, upon the treasury of the United States. This responsible and lucrative office now engages the time and talents of Col. Suggs, who may be seen every winter at Washington, faithfully and laboriously engaged with members of Congress and in the departments, urging the matters of his mission upon the dull sense of the Janitors of the Federal Treasury.

May his shadow never grow less; and may the Indians live to get their dividends of the arrears paid to their agent.

Thomas Bangs Thorpe (1815-1878)

A native of Massachusetts, Thomas Bangs Thorpe grew up in Albany and New York City, and at the age of fifteen studied painting with artist John Quidor. Painting would remain a major part of his life even as he pursued other professional interests. He attended Wesleyan University in Connecticut for two years before seeking in 1837 a climate better suited to his poor health. He found it in Louisiana, which would be his home for the next seventeen years. Painting portraits of wealthy patrons, editing at least five newspapers, serving during the Mexican War, and becoming involved in Whig politics kept him busy without making him wealthy. Returning to New York in 1854, painting and writing for several prominent periodicals, such as the *Spirit of the Times, Harper's, Graham's,* and *Knickerbocker Magazine* occupied his time as he sought a career in political preferment. He worked in the New York Custom House, returned to New Orleans as a federal customs agent during the Civil War, and served in a variety of capacities there and back in New York for the remainder of his life. Less than a year before his death in 1878, he resigned from the New York Custom House under threat of being fired over dishonest transactions.

Thorpe's first story, "Tom Owen, the Bee-Hunter," was published in 1839 in the New York *Spirit of the Times* while he was resident in New Orleans. It was widely reprinted in other papers and brought him a degree of popular success as a writer. During his lifetime, Thorpe would publish at least five books and over 150 stories, sketches, and essays. While his humorous character study of Tom Owen in mock-heroic style as an example of the Louisiana backwoodsman was striking, if much in the style of Washington Irving, there was little in his other work to predict the culmination of his talent in "The Big Bear of Arkansas," published in the *Spirit of the Times* in March 1841. Myth, symbol, and psychological insight somehow coalesced into a powerful story, written with complex skill, that captured the entire spirit of the American frontier experience and national character. It has remained one of the best pieces of American short fiction ever written and the major example of the humor of the Old Southwest, thus the often applied epithet, "The Big Bear School of Humor."

The story was collected as the lead piece in William T. Porter's anthology, *The Big Bear of Arkansas, and Other Sketches,* in 1845, was reprinted in Thorpe's own second book, *The Hive of the "Bee-Hunter,"* in 1854, and has been included in numerous anthologies ever since. Many American writers have acknowledged the power of its influence, including William Faulkner, who said, "A writer is afraid of a story like that," but went on to create his own version one hundred years later in *The Bear* in 1942. While none of Thorpe's other works achieved the rich texture of this one, a constant theme is the passing away of the wilderness and nature in the face of civilization. But he did show a special talent for parody in his series of twelve mock letters about a hunting expedition published as "Letters from the Far West" in the Louisiana *Concordia Intelligencer* in 1843 and 1844 and subsequently reprinted in the *Spirit of the Times.*

Texts: "The Big Bear of Arkansas," from *The Hive of the "Bee-Hunter," a Repository of Sketches, Including Peculiar American Character, Scenery, and Rural Sports* (New York: D. Appleton, 1854). "Letters from the Far West," Letters 2, 7, 10, and 12, from *Concordia Intelligencer,* August 12, 1843; October 14, 1843; December 16, 1843; and February 10, 1844.

The Big Bear of Arkansas

A steamboat on the Mississippi, frequently, in making her regular trips, carries between places varying from one to two thousand miles apart; and, as these boats advertise to land passengers and freight at "all intermediate landings," the heterogeneous character of the passengers of one of these up-country boats can scarcely be imagined by one who has never seen it with his own eyes.

Starting from New Orleans in one of these boats, you will find yourself associated with men from every State in the Union, and from every portion of the globe; and a man of observation need not lack for amusement or instruction in such a crowd, if he will take the trouble to read the great book of character so favorably opened before him.

Here may be seen, jostling together, the wealthy Southern planter and the pedler of tin-ware from New England—the Northern merchant and the Southern jockey—a venerable bishop, and a desperate gambler—the land speculator, and the honest farmer—professional men of all creeds and characters—Wolvereens, Suckers, Hoosiers, Buckeyes, and Corn-crackers, beside a "plentiful sprinkling" of the half-horse and half-alligator species of men, who are peculiar to "old Mississippi," and who appear to gain a livelihood by simply going up and down the river. In the pursuit of pleasure or business, I have frequently found myself in such a crowd.

On one occasion, when in New Orleans, I had occasion to take a trip of a few miles up the Mississippi, and I hurried on board the well-known "high-pressure-and-beat-every-thing" steamboat "Invincible," just as the last note of the last bell was sounding; and when the confusion and bustle that is natural to a boat's getting under way had subsided, I discovered that I was associated in as heterogeneous a crowd as was ever got together. As my trip was to be of a few hours' duration only, I made no endeavors to become acquainted with my fellow-passengers, most of whom would be together many days. Instead of this, I took out of my pocket the "latest paper," and more critically than usual examined its contents; my fellow-passengers, at the same time, disposed of themselves in little groups.

While I was thus busily employed in reading, and my companions were more busily still employed, in discussing such subjects as suited their humors best, we were most unexpectedly startled by a loud Indian whoop, uttered in the "social hall," that part of the cabin fitted off for a bar; then was to be heard a loud crowing, which would not have continued to interest us—such sounds being quite common in that *place of spirits*—had not the hero of these windy accomplishments stuck his head into the cabin, and hallooed out, "Hurra for the Big Bear of Arkansaw!"

Then might be heard a confused hum of voices, unintelligible, save in such broken sentences as "horse," "screamer," "lightning is slow," &c.

As might have been expected, this continued interruption, attracted the attention of every one in the cabin; all conversation ceased, and in the midst of this surprise, the "Big Bear" walked into the cabin, took a chair, put his feet on the stove, and looking back over his shoulder, passed the general and familiar salute—"Strangers, how are you?"

He then expressed himself as much at home as if he had been at "the Forks of Cypress," and "prehaps a little more so."

Some of the company at this familiarity looked a little angry, and some astonished; but in a moment every face was wreathed in a smile. There was something about the intruder that won the heart on sight. He appeared to be a man enjoying perfect health and contentment; his eyes were as sparkling as diamonds, and good-natured to simplicity. Then his perfect confidence in himself was irresistibly droll.

"Prehaps," said he, "gentlemen," running on without a person interrupting, "prehaps you have been to New Orleans often; I never made *the first visit before*, and I don't intend to make another in a crow's life. I am thrown away in that ar place, and useless, that ar a fact. Some of the gentlemen thar called me *green*—well, prehaps I am, said I, *but I arn't so at home*; and if I ain't off my trail much, the heads of them perlite chaps themselves weren't much the hardest; for according to my notion, they were *real know-nothings*, green as a pumpkin-vine—couldn't, in farming, I'll bet, raise a crop of turnips; and as for shooting, they'd miss a barn if the door was swinging, and that, too, with the best rifle in the country. And then they talked to me 'bout hunting, and laughed at my calling the principal game in Arkansaw poker, and high-low-jack.

"'Prehaps,' said I, 'you prefer checkers and roulette;' at this they laughed harder than ever, and asked me if I lived in the woods, and didn't know what *game* was?

"At this, I rather think *I* laughed.

"'Yes,' I roared, and says, I, 'Strangers, if you'd ask me *how we got our meat* in Arkansaw, I'd a told you at once, and given you a list of varmints that would make a caravan, beginning with the bar, and ending off with the cat; that's *meat* though, not game.

"Game, indeed,—that's what city folks call it; and with them it means chippen-birds and shite-pokes; may be such trash live in my diggins, but I arn't noticed them yet: a bird anyway is too trifling. I never did shoot at but one, and I'd never forgiven myself for that, had it weighted less than forty pounds. I wouldn't draw a rifle on anything less heavy than that; and when I meet with another wild turkey of the same size, I will drap him."

"A wild turkey weighting forty pounds!" exclaimed twenty voices in the cabin at once.

"Yes, strangers, and wasn't it a whopper? You see, the thing was so fat that it couldn't fly far; and when he fell out of the tree, after I shot him, on striking the ground he bust open behind, and the way the pound gobs of tallow rolled out of the opening was perfectly beautiful."

"Where did all that happen?" asked a cynical-looking Hoosier.

"Happen! happened in Arkansaw: where else could it have happened, but in the creation State, the finishing-up country—a State where the *sile* runs down to the centre of the 'arth, and government gives you a title to every inch of it? Then it airs—just breathe them, and they will make you snort like a horse. It's a State without a fault, it is."

"Excepting mosquitoes," cried the Hoosier.

"Well, stranger, except them; for it ar a fact that they are rather *enormous,* and do push themselves in somewhat troublesome. But, stranger, they never stick twice in the same place; and give them a fair chance for a few months, and you will get as much above noticing them as an alligator. They can't hurt my feelings, for they lay under the skin; and I never knew but one case of injury resulting from them, and that was to a Yankee: and they take worse to foreigners, any how, than they do to natives. But the way they used that fellow up! First they punched him until he swelled up and busted; then he sup-per-a-ted, as the doctor called it, until he was as raw as beef; then, owing to the warm weather, he tuck the ager, and finally he tuck a steamboat and left the country. He was the only man that ever tuck mosquitoes at heart that I knowd of.

"But mosquitoes is nature, and I never find fault with her. If they ar large, Arkansaw is large, her varmints ar large, her trees ar large, her rivers ar large, and a small mosquito would be of no more use in Arkansaw than preaching in a cane-brake."

This knock-down argument in favor of big mosquitoes used the Hoosier up, and the logician started on a new track, to explain how numerous bear were in his "diggins," where he represented them to be "about as plenty as blackberries, and a little plentifuller."

Upon the utterance of this assertion, a timid little man near me inquired, if the bear in Arkansaw ever attacked the settlers in numbers.

"No," said our hero, warming with the subject, "no, stranger, for you see it ain't the natur of bear to go in droves; but the way they squander about in pairs and single ones is edifying.

"And then the way I hunt them—the old black rascals know the crack of my gun as well as they know a pig's squealing. They grow thin in our parts, it frightens them so, and they do take the noise dreadfully, poor things. That gun of mine is a perfect *epidemic among bear:* if not watched closely, it will go off as quick on a warm scent as my dog Bowieknife will: and then that dog— whew! Why the fellow thinks that the world is full of bear, he finds them so easy. It's lucky he don't talk as well as think; for with his natural modesty, if he should suddenly learn how much he is acknowledged to be ahead of all other dogs in the universe, he would be astonished to death in two minutes.

"Strangers, that dog knows a bear's way as well as a horse-jockey knows a woman's: he always barks at the right time, bites at the exact place, and whips without getting a scratch.

"I never could tell whether he was made expressly to hunt bear, or whether bear was made expressly for him to hunt; any way, I believe they were ordained to go together as naturally as Squire Jones says a man and woman is, when he moralizes in marrying a couple. In fact, Jones once said, said he, 'Marriage according to law is a civil contract of divine origin; it's common to all countries as well as Arkansaw, and people take to it as naturally as Jim Doggett's Bowieknife takes to bear.'"

"What season of the year do your hunts take place?" inquired a gentlemanly foreigner, who, from some peculiarities of his baggage, I suspected to be an Englishman, on some hunting expedition, probably at the foot of the Rocky Mountains.

"The season for bear hunting, stranger," said the man of Arkansaw, "is generally all the year round, and the hunts take place about as regular. I read in history that varmints have their fat season, and their lean season. That is not the case in Arkansaw, feeding as they do upon the *spontenacious* productions of the sile, they have one continued fat season the year round; though in winter things in this way is rather more greasy than in summer, I must admit. For that reason bear with us run in warm weather, but in winter they only waddle.

"Fat, fat! It's an enemy to speed; it tames every thing that has plenty of it. I have seen wild turkeys, from its influence, as gentle as chickens. Run a bear in this fat condition, and the way it improves the critter for eating is amazing; it sort of mixes the ile up with the meat, until you can't tell t'other from which. I've done this often.

"I recollect one perty morning in particular, of putting an old he fellow on the stretch, and considering the weight he carried, he run well. But the dogs soon tired him down, and when I came up with him wasn't he in a beautiful sweat—I might say fever; and then to see his tongue sticking out of his mouth a feet, and his sides sinking and opening like a bellows, and his cheeks so fat that he couldn't look cross. In this fix I blazed at him, and pitch me naked into a briar patch, if the steam didn't come out of the bullet-hole ten foot in a straight line. The fellow, I reckon, was made on the high-pressure system, and the lead sort of bust his bilier."

"That column of steam was rather curious, or else the bear must have been very *warm*," observed the foreigner, with a laugh.

"Stranger, as you observe, that bear was WARM, and the blowing off of the steam show'd it, and also how hard the varmint had been run. I have no doubt if he had kept on two miles farther his insides would have been stewed; and I expect to meet with a varmint yet of extra bottom, that will run himself into a skinfull of bear's grease: it is possible; much onlikelier things have happened."

"Whereabouts are these bears so abundant?" inquired the foreigner, with increasing interest.

"Why, stranger, they inhabit the neighborhood of my settlement, one of the prettiest places on old Mississipp—a perfect location, and no mistake; a place that had some defects until the river made the 'cut-off' at 'Shirttail bend,' and that remedied the evil, as it brought my cabin on the edge of the river—a great advantage in wet weather, I assure you, as you can now roll a barrel of whiskey into my yard in high water from a boat, as easy as falling off a log. It's a great improvement, as toting it by land in a jug, as I used to do, *evaporated* it too fast, and it became expensive.

"Just stop with me, stranger, a month or two, or a year, if you like, and you will appreciate my place. I can give you plenty to eat; for beside hog and hominy, you can have bear-ham, and bear-sausages, and a mattrass of bear-skins to sleep on, and a wildcat-skin, pulled off hull, stuffed with corn-shucks, for a pillow. That bed would put you to sleep if you had the rheumatics in every joint in your body. I call that ar bed, a *quietus.*

"Then look at my 'pre-emption'—the government ain't got another like it to dispose of. Such timber, and such bottom land,—why you can't preserve anything natural you plant in it unless you pick it young, things thar will grow out of shape so quick.

"I once planted in those diggins a few potatoes and beets; they took a fine start, and after that, an ox team couldn't have kept them from growing. About that time I went off to old Kaintuck on business, and did not hear from them things in three months, when I accidentally stumbled on a fellow who had drapped in at my place, with an idea of buying me out.

"'How did you like things?' said I.

"'Pretty well,' said he; 'the cabin is convenient, and the timber land is good; but that bottom land ain't worth the first red cent.'"

"'Why?' said I.

"''Cause,' said he.

"''Cause what?' said I.

"''Cause it's full of cedar stumps and Indian mounds, and *can't be cleared.*'

"'Lord,' said I, 'them ar "cedar stumps" is beets, and them ar "Indian mounds" tater hills.'

"As I had expected, the crop was overgrown and useless: the sile is too rich, *and planting in Arkansaw is dangerous.*

"I had a good-sized sow killed in that same bottom land. The old thief stole an ear of corn, and took it down to eat where she slept at night. Well, she left a grain or two on the ground, and lay down on them: before morning the corn shot up, and the percussion killed her dead. I don't plant any more: natur intended Arkansaw for a hunting ground, and I go according to natur."

The questioner, who had thus elicited the description of our hero's settlement, seemed to be perfectly satisfied, and said no more; but the "Big Bear of Arkansaw" rambled on from one thing to another with a volubility perfectly astonishing, occasionally disputing with those around him, particularly with a "live Sucker" from Illinois, who had the daring to say that our Arkansaw friend's stories "smelt rather tall."

The evening was nearly spent by the incidents we have detailed; and conscious that my own association with so singular a personage would probably end before morning, I asked him if he would not give me a description of some particular bear hunt; adding, that I took great interest in such things, though I was no sportsman. The desire seemed to please him, and he squared himself round towards me, saying, that he could give me an idea of a bear hunt that was never beat in this world, or in any other. His manner was so singular, that half of his story consisted in his excellent way of telling it, the great peculiarity of which was, the happy manner he had of emphasizing the prominent parts of his conversation. As near as I can recollect, I have italicized the words, and given the story in his own way.

"Stranger," said he, "in bear hunts *I am numerous,* and which particular one as you say, I shall tell, puzzles me.

"There was the old she devil I shot at the Hurricane last fall—then there was the old hog thief I popped over at the Bloody Crossing, and then—Yes, I have it! I will give you an idea of a hunt, in which the greatest bear was killed that ever lived, *none excepted;* about an old fellow that I hunted, more or less, for two or three years; and if that ain't a *particular bear hunt,* I ain't got one to tell.

"But in the first place, stranger, let me say, I am pleased with you, because you ain't ashamed to gain information by asking and listening; and that's what I say to Countess's pups every day when I'm home; and I have got great hopes of them ar pups, because they are continually *nosing* about; and though they stick it sometimes in the wrong place, they gain experience any how, and may learn something useful to boot.

"Well, as I was saying about this big bear, you see when I and some more first settled into our region, we were drivin to hunting naturally; we soon liked it, and after that we found it an easy matter to make the thing our business. One old chap who had pioneered 'afore us, gave us to understand that we had settled in the right place. He dwelt upon its merits until it was affecting, and showed us, to prove his assertions, more scratches on the bark of the sassafras trees, than I ever saw chalk marks on a tavern door 'lection time.

"'Who keeps thar ar reckoning?' said I.

"'The bear,' said he.

"'What for?' said I.

"'Can't tell,' said he; 'but so it is: the bear bite the bark and wood too, at the highest point from the ground they can reach, and you can tell, by the marks,' said he, 'the length of the bear to an inch.'

"'Enough,' said I; 'I've learned something here a'ready, and I'll put it in practice.'

"Well, stranger, just one month from that time I killed a bear, and told its exact length before I measured it, by those very marks; and when I did that, I swelled up considerably—I've been a producer man ever since.

"So I went on, larning something every day, until I was reckoned a buster, and allowed to be decidedly the best bear hunter in my district; and that is a reputation as much harder to earn than to be reckoned first man in Congress, as an iron ramrod is harder than a toadstool.

"Do the varmints grow over-cunning by being fooled with by greenhorn hunters, and by this means get troublesome, they send for me, as a matter of course, and thus I do my own hunting, and most of my neighbors'. I walk into the varmints though, and it has become about as much the same to me as drinking. It is told in two sentences—

"A bear is started, and he is killed.

"The thing is somewhat monotonous now—I know just how much they will run, where they will tire, how much they will growl, and what a thundering time I will have in getting their meat home. I could give you the history of the chase with all the particulars at the commencement, I know the signs so well—*Stranger, I'm certain.* Once I met with a match, though, and I will tell you about it; for a common hunt would not be worth relating.

"On a fine fall day, long time ago, I was trailing about for bear, and what should I see but fresh marks on the sassafras trees, about eight inches above any in the forests that I knew of. Says I, 'Them marks is a hoax, or it indicates the d—t bear that was ever grown.' In fact, stranger, I couldn't believe it was real, and I went on. Again I saw the same marks, at the same height, and *I knew the thing lived.* That conviction came home to my soul like an earthquake.

"Says I, 'here is something a-purpose for me: that bear is mine, or I give up the hunting business.' The very next morning, what should I see but a number of buzzards hovering over my corn-field. 'The rascal has been there,' said I, 'for that sign is certain'; and, sure enough, on examining, I found the bones of what had been as beautiful a hog the day before, as was ever raised by a Buckeye. Then I tracked the critter out of the field to the woods, and all the marks he left behind, showed me that he was *the bear.*

"Well, stranger, the first fair chase I ever had with that big critter, I saw him no less than three distinct times at a distance; the dogs run him over eighteen miles and broke down, my horse gave out, and I was as nearly used up as a man can be, made on *my* principle, *which is patent.*

"Before this adventure, such things were unknown to me as possible; but, strange as it was, that bear got me used to it before I was done with him; for he got so at last, that he would leave me on a long chase *quite easy.* How he did it, I never could understand.

"That a bear runs at all, is puzzling; but how this one could tire down and bust up a pack of hounds and a horse, that were used to overhauling everything they started after in no time, was past my understanding. Well, stranger, that bear finally got so sassy, that he used to help himself to a hog off my premises whenever he wanted one; the buzzards followed after what he left, and so, between *bear and buzzard,* I rather think I got *out of pork.*

"Well, missing that bear so often took hold of my vitals, and I wasted away. The thing had been carried too far, and it reduced me in flesh faster than an ager. I would see that bear in every thing I did: *he hunted me,* and that, too, like a devil, which I began to think he was.

"While in this shaky fix, I made preparations to give him a last brush, and be done with it. Having completed everything to my satisfaction, I started at sunrise, and to my great joy, I discovered from the way the dogs run, that they were near him. Finding his trail was nothing, for that had become as plain to the pack as a turnpike road.

"On we went, and coming on an open country, what should I see but the bear very leisurely ascending a hill, and the dogs close at his heels, either a match for him this time in speed, or else he did not care to get out of their way—I don't know which. But wasn't he a beauty, though! I loved him like a brother.

"On he went, until he came to a tree, the limbs of which formed a crotch about six feet from the ground. Into this crotch he got and seated himself, the dogs yelling all around it; and there he sat eyeing them as quiet as a pond in low water.

"A greenhorn friend of mine, in company, reached shooting distance before me, and blazed away, hitting the critter in the centre of his forehead. The bear shook his head as the ball struck it, and then walked down from that tree, as gently as a lady would from a carriage.

"'Twas a beautiful sight to see him do that—he was in such a rage, that he seemed to be as little afraid of the dogs as if they had been sucking pigs; and the dogs warn't slow in making a ring around him at a respectful distance, I tell you; even Bowieknife himself, stood off. Then the way his eyes flashed!—why the fire of them would have singed a cat's hair; in fact, that bear was in a *wrath all over.* Only one pup came near him, and he was brushed out so totally with the bear's left paw, that he entirely disappeared; and that made the old dogs more cautious still. In the mean time, I came up, and taking deliberate aim, as a man should do, at his side, just back of his foreleg, *if my gun did not snap,* call me a coward, and I won't take it personal.

"Yes, stranger, *it snapped,* and I could not find a cap about my person. While in this predicament, I turned round to find my fool friend—'Bill,' says I, 'you're an ass—you're a fool—you might as well have tried to kill that bear by barking the tree under his belly, as to have done it by hitting him in the head. Your shot has made a tiger of him; and blast me, if a dog gets killed or wounded when they come to blows, I will stick my knife into your liver, I will—.' My wrath was up. I had lost my caps, my gun had snapped, the fellow with me had fired at the bear's head, and I expected every moment to see him close in with the dogs and kill a dozen of them at least. In this thing I was mistaken; for the bear leaped over the ring formed by the dogs, and giving a fierce growl, was off—the pack, of course, in full cry after him. The run this time was short, for coming to the edge of a lake, the varmint jumped in, and swam to a little island in the lake, which it reached, just a moment before the dogs.

"'I'll have him now,' said I, for I had found my caps in the *lining of my coat*—so, rolling a log into the lake, I paddled myself across to the island, just as the dogs had cornered the bear in a thicket. I rushed up and fired—at the same time the critter leaped over the dogs and came within three feet of me, running like mad; he jumped into the lake, and tried to mount the log I had just deserted, but every time he got half his body on it, it would roll over and send him under; the dogs, too, got around him, and pulled him about, and finally Bowieknife clenched with him, and they sunk into the lake together.

"Stranger, about this time I was excited, and I stripped off my coat, drew my knife, and intended to have taken a part with Bowieknife myself, when the bear rose to the surface. But the varmint staid under—Bowieknife came up alone, more dead than alive, and with the pack came ashore.

"'Thank God!' said I, 'the old villain has got his deserts at last.'

"Determined to have the body, I cut a grape-vine for a rope, and dove down where I could see the bear in the water, fastened my rope to his leg, and fished him, with great difficulty, ashore. Stranger, may I be chawed to death by young alligators, if the thing I looked at wasn't a *she bear, and not the old critter after all.*

"The way matters got mixed on that island was onaccountably curious, and thinking of it made me even more than ever convinced that I was hunting the devil himself. I went home that night and took to my bed—the thing was killing me. The entire team of Arkansaw in bear-hunting acknowledged himself used up, and the fact sunk into my feelings as a snagged boat will in the Mississippi. I grew as cross as a bear with two cubs and a sore tail. The thing got 'mong my neighbors, and I was asked how come on that individ-u-al didn't wear telescopes when he turned a she-bear, of ordinary size, into an old he one, a little larger than a horse?

"'Prehaps,' said I, 'friends'—getting wrathy—'prehaps you want to call somebody a liar?'

"'Oh, no,' said they, 'we only heard of such things being *rather common* of late, but we don't believe one word of it; oh, no,'—and then they would ride off, and laugh like so many hyenas over a dead nigger.

"It was too much, and I determined to catch that bear, go to Texas, or die,—and I made my preparations accordin.'

"I had the pack shut up and rested. I took my rifle to pieces, and iled it.

"I put caps in every pocket about my person, *for fear of the lining.*

"I then told my neighbors, that on Monday morning—naming the day—I would start THAT BEAR, and bring him home with me, or they might divide my settlement among them, the owner having disappeared.

"Well, stranger, on the morning previous to the great day of my hunting expedition, I went into the woods near my house, taking my gun and Bowieknife along, just *from habit,* and there sitting down, also from habit, what should I see, getting over my fence, but *the bear!* Yes, the old varmint was within a hundred yards of me, and the way he walked *over that fence*—stranger; he loomed up like a *black mist,* he seemed so large, and he walked right towards me.

"I raised myself, took deliberate aim, and fired. Instantly the varmint wheeled, gave a yell, and *walked through the fence,* as easy as a falling tree would through a cobweb.

"I started after, but was tripped up by my inexpressibles, which, either from habit or the excitement of the moment, were about my heels, and before I had really gathered myself up, I heard the old varmint groaning, like a thousand sinners, in a thicket near by, and, by the time I reached him, he was a corpse.

"Stranger, it took five niggers and myself to put that carcass on a mule's back, and old long-ears waddled under his load, as if he was foundered in every leg of his body; and with a common whopper of a bear, he would have trotted off, and enjoyed himself.

"'Twould astonish you to know how big he was: I made a *bedspread of his skin,* and the way it used to cover my bear mattress, and leave several feet on each side to tuck up, would have delighted you. It was, in fact, a creation bear, and if it had lived in Samson's time, and had met him in a fair fight, he would have licked him in the twinkling of a dice-box.

"But, stranger, I never liked the way I hunted him, *and missed him.* There is something curious about it, that I never could understand,—and I never was satisfied at his giving in *so easy at last.* Prehaps he had heard of my preparations to hunt him the next day, so he jist guv up, like Captain Scott's coon, to save his wind to grunt with in dying; but that ain't likely. My private opinion is, that that bear was an *unhuntable bear, and died when his time come.*"

When this story was ended, our hero sat some minutes with his auditors, in a grave silence; I saw there was a mystery to him connected with the bear whose death he had just related, that had evidently made a strong impression on his mind. It was also evident that there was some superstitious awe connected with the affair,—a feeling common with all "children of the wood," when they meet with any thing out of their every-day experience.

He was the first one, however, to break the silence, and, jumping up, he asked all present to "liquor" before going to bed,—a thing which he did, with a number of companions, evidently to his heart's content.

Long before day, I was put ashore at my place of destination, and I can only follow with the reader, in imagination, our Arkansas friend, in his adventures at the "Forks of Cypress," on the Mississippi.

Letters from the Far West: Letter 2

Prospect of sport; Frontier Temperance Society; a real wild Indian; his natural eloquence and its power; meeting with Buffaloes; their peculiar behavior; my first hunt; head-work; a joke of misfortunes.

ABOVE THE YELLOW STONE, *June* 6, 1843.

In my last letter you could easily perceive that we were getting on the buffalo hunting grounds, in fact I thought for several days that I could hear the bulls bellowing in the night, but my companions told me it was only owing to my glowing imagination. The prospect of sport inspirited all of us, especially after the whiskey jug had been freely passed around, previous to the grand temperance society we shall form after we get out of liquor. We have had a great many savages with us one time and another, but most of them are more than half-civilized, as they will get drunk and steal as quick as any white man I ever saw. Yesterday, however, we were blessed with the sight of a real wild chap, he came into the encampment looking like a corn field scare-cow, dressed up in a coat of feathers; a man with us from Arkansas, said it would improve his appearance very much in his estimation if the feathers had been stuck on with a coat of tar; Audubon said he put him in mind of a sick Pelican, in the moulting season. This Indian was a brave looking fellow, though, walked splendidly, evidently imitated Forrest the actor in Metamora, or a parrot, I don't know which. He was short thick set, and smelt strongly of rancid bear's oil, which he used as we do cologne; he is said to be the blackest Indian of his tribe; his name I learned, was Tar-pot-wan-ja, which means literally translated, *the tall white Crane.* I took to him naturally; there was something that pleased me in his eye, and the grateful expression of his face, as I gave him a drink out of my canteen; I asked him if he ever had been in war, at the question he started back, placed himself in a most elegant attitude, a perfect representation of a corpulent Apollo, then tracing the sun's course with his finger through the heavens, he turned his face full towards me, uttered a guttural "ugh!" took a plug of tobacco out of my hand, stuck it in the folds of his blanket, and quietly walked out of the tent, to attend to the sale of some venison at a dime a hind quarter; I never saw a more noble, and beautiful exhibition of savage life. Yesterday was an era in our history, the first of our seeing Buffalo, which are now skirting along the horizon as if we were in a great farm yard of fine cattle. It's a mighty great idea that a fellow owns as many of these monsters as he can catch, though the latter is more difficult than you would at first imagine. I was determined to be at last, first, as I was always before behind in every thing, so I mounted my horse unbeknown to my companions and sallied out, pretty soon I got near the reptiles, and oh! thunder and turf, such looking beasts as they were, no more like decently behaved cattle than I am like a flat-head. There they were, bless their souls, looking at me through their sweet little eyes, and seeming as willing to tuck me up with their fine little horns, as if I had been a bundle of prairie grass. Buffalo indeed, they all looked like Aesop's donkey in the lion skin, they were so shaggy in front the villains, and so slick and smooth behind. My horse at first did not seem to mind them, but all of a sudden he pricked up his ears; came to a stand still and snorted; as he did this, the buffaloes raised their elegant countenances, and stopped eating; the biggest ones sort of forming a half circle round me, and making obeisances by lowering their heads, and scarping their left fore feet in the ground. "Good manners to you," said I, taking off my hat, determined not to be out-done in politeness; as I did this, I thought I heard thunder; I just got a glimpse of some confused thing in a big dust, and here and there, a swab sticking in the air, that I now believe to be buffalo tails. My horse, all this time, was not idle; he took to his heels, started off, first spilling my gun, then my hat, bad luck to it, then me, and afterwards my saddle; I came to the ground under the impression I had been struck with lightning, but recovering myself I found that the top of my head had just come exactly on top of a buffalo skull, cracking it into three halves, and driving them into the ground. If you had seen me the next day, you would have thought I had painted myself in imitation of the savages; my face, particularly round my eyes, was of so many colors. It may be set down as a fact in natural history, that human heads are not generally as hard as a buffalo's. I gathered up my gun, hat and saddle, and walked towards the encampment. "Did you catch a buffalo bull," said one to me, as I presented myself, half dead with the fall, and the foot travel. "It was an Irish bull he was after," said Mat Field. "Out upon you, you unfeeling blackguard of a wit," said I, getting good humored in a minute. "It's Mat, is it, that cracks his wit, on my cracked head?" but I'll forgive him, hoping he may run his own against a live bull, that 'ill pay him for all his sins, bless his soul. Thus ended my first hunt, and as I shall go properly prepared to-morrow, I trust you will hear that I have done myself honor in bringing down as big a critter, as ever run over these big grass plots, called "prairies."   P.O.F.

P.S.—I am happy to say, as this letter did not go on the day I sealed it up, that I have had a fair view of the far-famed *one horned* buffalo, that has kept undisturbed possession of this country and has never yet been killed. He is known from the mouth of the Yellow Stone to the tributaries of the Columbia, as the "one horned buffalo of the prairies." I shall take great pains to learn all the anecdotes respecting him, particularly how he lost his duplicate horn. Sir William Stuart has put us all under "martial law," and some of the "young uns" make wry faces at it; but he is an old campaigner, and I think knows as much about the ways of this heathen world, as any one about here. So I sing "Scots wa ha," and go ahead.

Letters from the Far West: Letter 7

Interesting situation; Our appearance; Danger from the backwoods; Dresses; Singular appearance; Anecdotes; Reflections.

ABOVE THE HEAD OF PLATTE, Aug. 21, 1843.

It is an elegant way of living we have in this far west. Here is Sir William, as rich as a Santa Fe nabob, traveling about, talking Indian, and looking like Robinson Crusoe; and here is myself, bad luck to my enterprise, out here too, dressed up in clothes made of skins, and looking like a scare-crow out of a corn-field. "It's sport we have," said Mat Field, with a big twine round his front tooth, trying to pull it out. "It's hu-wah-me-kas-haw," says Tar-pot-wan-ja, the villain, looking as comfortable as a setting hen. "It's all kind of scrapes that I am getting into continually," thought I, as I reflected on the elegant adventure of which I was the hero. You see it had rained some four weeks steadily, and my raw deer skin clothes, hair outside, were as loose and comfortable as an Ottoman's. Six times since I wore them, have I been near being shot for an Elk, which makes my situation very pleasant indeed; but to the adventure. I was out on a hunting expedition, which took me a full day's journey from the camp, and was detained over night—sleeping on the ground in about two inches of water. In the morning I started for home, and to my great relief, the sun came out hot, and magnificent; if you could just have seen me traveling across the prairie, and drying slowly, and sending up steam like a locomotive. I ate dinner that day with great relish—the sun so inspired my appetite, and I indulged myself for the first time in some of Tar-pot-wan-ja's dishes, who was with me. It might have been three o'clock in the evening, when I felt a singular rush of blood to my head, a want of breath, and other unpleasant signs; presently my clothes seemed to grow *too small,* and kept tightening in an alarming manner. "How do people feel that are poisoned?" said I to Audubon. "Like a stuffed bird's skin," said he. "Then," said I, growing pale, "my mother's son will leave his bones among heathen." He enquired, with interest, what I ate for dinner, I told him some Indian dish; he rolled up his eyes with astonishment, and bid me hurry to the camp. I pushed on, all my alarming symptoms increasing with violence, until it seemed as if my legs and my head would burst. When I got to the camp, I was so stiff I had to be lifted off my horse, and laid upon my back. A consultation was held within sight, but not in hearing, in which Tar-pot-wan-ja, pulling out a sharp knife, and shaking it at me, took a very active part. My feelings were indescribable. How I had offended the Red man, I could not imagine, for it was now evident he had poisoned me, and wished to finish the job, by cutting my throat. Not a soul pitied me, but looked upon the whole affair as a pleasant joke. "*Soak it out of him,*" said Sir William finally; and to my horror, Tar-pot-wan-ja my enemy, and another Indian, took me up and laid me in a neighboring stream, just leaving my head out of the water. "They are all savages thought I," closing my eyes, and when I opened them the Indians were gone. "Is this the way to treat a sick man, pitch him into the river to die like a dog, for fear of a little trouble?" "Soak it out of him," indeed; it's the breath they alluded to! Such were my thoughts, when, to my astonishment, I began to feel relieved—the blood seemed to leave my head, and limbs, and I began to have some power of locomotion—less than half an hour elapsed before I got up and walked as well as usual. I went to the camp, wet as I was, burning with vengeance; as I approached it, a general shout of laughter saluted me. "Oh you unchristian bastes that you are," said I, shaking my fist at the whole of them, "is it for you to leave a sick friend to die, you savages; but I've got well, and can whip the whole of ye." "*Not if you'r deer skin clothes dry up in the sun until you can't move,*" said somebody, when the truth flashed upon me, that Tar-pot-wan-ja wished to cut me out of them, instead of out of my breath, and not "soak me out," as proposed by Sir William. My feelings altered at once, and I joined in the laugh; it only being one of those pleasant jokes peculiar to the *sport* of this part of the world. I find upon inquiry into accidents resulting from a precipitate use of deer skin clothing, that the most dreadful things have happened. An old hunter informed me that a whole party of white men, who were thus dressed, were caught by a sudden coming out of a hot sun, while eating their dinner; they were rendered helpless, before they were conscious of the reason, and sat staring at each other, with a buffalo steak in each hand, until they starved to death, their clothes not permitting them to move; and what made it more awful, after they were dead, damp weather came on—they melted down on the ground, and remained prostrate until the next sun shine—they then, as their skin clothing contracted by the heat, came up right again, in all imaginable positions, exhibiting one of the most melancholy spectacles that ever greeted the eye of humanity. The escape I made was miraculous indeed, for which I cannot be too thankful. And here, permit me to say one word, as I feel in a moral mood about the fitness of nature, the buffaloes it seems, from the inquiries I have made, are dressed in raw skins, as I was—hair outside—they are fond of water, and also fond of the sunshine. To avoid the fatal accidents that overtake the human species, they are provided over the shoulder with a *large hump,* containing nothing but fat. When indulging in the sun, this fat melts, runs over the skin, and keeps the water from penetrating the pores, so as to make the texture, when drying, susceptible to the sun's rays. Taking advantage of this beautiful law, I grease my clothes every morning with buffalo grease; and although they smell exceedingly rancid, and compel me to associate entirely with Tar-pot-wan-ja, still I had rather do this, than endanger my life as I have already done.   P.O.F.

P.S.—The wild turkies of last year, were all killed by the rains, so that this season there are none to be met with; all sorts of game are very scarce. I bear up under my misfortunes, like a man, as I frequently hear the remark, I am *such game.*

Letters from the Far West: Letter 10

CROSS TIMBERS, October 2, 1843.

Throwing the Laso; Unintelligible Jokes; Far West Fun; Singular Phenomenon; New way to catch Wild Game; Escape from Indians; Scientific failures; Prospects for immorality.

In my last, I mentioned the addition to our party of the famous laso thrower, *Don Desparato;* as a catcher of wild horses, and even deer, he has no equal. The day following my ride on the bear, we halted on our way to the "Cross Timbers," upon a very beautiful hillock that, but for its extent, might have been taken for an Indian mound. Desperato, who was idle, and vain of his accomplishment, amused himself by throwing his laso over "Spanish quarters," which he did with great precision at thirty yards, and in that way won a pocket full of silver coin. Sir William proposed for amusement to turn one of his saddle horses loose on the plain, and that Desparato should, at full gallop catch the horse with the laso by the hind foot. The thing was encouraged, and was soon ready for execution. The Spaniard mounted his "Indian poney," that, from its small size, compared with the big saddle on his back, looked at a distance as if it was standing under a shed, and gave the word. I let go Sir William's horse, and hit him a severe lick to send him ahead; but the animal, instead of running off, turned round, and walked back to the baggage wagons. We were not to be thus disappointed, and at the suggestion of several, I mounted the horse myself, and putting whip to his flanks, dashed off, down the hillock, but circling round the base, so as to give all the party at the top, a fair chance to see the Spaniard catch the horse by the *hind foot.* On he came, shouting like a Pawnee, and making the diameter of my circle, of course he soon came up, threw the laso, and missed. A shout of derision followed this failure, and as my blood was up, I laughed myself, and went on the harder. Now my horse had the heels, and I bothered him tremendously; I could hear him muttering big words, that I knew was Spanish, for swearing. Presently he came near me again and threw his laso; I felt a slight tap on the head, heard a great shout and laughter, then my respiration stopped, and I realized a shock over my whole system, that felt as if I had been caught under a falling tree. Respiration returned, and on opening my eyes, there sat Desparato on his poney, I on the ground, the laso round my neck, and he holding on the opposite end of it, grinning at me like an enraged monkey.

"Halloo!" said I.

"Senior Necio!" he growled.

"Let me up," cried I, with alarm, seizing hold of the laso. Hereupon he gave it a jerk that tightened it up, and I concluded the dog intended hanging me—the motion, however, exposed a piece of tobacco that was in my pocket—so, getting down, he very quietly took the quid, released my neck, and mounted his horse, and rode towards the party on the hillock. I was so bruised by the fall from my horse, and so sore about the neck, that I could with difficulty get up the hill. "Haw, haw, haw," uttered all the party when I got among them.

"Villians!" gnashed I, through my teeth.

"Don't get mad, that was a *Spanish joke,*" said somebody.

"And he don't understand the language well enough to enjoy the wit of it," said every body.

For the fifteenth time since I have been out here, I saw there was no use at being offended at merely being killed, if it was done in fun, so I joined in the laugh, but in my heart execrated Spanish jokes and lasos.

As was anticipated by some of our old hunters, the "mast," which means the fruit of the forest trees, is very scarce, and we find ourselves, since our arrival here at the "Cross Timbers," nearly starved. Nothing is found in the woods but the Pine burr—the tree which bears it, flourishing here in its most magnificent grandeur. As we relied principally, upon the wild turky for food, and they having been compelled, from necessity, to eat these pine burrs for food for a long time, they become so impregnated with turpentine, that they caught fire whenever we attempted to roast them, and burnt up. I really believe we should have starved to death but for the ingenuity of an old fellow with us, who said he was originally from Bunkum, North Carolina. He took some dozen turkies, well cleaned, covered them with about six inches of dirt, and then built a large fire over the pile. In the course of the day, small streams of clear tar were seen running out of the heap, and when evening came, the turkies, shrunk up to the size of chickens, were taken from "the kiln," and eaten—tolerably fair food, but, as might be imagined, *very dry.*

This singular impregnation of wild game, with the article of food on which it exists, has been strangely overlooked by naturalists. I would in this connection, relate a singular escape made by a party of hunters connected with these "turpentine birds." It seems that while they were out hunting they were attacked by a large number of Soshonees, and surrounded. Protected by a small skirt of woods, they entrenched themselves for the night, expecting in the morning to have their scalps hung on long poles, and dried in the smoke like Dutch herring—an idea, by the way, that makes my head ache—just to think of. Well, in the night there came up a terrible storm, in the midst of which, the lightning struck a tree near the white hunter's camp, on which were roosting several of these pine burr fed turkies. The birds, as the lightning descended, were instantly on fire, and flying towards the Indians, fell blazing, and hissing among them, such an exhibition struck them with consternation, and supposing the white men had the means of destruction they were not acquainted with, the Indians fled, and left the hunters in peaceable possession of the country, and, I am sorry to add, they were found afterwards starved to death, from the great inclemency of the season.

As may be imagined, a person of my enquiring mind and aptness to learn, would pick up many many useful hints in this wild country. I have among other things, as leisure permitted, practised much to get the art of preserving birds and animals. Now Audubon will take either, and in an incredible short space of time, make the expressionless mass of skin, teem with life, as if the bird or beast had been suddenly petrified in some graceful action. But, some how, I cannot get the hang of it—my quadrupeds look like sausages, and my birds like a roll of dough. I have got a crane with a neck as big as his body, and a wild cat that resembles a gigantic weasel.

Sir William says he would not trust me to stuff a pillow. I intend to keep my "specimens" as works of art, if not of nature, and when I get home, if they are mistaken by some natural history society for *new species,* of course I shall be mum, and they will receive unpronounceable names, and my memory will be handed down to posterity, preserved in a dead language. P.O.F.

P.S.—Tar-pot-wan-ja is very anxious for me to stuff for him a buffalo skin; he says if I will do it, it will be "Knochanee-shokbou-nahoola," which literally translated, signifies buffalo made ugly will be handsome "heap."

Letters from the Far West: Letter 12

BEYOND THE CROSS TIMBERS, Oct., 1843

An amiable mule; Tar-pot-wan-ja's astonishment; Transmigration; New troubles; Fun alive; A fix peculiar; A dream; End of the days' work.

Our party halted with pleasure the announcement that we were to leave the "cross timbers," and take up our line of march towards the fine country lying beyond them. We packed up with alacrity, and as the bright morning sun in long reaching rays, lit up the prairie, we were in motion. Every thing went ahead, but a long eared mule in one of the baggage waggons—a stubborn representative, that did honor in this respect to his respectable progenitor, whoever he was. Don Desparato pounded him on one side, and Tar-pot-wan-ja, voluntarily, for an Indian never works by compulsion, labored on the other.

"Fire-consume-your-heart," said Desparato in Spanish, hitting the brute across the head.

"Ah-whooh-hah!" grunted Tar-pot, as he followed the example; here the mule laid down, and turning his head over his harness collar, and eying his tormenters very coolly, gave a loud bray, extended himself at full length on the ground, and seemed inclined to go to sleep under the hands of his tormenters, as a Turk will while under the process of shampooing. All this seemed to amuse the red man highly; between every blow, he would place his extended hands over his ears, and flap them, as if in imitation of wings; then laugh heartily, and hit the mule again. Desparato in the mean time, gathered some light wood, kindled a fire around and near the beast's body, and as the curling flame increased in force, and the rough hair began to singe, and smoke, while the animal paid no attention to it, Tar-pot's enthusiasm extended into admiration; his vivid imagination pictured the animal possessed of a soul of some Indian warrior, who defied blows and the faggot—kicking the fire about the prairie, he rushed forward and embraced the animal; muley not understanding the nature of the hug, got upon his feet and commenced kicking in a most violent manner. Tar-pot sprang out of the way of the dangerous heels, fully convinced that a mule and an Indian were of the same identical breed.

In time we fairly got under way, and the horsemen, including myself, instead of following the wagon trail, took a short cut through some low, swampy land, covered by what is known out here as the "scrub-oaks;" they are the same kind of trees I mentioned as peculiar to the "yallah stun" in one of my first letters. When we got fairly among them, we noticed them covered with little balls of earth, as we thought; but upon close examination they proved to be hornet's nests, which, disturbed by our intrusion, commenced issuing out in formidable numbers. Now a hornet is decidedly a very passionate yellow coated insect, and pitching into us with a vehemence truly commendable, attacked us in the front and rear. A general *scrub race* commenced—the horses flew through the low growth of brush, the tallest of which only came up to their breasts, as if they were pursued by torches of fire. Sir William Stewart's grey horse, which was the most powerful animal, snorted like a hurricane; while Desparato, swearing in Indian and Spanish, threw his arms about like a wind-mill. Tar-pot-wan-ja, Indian like, took it more coolly—he and his horse seemed above complaining, except as evinced by the poor animal's tail, that kept whirling around like a piece of fire works. On we went, knocking at every step, the little mud balls on the ground, as rapidly as if we were dropping potatoes from a cart, while the inhabitants, first astonished, would for a moment confusedly crawl about, and then with unerring instinct make a straight line for the luckless invaders of their homes. My horse, not at any time one of the best, coming to a hole in the earth, caught his foot and fell to the ground; before I could recover myself, my companions were some distance ahead of me, and the hornets, to my horror, instead of pursuing on, turned back and made a general attack on me. My horse, infuriated by the hornets, would keep running around me, kicking and snorting, and raising up new enemies every instant; I finally mounted and pushed on, enveloped in a cloud of burning stings. Whatever might have been my troubles in my search of sport out in the Far West, this excelled every thing in my unfortunate experience. I fought and knocked about, expecting every moment to fall from mere paid, when my horse again stumbled, and threw me in a hole about five feet deep,—the hornets buzzed above me for a moment like a thin mist, and then, as if afraid to descend, where I lay, separated to their dilapidated nests. Bruised and poisoned, I felt some relief from the absence of the hornets; no part of my body, but my face and hands, was much stung. Presently my face began to swell, my eyes closed up, and I was left in total darkness. In this situation, covered head, neck and heels with mud, for the hole into which I had fallen, was, at its bottom, composed of it, exhausted with pain, and sightless, from the swollen state of my face, I gradually swooned away and lost myself. While thus, I dreamed that the learned members of the Royal Society, London, had issued a circular, offering a thousand pounds reward for a "perpetual motion," and a display of the most foolish thing in the world; and I dreamed that I gave to the society a journal of my adventures "Out West," and proved that I went out there for the purpose of "sport," and the society unanimously awarded to me the thousand pounds. Taking the money, I awoke with joy, and discovered that my eyes would open—that I was much relieved of the pain in my face, and that the sun was just setting. Crawling out of the hole, as the chilly air of the night came on, I found the hornets benumbed with cold; I lit a fire by flashing powder in the pan of my pistol, and sat down beside it, and from the fix I was in when thoroughly warmed, I resembled a huge hornets' nest , from my close resemblance to a ball of mud. About midnight, I discovered the camp fire of my fellow travelers, about two miles off, and made towards it, the most miserable dog that ever went sport-seeking in the Far West.   P.O.F.

Henry Clay Lewis (1825-1850)

Born in Charleston, South Carolina, into a large family, Henry Clay Lewis had a more cosmopolitan and European-informed background than most of the other humorists as his parents were of French and Italian Jewish descent. He was only six when his mother died, and afterward he was raised haphazardly by family members when he was not on his own working on boats on the Ohio, Mississippi, and Yazoo rivers or in the cotton fields in Mississippi. After an apprenticeship to a physician, Lewis entered the Louisville Medical Institute and before the age of twenty-one had graduated with his medical degree. He settled to practice medicine in a backwoods community in Louisiana where he lived in a log cabin, donned boots and a coonskin cap, and became a "swamp doctor" to the often malnourished and fever-ridden inhabitants at the intersection between the Tensas River and Bayou Despair in the northeastern part of the state. He prospered and became active in Whig politics , but during the cholera epidemic of 1850 while returning home from a medical call, Lewis accidentally fell into a flooded bayou and drowned.

Lewis is remembered only because of his stories based on his experiences as a medical student and a physician in the Louisiana swamps. His first sketch appeared in the New York *Spirit of the Times* in August 1845 and launched a series of dark, grotesque, and demonic narratives startling to readers then and now for their gothic sensibility. They recount the experiences of a young doctor, recalled in retrospect by an older narrator, as he comes to grips with life at the margins of society, where brutality and the struggle for survival have not yet been replaced by civility and social restraint. In their psychological depth and disturbing imagery, they have more in common with the fiction of his contemporaries Edgar Allan Poe and Herman Melville than with that of the other humorists of the frontier. Nine of his stories appeared in the New York sporting journal, but he wrote a good many more, obviously intent from the start on producing a full-scale book which appeared in 1850 as *Odd Leaves from the Life of a Louisiana "Swamp Doctor"* under the pseudonym "Madison Tensas, M.D., Ex. V. P. M. S. U. Ky."

> Lewis did not live to see the full success and popularity of his book which went through six reprintings before the end of the century.
> Texts: "A Tight Race Considerin,'" "The Indefatigable Bear Hunter," and "A Struggle for Life," from *Odd Leaves from the Life of a Louisiana "Swamp Doctor"* (Philadelphia: A. Hart, 1850).

A Tight Race Considerin'

During my medical studies, passed in a small village in Mississippi, I became acquainted with a family named Hibbs (a *nom de plume* of course), residing a few miles in the country. The family consisted of Mr. and Mrs. Hibbs and son. They were plain, unlettered people, honest in intent and deed, but overflowing with that which amply made up for all their deficiencies of education, namely, warmhearted hospitality, the distinguishing trait of Southern character. They were originally from Virginia, from whence they had emigrated in quest of a clime more genial and a soil more productive than that in which their fathers toiled. Their search had been rewarded, their expectations realized, and now in their old age, though not wealthy in the "Astorian" sense, still they had sufficient to keep the wolf from the door and could drop something more substantial than condolence and tears in the hat that poverty hands round for the kind offerings of humanity.

The old man was like the generality of old planters, men whose ambition is embraced by the family or social circle and whose thoughts turn more on the relative value of "Sea Island" and "Mastodon" and the improvement of their plantations than the "glorious victories of Whiggery in Kentucky" or the "triumphs of democracy in Arkansas."

The old lady was a shrewd, active dame, kindhearted and long-tongued, benevolent and impartial, making her coffee as strong for the poor pedestrian with his all upon his back as the broadcloth sojourner with his "up-country pacer." She was a member of the church, as well as the daughter of a man who had once owned a race horse; and these circumstances gave her an indisputable right, she thought, to "let on all she knew" when religion or horseflesh was the theme. At one moment she would be heard discussing whether the new "circus rider" (as she always called him) was as affecting in Timothy as the old one was pathetic in Paul, and anon (not anonymous, for the old lady did everything above board, except rubbing her corns at supper) protecting dad's horse from the invidious comparison of some visitor who having heard, perhaps, that such horses as Fashion and Boston existed, thought himself qualified to doubt the old lady's assertion that her father's horse "Shumach" had run a mile on one particular occasion. "Don't tell *me*," was her never failing reply to their doubts, "Don't tell *me* 'bout Fashun or Bosting or any other beating 'Shumach' a fair race, for the thing was unfesible: didn't he run a mile a minute by Squire Dim's watch, which always stopt 'zactly at twelve, and didn't he start a minute afore and git out, jes as the long hand war givin' its last quiver on ketchin' the short leg of the watch? And didn't he beat everything in Virginny 'cept once? Dad and the folks said he'd beat them, if young Mr. Spotswood hadn't give 'old Swaga,' Shumach's rider, some of the 'Croton water' (that them Yorkers is makin' sich a fuss over as bein' so good, when gracious knows, nothin' but what the doctors call interconception could git me to take a dose), and jis 'fore the race Swage or Shumach, I don't 'stinctly 'member which, but one of them had to *let down*, and so dad's hoss got beat."

The son I will describe in few words. Imbibing his parents' contempt for letters, he was very illiterate, and as he had not enjoyed the equivalent of travel was extremely ignorant on all matters not relating to hunting or plantation duties. He was a stout, active fellow with a merry twinkling of the eye, indicative of humor and partiality for practical joking. We had become very intimate, he instructing me in "forest lore," and I, in return, giving amusing stories or, what was as much to his liking, occasional introductions to my hunting flask.

Now that I have introduced the "Dramatis Personae," I will proceed with my story. By way of relaxation and to relieve the tedium incident more or less to a student's life, I would take my gun, walk out to old Hibbs's, spend a day or two, and return refreshed to my books.

One fine afternoon I started upon such an excursion, and as I had upon a previous occasion missed killing a fine buck, owing to my having nothing but squirrel shot, I determined to go this time for the "antlered monarch," by loading one barrel with fifteen "blue whistlers," reserving the other for small game.

At the near end of the plantation was a fine spring, and adjacent, a small cave, the entrance artfully or naturally concealed save to one acquainted with its locality. The cave was nothing but one of those subterraneous washes so common in the West and South and called "sink holes." It was known only to young H. and myself, and we, for peculiar reasons, kept it secret, having put it in requisition as the depository of a jug of "old Bourbon," which we favored. As the old folks abominated drinking, we had found convenient to keep the jug there whither we would repair to get our drinks and return to the house to hear them descant on the evils of drinking and vow no "drap, 'cept in doctor's truck," should ever come on their plantation.

Feeling very thirsty, I took my way by the spring that evening. As I descended the hill o'ertopping it, I beheld the hind parts of a bear slowly being drawn into the cave. My heart bounded at the idea of killing a bear, and my plans were formed in a second. I had no dogs—the house was distant—and the bear was becoming "small by degrees, and beautifully less." Every hunter knows, if you shoot a squirrel in the head when it's sticking out of a hole, ten to one he'll jump out; and I reasoned that if this were true regarding squirrels, might not the operation of the same principle extract a bear, applying it low down in the back?

Quick as thought I levelled my gun and fired, intending to give him the buckshot when his body appeared; but what was my surprise and horror, when, instead of a bear rolling out, the parts were jerked nervously in and the well-known voice of young H. reached my ears.

"Murder! Hingins! h—1and kuckle-burs! Oh! Lordy! 'nuff—'nuff!—take him off! Jist let me off this wunst, dad, and I'll never run Mam's colt again! Oh! Lordy! Lordy! *all my brains blowed clean out!* Snakes! snakes!" yelled he, in a shriller tone, if possible, "H—1n the outside and snakes in the sink-hole! I'll die a Christian anyhow, and if I die before I wake," and out scrambled poor H., pursued by a large black snake.

If my life had depended on it, I could not have restrained my laughter. Down fell the gun, and down dropped I shrieking convulsively. The hill was steep, and over and over I went until my head striking against a stump at the bottom stopped me, half senseless. On recovering somewhat from the stunning blow, I found Hibbs upon me, taking satisfaction from me for having "blowed out his brains." A contest ensued and H. finally relinquished his hold, but I saw from the knitting of his brows that the bear-storm, instead of being over, was just brewing. "Mr. Tensas," he said with awful dignity, "I'm sorry I put into you 'fore you cum to, but you're at yourself now, and as you've tuck a shot at me, it's no more than far I should have a chance 'fore the hunt's up."

It was with the greatest difficulty I could get H. to bear with me until I explained the mistake, but as soon as he learned it he broke out in a huge laugh. "Oh, Dod busted! that's 'nuff; you has my pardon. I ought to know'd you didn't 'tend it; 'sides, you jis scraped the skin. I war wus skeered than hurt, and if you'll go to the house and beg me off from the old folks, I'll never let on you cuddent tell copperas breeches from bar-skin."

Promising that I would use my influence, I proposed taking a drink and that he should tell me how he had incurred his parents' anger. He assented, and after we had inspected the cave and seen that it held no other serpent than the one we craved, we entered its cool recess and H. commenced.

"You see, Doc, I'd heered so much from Mam 'bout her dad's Shumach and his nigger Swage, and the mile a minute, and the Croton water that was gin him, and how she bleved that if it warn't for bettin', and the cussin' and fightin', running race hosses warn't the sin folks said it war; and if they war anything to make her 'gret gettin' religion and jinin' the church, it war cos she couldn't 'tend races and have a race colt of her own to comfort her 'clinin' years, sich as her daddy had afore her, till she got me; so I couldn't rest for wantin' to see a hoss race, and go shares, p'raps, in the colt she war wishin' for. And then I'd think what sort of a hoss I'd want him to be—a quarter nag, a mile critter, or a hoss wot could run (fur all Mam says it can't be did) a whole four mile at a stretch. Sometimes I think I'd rather own a quarter nag, for the suspense wouldn't long be hung, and then we could run up the road to old Nick Bamer's cowpen, and Sally is almost allers out thar in the cool of the evenin'; and in course we wouldn't be so cruel as to run the poor critter in the heat of the day. But then agin, I'd think I'd rather have a miler—for the 'citement would be greater—and we could run down the road to old Wither's orchard, an' his gal Miry is frightfully fond of sunnin' herself thar when she 'spects me 'long, and she'd hear of the race, certain; but then thar war the four-miler for my thinkin', and I'd knew'd in such case the 'citement would be the greatest of all, and you know, too, from dad's stable to the grocery is jist four miles, an' in case of any 'spute, all hands would be willin' to run over, even if it had to be tried a dozen times. So I never could 'cide on which sort of a colt to wish for. It was fust one, then t'others, till I was nearly 'stracted, and when Mam, makin' me religious, told me one night to say grace, I jes shut my eyes, looked pious, and yelled out, 'D—n it, go!' and in 'bout five minutes arter, came near kickin' dad's stumak off, under the table, thinkin' I war spurrin' my critter in a tight place. So I found the best way was to get the hoss fust, and then 'termine whether it should be Sally Bamers and the cowpen, Miry Withers and the peach orchard, or Spillman's grocery with the bald face.

"You've seed my black colt, that one that dad's father gin me in his will when he died, and I 'spect the reason he wrote that will war that he might have wun then, for it's more than he had when he was alive, for granma war a monstrus overbearin' woman. The colt would cum up in my mind every time I'd think whar I was to git a hoss. 'Git out!' said I at fust—*he* never could run, and 'sides if he could, Mam rides him now, an' he's too old for anything, 'cept totin her and bein' called mine; for you see, though he war named Colt, yet for the old lady to call him old would bin like the bar 'fecting contempt for the rabbit on account of the shortness of his tail.

"Well, thought I, it does look sorter unpromisin', but it's Colt or none; so I 'termined to put him in trainin' the fust chance. Last Saturday, who should cum ridin' up but the new cirkut preacher, a long-legged, weakly, sickly, never-contented-onless-the-best-on-the-plantation-war-cooked-fur-him sort of a man; but I didn't look at him twice, his hoss was the critter that took my eye; for the minute I looked at him, I knew him to be the same hoss as Sam Spooner used to win all his splurgin' dimes with, the folks said, and wot he used to ride past our house so fine on. The hoss war a heap the wuss for age and change of masters; for preachers, though they're mity 'ticular 'bout thar own comfort, seldom tends to thar hosses, for one is privit property and 'tother generally borried. I seed from the way the preacher rid that he didn't know the animal he war straddlin'; but I did and I 'termined I wouldn't lose sich a chance of trainin' Colt by degrees the side of a hoss wot had run real races. So that night, arter prayers and the folks was abed, I and Nigger Bill tuck the hosses and carried them down to the pastur.' It war a forty-aker lot, and consequently jist a quarter across—for I thought it best to promote Colt by degrees to a four-miler. When we got thar, the preacher's hoss showed he war willin'; but Colt, dang him, commenced nibblin' a fodder stack over the fence. I nearly cried for vexment, but an idea struck me; I hitched the critter and told Bill to get on Colt and stick tight wen I giv' the word. Bill got reddy, and unbeknownst to him I pulled up a bunch of nettles, and, as I clapped them under Colt's tail, yelled, 'Go!' Down shut his graceful like a steel trap, and away he shot so quick an' fast that he jumpt clean out from under Bill and got nearly to the end of the quarter 'fore the nigger toch the ground. He lit on his head and in course warn't hurt—so we cotched Colt, an' I mounted him.

"The next time I said 'go' he showed that age hadn't spiled his legs or memory. Bill an' me 'greed we could run him now, so Bill mounted Preacher and we got ready. Thar war a narrer part of the track 'tween two oaks, but as it war near the end of the quarter, I 'spected to pass Preacher 'fore we got thar, so I warn't afraid of barkin' my shins.

"We tuck a fair start, and off we went like a peeled ingun, an' I soon 'scovered that it warn't such an easy matter to pass Preacher, though Colt dun delightful. We got nigh the trees, and Preacher warn't past yet, an' I 'gan to get skeered, for it warn't more than wide enuf for a horse and a half. So I hollered to Bill to hold up, but the imperdent nigger turned his ugly pictur and said he'd be cussed if he warn't goin' to play his han' out. I gin him to understand he'd better fix for a foot race when we stopt and tried to hold up Colt, but he wouldn't stop. We reached the oaks, Colt tried to pass Preacher, Preacher tried to pass Colt, and cowollop, crosh, cochunk! we all cum down like 'simmons arter frost. Colt got up and won the race; Preacher tried hard to rise, but one hind leg had got threw the stirrup, and 'tother in the head stall, an' he had to lay still, doubled up like a long nigger in a short bed. I lit on my feet, but Nigger Bill war gone entire. I looked up in the fork of one of the oaks, and thar he war sittin', lookin' very composed on surroundin' nature. I couldn't git him down till I promised not to hurt him for disobeyin' orders when he slid down. We'd 'nuff racin' for that night, so we put up the hosses and went to bed.

"Next morning the folks got ready for church, when it was diskivered that the hosses had got out. I an' Bill started off to look for them; we found them cleer off in the field, tryin' to git in the pastur' to run the last night's race over, old Blaze, the Reverlushunary mule, bein' along to act as judge.

"By the time we got to the house it war nigh on to meetin' hour; and dad had started to the preachin' to tell the folks to sing on as preacher and Mam would be 'long bimeby. As the passun war in a hurry and had been complainin' that his creetur war dull, I 'suaded him to put on Uncle Jim's spurs what he fotch from Mexico. I saddled the passun's hoss, takin' 'ticular pains to let the saddle blanket come down low in the flank. By the time these fixins war threw, Mam war 'head nigh on to a quarter. 'We must ride on, passun,' I said, 'or the folks'll think we is lost.' So I whipt up the mule I rid, and the passun chirrupt and chuct to make his crittur gallop, but the animal didn't mind him a pic. I 'gan to snicker, an' the passun 'gan to git vext; sudden he thought of his spurs so he ris up an' drove them *vim* in his hoss's flanx till they went through his saddle blanket and like to bored his nag to the holler. By gosh! but it war a quickener—the hoss kickt till the passun had to hug him round the neck to keep from pitchin' him over the head. He next jumpt up 'bout as high as a rail fence, passun holdin' on and tryin' to git his spurs out—but they war lockt—his breeches split plum across with the strain, and the piece of wearin' truck wot's next the skin made a monstrous putty flag as the old hoss, like drunkards to a barbecue, streakt it up the road.

"Mam war ridin' slowly along, thinkin' how sorry she was cos Chary Dolin, who always led her off, had sich a bad cold an' wouldn't be able to 'sist her singin' today. She war practisin' the hymns and had got as far as whar it says, 'I have a race to run,' when the passun huv in sight, an' in 'bout the dodgin' of a diedapper, she found thar war truth in the words, for the colt, hearin' the hoss cumin' up behind, began to show symptoms of runnin'; but when he heard the passun holler 'wo! wo!' to his hoss, he thought it war me shoutin' 'go!' and sure 'nuff off they started jis as the passun got up even; so it war a fair race. Whoop! git out, but it war egsitin'—the dust flew, and the rail fence appeared strate as a rifle. Thar war the passun, his legs fast to the critter's flanx, arms lockt round his neck, face as pale as a rabbit's belly, and the white flag streemin' far behind—and thar war Mam, fust on one side, then on t'other, her new caliker swelled up round her like a bear with the dropsy, the old lady so much surprized she cuddent ride steddy, an' tryin' to stop her colt, but he war too well trained to stop while he heard 'go!' Mam got 'sited at last, and her eyes 'gan to glimmer like she seen her daddy's gost axin' if he ever trained up a child or a race hoss to be 'fraid of a small brush on a Sunday, and she commenced ridin' beautiful; she braced herself up in the saddle and began to make calkerlations how she war to win the race, for it war nose and nose, and she saw the passun spurrin' his critter every jump. She tuk off her shoe, and the way a number ten go-to-meetin' brogan commenced givin' a hoss particular Moses were a caution to hossflesh—but still it kept nose and nose. She found she war carryin' too much weight for Colt, so she 'gan to throw off plunder till nuthin' was left but her saddle and close, and the spurs kept tellin' still. The old woman commenced strippin' to lighten till it wouldn't bin the clean thing for her to have taken off one dud more; an' then when she found it war no use while the spurs lasted, she got cantankerous. 'Passun,' said she, 'I'll be cust if it's fair or gentlemanly for you, a preacher of the gospel, to take advantage of an old woman this way, usin' spurs when you know *she* can't wear 'em—'taint Christian-like nuther,' and she burst into cryin.' 'Wo! Miss Hibbs! Wo! Stop! Madam! Wo! Your son!'—he attempted to say, when the old woman tuck him on the back of the head, fillin' his mouth with right smart of a saddle horn and stoppin' the talk as far as his share went for the present.

"By this time they'd got nigh on to the meetin'house, and the folks were harkin' away on 'Old Hundred and wonderin' what could have become of the passun and Mam Hibbs. One sister in a long beard axt another brethren in church if she'd heered anything 'bout that New York preacher runnin' way with a woman old enough to be his muther. The brethrens gin a long sigh an' groaned, 'It ain't possible! marciful heavens! you don't 'spicion?' wen the sound of the hosses comin' roused them up like a touch of the agur an' broke off their sarpent talk. Dad run out to see what was to pay, but when he seed the hosses so close together, the passun spurrin' and Mam ridin' like close war skase whar she cum, he knew her fix in a second and 'tarmined to help her; so clinchin' a sapplin,' he hid 'hind a stump 'bout ten steps off and held on for the hosses. On they went in beautiful style, the passun's spurs tellin' terrible and Mam's shoe operatin' 'no small pile of punkins'—passun stretched out the length of two hosses while Mam sot as stiff and strate as a bull yearling in his fust fight, hittin' her nag, fust on one side, next on t'other, and the third for the passun, who had chawed the horn till little of the saddle and less of his teeth war left, and his voice sounded as holler as a jackass-nicker in an old sawmill.

"The hosses war nose and nose, jam up together so close that Mam's last kiverin' and passun's flag had got lockt an' 'tween bleached domestic and striped linsey made a beautiful banner for the pious racers.

"On they went like a small arthquake, an' it seemed like it war goin' to be a draun race; but dad, when they got to him, let down with all his might on Colt, scarin' him so bad that he jumpt clean ahead of passun, beatin' him by a neck, buttin' his own head agin the meetin'house, an' pitchin' Mam, like a ham for the sacryfise, plum through the winder 'mongst the mourners, leavin' her only garment flutterin' on a nail in the sash. The men shot their eyes and scrambled outen the house, an' the women gin Mam so much of their close that they like to put themselves in the same fix.

"The passun quit the circuit, and I haven't been home yet."

The Indefatigable Bear Hunter

In my round of practice, I occasionally meet with men whose peculiarities stamp them as belonging to a class composed only of themselves. So different are they in appearance, habit, and taste from the majority of mankind that it is impossible to classify them, and you have therefore to set them down as queer birds of a feather that none resemble sufficiently to associate with.

I had a patient once who was one of these queer ones—gigantic in stature, uneducated, fearless of real danger yet timorous as a child of superstitious perils, born literally in the woods, never having been in a city in his life and his idea of one being that it was a place where people met together to make whiskey and form plans for swindling country folks. To view him at one time, you would think him only a whiskey-drinking, bear-fat-loving mortal. At other moments he would give vent to ideas proving that beneath his rough exterior there ran a fiery current of high enthusiastic ambition.

It is a favorite theory of mine—and one that I am fond of consoling myself with for my own insignificance—that there is no man born who is not capable of attaining distinction and no occupation that does not contain a path leading to fame. To bide our time is all that is necessary. I had expressed this view in the hearing of Mik-hoo-tah, for so was the subject of this sketch called, and it seemed to chime in with his feelings exactly. Born in the woods and losing his parents early, he had forgotten his real name, and the bent of his genius inclining him to the slaying of bears, he had been given even when a youth the name of Mik-hoo-tah, signifying "the grave of bears" by his Indian associates and admirers.

To glance in and around his cabin, you would have thought that the place had been selected for ages past by the bear tribe to yield up their spirits in, so numerous were the relics. Little chance, I ween, had the cold air to whistle through that hut, so thickly it was tapestried with the soft, downy hides, the darkness of the surface relieved occasionally by the skin of a tender fawn or the short-haired irascible panther. From the joists depended bear hams and tongues innumerable, and the ground outside was literally white with bones. Ay, he was a bear hunter in its most comprehensive sense—the chief of that vigorous band, whose occupation is nearly gone, crushed beneath the advancing strides of romance-destroying civilization. When its horn sounded—so tradition ran—the bears began to draw lots to see who should die that day, for painful experience had told them the uselessness of all endeavoring to escape. The "Big Bear of Arkansas" would not have given him an hour's extra work or raised a fresh wrinkle on his already care-corrugated brow. But, though almost daily imbruing his hands in the blood of Bruin, Mik-hoo-tah had not become an impious or cruel-hearted man. Such was his piety that he never killed a bear without getting down on his knees—to skin it—and praying to be d—ned if it "warn't a buster." Such was his softness of heart that he often wept when he, by mistake, had killed a suckling bear, depriving her poor offspring of a mother's care, and found her too poor to be eaten. So indefatigable had he become in his pursuit that the bears bid fair to disappear from the face of the swamp and be known to posterity only through the one mentioned in Scripture that assisted Elisha to punish the impertinent children, when an accident occurred to the hunter which raised their hopes of not being entirely exterminated.

One day Mik happened to come unfortunately in contact with a stray grizzly fellow who, doubtless in the indulgence of an adventurous spirit, had wandered away from the Rocky Mountains and formed a league for mutual protection with his black and more effeminate brethren of the swamp. Mik saluted him as he approached with an ounce ball in the forehead to avenge half a dozen of his best dogs who lay in fragments around. The bullet flattened upon his impenetrable skull, merely infuriating the monster, and before Mik could reload it was upon him. Seizing him by the leg, it bore him to the ground and ground the limb to atoms. But before it could attack a more vital part, the knife of the dauntless hunter had cloven its heart, and it dropped dead upon the bleeding form of its slayer in which condition they were shortly found by Mik's comrades. Making a litter of branches, they placed Mik upon it and proceeded with all haste to their camp, sending one of the company by a near cut for me as I was the nearest physician. When I reached their temporary shelter I found Mik doing better than I could have expected, with the exception of his wounded leg, and that, from its crushed and mutilated condition, I saw would have to be amputated immediately, of which I informed Mik. As I expected, he opposed it vehemently, but I convinced him of the impossibility of saving it, assuring him if it were not amputated he would certainly die, and appealed to his good sense to grant permission, which he did at last. The next difficulty was to procure amputating instruments, the rarity of surgical operations and the generally slender purse of the Swamp Doctor not justifying him in purchasing expensive instruments. A couple of bowie knives, one ingeniously hacked and filed into a saw, a tourniquet made of a belt and piece of stick, a gun screw converted for the time into a tenaculum, and some buckskin slips for ligatures completed my case of instruments for amputation. The city physician may smile at this recital, but I assure him many a more difficult operation than the amputation of a leg has been performed by his humble brother in the swamp with far more simple means than those I have mentioned. The preparations being completed, Mik refused to have his arms bound and commenced singing a bear song, and throughout the whole operation which was necessarily tedious he never uttered a groan or missed a single stave. The next day I had him conveyed by easy stages to his pre-emption, and with my tending assiduously in the course of a few weeks he had recovered sufficiently for me to cease attentions. I made him a wooden leg which answered a good purpose, and with a sigh of regret for the spoiling of such a good hunter I struck him from my list of patients.

A few moments passed over and I heard nothing more of him. Newer but not brighter stars were in the ascendant, filling with their deeds the clanging trump of bear-killing fame, and, but for the quantity of bear blankets in the neighboring cabins and the painful absence of his usual present of bear hams, Mik-hoo-tah bid fair to suffer that fate most terrible to aspiring ambitionists— forgetfulness during life.

The sun, in despair at the stern necessity which compelled him to yield up his tender offspring, day, to the gloomy cave of darkness, had stretched forth his long arms, and, with the tenacity of a drowning man clinging to a straw, had clutched the tender whispering straw-like topmost branches of the trees—in other words it was near sunset—when I arrived at home from a long wearisome semi-ride-and-swim through the swamp. Receiving a negative to my inquiry whether there were any new calls, I was felicitating myself upon a quiet night beside my tidy bachelor hearth, undisturbed by crying children, babbling women, or amorous cats—the usual accompaniments of married life—when, like a poor henpecked Benedick crying for peace when there is no peace, I was doomed to disappointment. Hearing the splash of a paddle in the bayou running before the door, I turned my head towards the bank and soon beheld, first the tail of a coon, next his body, a human face, and, the top of the bank being gained, a full-proportioned form clad in the garments which better than any printed label wrote him down as raftsman, trapper, bear hunter. He was a messenger from the indefatigable bear hunter, Mik-hoo-tah. Asking him what was the matter, as soon as he could get the knots untied which two-thirds drunkenness had made in his tongue, he informed me, to my sincere regret, that Mik went out that morning on a bear hunt and in a fight with one had got his leg "broke all to flinders" if possible worse than the other and that he wanted me to come quickly. Getting into the canoe which awaited me, I wrapped myself in my blanket and yielding to my fatigue was soon fast asleep. I did not awaken until the canoe striking against the bank as it landed at Mik's preemption nearly threw me in the bayou and entirely succeeded with regard to my half-drunken paddler, who—like the sailor who circumnavigated the world and then was drowned in a puddle hole in his own garden—had escaped all the perils of the tortuous bayou to be pitched overboard when there was nothing to do but step out and tie the dugout. Assisting him out of the water, we proceeded to the house when to my indignation I learnt that the drunken messenger had given me the long trip for nothing, Mik only wanting me to make him a new wooden leg, the old one having been completely demolished that morning.

Relieving myself by a satisfactory oath, I would have returned that night, but the distance was too great for one fatigued as I was. I had to content myself with such accommodations as Mik's cabin afforded, which, to one blessed like myself with the happy faculty of ready adaptation to circumstances, was not a very difficult task.

I was surprised to perceive the change in Mik's appearance. From nearly a giant, he had wasted to a mere huge bony framework. The skin of his face clung tightly to the bones and showed nothing of those laughter-moving features that were wont to adorn his visage. Only his eye remained unchanged, and it had lost none of its brilliancy—the flint had lost none of its fire.

"What on earth is the matter with you, Mik? I have never seen anyone fall off so fast. You have wasted to a skeleton—surely you must have the consumption."

"Do you think so, Doc? I'll soon show you whether the old bellows has lost any of its force!" Hopping to the door which he threw wide open, he gave a death-hug rally to his dogs in such a loud and piercing tone that I imagined a steam whistle was being discharged in my ear and for several moments could hear nothing distinctly.

"That will do! Stop!" I yelled as I saw Mik drawing in his breath preparatory to another effort of his vocal strength. "I am satisfied you have not got consumption, but what has wasted you so, Mik? Surely, you ain't in love?"

"Love! h—ll! you don't suppose, Doc, even if I was 'tarmined to make a cussed fool of myself that there is any gal in the swamp that could stand that hug, do you?" and catching up a huge bulldog who lay basking himself by the fire, he gave him such a squeeze that the animal yelled with pain and for a few moments appeared dead. "No, Doc, it's grief, pure sorrur, sorrur, Doc! When I looks at what I is now and what I used to be! Jes think, Doc, of the fust hunter in the swamp having his sport spilte like bar meat in summer without salt! Jes think of a man standin' up one day and blessing old Master for having put bar in creation and the next cussing high heaven and low h—ll 'cause he couldn't 'sist in puttin' them out! Warn't it enough to bring tears to the eyes of an Injun tater, much less take the fat off a bar hunter? Doc, I fell off like 'simmons arter frost, and folks as doubted me needn't had asked whether I war 'ceitful or not for they could have seed plum threw me! The bar and painter got so saucy that they'd cum to the t'other side of the bayou and see which could talk the impudentest! 'Don't you want some bar meat or painter blanket?' they'd ask. 'Bars is monstrous fast and painter's hide is mighty warm!' Oh! Doc, I was a miserable man! The sky warn't blue for me, the sun war always cloudy, and the shade trees gin no shade for me. Even the dogs forgot me, and the little children quit coming and asking, 'Please, Mr. Bar-Grave, cotch me a young bar or a painter kitten.' Doc, the tears would cum in my eyes and the hot blood would cum biling up from my heart when I'd hobble out of a sundown and hear the boys tell, as they went by, of the sport they'd had that day, and how the bar fit 'fore he was killed, and how fat he war arter he was slayed. Long arter they was gone and the whippoorwill had eat up their voices, I would sit out there on the old stump and think of the things that used to hold the biggest place in my mind when I was a boy and p'raps sense I've bin a man.

"I'd heard tell of distinction and fame and people's names never dying and how Washington and Franklin and Clay and Jackson and a heap of political dicshunary folks would live when their big hearts had crumbled down to a rifle charge of dust. And I begun, too, to think, Doc, what a pleasant thing it would be to know folks a million years off would talk of me like them, and it made me 'tarmine to 'stinguish myself and have my name put in a book with a yaller kiver. I warn't a genus, Doc, I nude that, nor I warn't dicshunary. So I determined to strike out in a new track for glory and 'title myself to be called the 'bear hunter of Ameriky.' Doc, my heart jumpt up, and I belted my hunting shirt tighter for fear it would lepe out when I fust spoke them words out loud.

"'The bar hunter of Ameriky!' Doc, you know whether I war ernin' the name when I war ruined. There is not a child—white, black, Injun, or nigger—from the Arkansas line to the Trinity but what has heard of me, and I were happy when"—here a tremor of his voice and a tear glistening in the glare of the fire told the old fellow's emotion—"when—but les take a drink—Doc, I found I was dying—I war gettin' weaker and weaker—I nude your truck warn't what I needed, or I'd sent for you. A bar hunt war the medsin that my systum required, a fust class bar hunt—the music of the dogs, the fellers a-screaming, the cane poppin', the rifles crackin', the bar growlin', the fight hand to hand, slap goes the paw, and a dog's hide hangs on one cane and his body on another, the knife glistenin' and then goin' plump up to the handle in his heart! Oh! Doc, this was what I needed, and I swore, since death were huggin' me anyhow, I mite as well feel his last grip in a bar hunt.

"I seed the boys goin' long one day and haled them to wait awhile as I believed I would go along too. I war frade if I kept out of a hunt much longer I wood get outen practis. They laughed at me, thinkin' I war jokin', for wat cood a sick, old, one-legged man do in a bar hunt? How cood he get threw the swamp, and vines, and canes, and backwater? And s'pose he mist the bar, how war he to get outen the way?

"But I war 'tarmined on goin'. My dander was up, and I swore I wood go, tellin' them if I coodent travel 'bout much I could take a stand. Seein' it war no use tryin' to 'swade me, they saddled my poney and off we started. I felt better right off. I knew I cuddent do much in the chase, so I told the fellers I would go to the cross path stand and wate for the bar as he would be sarten to cum by thar. You have never seed the cross path stand, Doc. It's the singularest place in the swamp. It's rite in the middle of a canebrake, thicker than har on a barhide, down in a deep sink that looks like the devil had cummenst diggin' a skylite for his pre-emption. I knew it war a dangersome place for a well man to go in, much less a one-leg cripple, but I war 'tarmined that time to give a deal on the dead wood and play my hand out. The boys gin me time to get to the stand and then cummenst the drive. The bar seemed 'tarmined on disappinting me, for the fust thing I heard of the dogs and bar they was outen hearing. Everything got quiet, and I got so wrathy at not being able to foller up the chase that I cust till the trees cummenst shedding their leaves and small branches, when I herd them lumbrin' back and I nude they war makin' to me. I primed old 'bar death' fresh and rubbed the frizin, for it war no time for rifle to get to snappin'. Thinks I, if I happen to miss, I'll try what virtue there is in a knife—when, Doc, my knife war gone. H——ll! bar, for God's sake have a soft head, and die easy, for I *can't* run!

"Doc, you've hearn a bar bustin' threw a canebrake and know how near to a harrycane it is. I almost cummenst dodgin' the trees, thinkin' it war the best-in-the-shop one a-comin'—for it beat the loudest thunder ever I heard, that ole bar did—comin' to get his death from an ole, one-legged cripple what had slayed more of his brethren than his nigger foot had ever made trax in the mud. Doc, he heerd a *monstrus long ways ahead of the dogs*. I warn't skeered, but I must own, as I had but one shot an' no knife, I wud have prefurd they had been closer. But here he cum! He-bar—big as a bull—boys off h——llwards—dogs nowhar—no knife—but one shot—*and only one leg that cood run!*

"The bar 'peered s'prised to see me standin' ready for him in the openin'— for it war currently reported 'mong his brethren that I war either dead or no use for bar. I thought fust he war skeered, and, Doc, I b'leve he war till he cotch a sight of my wooden leg and that toch his pride for he knew he would be hist outen every she-bear's company ef he run from a poor, sickly, one-legged cripple. So on he cum, a small river of slobber pourin' from his mouth and the blue smoke curlin' outen his ears. I tuck good aim at his left and let drive. The ball struck him on the eyebrow and glanced off, only stunnin' him for a moment, jes givin' me time to club my rifle, an' on he kum as fierce as an old grizzly. As he got in reach, I gin him a lick 'cross the temples, brakin' the stock in fifty pieces an' knockin' him senseless. I struv to foller up the lick when, Doc, I war fast—my timber-toe had run inter the ground and I cuddent git out though I jerked hard enuf almost to bring my thigh out of joint. I stuped to unscrew the infurnal thing when the bar cum to and cum at me agen. Vim! I tuck him over the head, and cochunk, he keeled over. H——ll! but I cavorted and pitched. Thar war my wust enemy waitin' for me to giv him a finisher an' I *cuddent* git at him. I'd cummense unscrewin' leg—here cum bar—vim—cochunk—he'd fall out of reach—and, Doc, *I cuddent git to him.* I kept workin' my body round so as to unscrew the leg and keep the bar off till I cood 'complish it, when jes as I tuck the last turn and got loose from the d——d thing, here cum bar more venimous than ever, and I nude thar war death to one out and comin' shortly. I let him get close an' then cum down with a perfect tornado on his head, as I thought. But the old villain had learnt the dodge—the barrel jes struck him on the side of the head and glanst off, slinging itself out of my hands 'bout twenty feet 'mongst the thick cane, and thar I war in a fix sure. Bar but little hurt—no gun—no knife—no dogs—no frens—no chance to climb—*an' only one leg that cood run.* Doc, I jes cummenst makin' 'pologies to ole Master when an idee struck me. Doc, did you ever see a piney woods nigger pullin' at a sassafras root, or a suckin' pig in a tater patch arter the big yams? You has! Well, you can 'magin how I jurkt at that wudden leg, for it war the last of pea time with me, sure, if I didn't rise 'fore bar did. At last, they both cum up, 'bout the same time, and I braced myself for a death struggle.

"We fit all round that holler! Fust I'd foller bar and then bar would chase me! I'd make a lick—he'd fend off and showin' a set of teeth that no doctor 'cept natur had ever wurkt at, cum tearin' at me! We both 'gain to git tired. I heard the boys and dogs cumin, so did bar, and we were both anxshus to bring the thing to a close 'fore they cum up, though I wuddent thought they were intrudin' ef they had cum up some time afore.

"I'd worn the old leg pretty well off to the second jint, when, jest 'fore I made a lick, the noise of the boys and the dogs cummin' sorter confused bar and he made a stumble, and bein' off his guard I got a fair lick! The way that bar's flesh giv in to the soft impresshuns of that leg war an honor to the mederkal perfeshun for having invented sich a weepun! I hollered—but you have heered me holler an' I won't describe it. I had whipped a bar in a fair hand to hand fight—me, an old, sickly, one-legged bar hunter! The boys cum up and when they seed the ground we had fit over, they swore they would hav thought 'stead of a bar fight that I had been cuttin' cane and deadenin' timber for a corn patch, the sile war so worked up. They then handed me a knife to finish the work.

"Doc, les licker. It's a dry talk. When will you make me another leg? Bar meat is not over plenty in the cabin and I feel like tryin' another!"

A Struggle for Life

It was the spring of 183—. The water from the Mississippi had commenced overflowing the low swamps and rendering travelling on horseback very disagreeable. The water had got to that troublesome height, when it was rather too high for a horse and not high enough for a canoe or skiff to pass easily over the submerged grounds.

I was sitting out under my favorite oak congratulating myself that I had no travelling to do just then—it was very healthy—when my joy was suddenly nipped in the bud by a loud hallo from the opposite side of the bayou. Looking over and answering the hail, I discerned first a mule and then something which so closely resembled an ape or an orang-outang that I was in doubt whether the voice had proceeded from it until a repetition of the hail, this time coming unmistakably from it, assured me that it was a human.

"Massa Doctor at home?" yelled the voice.

"Yes, I am the doctor. What do you want?"

"Massa sent me with a letter to you."

Jumping in the skiff, a few vigorous strokes sent me to the opposite shore where the singular being awaited my coming.

He was a Negro dwarf of the most frightful appearance. His diminutive body was garnished with legs and arms of enormously disproportionate length. His face was hideous—a pair of tushes projected from either side of a double harelip. Taking him altogether, he was the nearest resemblance to the orang-outang mixed with the devil that human eyes ever dwelt upon. I could not look at him without feeling disgust.

"Massa Bill sent me with a letter," was his reply to my asking him his business.

Opening it, I found a summons to see a patient, the mother of a man named Disney, living some twenty miles distant by the usual road. It was in no good humor that I told the dwarf to wait until I could swim my horse over and I would accompany him.

By the time I had concluded my preparations and put a large bottle of brandy in my pocket, my steed was awaiting me upon the opposite shore.

"Massa tole me to tell you ef you didn't mine swimming a little you had better kum de nere way."

"Do you have to swim much?"

"Oh no, Massa, onely swim Plurisy Lake and wade de backwater a few miles, you'll save haf de way at leste."

I looked at the sun. It was only about two hours high, and the roads were in such miserable condition that six miles an hour would be making fine speed. So I determined to go the near way and swim "Pleurisy slough."

"You are certain you know the road, boy?"

"Oh, yes, Massa, me know um ebery inch ob de groun', hunted 'possum an' coon ober him many a night. Massa, you ain't got any 'baccy, is you?"

"There's a chaw—and here's a drink of brandy. I'll give you another if you pilot me safe through and a good pounding if you get lost."

"Dank you, Massa, um's good. No fere I lose you, know ebery inch of de groun.'"

I had poured him out a dram, not considering his diminutive stature, sufficient to unsettle the nerves of a stout man, but he drank it off with great apparent relish. By this time, everything being ready, we commenced ploughing our way through the muddy roads.

We made but slow progress. I would dash on and then have to wait for the dwarf, who, belaboring his mule with a cudgel almost as large as himself, strove in vain to keep up.

The road was directly down the bayou for some miles. There were few settlers on it then and the extent of their clearing consisted of a corn patch. They were the pre-emptioners or squatters, men who settled upon government land before its survey and awaited the incoming of planters with several Negroes to buy their claims, themselves to be bought out by more affluent emigrants. To one of the first-mentioned class—the pre-emptioner—my visit was directed, or rather to his mother, who occupied an intermediate grade between the squatter and the small planter in as much as she possessed one Negro, the delectable morsel for whom I was waiting every few hundred yards.

It wanted but an hour to sundown when we reached the place where it was optional with me either to go the longer route by the bayou or save several miles by cutting across the bend of the stream, having, however, to swim "Pleurisy slough" if I did so.

The path across was quite obscure, and it would be dark by the time we crossed. But the Negro declared he knew every inch of the way, and as saving distance was a serious consideration, I determined to try it and "Pleurisy slough."

Taking a drink to warm me for the dew that had commenced to fall was quite chilling, I gave one to the Negro, not noticing the wild sparkle of his eye or the exhilaration of his manner.

We pressed on eagerly, I ahead as long as the path lasted, but it giving out at the edge of the backwater, it became necessary for the Negro to precede and pilot the way.

I followed him mechanically for some distance, relying on his intimate knowledge of the scamp, our steeds making but slow progress through the mud and water.

When we entered the swamp I had remarked that the sun was in our faces, and great was my astonishment when we had travelled some time, on glancing my eye upwards to see if it had left the tree tops, to perceive its last beams directly at my back, the very reverse of what it should have been. Thinking perhaps that it was some optical illusion, I consulted the moss on the trees, and its indication was that we were taking the back track. I addressed the Negro very sharply for having misled me, when, instead of excusing himself, he turned on me his hideous countenance and chuckled the low laugh of drunkenness. I saw that I had given him too much brandy for his weak brain and that he was too far gone to be of any assistance to me in finding the way.

Mine was a pleasant situation truly. To return home would be as bad as to endeavor to go on. It would be night at any rate before I could get out of the swamp, and after it fell, as there was no moon, it would be dangerous to travel as the whole country was full of lakes and sloughs and we might be precipitated suddenly into one of them, losing our animals if not being drowned ourselves.

It was evident that I would have to pass the night in the swamp, my only companion the drunken dwarf. I had nothing to eat and no weapons to protect myself if assailed by wild beasts, but the swamp was high enough to preclude the attack of anything but alligators, and their bellow was resounding in too close proximity to be agreeable.

Fortunately, being a cigar smoker, I had a box of matches in my pocket, and so I would have a fire at least. My next care was to find a ridge sufficiently above the water to furnish a dry place for building a fire and camp. After considerable search, just at nightfall the welcome prospect of a cane ridge above the overflow met my gaze. Hurrying up the Negro, who by this time was maudlin drunk, I reached the cane and forcing my way with considerable difficulty through it until I got out of the reach of the water, dismounted, and tying my horse took the Negro down and performed the same office for his mule.

My next care was to gather materials for a fire before impenetrable darkness closed over the swamp. Fortunately for me, a fallen oak presented itself not ten steps from where I stood. To have a cheerful blazing fire was the work of a few minutes. Breaking off sufficient cane tops to last the steeds till morning, I stripped my horse—the mule had nothing on but a bridle—and with the saddle and cane leaves made me a couch that a monarch, had he been as tired as I was, would have found no fault with. As the Negro was perfectly helpless and nearly naked, I gave him my saddle blanket and making him a bed at a respectful distance bade him go to sleep.

Replenishing the fire with sufficient fuel to last till morning, I lit a cigar, and throwing myself down upon my fragrant couch, gave myself up to reflections upon the peculiarity of my situation. Had it been a voluntary bivouac with a set of chosen companions, it would not have awakened half the interest in my mind that it did, for the attending circumstances imparted to it much of the romantic.

There, far from human habitation, my only companion a hideous dwarf, surrounded with water, and the night draperied darkly around, I lay, the cane leaves for my bed, the saddle for my pillow, the huge fire lighting up the darkness for a space around, giving natural objects a strange, distorted appearance, and bringing the two steeds into high relief against the dark background of waving cane which nodded over, discoursing a wile, peculiar melody of its own. Occasionally a loud explosion would be heard as the fire communicated with a green reed. The wild hoot of an owl was heard and directly I almost felt the sweep of his wings as he went sailing by and alighted upon an old tree just where the light sank mingling with the darkness. I followed him with my eye, and as he settled himself, he turned his gaze toward me. I moved one of the logs, and his huge eyes fairly glistened with light as the flames shot up with increased vigor. The swamp moss was flowing around him in long, tangled masses, and as a more vivid gleam uprose, I gazed and started involuntarily. Had I not known it was an owl surrounded with moss that sat upon that stricken tree, I would have sworn it was the form of an old man, clad in a sombre flowing mantle, his arm raised in an attitude of warning, that I gazed upon. A cane exploding startled the owl and with a loud tu-whit, tu-whoo he went sailing away in the darkness. The unmelodious bellow of the alligator and the jarring cry of the heron arose from a lake on the opposite side of the cane, whilst the voices of a myriad of frogs and the many undistinguishable sounds of the swamp made the night vocal with discordancy.

My cigar being by this time exhausted, I took the bottle from my pocket and taking a hearty drink to keep the night air from chilling me when asleep was about to restore it to its place and commend myself to slumber, when glancing at the dwarf, I saw his eyes fixed upon me with a demoniac expression that I shall never forget.

"Give me a dram," he said very abruptly, not prefacing the request by those deferential words never omitted by the slave when in his proper mind.

"No, sir, you have already taken too much. I will give you no more," I replied.

"Give me a dram," he again said, more fiercely than before.

Breaking off a cane, I told him that if he spoke to me in that manner again I would give him a severe flogging.

But to my surprise he retorted, "D—n you, white man, I will kill you ef you don't give me more brandy," his eyes flashing and sparkling with electric light.

I rose to correct him but a comparison of my well developed frame with his stunted deformed proportions and the reflection that his drunkenness was attributable to my giving him the brandy deterred me.

"I will kill you," he again screamed, his fangs clashing and the foam flying from his mouth, his long arms extended as if to clutch me and the fingers quivering nervously.

I took a hasty glance of my condition. I was lost in the midst of the swamp, an unknown watery expanse surrounding me, remote from any possible assistance. The swamps were rapidly filling with water, and if we did not get out tomorrow or next day we would in all probability be starved or drowned. The Negro was my only dependence to pilot me to the settlements, and he was threatening my life if I did not give him more brandy. Should I do it or not? Judging from the effects of the two drinks I had given him, if he got possession of the bottle it might destroy him, or at least render him incapable of travelling until starvation and exposure would destroy us. My mind was resolved upon that subject. I would give him no more. There was no alternative, I would have to stand his assault. Considering I was three times his size, a fearful adventure, truly thought I, not doubting a moment but that my greater size would give me proportionate strength, I must not hurt him, but will tie him until he recovers.

The dwarf, now aroused to maniacal fury by the persistence in my refusal, slowly approached me to carry his threat into execution. The idea of such a diminutive object destroying without weapons a man of my size presented something ludicrous, and I laughingly awaited his attack, ready to tie his hands before he could bite or scratch me. Woefully I underrated his powers!

With a yell like a wild beast's, he precipitated himself upon me. Evading my blow, he clutched with his long fingers at my throat, burying his talons in my flesh and writhing his little body around mine strove to bear me to earth.

I summoned my whole strength and endeavored to shake him off. But possessing the proverbial power of the dwarf increased by his drunken mania to an immense degree, I found all my efforts unavailing—and oh God! horrors of horrors—what awful anguish was mine when I found him bearing me slowly to earth and his piercing talons buried in my throat, cutting off my breath! My eyes met his with a more horrid gleam than that he glared upon me. His was the fire of brutal nature aroused by desire to intense malignancy, and mine the gaze of despair and death. Closer and firmer his grip closed upon my throat, barring out the sweet life's breath. I strove to shriek for help but could not. How shall I describe the racking agony that tortured me? A mountain, heavier than any earth's bosom holds, was pressing upon my breast, slowly crushing me to fragments. All kinds of colors first floated before my eyes and then everything wore a settled, intensely fiery red. I felt my jaw slowly dropping and my tongue protruding till it rested on the hellish fangs that encircled my throat. I could hear distinctly every pulsation of even the minutest artery in my frame. Its wild singing was in my ears like the ocean wave playing over the shell-clad shore. I remember it all perfectly, for the mind through all this awful struggle remained full of thought and clearness. Closer grew the grip of those talons around my throat, and I knew that I could live but a few moments more.

I did not pray. I did not commend my soul to God. I had not a fear of death. But oh! awful were my thoughts at dying in such a way—suffocated by a hellish Negro in the midst of the noisome swamp, my flesh to be devoured by the carrion crow, my bones to whiten where they lay for long years and then startle the settler, when civilization had strode into the wilderness and the cane that would conceal my bones would be falling before the knife of the cane cutter. I ceased to breathe. I was dead. I had suffered the last pangs of that awful hour, and either it was the soul not yet resigned to leave its human tenement or else immortal mind triumphing over death, but I still retained the sentient principle within my corpse. I remember distinctly when the demon relaxed his clutch and shaking me to see if I were really dead broke into a hellish laugh. I remember distinctly when tearing the bottle from me, he pulled my limber body off my couch and stretched himself upon it.

And what were my thoughts? I was dead—yet am living now. Ay, dead as human ever becomes. My lungs had ceased to play, my heart was still, my muscles were inactive, and even my skin had the dead clammy touch. Had men been there, they would have placed me in a coffin and buried me deep in the ground. The worm would have eaten me, and the death rats made nests in my heart, and what was lately a strong man would have become a loathsome mass. But still in that coffin amidst those writhing worms would have been the immortal mind, and still would it have thought and pondered on till the last day was come. For such is the course of soul and death, as my interpretation has it. I was dead in all but my mind and that still thought on as vividly, as ramblingly as during life. My body lay dead in that murderer's swamp—my mind roamed far away in thought, reviewing my carnal life. I stood, as when a boy, by my mother's grave. The tall grass was waving over it and the green sod smiled at my feet. "Mother," I whispered, "your child is weary—the world looks harsh upon him—coldness comes from those who should shelter the orphan. Mother, open your large black eyes and smile upon your child." Again, I stood upon the steamer a childish fugitive, giving a last look upon my fleeing home and mingling my tears with the foaming wave beneath. I dragged my exhausted frame through the cotton fields of the South. My back was wearied with stooping—we were picking the first opening—and as dreams of future distinction would break upon my soul, the strap of the cotton sack, galling my shoulder, recalled me to myself. All the phases of my life were repeated until they ended where I lay dead—dead as mortal ever becomes. I thought what will my friends say when they hear, that on a visit to the sick, I disappeared in the swamp and was never heard of more—drowned or starved to death? Will they weep for me? Not many, I ween, will be the tears that will be shed for me. Then, after the lapse of long years, my bones will be found. I wonder who will get my skull? Perhaps an humble doctor like myself, who, meditating upon it, will not think that it holds the mind of a creature of his own ambition—his own lofty instincts. He will deem it but an empty skull and little dream that it held a sentient principle. But I know that the mind will still tenant it.

Ha, ha! how that foul ape is gurgling his blood-bought pleasure. I would move if I could and wrench the bottle from him, but mine is thought, not action. Hark! there is a storm arising. I hear with my ear that is pressed on the earth the thunder of the hurricane. How the trees crash beneath it! Will it prostrate those above me! Hark! what awful thunder! Ah me! what fierce pang is that piercing my very vitals? There is a glimmering of light before my eyes. Can it be that I the dead am being restored to human life? Another thunder peal! 'Tis the second stroke of my heart—my blood is red hot—it comes with fire through my veins—the earth quakes—the mountain is rolling off my chest—I live!—I breathe!—I see!—I hear!—where am I? Who brought me here? I hear other sounds but cannot my own voice. Where am I? Ah! I remember the dwarf strangled me. Hark! where is he? Is that the sunbeam playing over the trees? What noisome odor like consuming flesh is that which poisons the gale? Great God! can that disfigured, half-consumed mass be my evil genius?

I rose up and staggering fell again. My strength was nearly gone. I lay until I thought myself sufficiently recruited to stand and then got up and surveyed the scene. The animals were tied as I left them and were eating their cane unconcernedly, but fearfully my well-nigh murderer had paid for his crime and awful was the retribution. Maddened by the spirits, he had rushed into the flames and in the charred and loathsome mass nothing of the human remained. He had died the murderer's death and been buried in his grave—a tomb of fire.

To remain longer in the horrid place was impossible. My throat pained me excessively where the talons had penetrated the flesh, and I could not speak above a whisper. I turned the mule loose, thinking that it would return home and conduct me out of the swamp. I was not incorrect in my supposition. The creature led me to his owner's cabin. The patient had died during the night.

My account of the dwarf's attack did not surprise the family. He had once, when in a similar condition, made an attack upon his mistress and would have strangled her had assistance not been near.

His bones were left to bleach where they lay. I would not for the universe have looked again upon the place, and his mistress being dead, there were none to care for giving him the rites of sepulture.

Samuel Langhorne Clemens (1835-1910)

The receding frontier was a shaping influence on both the life and career of Samuel Clemens as he reconfigured his persona into Mark Twain, the white-haired and white-suited (in his final years) patriarch of American literary humor who voiced the spirit and character of the nation. Early on, however, his boyhood experiences in Hannibal, Missouri; his brief career as a steamboat pilot when he became acquainted, he wrote, "with all the different types of human nature that are found in fiction, biography, or history"; and his work as a miner in the frontier territory of Nevada—all contributed to his self-nurtured reputation as a wild man of the West, lately captured and civilized for the edification and entertainment of eastern audiences. Another side of his personality that emerged was one that aspired to respect from genteel literati, to success as a publisher and businessman, and to recognition as an accomplished novelist and author.

It was while working for Mississippi valley and western newspapers that Clemens encountered the humor of the Old Southwest, where it was reprinted in their columns. He reviewed favorably *Sut Lovingood: Yarns* by George Washington Harris in a California newspaper in 1867, and he would borrow some scenes from a story in that collection, as well as a chapter from *Some Adventures of Captain Simon Suggs* by Johnson Jones Hooper, for use in two of his later books. Most importantly, Clemens learned how to write by trying his hand at imitating them. Most of the things that would characterize his contributions to American literature he borrowed from them: the effective use of first-person narrators, the use of American language and vernacular in fiction, and an accurate rendition of the brutal and mean nature of existence at the bottom of society. In a sense he was the culmination of the tradition of the humor of the Old Southwest, at once its brightest exemplar and its most important product. It is in that spirit that he is included here with some pieces that reflect his participation in that tradition.

Texts: "The Celebrated Jumping Frog of Calaveras County" from *The Celebrated Jumping Frog of Calaveras County, and Other Sketches* (New York: C. H. Webb, 1867). "The Story of the Old Ram" from *Roughing It* (Hartford: American, 1872). "Frescoes from the Past" from *Life on the Mississippi* (Boston: James R. Osgood, 1883).

The Celebrated Jumping Frog of Calaveras County

In compliance with the request of a friend of mine, who wrote me from the East, I called on good-natured, garrulous old Simon Wheeler, and inquired after my friend's friend, *Leonidas W.* Smiley, as requested to do, and I hereunto append the result. I have a lurking suspicion that *Leonidas W.* Smiley is a myth; that my friend never knew such a personage; and that he only conjectured that, if I asked old Wheeler about him, it would remind him of his infamous *Jim* Smiley, and he would go to work and bore me nearly to death with some infernal reminiscence of him as long and tedious as it should be useless to me. If that was the design, it certainly succeeded.

I found Simon Wheeler dozing comfortably by the bar-room stove of the old, dilapidated tavern in the ancient mining camp of Angel's, and I noticed that he was fat and bald-headed, and had an expression of winning gentleness and simplicity upon his tranquil countenance. He roused up and gave me good-day. I told him a friend of mine had commissioned me to make some inquiries about a cherished companion of his boyhood named *Leonidas W.* Smiley—*Rev. Leonidas W.* Smiley—a young minister of the Gospel, who he had heard was at one time a resident of Angel's Camp. I added that, if Mr. Wheeler could tell me any thing about this Rev. Leonidas W. Smiley, I would feel under many obligations to him.

Simon Wheeler backed me into a corner and blockaded me there with his chair, and then sat me down and reeled off the monotonous narrative which follows this paragraph. He never smiled, he never frowned, he never changed his voice from the gentle-flowing key to which he tuned the initial sentence, he never betrayed the slightest suspicion of enthusiasm; but all through the interminable narrative there ran a vein of impressive earnestness and sincerity, which showed me plainly that, so far from imagining that there was any thing ridiculous or funny about this story, he regarded it as a really important matter, and admired its two heroes as men of transcendent genius in *finesse.* To me, the spectacle of a man drifting serenely along through such a queer yarn without ever smiling, was exquisitely absurd. As I said before, I asked him to tell me what he knew of Rev. Leonidas W. Smiley, and he replied as follows. I let him go on in his own way, and never interrupted him once:

There was a feller here once by the name of *Jim* Smiley, in the winter of '49—or maybe it was the spring of '50—I don't recollect exactly, somehow, though what makes me think it was one or the other is because I remember the big flume wasn't finished when he first came to the camp; but any way, he was the curiosest man about always betting on any thing that turned up you ever see, if he could get any body to bet on the other side; and if he couldn't, he'd change sides. Any way that suited the other man would suit him—any way just so's he got a bet, *he* was satisfied. But still he was lucky, uncommon lucky; he most always come out winner. He was always ready and laying for a chance; there couldn't be no solitry thing mentioned but that feller'd offer to bet on it, and take any side you please, as I was just telling you. If there was a horse-race, you'd find him flush, or you'd find him busted at the end of it; if there was a dog-fight, he'd bet on it; if there was a cat-fight, he'd bet on it; if there was a chicken-fight, he'd bet on it; why, if there was two birds setting on a fence, he would bet you which one would fly first; or if there was a camp-meeting, he would be there reg'lar, to bet on Parson Walker, which he judged to be the best exhorter about here, and so he was too, and a good man. If he even seen a straddle-bug start to go anywheres, he would bet you how long it would take him to get wherever he was going to, and if you took him up, he would foller that straddle-bug to Mexico but what he would find out where he was bound for and how long he was on the road. Lots of the boys here has seen that Smiley, and can tell you about him. Why, it never made no difference to *him*—he would bet on *any* thing—the dangdest feller. Parson Walker's wife laid very sick once, for a good while, and it seemed as if they warn't going to save her; but one morning he came in, and Smiley asked how she was, and he said she was considerable better—thank the Lord for his inf'nit mercy—and coming on so smart that, with the blessing of Prov'dence, she'd get well yet; and Smiley, before he thought, says, "Well, I'll risk two-and-a-half that she don't, any way."

Thish-yer Smiley had a mare—the boys called her the fifteen-minute nag, but that was only in fun, you know, because, of course, she was faster than that—and he used to win money on that horse, for all she was so slow and always had the asthma, or the distemper, or the consumption, or something of that kind. They used to give her two or three hundred yards start, and then pass her under way; but always at the fag-end of the race she'd get excited and desperate-like, and come cavorting and straddling up, and scattering her legs around limber, sometimes in the air, and sometimes out to one side amongst the fences, and kicking up m-o-r-e dust, and raising m-o-r-e racket with her coughing and sneezing and blowing her nose—and always fetch up at the stand just about a neck ahead, as near as you could cipher it down.

And he had a little small bull pup, that to look at him you'd think he wan't worth a cent, but to set around and look ornery, and lay for a chance to steal something. But as soon as money was up on him, he was a different dog; his under-jaw'd begin to stick out like the fo'castle of a steamboat, and his teeth would uncover, and shine savage like the furnaces. And a dog might tackle him, and bully-rag him, and bite him, and throw him over his shoulder two or three times, and Andrew Jackson—which was the name of the pup—Andrew Jackson would never let on but what *he* was satisfied, and hadn't expected nothing else—and the bets being doubled and doubled on the other side all the time, till the money was all up; and then all of a sudden he would grab that other dog jest by the j'int of his hind leg and freeze to it—not chaw, you understand, but only jest grip and hang on till they throwed up the sponge, if it was a year. Smiley always come out winner on that pup, till he harnessed a dog once that didn't have no hind legs, because they'd been sawed off by a circular saw, and when the thing had gone along far enough, and the money was all up, and he come to make a snatch for his pet holt, he saw in a minute how he'd been imposed on, and how the other dog had him in the door, so to speak, and he 'peared surprised, and then he looked sorter discouraged-like, and didn't try no more to win the fight, and he got shucked out bad. He gave Smiley a look, as much as to say his heart was broke, and it was *his* fault, for putting up a dog that hadn't no hind legs for him to take holt of, which was his main dependence in a fight, and then he limped off a piece and laid down and died. It was a good pup, was that Andrew Jackson, and would have made a name for hisself if he'd lived, for the stuff was in him, and he had genius—I know it, because he hadn't no opportunities to speak of, and it don't stand to reason that a dog could make such a fight as he could under them circumstances, if he hadn't no talent. It always makes me feel sorry when I think of that last fight of his'n, and the way it turned out.

Well, thish-yer Smiley had rat-tarriers, and chicken cocks, and tom-cats, and all them kind of things, till you couldn't rest, and you couldn't fetch nothing for him to bet on but he'd match you. He ketched a frog one day, and took him home, and said he cal'klated to edercate him; and so he never done nothing for three months but set in his back yard and learn that frog to jump. And you bet you he *did* learn him, too. He'd give him a little punch behind, and the next minute you'd see that frog whirling in the air like a doughnut—see him turn one summerset, or may be a couple, if he got a good start, and come down flat-footed and all right, like a cat. He got him up so in the matter of catching flies, and kept him in practice so constant, that he'd nail a fly every time as far as he could see him. Smiley said all a frog wanted was education, and he could do most any thing—and I believe him. Why, I've seen him set Dan'l Webster down here on this floor—Dan'l Webster was the name of the frog—and sing out, "Flies, Dan'l, flies!" and quicker'n you could wink, he'd spring straight up, and snake a fly off'n the counter there, and flop down on the floor again as solid as a gob of mud, and fall to scratching the side of his head with his hind foot as indifferent as if he hadn't no idea he'd been doin' any more'n any frog might do. You never see a frog so modest and straightfor'ard as he was, for all he was so gifted. And when it come to fair and square jumping on a dead level, he could get over more ground at one straddle than any animal of his breed you ever see. Jumping on a dead level was his strong suit, you understand; and when it come to that, Smiley would ante up money on him as long as he had a red. Smiley was monstrous proud of his frog, and well he might be, for fellers that had traveled and been everywheres, all said he laid over any frog that ever *they* see.

Well, Smiley kept the beast in a little lattice box, and he used to fetch him down town sometimes and lay for a bet. One day a feller—a stranger in the camp, he was—come across him with his box, and says:

"What might it be that you've got in the box?"

And Smiley says, sorter indifferent like, "It might be a parrot, or it might be a canary, may be, but it an't—it's only just a frog."

And the feller took it, and looked at it careful, and turned it round this way and that, and says, "H'm—so 'tis. Well, what's *he* good for?"

"Well," Smiley says, easy and careless, "He's good enough for *one* thing, I should judge—he can outjump ary frog in Calaveras county."

The feller took the box again, and took another long, particular look, and give it back to Smiley, and says again, very deliberate, "Well, I don't see no p'ints about that frog that's any better'n any other frog."

"May be you don't," Smiley says. "May be you understand frogs, and may be you don't understand 'em; may be you've had experience and may be you an't only a amature, as it were. Anyways, I've got *my* opinion, and I'll risk forty dollars that he can outjump any frog in Calaveras county"

And the feller studied a minute, and then says, kinder sad like, "Well, I'm only a stranger here, and I an't got no frog; but if I had a frog, I'd bet you."

And then Smiley says, "That's all right—that's all right—if you'll hold my box a minute, I'll go and get you a frog." And so the feller took the box, and put up his forty dollars along with Smiley's, and set down to wait.

So he set there a good while thinking and thinking to hisself, and then he got the frog out and prized his mouth open and took a teaspoon and filled him full of quail shot—filled him pretty near up to his chin—and set him on the floor. Smiley he went to the swamp and slopped around in the mud for a long time, and finally he ketched a frog, and fetched him in, and give him to this feller, and says:

"Now, if you're ready, set him alongside of Dan'l, with his fore-paws just even with Dan'l, and I'll give the word." Then he says, "One—two—three—jump!" and him and the feller touched up the frogs from behind, and the new frog hopped off, but Dan'l gave a heave, and hysted up his shoulders—so—like a Frenchman, but it wan't no use—he couldn't budge; he was planted as solid as an anvil, and he couldn't no more stir than if he was anchored out. Smiley was a good deal surprised, and he was disgusted too, but he didn't have no idea what the matter was, of course.

The feller took the money and started away; and when he was going out at the door, he sorter jerked his thumb over his shoulders—this way—at Dan'l, and says, very deliberate, "Well, *I* don't see no p'ints about that frog that's any better'n any other frog."

Smiley he stood scratching his head and looking down at Dan'l a long time, and at last he says, "I do wonder what in the nation that frog throw'd off for—I wonder if there an't something the matter with him—he 'pears to look mighty baggy, somehow." And he ketched Dan'l by the nap of the neck, and lifted him up and says, "Why, blame my cats, if he don't weigh five pound!" and turned him upside down, and he belched out a double handful of shot. And then he see how it was, and he was the maddest man—he set the frog down and took out after that feller, but he never ketched him. And——

[Here Simon Wheeler heard his name called from the front yard, and got up to see what was wanted.] And turning to me as he moved away, he said: "Jest set where you are, stranger, and rest easy—I an't going to be gone a second."

But, by your leave, I did not think that a continuation of the history of the enterprising vagabond *Jim* Smiley would be likely to afford me much information concerning the Rev. *Leonidas W.* Smiley, and so I started away.

At the door I met the sociable Wheeler returning, and he buttonholed me and recommenced:

"Well, thish-yer Smiley had a yaller one-eyed cow that didn't have no tail, only jest a short stump like a bannanner, and—"

"Oh! hang Smiley and his afflicted cow!" I muttered, good-naturedly, and bidding the old gentleman good-day, I departed.

The Story of the Old Ram

Every now and then, in these days, the boys used to tell me I ought to get one Jim Blaine to tell me the stirring story of his grandfather's old ram—but they always added that I must not mention the matter unless Jim was drunk at the time—just comfortably and sociably drunk. They kept this up until my curiosity was on the rack to hear the story. I got to haunting Blaine; but it was of no use, the boys always found fault with his condition; he was often moderately but never satisfactorily drunk. I never watched a man's condition with such absorbing interest, such anxious solicitude; I never so pined to see a man uncompromisingly drunk before. At last, one evening I hurried to his cabin, for I learned that this time his situation was such that even the most fastidious could find no fault with it—he was tranquilly, serenely, symmetrically drunk—not a hiccup to mar his voice, not a cloud upon his brain thick enough to obscure his memory. As I entered, he was sitting upon an empty powder-keg, with a clay pipe in one hand and the other raised to command silence. His face was round, red, and very serious; his throat was bare and his hair tumbled; in general appearance and costume he was a stalwart miner of the period. On the pine table stood a candle, and its dim light revealed "the boys" sitting here and there on bunks, candle-boxes, powder-kegs, etc. They said:

"Sh—! Don't speak—he's going to commence."
THE STORY OF THE OLD RAM
I found a seat at once, and Blaine said:
"I don't reckon them times will ever come again. There never was a more bullier old ram than what he was. Grandfather fetched him from Illinois—got him of a man by the name of Yates—Bill Yates—maybe you might have heard of him; his father was a deacon—Baptist—and he was a rustler, too; a man had to get up ruther early to get the start of old Thankful Yates; it was him put the Greens up to jining teams with my grandfather when he moved West. Seth Green was prob'ly the pick of the flock; he married a Wilkerson—Sarah Wilkerson—good cretur, she was—one of the likeliest heifers that was ever raised in old Stoddard, everybody said that knowed her. She could heft a bar'l of flour as easy as I can flip a flapjack. And spin? Don't mention it! Independent? Humph! When Sile Hawkins come abrowsing around her, she let him know that for all his tin he couldn't trot in harness alongside of *her*. You see, Sile Hawkins was—no, it warn't Sile Hawkins, after all—it was a galoot by the name of Filkins—I disremember his first name; but he *was* a stump—come into pra'r meeting drunk, one night, hooraying for Nixon, becuz he thought it was a primary; and old deacon Ferguson up and scooted him through the window and he lit on old Miss Jefferson's head, poor old filly. She was a good soul—had a glass eye and used to lend it to old Miss Wagner, that hadn't any, to receive company in; it warn't big enough, and when Miss Wagner warn't noticing, it would get twisted around in the socket, and look up, maybe, or out to one side, and every which way, while t'other one was looking as straight ahead as a spyglass. Grown people didn't mind it, but it most always made the children cry, it was so sort of scary. She tried packing it in raw cotton, but it wouldn't work, somehow—the cotton would get loose and stick out and look so kind of awful that the children couldn't stand it no way. She was always dropping it out, and turning up her old dead-light on the company empty, and making them oncomfortable, becuz *she* never could tell when it hopped out, being blind on that side, you see. So somebody would have to hunch her and say, 'Your game eye has fetched loose, Miss Wagner dear'—and then all of them would have to sit and wait till she jammed it in again—wrong side before, as a general thing, and green as a bird's egg, being a bashful cretur and easy sot back before company. But being wrong side before warn't much difference, anyway, becuz her own eye was sky-blue and the glass one was yaller on the front side, so whichever way she turned it it didn't match nohow. Old Miss Wagner was considerable on the borrow, she was. When she had a quilting, or Dorcas S'iety at her house she gen'ally borrowed Miss Higgins's wooden leg to stump around on; it was considerable shorter than her other pin, but much *she* minded that. She said she couldn't abide crutches when she had company, becauz they were so slow; said when she had company and things had to be done, she wanted to get up and hump

herself. She was as bald as a jug, and so she used to borrow Miss Jacops's wig—Miss Jacops was the coffin-peddler's wife—a ratty old buzzard, he was, that used to go roosting around where people was sick, waiting for 'em; and there that old rip would sit all day, in the shade, on a coffin that he judged would fit the can'idate; and if it was a slow customer and kind of uncertain, he'd fetch his rations and a blanket along and sleep in the coffin nights. He was anchored out that way, in frosty weather, for about three weeks, once, before old Robbins's place, waiting for him; and after that, for as much as two years, Jacops was not on speaking terms with the old man, on account of his disapp'inting him. He got one of his feet froze, and lost money, too, becuz old Robbins took a favorable turn and got well. The next time Robbins got sick, Jacops tried to make up with him, and varnished up the same old coffin and fetched it along; but old Robbins was too many for him; he had him in, and 'peared to be powerful weak; he bought the coffin for ten dollars and Jacops was to pay it back and twenty-five more besides if Robbins didn't like the coffin after he'd tried it. And then Robbins died, and at the funeral he bursted off the lid and riz up in his shroud and told the parson to let up on the performances, becuz he could *not* stand such a coffin as that. You see he had been in a trance once before, when he was young, and he took the chances on another, cal'lating that if he made the trip it was money in his pocket, and if he missed fire he couldn't lose a cent. And by George he sued Jacops for the rhino and got jedgment; and he set up the coffin in his back parlor and said he 'lowed to take his time, now. It was always an aggravation to Jacops, the way that miserable old thing acted. He moved back to Indiany pretty soon—went to Wellsville—Wellsville was the place the Hogadorns was from. Mighty fine family. Old Maryland stock. Old Squire Hogadorn could carry around more mixed licker, and cuss better than most any man I ever see. His second wife was the widder Billings—she that was Becky Martin; her dam was deacon Dunlap's first wife. Her oldest child, Maria, married a missionary and died in grace—et up by the savages. They et *him*, too, poor feller—biled him. It warn't the custom, so they say, but they explained to friends of his'n that went down there to bring away his things, that they'd tried missionaries every other way and never could get any good out of 'em—and so it annoyed all his relations to find out that that man's life was fooled away just out of a dern'd experiment, so to speak. But mind you, there ain't anything ever reely lost; everything that people can't understand and don't see the reason of does good if you only hold on and give it a fair shake; Prov'dence don't fire no blank ca'tridges, boys. That there missionary's substance, unbeknowns to himself, actu'ly converted every last one of them heathens that took a chance at the barbecue. Nothing ever fetched them but that. Don't tell *me* it was an accident. When my uncle Lem was leaning up agin a scaffolding once, sick, or drunk, or suthin, an Irishman with a hod full of bricks fell on him out of the third story and broke the old man's back in two places. People said it was an accident. Much accident there was about that. He didn't know what he was there for, but he was there for a good object. If he hadn't been there the Irishman would have been killed. Nobody can ever make me believe anything different from that. Uncle Lem's dog was there. Why didn't the Irishman fall on the dog? Becuz the dog would a seen him a-coming and stood from under. That's the reason the dog warn't appinted. A dog can't be depended on to carry out a special providence. Mark my words it was a put-up thing. Accidents don't happen, boys. Uncle Lem's dog—I wish you could a seen that dog. He was a reglar shepherd—or ruther he was part bull and part shepherd—splendid animal; belonged to parson Hagar before Uncle Lem got him. Parson Hagar belonged to the Western Reserve Hagars; prime family; his mother was a Watson; one of his sisters married a Wheeler; they settled in Morgan County, and he got nipped by the machinery in a carpet factory and went through in less than a quarter of a minute; his widder bought the piece of carpet that had his remains wove in, and people come a hundred mile to 'tend the funeral. There was fourteen yards in the piece. She wouldn't let them roll him up, but planted him just so—full length. The church was middling small where they preached the funeral, and they had to let one end of the coffin stick out of the window. They didn't bury him—they planted one end, and let him stand up, same as a monument. And they nailed a sign on it and put—put on—put on it—sacred to—the m-e-m-o-r-y—of fourteen y-a-r-d-s—of three-ply—car——pet—containing all that was—m-o-r-t-a-l—of—of—W i –1–1 -i-a-m—W-h-e—"

Jim Blaine had been growing gradually drowsy and drowsier—his head nodded, once, twice, three times—dropped peacefully upon his breast, and he fell tranquilly asleep. The tears were running down the boys' cheeks—they were suffocating with suppressed laughter—and had been from the start, though I had never noticed it. I perceived that I was "sold." I learned then that Jim Blaine's peculiarity was that whenever he reached a certain stage of intoxication, no human power could keep him from setting out, with impressive unction, to tell about a wonderful adventure which he had once had with his grandfather's old ram—and the mention of the ram in the first sentence was as far as any man had ever heard him get, concerning it. He always maundered off, interminably, from one thing to another, till his whisky got the best of him and he fell asleep. What the thing was that happened to him and his grandfather's old ram is a dark mystery to this day, for nobody has ever yet found out.

Frescoes from the Past

Apparently the river was ready for business, now. But no, the distribution of a population along its banks was as calm and deliberate and time-devouring a process as the discovery and exploration had been.

Seventy years elapsed, after the exploration, before the river's borders had a white population worth considering; and nearly fifty more before the river had a commerce. Between La Salle's opening of the river and the time when it may be said to have become the vehicle of anything like a regular and active commerce, seven sovereigns had occupied the throne of England, America had become an independent nation, Louis XIV. and Louis XV. had rotted and died, the French monarchy had gone down in the red tempest of the revolution, and Napoleon was a name that was beginning to be talked about. Truly, there were snails in those days.

The river's earliest commerce was in great barges—keelboats, broadhorns. They floated and sailed from the upper rivers to New Orleans, changed cargoes there, and were tediously warped and poled back by hand. A voyage down and back sometimes occupied nine months. In time this commerce increased until it gave employment to hordes of rough and hardy men; rude, uneducated, brave, suffering terrific hardships with sailor-like stoicism; heavy drinkers, coarse frolickers in moral sties like the Natchez-under-the-hill of that day, heavy fighters, reckless fellows, every one, elephantinely jolly, foul-witted, profane; prodigal of their money, bankrupt at the end of the trip, fond of barbaric finery, prodigious braggarts; yet, in the main, honest, trustworthy, faithful to promises and duty, and often picturesquely magnanimous.

By and by the steamboat intruded. Then, for fifteen or twenty years, these men continued to run their keelboats down-stream, and the steamers did all of the up-stream business, the keelboatmen selling their boats in New Orleans, and returning home as deck passengers in the steamers.

But after a while the steamboats so increased in number and in speed that they were able to absorb the entire commerce; and then keelboating died a permanent death. The keelboatman became a deck hand, or a mate, or a pilot on the steamer; and when steamer-berths were not open to him, he took a berth on a Pittsburgh coal-flat, or on a pineraft constructed in the forests up toward the sources of the Mississippi.

In the heyday of the steamboating prosperity, the river from end to end was flaked with coal-fleets and timber rafts, all managed by hand, and employing hosts of the rough characters whom I have been trying to describe. I remember the animal processions of mighty rafts that used to glide by Hannibal when I was a boy,—an acre or so of white, sweet-smelling boards in each raft, a crew of two dozen men or more, three or four wigwams scattered about the raft's vast level space for storm-quarters,—and I remember the rude ways and the tremendous talk of their big crews, the ex-keelboatmen and their admiringly patterning successors; for we used to swim out a quarter or third of a mile and get on these rafts and have a ride.

By way of illustrating keelboat talk and manners, and that now-departed and hardly-remembered raft-life, I will throw in, in this place, a chapter from a book which I have been working at, by fits and starts, during the past five or six years, and may possibly finish in the course of five or six more. The book is a story which details some passages in the life of an ignorant village boy, Huck Finn, son of the town drunkard of my time out west, there. He has run away from his persecuting father, and from a persecuting good widow who wishes to make a nice, truth-telling, respectable boy of him; and with him a slave of the widow's has also escaped. They have found a fragment of a lumber raft (it is high water and dead summer time), and are floating down the river by night, and hiding in the willows by day,—bound for Cairo,—whence the negro will seek freedom in the heart of the free States. But in a fog, they pass Cairo without knowing it. By and by they begin to suspect the truth, and Huck Finn is persuaded to end the dismal suspense by swimming down to a huge raft which they have seen in the distance ahead of them, creeping aboard under cover of the darkness, and gathering the needed information by eavesdropping:—

But you know a young person can't wait very well when he is impatient to find a thing out. We talked it over, and by and by Jim said it was such a black night, now, that it wouldn't be no risk to swim down to the big raft and crawl aboard and listen,—they would talk about Cairo, because they would be calculating to go ashore there for a spree, maybe, or anyway they would send boats ashore to buy whiskey or fresh meat or something. Jim had a wonderful level head, for a nigger: he could most always start a good plan when you wanted one.

I stood up and shook my rags off and jumped into the river, and struck out for the raft's light. By and by, when I got down nearly to her, I eased up and went slow and cautious. But everything was all right—nobody at the sweeps. So I swum down along the raft till I was most abreast the camp fire in the middle, then I crawled aboard and inched along and got in amongst some bundles of shingles on the weather side of the fire. There was thirteen men there—they was the watch on deck of course. And a mighty rough-looking lot, too. They had a jug, and tin cups, and they kept the jug moving. One man was singing—roaring, you may say; and it wasn't a nice song—for a parlor anyway. He roared through his nose, and strung out the last word of every line very long. When he was done they all fetched a kind of Injun war-whoop, and then another was sung. It begun:—

> There was a woman in our towdn,
> In our towdn did dwed'l (dwell,)
> She loved her husband dear-i-lee,
> But another man twyste as wed'l.

> Singing too, riloo, riloo, riloo,
> Ri-too, riloo, rilay—-e,
> She loved her husband dear-i-lee,
> But another man twyste as wed'l.

And so on—fourteen verses. It was kind of poor, and when he was going to start on the next verse, one of them said it was the tune the old cow died on; and another one said, "Oh, give us a rest." And another one told him to take a walk. They made fun of him till he got mad and jumped up and began to cuss the crowd, and said he could lam any thief in the lot.

They was all about to make a break for him, but the biggest man there jumped up and says:—

"Set whar you are, gentlemen. Leave him to me; he's my meat."

Then he jumped up in the air three times and cracked his heels together every time. He flung off a buckskin coat that was all hung with fringes, and says, "You lay thar tell the chawin-up's done;" and flung his hat down, which was all over ribbons, and says, "You lay thar tell his sufferins is over."

Then he jumped up in the air and cracked his heels together again and shouted out:—

"Whoo-oop! I'm the old original iron-jawed, brass-mounted, copper-bellied corpse-maker from the wilds of Arkansaw!—Look at me! I'm the man they call Sudden Death and General Desolation! Sired by a hurricane, dam'd by an earthquake, half-brother to the cholera, nearly related to the small-pox on the mother's side! Look at me! I take nineteen alligators and a bar'l of whiskey for breakfast when I'm in robust health, and a bushel of rattlesnakes and a dead body when I'm ailing! I split the everlasting rocks with my glance, and I squench the thunder when I speak! Whoo-oop! Stand back and give me room according to my strength! Blood's my natural drink, and the wails of the dying is music to my ear! Cast your eye on me, gentlemen!—and lay low and hold your breath, for I'm bout to turn myself loose!"

All the time he was getting this off, he was shaking his head and looking fierce, and kind of swelling around in a little circle, tucking up his wrist-bands, and now and then straightening up and beating his breast with his fist, saying, "Look at me, gentlemen!" When he got through, he jumped up and cracked his heels together three times, and let off a roaring "whoo-oop! I'm the bloodiest son of a wildcat that lives!"

Then the man that had started the row tilted his old slouch hat down over his right eye; then he bent stooping forward, with his back sagged and his south end sticking out far, and his fists a-shoving out and drawing in in front of him, and so went around in a little circle about three times, swelling himself up and breathing hard. Then he straightened, and jumped up and cracked his heels together three times before he lit again (that made them cheer), and he begun to shout like this:—

"Whoo-oop! bow your neck and spread, for the kingdom of sorrow's a-coming! Hold me down to the earth, for I feel my powers a-working! whoo-oop! I'm a child of sin, *don't* let me get a start! Smoked glass here, for all! Don't attempt to look at me with the naked eye, gentlemen! When I'm playful I use the meridians of longitude and parallels of latitude for a seine, and drag the Atlantic Ocean for whales! I scratch my head with the lightning and purr myself to sleep with the thunder! When I'm cold, I bile the Gulf of Mexico and bathe in it; when I'm hot, I fan myself with an equinoctial storm; when I'm thirsty I reach up and suck a cloud dry like a sponge; when I range the earth hungry, famine follows in my tracks! Whoo-oop! Bow your neck and spread! I put my hand on the sun's face and make it night in the earth; I bite a piece out of the moon and hurry the seasons; I shake myself and crumble the mountains! Contemplate me through leather—*don't* use the naked eye! I'm the man with a petrified heart and biler-iron bowels! The massacre of isolated communities is the pastime of my idle moments, the destruction of nationalities the serious business of my life! The boundless vastness of the great American desert is my enclosed property, and I bury my dead on my own premises!" He jumped up and cracked his heels together three times before he lit (they cheered him again), and as he come down he shouted out: "Whoo-oop! bow your neck and spread, for the pet child of calamity's a-coming!"

Then the other one went to swelling around and blowing again—the first one—the one they called Bob; next, the Child of Calamity chipped in again, bigger than ever; then they both got at it at the same time, swelling round and round each other and punching their fists most into each other's faces, and whooping and jawing like Injuns; then Bob called the Child names, and the Child called him names back again: next, Bob called him a heap rougher names and the Child come back at him with the very worst kind of language; next, Bob knocked the Child's hat off, and the Child picked it up and kicked Bob's ribbony hat about six foot; Bob went and got it and said never mind, this warn't going to be the last of this thing, because he was a man that never forgot and never forgive, and so the Child better look out, for there was a time a-coming, just as sure as he was a living man, that he would have to answer to him with the best blood in his body. The Child said no man was willinger than he was for that time to come, and he would give Bob fair warning, *now,* never to cross his path again, for he could never rest till he had waded in his blood, for such was his nature, though he was sparing him now on account of his family, if he had one.

Both of them was edging away in different directions, growling and shaking their heads and going on about what they was going to do; but a little black-whiskered chap skipped up and says:—

"Come back here, you couple of chicken-livered cowards, and I'll thrash the two of ye!"

And he done it, too. He snatched them, he jerked them this way and that, he booted them around, he knocked them sprawling faster than they could get up. Why, it warn't two minutes till they begged like dogs—and how the other lot did yell and laugh and clap their hands all the way through, and shout "Sail in, Corpse-Maker!" "Hi! at him again, Child of Calamity!" "Bully for you, little Davy!" Well, it was a perfect pow-wow for a while. Bob and the Child had red noses and black eyes when they got through. Little Davy made them own up that they was sneaks and cowards and not fit to eat with a dog or drink with a nigger; then Bob and the Child shook hands with each other, very solemn, and said they had always respected each other and was willing to let bygones be bygones. So then they washed their faces in the river; and just then there was a loud order to stand by for a crossing, and some of them went forward to man the sweeps there, and the rest went aft to handle the after-sweeps.

I laid still and waited for fifteen minutes, and had a smoke out of a pipe that one of them left in reach; then the crossing was finished, and they stumped back and had a drink around and went to talking and singing again. Next they got out an old fiddle, and one played, and another patted juba, and the rest turned themselves loose on a regular old-fashioned keel-boat break-down. They couldn't keep that up very long without getting winded, so by and by they settled around the jug again.

They sung "jolly, jolly raftman's the life for me," with a rousing chorus, and then they got to talking about differences betwixt hogs, and their different kind of habits; and next about women and their different ways; and next about the best ways to put out houses that was afire; and next about what ought to be done with the Injuns; and next about what a king had to do, and how much he got; and next about how to make cats fight; and next about what to do when a man has fits; and next about differences betwixt clear-water rivers and muddy-water ones. The man they called Ed said the muddy Mississippi water was wholesomer to drink than the clear water of the Ohio; he said if you let a pint of this yaller Mississippi water settle, you would have about a half to three-quarters of an inch of mud in the bottom, according to the stage of the river, and then it warn't no better than Ohio water—what you wanted to do was to keep it stirred up—and when the river was low, keep mud on hand to put in and thicken the water up the way it ought to be.

The Child of Calamity said that was so; he said there was nutritiousness in the mud, and a man that drunk Mississippi water could grow corn in his stomach if he wanted to. He says:—

"You look at the graveyards; that tells the tale. Trees won't grow worth shucks in a Cincinnati graveyard, but in a Sent Louis graveyard they grow upwards of eight hundred foot high. It's all on account of the water the people drunk before they laid up. A Cincinnati corpse don't richen a soil any."

And they talked about how Ohio water didn't like to mix with Mississippi water. Ed said if you take the Mississippi on a rise when the Ohio is low, you'll find a wide band of clear water all the way down the east side of the Mississippi for a hundred mile or more, and the minute you get out a quarter of a mile from shore and pass the line, it is all thick and yaller the rest of the way across. Then they talked about how to keep tobacco from getting mouldy, and from that they went into ghosts and told about a lot that other folks had seen; but Ed says—

"Why don't you tell something that you've seen yourselves? Now let me have a say. Five years ago I was on a raft as big as this, and right along here it was a bright moonshiny night, and I was on watch and boss of the stabboard oar forrard, and one of my pards was a man named Dick Allbright, and he come along to where I was sitting, forrard—gaping and stretching, he was—and stooped down on the edge of the raft and washed his face in the river, and come and set down by me and got out his pipe, and had just got it filled, when he looks up and says—

"'Why looky-here,' he says, 'ain't that Buck Miller's place, over yander in the bend?'

"'Yes,' says I, 'it is—why?' He laid his pipe down and leant his head on his hand, and says,—

"'I thought we'd be furder down.' I says,—

"'I thought it too, when I went off watch'—we was standing six hours on and six off—'but the boys told me,' I says, 'that the raft didn't seem to hardly move, for the last hour,' says I, 'though she's a slipping along all right, now,' says I. He give a kind of a groan, and says,—

"'I've seed a raft act so before, along here,' he says, "'pears to me the current has most quit above the head of this bend durin' the last two years,' he says.

"Well, he raised up two or three times, and looked away off and around on the water. That started me at it, too. A body is always doing what he sees somebody else doing, though there mayn't be no sense in it. Pretty soon I see a black something floating on the water away off to stabboard and quartering behind us. I see he was looking at it, too. I says,—

"'What's that?' He says, sort of pettish,—

'Tain't nothing but an old empty bar'l.'

"'An empty bar'l!' says I, 'why,' says I, 'a spy-glass is a fool to *your* eyes. How can you tell it's an empty bar'l?' He says,—

"'I don't know; I reckon it ain't a bar'l, but I thought it might be,' says he.

"'Yes,' I says, 'so it might be, and it might be anything else, too; a body can't tell nothing about it, such a distance as that,' I says.

"We hadn't nothing else to do, so we kept on watching it. By and by I says,—

"'Why looky-here, Dick Allbright, that thing's a-gaining on us, I believe.'

"He never said nothing. The thing gained and gained, and I judged it must be a dog that was about tired out. Well, we swung down into the crossing, and the thing floated across the bright streak of the moonshine, and, by George, it *was* bar'l. Says I,—

"'Dick Allbright, what made you think that thing was a bar'l, when it was a half a mile off,' says I. Says he,—

"'I don't know.' Says I,—

"'You tell me, Dick Allbright.' He says,—

"'Well, I knowed it was a bar'l; I've seen it before; lots has seen it; they says it's a haunted bar'l.'

"I called the rest of the watch, and they come and stood there, and I told them what Dick said. It floated right along abreast, now, and didn't gain any more. It was about twenty foot off. Some was for having it aboard, but the rest didn't want to. Dick Allbright said rafts that had fooled with it had got bad luck by it. The captain of the watch said he didn't believe in it. He said he reckoned the bar'l gained on us because it was in a little better current than what we was. He said it would leave by and by.

"So then we went to talking about other things, and we had a song, and then a breakdown; and after that the captain of the watch called for another song; but it was clouding up, now, and the bar'l stuck right thar in the same place, and the song didn't seem to have much warm-up to it, somehow, and so they didn't finish it, and there warn't any cheers, but it sort of dropped flat, and nobody said anything for a minute. Then everybody tried to talk at once, and one chap got off a joke, but it warn't no use, they didn't laugh, and even the chap that made the joke didn't laugh at it, which ain't usual. We all just settled down glum, and watched the bar'l, and was oneasy and oncomfortable. Well, sir, it shut down black and still, and then the wind begin to moan around, and next the lightning begin to play and the thunder to grumble. And pretty soon there was a regular storm, and in the middle of it a man that was running aft stumbled and fell and sprained his ankle so that he had to lay up. This made the boys shake their heads. And every time the lightning come, there was that bar'l with the blue lights winking around it. We was always on the look-out for it. But by and by, towards dawn, she was gone. When the day come we couldn't see her anywhere, and we warn't sorry, neither.

"But next night about half-past nine, when there was songs and high jinks going on, here she comes again, and took her old roost on the stabboard side. There warn't no more high jinks. Everybody got solemn; nobody talked; you couldn't get anybody to do anything but set around moody and look at the bar'l. It begun to cloud up again. When the watch changed, the off watch stayed up, 'stead of turning in. The storm ripped and roared around all night, and in the middle of it another man tripped and sprained his ankle, and had to knock off. The bar'l left towards day, and nobody see it go.

"Everybody was sober and down in the mouth all day. I don't mean the kind of sober that comes of leaving liquor alone,—not that. They was quiet, but they all drunk more than usual,—not together,—but each man sidled off and took it private, by himself.

"After dark the off watch didn't turn in; nobody sung, nobody talked; the boys didn't scatter around, neither; they sort of huddled together, forrard; and for two hours they set there, perfectly still, looking steady in the one direction, and heaving a sigh once in a while. And then, here comes the bar'l again. She took up her old place. She staid there all night; nobody turned in. The storm come on again, after midnight. It got awful dark; the rain poured down; hail, too; the thunder boomed and roared and bellowed; the wind blowed a hurricane; and the lightning spread over everything in big sheets of glare, and showed the whole raft as plain as day; and the river lashed up white as milk as far as you could see for miles, and there was that bar'l jiggering along, same as ever. The captain ordered the watch to man the after sweeps for a crossing, and nobody would go,—no more sprained ankles for them, they said. They wouldn't even *walk* aft. Well then, just then the sky split wide open, with a crash, and the lightning killed two men of the after watch, and crippled two more. Crippled them how, says you? Why, *sprained their ankles!*

"The bar'l left in the dark betwixt lightnings, towards dawn. Well, not a body eat a bite at breakfast that morning. After that the men loafed around, in twos and threes, and talked low together. But none of them herded with Dick Allbright. They all give him the cold shake. If he come around where any of the men was, they split up and sidled away. They wouldn't man the sweeps with him. The captain had all the skiffs hauled up on the raft, alongside of his wigwam, and wouldn't let the dead men be took ashore to be planted; he didn't believe a man that got ashore would come back; and he was right.

"After night come, you could see pretty plain that there was going to be trouble if that bar'l come again; there was such a muttering going on. A good many wanted to kill Dick Allbright, because he'd seen the bar'l on other trips, and that had an ugly look. Some wanted to put him ashore. Some said, let's all go ashore in a pile, if the bar'l comes again.

"This kind of whispers was still going on, the men being bunched together forrard watching for the bar'l, when, lo and behold you, here she comes again. Down she comes, slow and steady, and settles into her old tracks. You could a heard a pin drop. Then up comes the captain, and says:—

"'Boys, don't be a pack of children and fools; I don't want this bar'l to be dogging us all the way to Orleans, and *you* don't; well, then, how's the best way to stop it? Burn it up,—that's the way. I'm going to fetch it aboard,' he says. And before anybody could say a word, in he went.

"He swum to it, and as he come pushing it to the raft, the men spread to one side. But the old man got it aboard and busted in the head, and there was a baby in it! Yes, sir, a stark naked baby. It was Dick Allbright's baby; he owned up and said so.

"'Yes,' he says, a-leaning over it, 'yes, it is my own lamented darling, my poor lost Charles William Allbright deceased,' says he,—for he could curl his tongue around the bulliest words in the language when he was a mind to, and lay them before you without a jint started, anywheres. Yes, he said he used to live up at the head of this bend, and one night he choked his child, which was crying, not intending to kill it,—which was prob'ly a lie,—and then he was scared, and buried it in a bar'l, before his wife got home, and off he went, and struck the northern trail and went to rafting; and this was the third year that the bar'l had chased him. He said the bad luck always begun light, and lasted till four men was killed, and then the bar'l didn't come any more after that. He said if the men would stand it one more night,—and was a-going on like that,—but the men had got enough. They started to get out a boat to take him ashore and lynch him, but he grabbed the little child all of a sudden and jumped overboard with it hugged up to his breast and shedding tears, and we never seen him again in this life, poor old suffering soul, nor Charles William neither."

"*Who* was shedding tears?" says Bob; "was it Allbright or the baby?"

"Why, Allbright, of course; didn't I tell you the baby was dead? Been dead three years—how could it cry?"

"Well, never mind how it could cry—how could it *keep* all that time?" says Davy. "You answer me that."

"I don't know how it done it," says Ed. "It done it though—that's all I know about it."

"Say—what did they do with the bar'l?" says the Child of Calamity.

"Why, they hove it overboard, and it sunk like a chunk of lead."

"Edward, did the child look like it was choked?" says one.

"Did it have its hair parted?" says another.

"What was the brand on that bar'l, Eddy?" says a fellow they called Bill.

"Have you got the papers for them statistics, Edmund?" says Jimmy.

"Say, Edwin, was you one of the men that was killed by the lightning?" says Davy.

"Him? O, no, he was both of 'em," says Bob. Then they all haw-hawed.

"Say, Edward, don't you reckon you'd better take a pill? You look bad—don't you feel pale?" says the Child of Calamity.

"O, come, now, Eddy," says Jimmy, "show up; you must a kept part of that bar'l to prove the thing by. Show us the bunghole—*do*—and we'll all believe you."

"Say, boys," says Bill, "less divide it up. Thar's thirteen of us. I can swaller a thirteenth of the yarn, if you can worry down the rest."

Ed got up mad and said they could all go to some place which he ripped out pretty savage, and then walked off aft cussing to himself, and they yelling and jeering at him, and roaring and laughing so you could hear them a mile.

"Boys, we'll split a watermelon on that," says the Child of Calamity; and he come rummaging around in the dark amongst the shingle bundles where I was, and put his hand on me. I was warm and soft and naked; so he says "Ouch!" and jumped back.

"Fetch a lantern or a chunk of fire here, boys—there's a snake here as big as a cow!"

So they run there with a lantern and crowded up and looked in on me.

"Come out of that, you beggar!" says one.

"Who are you?" says another.

"What are you after here? Speak up prompt, or overboard you go."

"Snake him out, boys. Snatch him out by the heels."

I began to beg, and crept out amongst them trembling. They looked me over, wondering, and the Child of Calamity says:—

"A cussed thief! Lend a hand and less heave him overboard!"

"No," says Big Bob, "less get out the paint-pot and paint him a sky blue all over from head to heel, and *then* heave him over!"

"Good! that's it. Go for the paint, Jimmy."

When the paint come, and Bob took the brush and was just going to begin, the others laughing and rubbing their hands, I begun to cry, and that sort of worked on Davy, and he says:—

"'Vast there! He's nothing but a cub. I'll paint the man that tetches him!"

So I looked around on them, and some of them grumbled and growled, and Bob put down the paint, and the others didn't take it up.

"Come here to the fire, and less see what you're up to here," says Davy. "Now set down there and give an account of yourself. How long have you been aboard here?"

"Not over a quarter of a minute, sir," says I.

"How did you get dry so quick?"

"I don't know, sir. I'm always that way, mostly."

"Oh, you are, are you? What's your name?"

I warn't going to tell my name. I didn't know what to say, so I just says:—

"Charles William Allbright, sir."

Then they roared—the whole crowd; and I was mighty glad I said that, because maybe laughing would get them in a better humor.

When they got done laughing, Davy says:—

"It won't hardly do, Charles William. You couldn't have growed this much in five year, and you was a baby when you come out of the bar'l, you know, and dead at that. Come, now, tell a straight story, and nobody'll hurt you, if you ain't up to anything wrong. What *is* your name?"

"Aleck Hopkins, sir. Aleck James Hopkins."

"Well, Aleck, where did you come from, here?"

"From a trading scow. She lays up the bend yonder. I was born on her. Pap has traded up and down here all his life; and he told me to swim off here, because when you went by he said he would like to get some of you to speak to a Mr. Jonas Turner, in Cairo, and tell him—"

"Oh, come!"

"Yes, sir; it's as true as the world; Pap he says—"

"Oh, your grandmother!"

They all laughed, and I tried again to talk, but they broke in on me and stopped me.

"Now, looky-here," says Davy; "you're scared, and so you talk wild. Honest, now, do you live in a scow, or is it a lie?"

"Yes, sir, in a trading scow. She lays up at the head of the bend. But I warn't born in her. It's our first trip."

"Now you're talking! What did you come aboard here, for? To steal?"

"No, sir, I didn't.—It was only to get a ride on the raft. All boys does that."

"Well, I know that. But what did you hide for?"

"Sometimes they drive the boys off."

"So they do. They might steal. Looky-here; if we let you off this time, will you keep out of these kind of scrapes hereafter?"

"'Deed I will, boss. You try me."

"All right, then. You ain't but little ways from shore. Overboard with you, and don't you make a fool of yourself another time this way.—Blast it, boy, some raftsmen would rawhide you till you were black and blue!"

I didn't wait to kiss good-bye, but went overboard and broke for shore. When Jim come along by and by, the big raft was away out of sight around the point. I swum out and got aboard, and was mighty glad to see home again.

David Crockett (1786-1836)

David Crockett was an example of the self-made man who rose to fame and popularity through his mother-wit and an ability to tell tales with effective comic exaggeration. Born in Greene County, Tennessee, in the midst of the westward frontier development, he denied himself formal education by being quarrelsome and restive and set off on his own, working at a number of odd jobs. Later he attended to his reading and writing, married, and settled down to farming and hunting, until he enlisted as a soldier in the Creek Indian War under Andrew Jackson. He returned home a hero with a reputation for courage and honesty and entered politics, where his humorous but level-headed speeches won him many supporters.

Crockett served twice in the Tennessee Legislature and was elected three times to the U. S. Congress. His popularity waned when he deserted the Jacksonian Democrats for the Whigs, and the Tennessee electorate rejected him in the 1835 congressional campaign. Crockett was reported to have said that the Tennessee voters could "all go to hell and I will go to Texas." Whether or not that is true, Crockett did indeed go to Texas to join the struggle for independence against Mexico. He died fighting at the Battle of the Alamo in March 1836.

His heroic death only added further to the number of myths and stories that had accrued around "Davy" Crockett during his lifetime. Along with Daniel Boone, he became the quintessential American frontiersman, known for his commonsense sayings and his superheroic struggles against the destructive forces of nature. While he himself was not given to written expression, a number of books and a series of almanacs appeared under his name describing his exploits. Nearly all were written by other hands, even though many of the events were based on things Crockett actually did or said.

The only book in which he actually participated was done in collaboration with Thomas Chilton, *A Narrative of the Life of David Crockett, of the State of Tennessee* in 1834. Because of their use of the native American vernacular, a focus on frontier life and society at the ground level, Crockett's tendency to exaggerate to mythic proportions, and his clever way with comic aphorisms and witty turns of phrase, the Crockett stories, both written and oral, contributed to the development of the conventions of the humor of the Old Southwest.

Texts: "Bear Hunting in Tennessee" from *A Narrative of the Life of David Crockett, of the State of Tennessee* (Philadelphia: Carey & Hart, 1834). "A Love Adventure and Uproarious Fight with a Stage Driver" from *Davy Crockett's Almanack* (Nashville, Tenn.: Published for the Author, 1836).

Bear Hunting in Tennessee

But the reader, I expect, would have no objection to know a little about my employment during the two years while my competitor was in Congress. In this space I had some pretty tuff times, and will relate some few things that happened to me. So here goes, as the boy said when he run by himself.

In the fall of 1825, I concluded I would build two large boats, and load them with pipe staves for market. So I went down to the lake, which was about twenty-five miles from where I lived, and hired some hands to assist me, and went to work; some at boat building, and others to getting staves. I worked on with my hands till the bears got fat, and then I turned out to hunting, to lay in a supply of meat. I soon killed and salted down as many as were necessary for my family; but about this time one of my old neighbours, who had settled down on the lake about twenty-five miles from me, came to my house and told me he wanted me to go down and kill some bears about in his parts. He said they were extremely fat, and very plenty. I know'd that when they were fat, they were easily taken, for a fat bear can't run fast or long. But I asked a bear no favours, no way, further than civility, for I now had *eight* large dogs, and as fierce as painters; so that a bear stood no chance at all to get away from them. So I went home with him, and then went on down towards the Mississippi, and commenced hunting.

We were out two weeks, and in that time killed fifteen bears. Having now supplied my friend with plenty of meat, I engaged occasionally again with my hands in our boat building, and getting staves. But I at length couldn't stand it any longer without another hunt. So I concluded to take my little son, and cross over the lake, and take a hunt there. We got over, and that evening turned out and killed three bears, in little or no time. The next morning we drove up four forks, and made a sort of scaffold, on which we salted up our meat, so as to have it out of the reach of the wolves, for as soon as we would leave our camp, they would take possession. We had just eat our breakfast, when a company of hunters came to our camp, who had fourteen dogs, but all so poor, that when they would bark they would almost have to lean up against a tree and take a rest. I told them their dogs couldn't run in smell of a bear, and they had better stay at my camp, and feed them on the bones I had cut out of my meat. I left them there, and cut out; but I hadn't gone far, when my dogs took a first-rate start after a very large fat old *he-bear,* which run right plump towards my camp. I pursued on, but my other hunters had heard my dogs coming, and met them, and killed the bear before I got up with him. I gave him to them, and cut out again for a creek called Big Clover, which wa'n't very far off. Just as I got there, and was entering a cane brake, my dogs all broke and went ahead, and, in a little time, they raised a fuss in the cane, and seemed to be going every way. I listened a while, and found my dogs was in two companies, and that both was in a snorting fight. I sent my little son to one, and I broke for t'other. I got to mine first, and found my dogs had a two-year-old bear down, a-wooling away on him; so I just took out my big butcher, and went up and slap'd it into him, and killed him without shooting. There was five of the dogs in my company. In a short time, I heard my little son fire at his bear; when I went to him he had killed it too. He had two dogs in his team. Just at this moment we heard my other dog barking a short distance off, and all the rest immediately broke to him. We pushed on too, and when we got there, we found he had still a larger bear than either of them we had killed, treed by himself. We killed that one also, which made three we had killed in less than half an hour. We turned in and butchered them, and then started to hunt for water, and a good place to camp. But we had no sooner started, than our dogs took a start after another one, and away they went like a thundergust, and was out of hearing in a minute. We followed the way they had gone for some time, but at length we gave up the hope of finding them, and turned back. As we were going back, I came to where a poor fellow was grubbing, and he looked like the very picture of hard times. I asked him what he was doing away there in the woods by himself? He said he was grubbing for a man who intended to settle there; and the reason why he did it was, that he had no meat for his family, and he was working for a little.

I was mighty sorry for the poor fellow, for it was not only a hard, but a very slow way to get meat for a hungry family; so I told him if he would go with me, I would give him more meat than he could get by grubbing in a month. I intended to supply him with meat, and also to get him to assist my little boy in packing in and salting up my bears. He had never seen a bear killed in his life. I told him I had six killed then, and my dogs were hard after another. He went off to his little cabin, which was a short distance in the brush, and his wife was very anxious he should go with me. So we started and went to where I had left my three bears, and made a camp. We then gathered my meat and salted, and scaffled it, as I had done the other. Night now came on, but no word from my dogs yet. I afterwards found they had treed the bear about five miles off, near to a man's house, and had barked at it the whole enduring night. Poor fellows! many a time they looked for me, and wondered why I didn't come, for they knowed there was no mistake in me, and I know they were as good as ever fluttered. In the morning, as soon as it was light enough to see, the man took his gun and went to them, and shot the bear, and killed it. My dogs, however, wouldn't have any thing to say to this stranger; so they left him, and came early in the morning back to me.

We got our breakfast, and cut out again; and we killed four large and very fat bears that day. We hunted out the week, and in that time we killed seventeen, all of them first-rate. When we closed our hunt, I gave the man over a thousand weight of fine fat bear-meat, which pleased him mightily, and made him feel as rich as a Jew. I saw him the next fall, and he told me he had plenty of meat to do him the whole year from his week's hunt. My son and me now went home. This was the week between Christmass and New-year that we made this hunt.

When I got home, one of my neighbours was out of meat, and wanted me to go back, and let him go with me, to take another hunt. I couldn't refuse; but I told him I was afraid the bear had taken to house by that time, for after they get very fat in the fall and early part of the winter, they go into their holes, in large hollow trees, or into hollow logs, or their cane-houses, or the harricanes; and lie there till spring, like frozen snakes. And one thing about this will seem mighty strange to many people. From about the first of January to about the last of April, these varments lie in their holes altogether. In all that time they have no food to eat; and yet when they come out, they are not an ounce lighter than when they went to house. I don't know the cause of this, and still I know it is a fact; and I leave it for others who have more learning than myself to account for it. They have not a particle of food with them, but they just lie and suck the bottom of their paw all the time. I have killed many of them in their trees, which enables me to speak positively on this subject. However, my neighbour, whose name was McDaniel, and my little son and me, went on down to the lake to my second camp, where I had killed my seventeen bears the week before, and turned out to hunting. But we hunted hard all day without getting a single start. We had carried but little provisions with us, and the next morning was entirely out of meat. I sent my son about three miles off, to the house of an old friend, to get some. The old gentleman was much pleased to hear I was hunting in those parts, for the year before the bears had killed a great many of his hogs. He was that day killing his bacon hogs, and so he gave my son some meat, and sent word to me that I must come in to his house that evening that he would have plenty of feed for my dogs, and some accommodations for ourselves; but before my son got back, we had gone out hunting, and in a large cane brake my dogs found a big bear in a cane-house, which he had fixed for his winter-quarters, as they sometimes do.

When my lead dog found him, and raised the yell, all the rest broke to him, but none of them entered his house until we got up. I encouraged my dogs, and they knowed me so well, that I could have made them seize the old serpent himself, with all his horns and heads, and cloven foot and ugliness into the bargain, if he would only have come to light, so that they could have seen him. They bulged in, and in an instant the bear followed them out, and I told my friend to shoot him, as he was mighty wrathy to kill a bear. He did so, and killed him prime. We carried him to our camp, by which time my son had returned; and after we got our dinners we packed up, and cut for the house of my old friend, whose name was Davidson.

We got there, and staid with him that night; and the next morning having salted up our meat, we left it with him, and started to take a hunt between the Obion lake and the Red-foot lake; as there had been a dreadful harricane, which passed between them, and I was sure there must be a heap of bears in the fallen timber. We had gone about five miles without seeing any sign at all; but at length we got on some high cany ridges, and, as we rode along, I saw a hole in a large black oak, and on examining it more closely, I discovered that a bear had clomb the tree. I could see his tracks going up, but none coming down, and so I was sure he was in there. A person who is acquainted with bear-hunting, can tell easy enough when the varment is in the hollow; for as they go up they don't slip a bit, but as they come down they make long scratches with their nails.

My friend was a little ahead of me, but I called him back, and told him there was a bear in that tree, and I must have him out. So we lit from our horses, and I found a small tree which I thought I could fall so as to lodge against my bear tree, and we fell to work chopping it with our tomahawks. I intended, when we lodged the tree against the other, to let my little son go up, and look into the hole, for he could climb like a squirrel. We had chop'd on a little time and stop'd to rest, when I heard my dogs barking mighty severe at some distance from us, and I told my friend I knowed they had a bear, for it is the nature of a dog, when he finds you are hunting bears, to hunt for nothing else; he becomes fond of the meat, and considers other game as "not worth a notice," as old Johnson said of the devil.

We concluded to leave our tree a bit, and went to my dogs, and when we got there, sure enough they had an eternal great big fat bear up a tree, just ready for shooting. My friend again petitioned me for liberty to shoot this one also. I had a little rather not, as the bear was so big, but I couldn't refuse; and so he blazed away, and down came the old fellow like some great log had fell. I now missed one of my dogs, the same that I before spoke of as having treed the bear by himself sometime before, when I had started the three in the cane brake. I told my friend that my missing dog had a bear somewhere, just as sure as fate; so I left them to butcher the one we had just killed, and I went up on a piece of high ground to listen for my dog. I heard him barking with all his might some distance off, and I pushed ahead for him. My other dogs hearing him broke to him, and when I got there, sure enough again he had another bear ready treed; if he hadn't, I wish I may be shot. I fired on him, and brought him down; and then went back, and help'd finish butchering the one at which I had left my friend. We then packed both to our tree where we had left my boy. By this time, the little fellow had cut the tree down that we intended to lodge, but it fell the wrong way; he had then feather'd in on the big tree, to cut that, and had found that it was nothing but a shell on the outside, and all dotted in the middle, as too many of our big men are in these days, having only an outside appearance. My friend and my son cut away on it, and I went off about a hundred yards with my dogs to keep them from running under the tree when it should fall. On looking back at the hole, I saw the bear's head out of it, looking down at them as they were cutting. I hollered to them to look up, and they did so; and McDaniel catched up his gun, but by this time the bear was out, and coming down the tree. He fired at it, and as soon as it touch'd ground the dogs were all round it, and they had a roll-and-tumble fight to the foot of the hill, where they stop'd him. I ran up, and putting my gun against the bear, fired and killed him. We now had three, and so we made our scaffold and salted them up.

In the morning I left my son at the camp, and we started on towards the harricane; and when we had went about a mile, we started a very large bear, but we got along mighty slow on account of the cracks in the earth occasioned by the earthquakes. We, however, made out to keep in hearing of the dogs for about three miles, and then we come to the harricane. Here we had to quit our horses, as old Nick himself couldn't have got through it without sneaking it along in the form that he put on, to make a fool of our old grandmother Eve. By this time several of my dogs had got tired and come back; but we went ahead on foot for some little time in the harricane, when we met a bear coming straight to us, and not more than twenty or thirty yards off. I started my tired dogs after him, and McDaniel pursued them, and I went on to where my other dogs were. I had seen the track of the bear they were after, and I knowed he was a screamer. I followed on to about the middle of the harricane; but my dogs pursued him so close, that they made him climb an old stump about twenty feet high. I got in shooting distance of him and fired, but I was all over in such a flutter from fatigue and running, that I couldn't hold steady; but, however, I broke his shoulder, and he fell. I run up and loaded my gun as quick as possible, and shot him again and killed him. When I went to take out my knife to butcher him, I found I had lost it in coming through the harricane. The vines and briers was so thick that I would sometimes have to get down and crawl like a varment to get through at all; and a vine had, as I supposed, caught in the handle and pulled it out. While I was standing and studying what to do, my friend came to me. He had followed my trail through the harricane, and had found my knife, which was mighty good news to me; as a hunter hates the worst in the world to lose a good dog, or any part of his hunting-tools. I now left McDaniel to butcher the bear, and I went after our horses, and brought them as near as the nature of the case would allow. I then took our bags, and went back to where he was; and when we had skin'd the bear, we fleeced off the fat and carried it to our horses in several loads. We then packed it up on our horses, and had a heavy pack of it on each one. We now started and went on till about sunset, when I concluded we must be near our camp; so I hollered and my son answered me, and we moved on in the direction to the camp. We had gone but a little way when I heard my dogs make a warm start again; and I jumped down from my horse and gave him up to my friend, and told him I would follow them. He went on to the camp, and I went ahead after my dogs with all my might for a considerable distance, till at last night came on. The woods were very rough and hilly, and all covered over with cane.

I now was compel'd to move on more slowly; and was frequently falling over logs, and into the cracks made by the earthquakes, so that I was very much afraid I would break my gun. However I went on about three miles, when I came to a good big creek, which I waded. It was very cold, and the creek was about knee-deep; but I felt no great inconvenience from it just then, as I was all over wet with sweat from running, and I felt hot enough. After I got over this creek and out of the cane, which was very thick on all our creeks, I listened for my dogs. I found they had either treed or brought the bear to a stop, as they continued barking in the same place. I pushed on as near in the direction to the noise as I could, till I found the hill was too steep for me to climb, and so I backed and went down the creek some distance till I came to a hollow, and then took up that, till I come to a place where I could climb up the hill. It was mighty dark, and was difficult to see my way or anything else. When I got up the hill, I found I had passed the dogs; and so I turned and went to them. I found, when I got there, they had treed the bear in a large forked poplar, and it was setting in the fork.

I could see the lump, but not plain enough to shoot with any certainty, as there was no moonlight; and so I set in to hunting for some dry brush to make me a light; but I could find none, though I could find that the ground was torn mightily to pieces by the cracks.

At last I thought I could shoot by guess, and kill him; so I pointed as near the lump as I could, and fired away. But the bear didn't come, he only clomb up higher, and got out on a limb, which helped me to see him better. I now loaded up again and fired, but this time he didn't move at all. I commenced loading for a third fire, but the first thing I knowed, the bear was down among my dogs, and they were fighting all around me. I had my big butcher in my belt, and I had a pair of dressed buckskin breeches on. So I took out my knife, and stood, determined, if he should get hold of me, to defend myself in the best way I could. I stood there for some time, and could now and then see a white dog I had, but the rest of them, and the bear, which were dark coloured, I couldn't see at all, it was so miserable dark. They still fought around me, and sometimes within three feet of me; but, at last, the bear got down into one of the cracks, that the earthquakes had made in the ground, about four feet deep, and I could tell the biting end of him by the hollering of my dogs. So I took my gun and pushed the muzzle of it about, till I thought I had it against the main part of his body, and fired; but it happened to be only the fleshy part of his foreleg. With this, he jumped out of the crack, and he and the dogs had another hard fight around me, as before. At last, however, they forced him back into the crack again, as he was when I had shot.

I had laid down my gun in the dark, and I now began to hunt for it; and, while hunting, I got hold of a pole, and I concluded I would punch him awhile with that. I did so, and when I would punch him, the dogs would jump in on him, when he would bite them badly, and they would jump out again. I concluded, as he would take punching so patiently, it might be that he would lie still enough for me to get down in the crack, and feel slowly along till I could find the right place to give him a dig with my butcher. So I got down, and my dogs got in before him and kept his head towards them, till I got along easily up to him; and placing my hand on his rump, felt for his shoulder, just behind which I intended to stick him. I made a lounge with my long knife, and fortunately stuck him right through the heart; at which he just sank down, and I crawled out in a hurry. In a little time my dogs all come out too, and seemed satisfied, which was the way they always had of telling me that they had finished him.

I suffered very much that night with cold, as my leather breeches, and every thing else I had on, was wet and frozen. But I managed to get my bear out of this crack after several hard trials, and so I butchered him, and laid down to try to sleep. But my fire was very bad, and I couldn't find any thing that would burn well to make it any better; and I concluded I should freeze, if I didn't warm myself in some way by exercise. So I got up, and hollered a while, and then I would just jump up and down with all my might, and throw myself into all sorts of motions. But all this wouldn't do; for my blood was now getting cold, and the chills coming all over me. I was so tired, too, that I could hardly walk; but I thought I would do the best I could to save my life, and then, if I died, nobody would be to blame. So I went to a tree about two feet through, and not a limb on it for thirty feet, and I would climb up it to the limbs, and then lock my arms together around it, and slide down to the bottom again. This would make the insides of my legs and arms feel mighty warm and good.

I continued this till daylight in the morning, and how often I clomb up my tree and slid down I don't know, but I reckon at least a hundred times.

In the morning I got my bear hung up so as to be safe, and then set out to hunt for my camp. I found it after a while, and McDaniel and my son were very much rejoiced to see me get back, for they were about to give me up for lost. We got our breakfasts, and then secured our meat by building a high scaffold, and covering it over. We had no fear of its spoiling, for the weather was so cold that it couldn't.

We now started after my other bear, which had caused me so much trouble and suffering; and before we got him, we got a start after another, and took him also. We went on to the creek I had crossed the night before and camped, and then went to where my bear was, that I had killed in the crack. When we examined the place, McDaniel said he wouldn't have gone into it, as I did, for all the bears in the woods.

We took the meat down to our camp and salted it, and also the last one we had killed; intending, in the morning, to make a hunt in the harricane again.

We prepared for resting that night, and I can assure the reader I was in need of it. We had laid down by our fire, and about ten o'clock there came a most terrible earthquake, which shook the earth so, that we were rocked about like we had been in a cradle. We were very much alarmed; for though we were accustomed to feel earthquakes, we were now right in the region which had been torn to pieces by them in 1812, and we thought it might take a notion and swallow us up, like the big fish did Jonah.

In the morning we packed up and moved to the harricane, where we made another camp, and turned out that evening and killed a very large bear, which made *eight* we had now killed in this hunt.

The next morning we entered the harricane again, and in little or no time my dogs were in full cry. We pursued them, and soon came to a thick cane-brake, in which they had stop'd their bear. We got up close to him, as the cane was so thick that we couldn't see more than a few feet. Here I made my friend hold the cane a little open with his gun till I shot the bear, which was a mighty large one. I killed him dead in his tracks. We got him out and butchered him, and in a little time started another and killed him, which now made *ten* we had killed; and we know'd we couldn't pack any more home, as we had only five horses along; therefore we returned to the camp and salted up all our meat, to be ready for a start homeward next morning.

The morning came, and we packed our horses with the meat, and had as much as they could possibly carry, and sure enough cut out for home. It was about thirty miles, and we reached home the second day. I had now accommodated my neighbour with meat enough to do him, and had killed in all, up to that time, fifty-eight bears, during the fall and winter.

As soon as the time come for them to quit their houses and come out again in the spring, I took a notion to hunt a little more, and in about one month I killed forty-seven more, which made one hundred and five bears I had killed in less than one year from that time.

A Love Adventure and Uproarious Fight with a Stage Driver

In the spring of '34 when I was going home from Congress I came the nearest being chawed up, that ever I did. After staying all night at Memphis, where I slept so *sound,* (i.e. made such a noise a snoring that the neighbors couldn't sleep for some distance from the hotel). From fatigue I was so drowsy they were obliged to open my eyes with a pickaxe. Well arter breakfast I started in the stage alone with the driver. At the distance of two or three miles from the house, at a point where the road was covered with stumps of trees, he drew up, and tying the reins up at the front window, he said to me, "look to the reins till I come back." He was obliged to go a little way to give out some sowing he said. Before I could say a word he was out of sight behind the trees. He kept me holding on to the reins for nearly half an hour, when I began to smell a rat, and was just on the point of getting out to go arter him, when he made his appearance from behind the trees. After he got on his box, I began to blow him up for staying so long. Says he, "the fact is I have a girl a little ways off; I always stop when I pass and make some of the passengers hold the horses. I have built a house and got a negro wench to wait on her." Thinks I what would the Post Master General say if he knew that the great Southern Mail was stopped half an hour every day or two to let a stage driver see his doxy. But says I to myself, Crockett keep dark and squat low. So on our arrival at the next hotel, instead of going on with him, I pretended I should stop till arternoon and take the stage to Natchez and go down the Mississippi. But no sooner had the driver started than I cut out for the gal's house in the woods. I quickly got into her good graces, as she was "nothing loth," as the poets say. I kept her company for two days, when as we were up in the loft of the house which had a ladder and trap door to get to it, all at once, whose voice should I hear but the stage driver's below, inquiring for his doxy. Zounds! here was a pretty predikyment. I must either play possum by jumping out of the window and running off, or jump down and fight. I found I must do the latter, as the window was so small I culdn't get out of it. As quick as the critter saw me, he flew into such a rage that he crooked up his neck and neighed like a stud horse, and dared me down. Says I, stranger! I'm the boy that can double up a dozen of you. I'm a whole team just from the roaring river.—I've rode through a crab apple orchard on a streak of lightning. I've squatted lower than a toad; and jumped higher than a maple tree; I'm all brimstone but my head, and that's aquafortis. At this he fell a cursing and stamping, and vowed he'd make a gridiron of my ribs to roast my heart on. I kicked the trap door aside, and got sight at the varmint; he was madder than a buffalo, and swore he'd set the house on fire. Says I take care how I lite on you; upon that I jumped right down upon the driver, and he tore my trowsers right off of me. I got hold of his whiskers and gave them such a twitch that his eyes stuck out like a lobster's. He fetched me a kick in the bowels that knocked all compassion out of them. I was driv almost distracted, and should have been used up, but luckily there was a poker in the fire which I thrust down his throat, and by that means mastered him. Says he, stranger you are the yellow flower of the forest. If ever you are up for Congress again, I'll come all the way to Duck river to vote for you. Upon this I bade them good morning, and proceeded on my journey. This adventure I never told to Mrs. Crockett.

"Riproarious Shemales"
Legendary Women of the Crockett Almanacs

The designation "riproarious shemales," coined by Davy Crockett scholar Michael A. Lofaro, refers to frontier women who performed phenomenal feats and who were featured in some of the anonymous tall tales published in the Crockett Almanacs between 1835 and 1856. These "half-horse, half-alligator" kind of women actually reflect characteristics of their male frontier counterparts in that they enjoy the freedom of men and exhibit the strength, independent spirit, courage, and self-confidence of males. These legendary frontier women, who acted out essentially a masculine script in accordance with the demands and necessities of frontier life, were the antithesis of the so-called sentimental woman associated with the nineteenth-century "cult of true womanhood," a figure revered for her passivity and submissiveness, helplessness, humility, emotionality, physical weakness—prevalent characteristics of women characters often featured in women's magazines and novels, gift annuals, and religious literature.

The Crockett Almanacs contain fifty-eight stories portraying variations of the "riproarious shemale" type. Characters like Katy Goodgrit, Florida Fury, the Mississippi Screamer Sal Fink, Sally Ann Whirlwind Crockett (Davy's wife), Lottie Ritchers, Nance Bowers, and Sal Fungus, who, though ironically created by male raconteurs, are empowered women, women who perform extraordinary feats, and thereby transcend the restrictive domain of the nineteenth-century ideal of womanhood. These are active women who work outdoors and show some of the same talents and capabilities associated with frontier men. They also know how to fight and hunt and how to use the skills necessary for survival in a wilderness society. Among these larger-than-life "shemales" are Nance Bowers, who "war seven feet tall out of her stockins . . . could wipe her feet with her hair . . . [and] swing on the top of a fifty foot hickory tree"; Judy Coon who let her toenails grow to an inch in length and went to a nest of wild cats and stomped them to death with her feet; Sal Fink who "fought a duel once with a thunderbolt all to flinders, an' gave the pieces to Uncle Sam's artillerymen, to touch off their cannon with"; Sal Fungus who could "laugh the bark off a tree . . . , dance a rock to pieces . . . [and] sing a wolf to sleep"; and Lottie Ritchers, "the flower of Gum Swamp" who "chased a crocodile one evening till his hide cum off . . . [and] carried twenty eyes in her work bag, at one time, that she had picked out of the heads of certain gals of her acquaintance," making them into a string of beads that she wore when she went to church.

While these mythic "shemales" are women with expanded roles, incredible strength, woodsman skills, and assertiveness—in many respects nearly the equal of the legendary frontiersmen—and while the anecdotes about them are among the earliest renderings of tall tales about women in American literature, the characters are never given voice to recount their own adventures in the first person. Nor do their attributes equal or exceed those of the mythic Davy Crockett, also featured in numerous tales in the Crockett Almanacs. Rather, the exploits of the "shemales" are narrated by anonymous male authors of these sketches who usually assume the persona and voice of Davy Crockett and who typically portray these female adventurers incongruously as being like men. Even so, these spectacular "riproarious shemales" do enlarge the boundaries of women's roles, and taken collectively the Crockett Almanac tales that feature them show a new dimension in the portrayal of women in antebellum southern humor, a perspective that challenges the gender politics of a patriarchal society, albeit humorously.

Texts: "Sal Fink, the Mississippi Screamer How She Cooked Injuns," *Crockett Almanac, 1854* (Philadelphia: Fisher and Brother, 1854). "Katy Goodgrit," *Ben Hardin's Crockett Almanac, 1842* (New York: Turner and Fisher, 1842). "One of Crockett's Infant Children Grinning Lightning at a Bear," *Crockett Almanac, 1845.* (Boston: James Fisher 1845). "The Flower of Gum Swamp," *Crockett Almanac, 1841* (Boston: James Fisher, 1841).

Sal Fink, the Mississippi Screamer, How She Cooked Injuns

I dar say you've all of you, if not more, frequently heerd this great she human crittur boasted of, an' pointed out as "*one o' the gals*"—but I tell you what, stranger, you have never really set your eyes on "*one of the gals*," till you have seen Sal Fink, the Mississippi screamer, whose miniature pictur I here give, about as nat'ral as life, but not half as handsome—an' if thar ever was a gal that desarved to be christened "*one o' the gals*," then this gal was that gal—and no mistake.

She fought a duel once with a thunderbolt, an' came off without a singe, while at the fust fire she split the thunderbolt all to flinders, an' gave the pieces to Uncle Sam's artillerymen, to touch off their cannon with. When a gal about six years old, she used to play see-saw on the Mississippi snags, and arter she war done she would snap 'em off, an' so cleared a large district of the river. She used to ride down the river on an alligator's back, standen upright, an' dancing *Yankee Doodle,* and could leave all the steamers behind. But the greatest feat she ever did, positively outdid anything that ever was did.

One day when she war out in the forest, making a collection o' wild cat skins for her family's winter beddin, she war captered in the most all-sneaken manner by about fifty Injuns, an' carried by 'em to Roast Flesh Hollow, whar the blood drinkin wild varmints detarmined to skin her alive, sprinkle a leetle salt over her, an' devour her before her own eyes; so they took an' tied her to a tree, to keep till mornin' should bring the rest o' thar ring-nosed sarpints to enjoy the fun. Arter that, they lit a large fire in the Holler, turned the bottom o' thar feet towards the blaze, Injun fashion, and went to sleep to dream o' thar mornin's feast; well, after the critturs got into a somniferous snore, Sal got into an all-lightnin' of a temper, and burst all the ropes about her like an apron string! She then found a pile o' ropes, took and tied all the Injuns' heels together all round the fire,—then fixin a cord to the shins of every two couple, she, with a suddenachous jerk, that made the intire woods tremble, pulled the intire lot o' sleepin' red-skins into that ar great fire, fast together, yellin, howlin, scramblin and singin,' that war ever seen or heerd on, since the great burnin' o' Buffalo prairie!

Katy Goodgrit

Katy Goodgrit war a favorite of mine, bekase when her spunk war up, she could grin a wild cat out of countenance, and make a streak of lightning back out. She didn't care for anything that went on four legs, nor anything that went on two legs. One day she war going out into the woods, and seed two wolves shying along like a snake in the grass, not a grate ways off; and she intarmined to put a stop to 'em, for they looked very obnoxious, and seemed to want to be tasting sumthing of the human kind. So she took up a club, and walked in between 'em. They begun to feel amazing skitish when they seed her coming with the club, but at last they come towards her.—She gave one of 'em a monstracious tap on the head with her club, and he squawked rite out. Before she had time to hit the other, she heered a pattering amongst the leaves, and when she lookt around, thar war about fifty wolves cuming towards her on the full trot. Sum gals wood hav ben skeered out of thar seven wits, but Katy always knowed it war the fust duty of a gal of Kaintuck to stand up to her lick log, salt or no salt. So she just squatted low for the present, and got up into a holler stump whar the wolves couldn't quite reach her, and they cum roaring around her, like the water boiling around Crocodile Rock, at Tumble Down Falls. They jumpt up evenmost to her face, and she spit at one so violent that it nocked his eye out. She cotch anuther by the scurf of his neck, and whipt his hed off agin the tree. So she kept stopping their wind, till the fust she knew thar war a pile of dead wolves around the tree, high enuff for the others to climb up on. Then she war obleeged to squat down, or they wood hav tore her hed off. She staid thar all nite; but early the nixt morning, she stuck up her head, and crowed, till she crowed and screamed all the wolves deff, and then they begun to cleer out, but she went arter 'em with a pole and killed haff of 'em before they got away.

One of Crockett's Infant Children, Grinning Lightning at a Bear

I always had the praise o' raisin the tallest and fattest, and sassyest gals in all America. They can out run, out jump, out fight, and out scream any critter in creation; an for scratchin, thar's not a hungry painter, or a patent horserake can hold a claw to 'em. The oldest one growed so etarnally tall that her head had got nearly out o'sight, when she got into an all storm fight with a thunder storm, that stunted her growth, and now I am afraid that she'll never reach her natural size; but still, it takes a hull winter's weavin to make her walkin and bed clothes; and when she goes to bed, she's so tarnal long, and sleeps so sound, that we can only waken her by degrees, and that's by choppen fire wood on her shins; but the youngest one o' them takes arter me, and is of the regular airthquake nater. Her body's flint rock, her soul's lightnin, and her fist is a thunderbolt, an her teeth can out cut any steam mill saw in creation. She is a perfect infant prodigy, being only six years old; she has the biggest foot and widest mouth in all the west, and when she grins, she is splendifferous; she shows most beautiful intarnals, an can scare a flock o' wolves to total terrifications. Well, one day, this sweet little infant was walking in the woods, and amusin herself by picking up walnuts, and cracking them with her front grindstones, when suddenaciously she stumbled over a thunderin great hungry he bar. The critter seein her fine red shoulders bare, showin an inviting feast, sprung at her as if determined to feast upon Crockett meat, he gin her a savaggerous hug, and was jist about bitin a regular buss out on her cheek, when the child resentin her insulted wartue, gin him a kick with her south fist, in his digestion, that made him buss the arth instanterly, and jist as he war a comin to her a second time, the little gal grinned sich a double streak o' blue lightnin into his mouth, that it cooked the critter to death as quick as think, an she brought him home for dinner. She'll be a thunderin fine gal when she gets her natural growth, if her stock o' Crockett lightnin don't burst her biler, and blow her up.

The Flower of Gum Swamp

The flower of Gum Swamp, war a gal by the name of Lotty Ritchers. She stood six foot in her shoes; but as she hadn't 'em on very often, she war not quite so high. She used to brag that she war a streak of litenin set up edgeways, and buttered with quicksilver. She chased a crockodile one evening till his hide cum off, and one day I met her in the forrest jist as she had killed a monstracious big bare; I seed it war too much for her great strength, so we laid holt together, she took the tail, and I the head part, and for this she treeted me to a slice of genuine steak. She still wears the shift that she made out of the varmint's skin. It is told on her that she carried twenty eyes in her work bag, at one time, that she had picked out of the heads of certain gals on her acquaintance. She always made them into a string of beads, when she went to church, and wore 'em round her neck. She never pared her nales, and had holes cut in her shoes, so that her toe nales could have room to grow. She war a real beauty; but the young fellers war shy of her, bekase she never cood kort long befour she wanted to box with her bo, and her thumb nale war grate for pullin out eyes. Finely she cort her death by standing two days up to her chin in the Massissippy to hale the steem botes as they past by.

Joseph Gault (1794-1879)

Joseph Gault is an unfamiliar name in the genre of Old Southwest humor, having published locally in Marietta, Georgia, only one book containing humorous material of the frontier variety, *Reports of Decisions in the Justice's Courts in the State of Georgia, from the Year of Our Lord 1820 to 1846*, a collection that its loftysounding title suggests is a compilation of serious accounts of cases in the justices of the peace court system in Georgia. The title is deceiving, for Gault's *Reports*, comprising thirty-seven sketches, is a burlesque, a valuable and amusing reservoir of sometimes lively, bizarre, and entertaining renderings of the proceedings that transpired in the justice-of-the-peace courts system with which Gault was associated and of various other anecdotes he witnessed or heard. Another clue to the humorously satiric focus of Gault's *Reports* may be found in the front matter. In the dedicatory preface to the 1846 edition to his fellow justice of the peace James McGee of Murray County, Georgia, Gault affects a tone of ironic mockery, indicating that his book contains a "large body of the most interesting and best authenticated cases tried in the Justice's Courts.... I consider them as being the last elegant *hifalluten* touch to the Judiciary system of our State." And in the preface, he notes that Georgia has no record of the cases tried in justices' courts, and in publishing his book, he hopes to fill this void. Along with his reports, Gault points out, half facetiously, "I have mingled some characteristic anecdotes, in order to relieve the tedium of legal detail and judicial narrative—interpolating the abstruse learning of the Justices' Courts with brilliant specimens of professional literature; and blending the hilarity of the convivial board with the soberness of the law."

Unlike many other antebellum humorists who published book-length collections of their sketches and tales, Gault did not initially publish any of his humorous anecdotes about the lower court system in newspapers. Nor were any reports of anecdotes reprinted in Porter's *Spirit of the Times*. Yet Gault's *Reports* went through four editions in his lifetime, and two other editions were published after his death, an indication that his book seemed to have some popular appeal.

Facts about Gault's life are few. He was born in the Union District of South Carolina on May 14, 1794. Before he married and moved to Georgia, he had been a teacher briefly in the Packolet River section of South Carolina. Shortly after Cobb County was established from former Indian territory in 1833, Gault started a law practice and in 1836 established a justice of the peace court in the county. Gault, in fact, became a justice of the peace himself and served in that capacity until 1860. Interestingly, Gault also achieved acclaim as a runner and often competed in foot races, both in South Carolina and Georgia.

Largely forgotten, some of Gault's *Reports* were published in *Studies in American Humor* and the *Mississippi Quarterly* in 1986 and 1998, respectively, by Stephen Meats; but before Meats's recovery work, there were few appraisals of Gault or of his *Reports*. Writing in 1935, Sarah Temple noted that Gault's *Reports* "reveal not only the personality of the author, but a picture of his times in which he lived. . . . He damned where damning was due; he praised where he deemed praise merited. That he escaped the penalties of the law of libel, or in earlier days a bullet from the gun of one of the individuals whom he did not hesitate to call by name, must be considered a tribute to his powers and the truth of the cases which he recited." Gault was an accomplished raconteur, and the significance of *Reports of Decisions in the Justice's Courts* ultimately lies, according to Stephen Meats, in his "portraits of backwoods attorneys and justices of the peace [that] are entertaining and have an authentic ring to them. His accounts of the rough-and-tumble chaos of the justices' courts are both funny and horrifying."

Texts: *Reports of Decisions in Justice's Courts, in the State of Georgia, from the Year of Our Lord 1820–1846* (Marietta, GA, 1846). "The Drunkard's Resurrection in His Mourning Shroud," *Joseph Gault's Fifth Edition of His Reports: Entitled A Coat of Many Arms* (Americus, GA, 1902).

A Constable Selling 'Coon Skins

This was a sale that took place shortly after the settling of Hall county. The Court house, which was a rail penn about seven feet high, covered with pine bark, and a slip-gap for the door, was situated in the woods, near Nancy's Cane Brake. Shortly after I arrived there, the constable came, and brought with him about fifty 'coon skins. I asked him what he intended to do with so many 'coon skins, and he told me that he was going to sell them by virtue of a fi. fa., but he feared they would not satisfy the debt. I asked him what was the amount of debt and cost; he said about three dollars. While we were conversing, an old lady walked up, with a basket in her hand, containing some dozen ginger cakes—and an old man, with a jug full of whiskey tied to the end of a stick and slung over his shoulder, and a pint goard and tin cup in one hand. The

Justice bought one goard full and the constable another, and they both drank as though they had a peculiar liking for it. After they had done drinking, the Justice ordered the constable to open Court, which he accordingly done. Court being now open, the Justice told the constable to sell the 'coon skins. The constable obeyed the order, and opened the sale instantly, by crying out: Oh, yes! oh, yes! oh, yes! all persons wishing to buy 'coon skins are requested to come forward and give a bid for them—and holding up a skin, he asked: How much for this one, and take fifty of them? One cent, said the Justice. Two cents, bid the constable. The Justice, finding the constable bidding against him, called to him and made the arrangement, that he would bid off the skins at three cents and divide them, and after Court adjourned, they would play the game of three-up to see which should have all. It was agreed upon, and the skins were knocked off to the Justice at three cents each. Now, said the Justice, adjourn Court, which was done. After adjourning Court, the constable walked up to the Justice and said: Let us divide them 'coon skins,—at the same time, pulling from his pocket an old deck of cards that had been in use, from all appearance, in a still-house for several years. They sat down and played the first game for a pint of whiskey, but some dispute arising about the game, they agreed to buy the whiskey between them, each paying half, and play for the 'coon skins. They bought a pint and set it between them on the board; the constable put up one 'coon skin as a stake, and said to the Justice: Damn you, if you have a mind to act the white man, stake up,—so the Justice covered his with another skin. They cut for deal, and the Justice won it, dealt the cards, and hearts came trumps; the constable begged, on the duce of trumps, the ace of clubs and a spade, and the Justice gave him one of the jack of trumps, the five of clubs and the six of diamonds; the constable led his heart, the Justice took it with his jack, and led his club, the constable took it with his ace, and swore he was out. Out, h—l, said the Justice; how come you out? Low, beg and the game! exclaimed the constable. It being late in the evening, I left them, still quarreling; but understood afterwards that they played all night by lightwood torches, and the constable won all the Justice's 'coon skins before breakfast next morning, the Sabbath.

A Justice Commanding the Peace

This was a case tried in Gwinnette county, in the year eighteen hundred and twenty before a Justice of the Peace. On the trial before the Justice, it appeared, by evidence, that Defendant B's. wife was sick a bed, and sent to the Plaintiff A's. wife for one pound of butter and a half grown chicken. A's wife sent the butter and chicken to B's wife according to her request; and in a short time thereafter, A's. wife sent a pair of shoes to B. and requested him to find leather and half sole her shoes, which B. accordingly done. And in a short time thereafter A. and B. had a difficulty, and A went to D. and C. Justices holding jurisdiction in said county, and prayed process against B. for the pound of butter and chicken at the price of 18 ¾ cents, which the Justices issued in accordance to the prayer of A.; and at the docket term of said case, the defendant B. answered the charge and pleaded a set-off and a larger debt, and prayed of the Court judgment for the balance due him. B's account against A. was 20 cents, for finding leather and half soleing A's. wife's shoes, and prayed judgment for 1 ¼ cents.

At the trial term of said case, the plaintiff A. proved his account by his own oath in due form of law, and closed. The defendant B. then proved his account by his own oath, and he closed for defendant. The plaintiff, A. then spoke to B. in Court, and swore that defendant B. was a damned rascal and a perjured villain. The defendant B. swore that A. was damn'd liar and a cow thief.

Justice D., in support of his office, and in the mildness of a Justice of the Peace, arose from his seat and exclaimed, I command the peace, God damn you both. The parties not obeying the judicial command of the Court, the Justice arose a second time and exclaimed, God damn you if I cannot keep the peace one way I will try another, and, drawing back his fist, struck the plaintiff on his left cheek bone and broke the skin. Down came the plaintiff on the floor—the Justice gave him several kicks on his head and side, and then said, damn you, I expect that next time you are commanded to keep the peace, you will do so! He then turned to the defendant, and said, damn you, I will give you a little, too. He then took the defendant by the throat and choked him until his eyes began to dance like a billiard ball, and his tongue ran out of his mouth at least four inches—and down came defendant on the floor. The Justice gave defendant a few kicks and then cried out, now, God damn you, I reckon you will hereafter learn how to behave yourself before the Judiciary, and learn to tell the truth, you damn'd rascal. He then took his seat and said to S.—I have made up my judgment—I believe them both to be damned rascals, and there is only 1 ¼ cents difference in their accounts, and I will give judgment against each of them for the cost, and add in a dollar in each judgment for my time and trouble for whipping the damn'd rascals—and accordingly done so. The memory was made in a fi. fa. at next term of the said court, and no appeal.

The Drunkard's Resurrection in His Morning Shroud

Recently, there was a young man, who resided near Marietta, by the name of B. He was a very industrious young man, but would at times indulge in drinking spirits to an excess. A few months since, he, as usual, takes an over-charge, and intending to go to Atlanta, he took the cars and directly found himself at Alatoona Station, sixteen miles on the other end of the road; and finding that he had not money enough to pay his fare until morning and freight back, he puts off a foot to Marietta. Late in the evening, with only 25 cents, he arrived in Marietta. About one hour before day-break he went to his brother's who lived near town, fatigued and hungry. Not wishing to interrupt the repose of his brother's family, he went into the kitchen, and, to his gratification found a large dish of Snap Beans and Bacon, and Bread and Buttermilk. He set in to satisfy his appetite, and did so by day light. When the family arose he told them what he had done. By being drunk that night, sleeping none, and eating a hearty supper, he found himself pretty sick early in the morning; he then struck for Marietta to get his morning bitters, and arrived there just as the grocery keepers opened. He went in and in a few minutes he drunk a pint of stump water wine, and in a very short time thereafter, he swallowed down a half pint of rat-tail whiskey, and then started for home to take a day's sleep. He had not got a half mile from town when he became so sick that he could not travel, and slipped into a thicket on the road side and lay down. At that time there was a man who resided in Lick Skillet, by the name of W. of the Methodist order, who was a firm and sturdy believer in a brimstone hell, and dealt largely in the article of brimstone, according to his means. On that morning I rode up to W.'s and saw a little boy, some eight or ten years old, running towards the house, his eyes rolling in his head, which appeared to be as large as billiard balls. W. ran to him exclaiming, what is the matter? what is the matter?—Why, said the boy, as I came from town I heard the birds making a fuss in the thicket back yonder, and I went out into it to find the nest, and had like to have stepped on a dead man. Is he dead? said W. Yes he is, for his head was in a heap of blood, and his brains are beat out and lying at his mouth, and the birds were eating them.

    I went on with W. and his son to the slaughter ground, and there lay B. He was a very red headed man, and had thrown up his late supper, stump water, and rat-tail, which made a pile as large as a quart bowl, and the jay birds, woodpeckers and old thrashers, were eating, fighting and frolicking over their early breakfast, derived from a late supper. Said W. here lies Alcohol; and laying his hand on B. said, arise Alcohol, you are not dead and are not ready to be buried yet, for you have no shroud but jay birds and wood-peckers.—[W. was a man wide between his knees, and his toes on each foot pointed to each other, and he had a very sharp nose; and if his face or head had been turned half way round he would have been remarkably full breasted.] B. arose, made a blow at W., but missed him, W. broke through the thicket. B. exclaimed, clear yourself from here you pigeon-toed bowlegged, brissel nosed, tarapan-backed hypocrit, or I will shroud you with a convoy of buzzards. W. got out of the thicket and said to me, before I would ever try to wake him again I would see him dead; yes, and let him lie until Gabriel's horn toots him up; yes sir'ee Bob, that I would.

James Edward Henry (1796-1850)

Born in Providence, Rhode Island, Henry migrated to Spartanburg, South Carolina, in 1816, taught school for several years, while at the same time he studied law, and in 1821 was admitted to the South Carolina Bar. A civic-minded person, Henry served on the first town council of Spartanburg in 1832, and became the first solicitor in 1838. He was also instrumental in founding a female academy in Spartanburg. A member of the Union Party, an opponent to the tariff and to nullification, and a proslavery advocate, Henry was elected to the South Carolina Legislature, first in 1828, and was reelected in 1832, 1840, 1846, and 1848. He was also selected an aid to Major General John Belton O'Neall, who appointed him to the rank of major.

Though a busy civil servant and lawyer, Henry, usually referred to as Major Henry by his friends and associates, pursued literary interests as well, his most important writing being in the genre of antebellum southern humor. He published sketches, anonymously and pseudonymously, in the *Southern Ladies' Book,* the *Magnolia,* Charleston *Southern Literary Journal,* Macon, Georgia, *Family Companion and Ladies Mirror,* and *The Orion* in the 1830s and 1840s. His works treat familiar subject areas of Old Southwest humor—courtship and marriage, intemperance, the clash of social classes, courtroom jests, practical jokes, and rascally misadventures. Henry himself had a serious drinking problem, and two of his *Magnolia* sketches—"Tetotality" and "The Jimplicate"—humorously treat this subject. These sketches and several other of his humorous pieces comprise the "Tales of the Packolette" series published in the *Magnolia* between December 1840 and December 1842. Henry also published a novelette, *Myra Cunningham: A Tale of 1780,* written between 1821 and 1825, and focusing on the Revolutionary War in upcountry South Carolina.

Henry has the notorious distinction of having been victimized intertextually by William Gilmore Simms in his posthumous backwoods tale "Bald-Head Bill Bauldy," when he has his frame narrator Big Lie berate a Major Henry as an inferior yarn-spinner compared to the more free-wheeling and entertaining hunter-raconteur Bill Baudy. And Big Lie's biographical details make clear that the object of his derision is none other than the real-life Henry.

Henry's first and most accomplished comic sketch, "My Man Dick," features a slave and body servant who is given extensive voice and space to mock, albeit innocuously, his master and thereby to gain centrality as a character and storyteller. Published in 1837 in the Charleston *Southern Literary Journal*, "My Man Dick" may be the earliest southwestern humor text to feature an African American slave given the liberty to derail comically the hierarchies of race and class.

While not in the first tier of the Old South's humorists, Major Henry was fondly remembered by some of his contemporaries, one of whom, former South Carolina governor Benjamin Franklin Perry, lauded him as "always in good spirits, full of wit and humor . . . , fond of a joke, told an anecdote well, and always most happy at repartee."

Text: Charleston *Southern Literary Journal and Monthly Magazine* 3 (February 1837).

My Man Dick

From the Unpublished "Tales of the Packolette."

That last glass was the thing. It had loosened my tongue, and I shall no further hesitate to comply with the requisition of our Commander-in-Chief. Let me think—what shall it be? Your examples so far are all auto-biographical, and I opine I must follow the lead. If I can make something out of nothing—well; if not, you will loose your time and I my trouble servant, so here goes for a sketch of the auto-biography of your humble servant, Tolliver Grinaway, junior, or, of his man Dick, which ever you may be disposed to christen my story.

My man Dick and I, were born on the same day and in the same hour, and our fortunes have been so intimately blended ever since, that I shall find it difficult to speak of myself without bringing in his name.

You see the copper-coloured rascal how he stands showing his ivory at me, which I take to be a base insinuation on his part that I am already, pretty much, how come ye so. It is false. Open that other bottle, Dick—this talking makes one thirsty—and have done, I enjoin you, with *looking* your slanders.

As I was saying, Dick, who was the fruit of a liaison between the overseer and head nurse, was born in the same hour with myself, and so remarkable did my worthy father consider the coincidence, that at three years of age he formally transferred Dick in fee, as the right and property of his son Tol. When the interesting fact was explained to me, I immediately asserted my right of property, by seizing Dick by the wool and dragging him to the floor. The contumacious little villain not having the fear of his lawful master before his eyes, resented the supposed insult, by mauling me most unmercifully, much to my annoyance, but greatly to the delight of my honored Pa, who swore Dick should have fair play, and that if Tol could not govern his own slaves no body else should.

A thousand bloody-nosed battles cemented the friendship between Dick and myself, and he became my protector against all the other little negroes on the plantation. True, he would thrash me himself whenever he took the notion—but then he respected my legal claims upon his duty so far, as to permit no other the same liberty.

When I was sent off to school, Dick was sent to the plough, and all rivalry between us from that time ceased. He did not intermit his interest in me, however, nor forget that I was his liege lord. My semi-annual visits to Moss Hill, always found Dick the first to welcome me home, and his joyful shouts of "Massa Toll's come," invariably brought out all the small fry to join in the kindly greeting.

Man and boy, we have lived together for the last fifty years.

"*Sixty*," interposed Dick, with decided emphasis.

"Hear the impudent scoundrel," rejoined the master, warmly. "Do you dare Mr. Copper-Skin to dispute my word in company? I say *fifty*, sir. You may be *sixty* for aught I know or care. I am not sure that you did not live out your three score and ten some twenty years since, and ought regularly to have been buried at that time. Confound the fellow, he has put me in a passion. Get out of my sight, sir. Get out I say, or—but open that other bottle before you and then—keep your place, and keep yourself quiet."

Various were the difficulties which Dick's zeal for the honor of his master, got me into. After I left college, he became my body servant, and so varied and multiplied were the lies he told, with a view of puffing me, that I was in constant dread of his detection; well knowing that however innocent myself, every body would believe me the instigator of the falsehood. The annoyance was almost insupportable—but Dick was incorrigible,—neither prayers nor threats could change or control him. He rejected with scorn the idea that I would either sell him or dispense with his personal services, and continued his system of lying, unmoved by my most vigorous attempts to prevent him.

I was travelling in one of the States to the South of us, and had determined to stop a few days in one of the principal towns. Amidst the great variety of company in the house, I, of course, passed almost unnoticed, and began to feel quite comfortable. But on the second day my annoyances began. The landlord attended the table in person, and was distressingly polite in his attentions—the servants seemed to have neither eyes nor ears for any commands beside my own. An unusual silence prevailed at the table. I was evidently the cause of this unpleasant effect, and began seriously to wish myself a thousand miles off. I knew full well it was all owing to some infernal lie of Dick's, but what was its character I could not imagine. There he stood behind my chair as dignified and as grave as a judge, discharging his duties with unwonted respect and attention. I longed for the opportunity, cowhide in hand, to force the secret out of him, as I firmly resolved on doing, soon after I left the table; but Dick seemed to have some misgivings of the charitable state of my mind, and until dinner time was among the missing. Then indeed he took his place as dignified and as grave as ever.

On rising from the table, I was happy in being saluted by an old college friend. We immediately adjourned to my room, where over our wine I laid open the griefs that annoyed me, and consulted him on the course I ought to pursue, in order to avoid the mortification of being scoffed at as a willful imposter. The table of petty distress delighted my friend Bob R., who swore he would have the secret out of Dick before night. I had no objection to his pumping Dick, whilst at the same time I feared that his waggish propensities might incline him to become a coadjutor of Dick's, in continuing the annoyance. However, I consented to send for Dick, and friend Bob placed himself at the head of the stairs to intercept him as he came forward to obey the call. I will give you the substance of their dialogue, which in part betrayed the secret of my greatness, and shows Dick's over-anxiety for the honor of his master.

"Well, Dick, how are you? Who do you belong to now?"

"Ky, massa! You know me—don't know I 'longs to massa Tol?"

"No, I didn't know but he had sold you. Is your master a gentleman?"

"Contraptions! Why you ask? Massa Tol best blood in Sout Calinee."

"Is he? Then I suppose he's a big man. Holds no office though, eh?"

"Sartin for true him duz. I and massa Tol go to Washentun next winter."

"Oh! he's a member of Congress, is he?"

"Contraptions! you no hear dat afore. Sartin for true."

"Well, but Carolina gentlemen when they travelled were Generals or Colonels, or at least Majors."

"Ky, massa," said Dick in a tone slightly contemptuous, "you no understand dem tings. Massa Tol no stood his draft yet."

"His *draft!* Why Dick do they *draft* their Generals and Colonels in South Carolina?"

"De zactly, massa. I tell you how tis, de peeples dey say Tol Grinaway rich man's son—he by all de unicorn, no feel it a single bit—we draft Tol for jinral. Massa Tol he make grand speech to de peeples. He say, me go to 'sembly to please you, me go to Kongrist to please you, why for you draft me for jinral? Spose you draft Bill Anvill for jinral; he good blacksmit—make good jinral too. Peeples dey say, hurrah for Bill Anvill; massa Tol treat to gallon whiskey. Peeples say, we no draft Tol Grinaway dis time, he too clever feller for dat. Gentlemens always call Mister—massa Tol tip top gentlemen, best blood in Sout Calinee; he farder kum from ole Firginny."

"Aye, I understand it *now*, Dick. So when a man is not rich enough and popular enough to avoid a draft, they make an officer of him whether he will or no."

"Contraptions! dats it, dezactly, massa."

I could stand it no longer—but sallying from my room, saluted Mr. Dick with the butt end of my sulky whip. Before the blow could be repeated, Dick had evaporated. Bob R. broke into an interminable horse laugh, which promised fair to arouse the whole house. To avoid such an *expose*, I drafted into my room, carefully locking the door after me.

Although extremely angry, I could not help feeling the folly of taking so seriously matters which, in themselves, presented a character perfectly ludicrous. I felt assured, and was not mistaken in the supposition, that Bob R. would, in mere sport, confirm every thing Dick had asserted, and began to conclude I had better submit with a good grace to the necessity of being considered a member of Congress. At the same time I was satisfied Dick had *tied on* some additional claim to the consideration of the boarders, who, I could not believe, were so little in the habit of meeting members of Congress, as to show on that account alone, so great a deference and respect in his presence. What the additional lie was I could not imagine, and knew it would be useless to question Dick on the subject.

I had hardly recovered my equanimity, when a respectful knock at the door announced some one in waiting. It was my landlord, who handing me a little rose coloured card, took the liberty of hoping I found my accommodations to my liking; and being answered in the affirmative, bowed and retired. The billet was to the following purport:

"Mr. and Mrs. Smith's compliments to the Honorable Mr. Grinaway of South Carolina, they respectfully and earnestly solicit the pleasure of his company at their house on to-morrow evening, 8 o'clock."

I did not stop to enquire who Mr. and Mrs. Smith were; but feeling the ridiculousness of my involuntary position, ordered my horses to be brought out instantly. These orders did not seem very acceptable to my man Dick, who raised a variety of objections to our evening's start. Rob Roy, he said, had cast a shoe and could not travel—Di Vernon was lame in a hind foot, and required more rest. But I was peremptory, and Dick reluctantly obeyed.

"I am sorry," remarked my landlord, as I went forward to pay my bill, "I am sorry that any thing has occurred to deprive us so soon of the pleasure of your company."

"Nothing has occurred on your part my friend," replied I, "I like your house—like your town—and would like to stay in it a few days longer, but my infernal lying servant would drive me from paradise, were he in attendance upon me. Let me tell you, sir, I have no disposition to pass for what I am not. I am a plain, unambitious man. I am no member of Congress, whatever my man Dick may assert to the contrary."

"Oh yes, I understand," said host, with a knowing smile, "you devote yourself exclusively to your literary pursuits."

"My literary pursuits! I am not aware I have any, unless attending to my own business, and reading the newspapers, can be called 'literary pursuits.'"

"What," asked Boniface, doubtingly, "are you not the author of———," naming the newest and most fashionable novel.

Death and the devil! here was the secret out with a vengeance. Mr. and Mrs. Smith wanted to lionize me at their party, as the gifted author of———. Dick, not contented with the honor of my being a member of Congress elect, had given me the paternity of our distinguished Cooper's very best production. I have never since ventured into the town of———, and would to this day ride an hundred miles to avoid that scene of my early honors.

Tolliver Grinaway, senior, like a dutiful parent, in due time presented his son Tolliver Grinaway, junior, with some thirty workers and a reasonable share of Moss Hill, and bade him go to planting as a gentleman should do. My man Dick was made head driver, and being really interested in my pecuniary success, as well as in my personal honor, assisted me very efficiently. In our neighborhood he had little scope for his puffing system, so that we got along for several years without my suffering any very great annoyance from his peculiar propensity.

But Dick had another foible which occasionally, in his great zeal for my character, produced an annoyance almost equal to his lying. He never could distinguish between a gentleman and a fashionable coat. A well dressed man was always in his estimation a gentleman, and entitled to his attention and respect. One plainly dressed was nobody, and precious little notice did Dick take of such a visitor to the house. His mistakes were often sufficiently mortifying even to himself, to have induced a correcter judgment—but experience could not improve him. "The *coat* was the standard of the man," and by that standard all my guests continued to be measured.

He once refused me to my estimable friend Governor M. The Governor's homespun coat and Indian poney were conclusive against his pretensions to the character of a gentleman—and most pertinaciously did Dick declare I was not at home. "Contraptions," exclaimed he, deeply mortified when he discovered his mistake, "contraptions, who eber seed a Gubner riding a tackey, afore now. He dress wusser an a poor man's oberseer."

Equally at fault, was Dick's judgment in my very next visitor who drove up to the house in a handsome sulkey, was fashionably dressed, and of course, thought Mr. Dick, "a gentleman." I had been through the plantation, and according to Dick's standard, was not in fitting time to meet the "great man" who waited an audience.

"Massa not at home," said Dick; although at the time I was in sight of the house, and approaching it to receive my visitor.

"Who is that gentleman?" asked the visitor.

"Dat's de oberseer," replied Dick promptly.

Had I been as regardful of appearances as my man Dick, I could have escaped the reproach of showing myself in soiled linen and a hunting shirt—but I was not, and entered the drawing room without changing my dress, notwithstanding Dick's most earnest entreaties to the contrary.

"I am sorry," said my visitor, "that I have missed the pleasure of seeing Mr. Grinaway—but I hope that my call will not prove an entire failure. Suffer me to show *you* the prospectus of a very valuable work for which I am soliciting subscriptions."

Dick looked aghast. He had palmed me off upon the itinerant as the overseer, and not only did he stand detected in the lie, but he experienced the shame of having once more so palpably mistaken a fine coat for a fine gentleman.

"Contraptions! Misser Pedler," said the enraged Dick, addressing my smiling, bowing visitor; "why de debble cant you tell a gentlemans from he oberseer. Dat's massa Tol heself."

I succeeded very well in my planting interest, had reached my thirty-fifth birth-day, when it accidentally came into my head that I might as well marry. I had never thought of the subject before, and the novelty of the idea kept me awake the greater part of the night. My determination, however, was soon made. I resolved to marry and take the chance of assisting to perpetuate the honorable blood of the Grinaways, but my cogitations were very much beclouded on the point. I had kept myself so much aloof from the ladies, that I could not recollect a single one with whom I had the honor of a personal acquaintance. I had no personal intimates with whom to consult, and was driven as a dernier resort to ask the opinion and advice of my man Dick.

I had entirely forgotten ever having heard that a Virginia cousin Miss Dolly Grinaway was not only an orphan, but an heiress. She must now have reached her thirtieth year in a state of single blessedness, if still unmarried. Dick's memory was more tenacious than mine; he had heard of the orphan heiress, and immediately suggested a visit to the "Old Dominion" to make the necessary enquiries after "Cousin Dolly." The plan struck me as quite feasible, and having good reason to recommend it, I had determined on taking to myself a wife, and Dolly Grinaway was as likely to suit me as any body else. My relationship would warrant me in visiting her, and render it more easy for me to make my proposals, than under other circumstances I might have found it. Beside, though not mercenary, I could not help thinking that the heiress's fortune would be a very comfortable addition to my own.

Imagine me, if you please, at the river on which the little town of ——, is situated. There Cousin Dolly made her residence, and that far had I proceeded in search of a wife. Dick was in attendance upon me, having solemnly promised before leaving home, not to misrepresent me on the journey. So far as I knew, he had kept his word and I had passed thus far with only the ordinary annoyances to which a private gentleman is always subjected in traveling.

I noticed that Dick and the ferryman were in close confab whilst we were crossing the river, but did not suspect the plot which was really brewing against my quiet.

Well, I was snugly ensconced in the principal hotel, thinking of nothing but my intended visit to Dolly in the morning, when my reveries were suddenly broken by a loud bawling at the door. Is *Jinral* Grinaway here? *Jinral* Grinaway left his cloak in the ferry boat, and I have brought it to him. It was shortly before supper time, and all the inmates of the house were lounging about the piazza and lower rooms, and consequently had an opportunity of learning the important fact that General Grinaway had arrived in town. It was one of Dick's infernal practical lies. He had bribed the ferryman to join in the plot, and between them, without ever having held a military commission, I was made a General for life. Dick now came forward and claimed the cloak—it belonged, he said, with becoming gravity, to his master, Jinral Grinaway of Sout Calina. The ferryman was rewarded for his rascality with a silver quarter, and Dick strutted into the house with the conscious importance attached to the body servant of a General.

I had entered my name as plain Tolliver Grinaway of South Carolina. On looking over the register the next morning I found the title of General prefixed in the hand writing as I supposed of my courteous landlord.

Dick it seems had changed his notion about military titles since the time in which he had asserted that all the gentlemen from South Carolina were called Mister. In addition to making me a general he had, as I afterwards discovered, given me the whole of Moss Hill with its hundred and seventy workers, wholly regardless of the just claims of my brothers and sisters on the life estate held and enjoyed by the senior Grinaway.

My reception by cousin Dolly was as flattering as I could have anticipated, though she betrayed her knowledge of my arrival previously to my call, by invariably addressing me as General Grinaway. This fact I thought argued favorably, beside she enquired in the kindest manner after the various members of my family, and seemed to take the deepest interest in every thing that concerned them.

How I sped in my wooing need not be told in detail. Day after day found me in Cousin Dolly's company, and continuing growing in her good graces. Having like an able tactician, made my advances with due caution and circumspection, I at length ventured to pop the question. We were near the river and in sight of the ferry at the very moment I made the tender of my hand and fortune. I had always prided myself on sustaining the character of an open candid gentleman. A sudden qualm of conscience, which no doubt a sight of the ferry man produced, reminded me that possibly the heiress might be acting under a mistaken idea as regarded my fortune and character.

Dolly very naturally "blushed, sighed, and hung down her head." I thought the answer would be favorable. Before you answer, cousin Dolly, said I, permit me to add a few words which my character as a gentleman requires me to speak--I would not willingly deceive you; I am no General unless the suffrage of yon rascally ferryman coupled with that of my own still more rascally attendant, can make me one. I am *not* the owner of Moss Hill and its gang of workers, but simply the proprietor of my own one sixth, to which I have made a reasonable addition since the ten years I have had it in possession. My man Dick has placed me before your towns-people in a false position, which in honor I cannot sustain with you.

"I admire your candor, Cousin Tolliver," replied she, "and honor your motives. Whether you are a General or not, cannot make the slightest difference. I will not deny that as a part of the gossip of the town I had heard you represented as a man of large fortune. Your own representations show your circumstances to be independent:—What more could any reasonable woman ask when tendered by a man of honor—but"

This speech of Cousin Dolly's certainly sounded very sensible. I had begun to felicitate myself on the certainty of success, when the added "*but*" fell like a damper on the bursting flame.

But, she continued, "come with me to the shade, I have much to say to you.—Let us sit down, and it may be that *my* candour may change your present views."

I obeyed in silence wholly ignorant of what the lady intended.

"I do not know," said she, when we had seated ourselves, "how far you are informed of my *true* situation. I must be satisfied on that point, and then am ready to answer you. Answer me truly, Cousin Tolliver, did you leave South Carolina with a view of visiting and addressing me?"

"I did."

"Of course you enquired into my character and fortune.—What was the result of those enquiries?"

"That you were a well educated, sensible young lady:—My father informed me that you were an orphan, that you had been left some fifty slaves, a valuable plantation and a considerable sum in ready money, that you had had many fine offers of marriage, which from some unknown cause, you had uniformly rejected, and that he supposed you would make an excellent wife, could I be so fortunate as to win your favour."

"Did he speak of no reverses, no misfortunes to the orphan heiress, whom he so kindly recommended to his son?"

"None."

"Then I must follow the candid example you have set me, and speak of them myself. Listen and judge for yourself. Report spoke truly of the amount of property left by my father. I was his only child, consequently, the sole heiress of his estate, but with his death my troubles began. A suit at law for the recovery of the plantation on which we resided, was soon afterwards commenced. By some legerdemain of the law, some unheard of minority in the claimants, some strangely kept back and long unknown better paper title, the plaintiffs succeeded. My patrimony was awarded to strangers by the supreme tribunal of the State. The large sum of ready money left by my father was expended in the payment of his debts and the necessary law expenses. How it happened that my father with his profuse and extravagant habits of expenditure could have accumulated so considerable a sum in cash was a matter of surprise not only to myself, but to all who knew him. I was not, however, long left in ignorance.—The money had been borrowed from the bank and secured by a deed of trust on all his slaves. The sequel may easily be anticipated. The closing of the business left me pennyless, my needle was my only resource from want and dependence. Such was the fate of the heiress of Bell Hall. I bore it with what fortitude I could, and have heretofore only anticipated the hapless destiny ever attendant on female poverty. The many fine offers of marriage of which your father spoke, *might* have been made, had I really continued an heiress. As it is, I cannot boast of any conquests or any rejected offers. You have heard my story cousin Tolliver. It remains for *you* to decide whether you will renew to the pennyless orphan the proposals you supposed you were making to the rich heiress."

"Is this a true story you have been telling me?" I asked.

"Yes."

"You have lost your plantation in a law-suit?"

"Yes."

"You have spent all your ready money in the payment of your father's debts and your legal expenses?"

"Yes."

"Your slaves have all been sold to foreclose a mortgage?"

"Yes."

"And you in truth and in fact are without a fortune?"

"Yes."

Whew! Thunder and Potomac, wasn't here a pretty kettle of fish. All my bright and airy castles dissolved as suddenly as the valley fog disappears before the beams of a summer sun. Dolly Grinaway after all was *no* heiress. How could I answer? dumbfounded as I was by the astounding discovery.

Dick, you dog, fill my glass once more, you stupid rascal,—had you had the eyes of a bat, you might have seen the true state of affairs and given me a hint in time,—but you were justly punished for your stupidity and your lying propensities by being subjected for twenty years to the caprices of a woman. Ah! you grin exultingly,—the annoyance is now over. Well, well! your mistress is gone to where there shall be no more—scolding. Out of respect to her memory, I'll take another glass.—I'll never marry again, nor lay aside my widower's weeds.

Excuse me, gentlemen, said Mr. Grinaway, after apostrophizing Dick until he had drunk three additional glasses of wine—Excuse me, I believe, anticipated the finale of my wooing. It is true, I carried home the portionless Dolly Grinaway as my bride; the secrets of matrimony shall not be told by me. Let that pass, all the fools a'nt dead yet, and we'll catch a heap more in the same net to bear us company.

There was something touching in my cousin's account of herself, which forbade me a brief withdrawal of my proposals. Beside, having made the offer I began to think I was bound in honor to renew it. I would have sung *te deum* had she rejected me; but of that I had little hope. One little stratagem, which I *called* acting candidly, I tried and failed most signally.

"My dear cousin," said I, so soon as I *could* speak, "I most sincerely lament your misfortunes. I beg you to believe, however, I could not think of withdrawing my proposals because I find you poor when I thought you rich. I admire your candour as much as you did mine. If you can afford to have me after coming to the knowledge of a single fact I will now make known to you,—say so, and name the wedding day."

"What is the fact you refer to?" asked Dolly, in evident agitation.

"Know then, cousin of mine, I am perfectly bald headed." So saying, I raised my wig, exposing the whole of my naked pate, with a secret hope it would disgust her into a rejection.

"I am rejoiced at it," cried Dolly, jumping up and clapping her hands in ecstasy. "It removes the last difficulty between us, and if you wish, I will marry you to-morrow. For know cousin of *mine,* I *too* am bald." And in proof of her assertion she raised *her* wig sufficiently to remove all doubt of the fact.

A man might as well laugh as cry at what he can't help. The mode in which I had been foiled in my little *finesse,*—the popping of our bald heads into each other's face, operated on my risibility, that I laughed long, loud, heartily and good humoredly. I submitted to my fate as a sensible man always will do when he finds it inevitable, and Dolly the next day became my wife.

"Contraptions, bad speck dat for Massa Tol," groaned Dick quite audibly.

General Tolliver Grinaway had by this time become pretty much fuddled,—his speech got thick and his mind oblivious of the particular subject under discussion, he attempted what no public speaker, ancient or modern, ever could do successfully, he attempted to compliment himself.

I am an orator, he said, I was born an orator, nothing but spite and malice has kept me thus long off the stage. I could teach Kean his A.B.C. in tragedy. Oh, great John of Roanoke, leave me thy mantle and a fig for thy high blooded stud, thy slaves and tobacco grounds. Modesty gentlemen—modesty is a jewel, invaluable for its rarity,—Had I a thimble full of impudence, I'd astonish you.

Dick, I'll retire, I am sometimes troubled with weakness in my limbs, which renders the aid of my man Dick necessary.

Good night, gentlemen, continued the General, as Dick mounted his master on his back. Good night to all.

Hippopotamus! Dick did you ever seen an hippopotamus?

"Contraption," muttered Dick as he bore his master out at the door "Contraption, Massa Tol's d—d drunk to-night."

Hamilton C. Jones (1798-1868)

As a humorist, Ham Jones was known by the byline under which he published his comic sketches and tales: "the Author of 'Cousin Sally Dilliard.'" "Cousin Sally Dilliard," Jones's first and most popular work, is a repetitive and rambling sketch, which initially appeared in *Atkinson's Saturday Evening Post* in 1831, and which was subsequently reprinted four times in William T. Porter's *Spirit of the Times* and in Porter's anthology of southern backwoods humor, *The Big Bear of Arkansas and Other Tales* (1845). A "shaggy dog story," set in North Carolina, "Cousin Sally Dilliard" depicts a court scene in which a lawyer calls upon a rustic witness, who likely has had too much to drink, to testify, his testimony an unexpected reversal since the witness keeps repeating the same nonsensical and irrelevant statement—"Captain Rice, he gin a treat, and cousin Sally Dilliard, she came over to our house and axed me if my wife, she moughtn't go."

Jones was born in Greenville County, Virginia, but with the death of his father a short time later, his mother moved the family to Stokes County, North Carolina, and married an influential and wealthy planter, Colonel James Martin, the brother of former North Carolina governor Alexander Martin. After attending the Chapel Hill, North Carolina Academy for boys, Jones entered the University of North Carolina, graduating in 1818. Then, after reading law in New Bern under the tutelage of William Gaston, one of the North Carolina's most exemplary attorneys, Jones married, obtained his law license, and practiced law in Salisbury in Rowan County. Jones subsequently became involved in state politics and was elected to the North Carolina House of Commons in 1827 and was reelected in 1828, 1838, and 1840.

In addition to his law practice and his political involvement, Ham Jones, like many other humorists of the Old South, tried his hand at journalism, founding in 1832 the Salisbury *Carolina Watchman*, a weekly newspaper, which supported Federalist and Whig ideologies, thereby countering the town's only other paper, the *Western Carolinian*, which was anti-Federalist and anti-Whig. As editor of the *Watchman* from 1832 to 1839, Jones printed material from other newspapers and wrote articles, editorials, humorous sketches, and anecdotes. The latter, under the heading "Salisbury Omnibus," began appearing in the newspaper in July of 1837, and provided a comic perspective on local happenings and activities. After the success of "Cousin Sally Dilliard," Jones wrote a number of humorous sketches, which were originally published in Porter's *Spirit of the Times*; these include "McAlpin's Trip to Charleston" (July 11, 1846), "Going to Muster in North Carolina" (July 18, 1846), "The Sandy Creek Literary Society" (August 15, 1846), "The Round Robin" (August 22, 1846), "The Frenchman and His Menagerie" (March 16, 1850), and "Abel Hucks in a Tight Place" (August 23, 1851).

While Jones was not a prolific writer of humorous sketches, his first story, "Cousin Sally Dilliard" (1831), was not only one of the earliest and best-known southern frontier humorous texts that Porter published in the *Spirit*, but it also pioneered some of the prominent features of the southwestern humor genre—the narrative frame, competing voices and discourses of the outlandish rural rustic and the effete town lawyer, and exaggeration of details.

Texts: "Cousin Sally Dilliard," *Atkinson's Saturday Evening Post*, August 6, 1831. "McAlpin's Trip to Charleston," New York *Spirit of the Times*, July 11, 1846.

Cousin Sally Dilliard

Scene—A Court of Justice, in No. Ca.

A beardless disciple of Themis rises, and thus addresses the court: May it please your Worships, and you, Gentlemen of the Jury, since it has been my fortune (good or bad I will not say) to exercise myself in legal disquisitions, it has never before befallen me to be obliged to denounce a breach of the peace so enormous and transcending as the one now claiming your attention. A more barbarous, direful, marked and malicious assault—a more wilful, violent, dangerous and murderous battery, and finally, a more diabolical breach of the peace has seldom happened in a civilized country, and I dare say it has seldom been your duty to pass upon one so shocking to benevolent feeling as this, which took place over at Captain Rice's, in this county, but you will hear from the witnesses. The witnesses being sworn, two or three were examined and deposed—one, that he heard the noise, but did'nt see the fight—another, that he saw the row, but don't know who struck first—and a third, that he was very drunk, and couldn't say much about the scrimmage.

Lawyer Chops.—I am sorry, gentlemen, to have occupied so much of your time with the stupidity of the witnesses examined. It arose, gentlemen, altogether from misapprehension on my part. Had I known, as I now do, that I had a witness in attendance, who was well acquainted with all the circumstances of the case, and who was able to make himself clearly and intelligibly understood by the court and jury, I should not so long have trespassed on your time and patience. Come forward, Mr. Harris, and be sworn.

So forward comes the witness, a fat, chuffy looking man, a *leetle corned*, and took his corporal oath with an air.

Chops. Mr. Harris, we wish you to tell all about the riot that happened the other day at Captain Rice's, and as a good deal of time has been already wasted in circumlocution, we wish you to be as compendious and at the same time as explicit as possible.

Edzacity,—giving the lawyer a knowing wink, at the same time clearing his throat—*Witness.* Captain Rice, he gin a treat, and cousin Sally Dilliard, she came over to our house and axed me if my wife, she mought'nt go—I told cousin Sally Dilliard that my wife was poorly, being as how she had a touch of the Rheumatics in the hip, and the big swamp was in the road, and the big swamp was up, for there had been a heap of rain lately; but howsomever as it was she, cousin Sally Dilliard, my wife, she mought go.—Well, cousin Sally Dilliard than axed me if Mose, he mought'nt go. I told cousin Sally Dilliard that Mose, he was the foreman of the crop, and the crop was smartly in the grass; but howsomever as it was she, cousin Sally Dilliard, Mose, he mout go.

Chops. In the name of common sense, Mr. Harris, what do you mean by this rigmarole?

Witness. Captain Rice, he gin a treat, and cousin Sally Dilliard, she came over to our house and axed me if my wife, she mout'nt go. I told Cousin Sally Dilliard—

Chops. Stop, sir, if you please. We don't want to hear anything about Cousin Sally Dilliard and your wife. Tell us about the fight at Captain Rice's.

Witness. Well, I will, sir, if you will let me.

Chops. Well, sir, go on.

Witness. Well, Captain Rice, he gin a treat, and cousin Sally Dilliard, she came over to our house and axed me if my wife, she mout'nt go—

Chops. There it is again,—witness, I say, witness, please to stop.

Witness. Well, sir, what as you want?

Chops. We want to know about the fight, and you must not proceed in this impertinent story—do you know any thing about the matter before the Court?

Witness. To be sure I do.

Chops. Will you go on and tell it, and nothing else?

Witness. Well, Captain Rice, he gin a treat—

Chops. This is intolerable! May it please the Court—I move that this witness be committed for a contempt,—he seems to me to be trifling with the court.

Court. Witness, you are now before a Court of Justice, and unless you behave yourself in a more becoming manner, you will be sent to jail; so begin and tell what you know about the fight at Captain Rice's.

Witness. (alarmed) Well, gentlemen, Captain Rice, he gin a treat, and cousin Sally Dilliard—

Chops. I hope that this witness may be ordered into custody.

Court. (after deliberating.) Mr. Attorney, the Court is of opinion that we may save time by telling the witness to go on in his own way.—Proceed, Mr. Harris, with your story, but stick to the point.

Witness. Yes, gentlemen: well, Captain Rice, he gin a treat, and cousin Sally Dilliard, she came over to our house, and axed me if my wife, she mout'nt go. I told cousin Sally Dilliard that my wife was poorly, being as how she had the Rheumatics in the hip, and the big swamp was in the road, and the big swamp was up; but howsomever, as it was she, cousin Sally Dilliard, my wife, she mout go. Well, cousin Sally Dilliard then axed me if Mose, he mout'nt go. I told cousin Sally Dilliard as how Mose, he was the foreman of the crop, and the crop was smartly in the grass; but howsomever, as it was she, cousin Sally Dilliard, Mose, he mout go. So on they goes together, Mose, my wife, and cousin Sally Dilliard, and they comes to the big swamp, and the big swamp was up, as I was telling you; but being as how there was a log across the big swamp, cousin Sally Dilliard and Mose, like genteel folks, they walks the log, but my wife, like a d—d fool, hoists up her petticoats and waded, and, gentlemen, that's the height of what I know about it.

McAlpin's Trip to Charleston

Written for the "Spirit of the Times" by the author of "Cousin Sally Dilliard."

In the county of Robison, in the State of North Carolina, there lived in times past a man by the name of BROOKS who kept a grocery for a number of years, and so had acquired most of the land around him. This was mostly pine barrens of small values, but nevertheless Brooks was looked up to as a great landholder and big man in the neighborhood. There was one tract, however, belonging to one Col. LAMAR, who lived in Charleston, that "*jammed in upon him so strong,*" and being withal better in quality than the average of his own domain, that Brooks had long wished to add it to his other broad acres. Accordingly he looked around him and employed, as he expressed it, "the smartest man in the neighborhood," to wit, one ANGUS McALPIN, to go to Charleston and negotiate with Col. Lamar for the purchase of this also. Being provided pretty well with bread, meat, and a bottle of *pale-face,* which were stowed away in a pair of leather saddle bags, and like all other great *Plenipotentiaries,* being provided with suitable instructions, Mac mounted a piney-wood-tacky (named Rasum) and hied him off to Charleston. The road was rather longer than Brooks had supposed, or his agent was less expeditious, or some bad luck had happened to him, or something was the matter that Angus did not get back until long after the day had transpired, which was fixed on for his return. Brooks in the meantime had got himself into a very fury of impatience. He kept his eyes fixed on the Charleston road—he was crusty towards his customers—harsh towards his wife and children, and scarcely eat or slept for several days and nights, for he had set his whole soul upon buying the Lamar land. One day, however, Angus was descried slowly and sadly wending his way up the long stretch of sandy road that made up to the grocery. Brooks went out to meet him, and, without, further ceremony, he accosted him.

"Well, Mac, have you got the land?"

The agent, in whose face was any thing but sunshine, replied somewhat gruffly that "he might let a body get down from his horse before he put at him with questions of business."

But Brooks was in a fever of anxiety and repeated the question—

"Did you get it?"

"Shaw, now, Brooks, don't press upon a body in this uncivil way. It is a long story and I must have time."

Brooks still urged and Mac still parried the question till they got into the house.

"Now, surely," thought Brooks, "he will tell me." But Mac was not quite ready.

"Brooks," says he, "have you any thing to drink?"

"To be sure I have," said the other, and immediately had some of his best forth-coming. Having moistened his clay, Mac took a seat and his employer another. Mac gave a preliminary hem! He then turned suddenly around to Brooks, looked him straight in the eyes, and slapped him on the thigh—

"Brooks," says he, "was you ever in Charleston?"

"Why, you know I never was," replied the other.

"Well, then, Brooks," says the agent, "you ought to go there. The greatest place upon the face of the earth! They've got houses there on both sides of the road for five miles at a stretch, and d—n the horse-track the whole way through! Brooks, I think I met five thousand people in a minute, and not a chap would look at me. They have got houses there on wheels. Brooks! I saw one with six horses hitched to it, and a big driver with a long whip going it like a whirl-wind. I followed it down the road for a mile and half, and when it stopt I looked and what do you think there was? nothing in it but one little woman sitting up in one corner. Well, Brooks, I turned back up the road, and as I was riding along I sees fancy looking chap with long curly hair hanging down his back, and his books as shiney as the face of an up-country nigger! I called him into the middle of the road and asked him a civil question—and a civil question, you know, Brooks, calls for a civil answer all over the world. I says, says I

'Stranger, can you tell me where Col. Lamar lives?' and what do you think was his answer—'*Go to h—l, you fool!!*'

"Well, Brooks, I knocks along up and down and about, until at last I finds out where Col. Lamar lived. I gets down and bangs away at the door. Presently the door was opened by as pretty, fine-spoken, well dressed a woman as ever you seed in your born days. Brooks, *Silks!* Silks *thar* every day. Brooks! Says I, 'Mrs. Lamar, I presume, Madam,' says I. "I am Mrs. Lamar, Sir.' Well, Madam,' says I, 'I have come all the way from North Carolina to see Colonel Lamar—to see about buying a tract of land from him that's up in our parts?' Then, she says, 'Col. Lamar has rode out in the country, but will be back shortly. Come in, Sir, and wait a while. I've no doubt the Colonel will soon return,' and she had a smile upon that pretty face of her's that reminded a body of a Spring morning. Well, Brooks, I hitched my horse to a brass thing on the door, and walked in. Well, when I got in I sees the floor all covered over with the nicest looking thing! Nicer than any patched-worked bedquilt you ever seed in your life, Brooks, I was trying to edge along around it, but presently I sees a big nigger come stepping right over it. Thinks I if that nigger can go it I can go it, too! So right over it I goes and takes my seat right before a picture which at first I thought was a little man looking in at a window. Well, Brooks, there I sot waiting and waiting for Col. Lamar, and *at* last—he didn't come, but they began to bring in dinner. Thinks I to myself, here's a scrape. But I made up my mind to tell her, if she axed me to eat—to tell her with a genteel bow that I *had no occasion to eat*. But, Brooks, she didn't ax me to eat—she axed me if I'd be so good as to carve that turkey for her, and she did it with one of them lovely smiles that makes the cold streaks run down the small of a feller's back. 'Certainly, Madam,' says I, and I walks up to the table—there was on one side of the turkey a great big knife as big as a bowie knife, and a fork with a trigger to it on the other side. Well, I falls to work, and in the first *e*-fort I slashed the gravy about two yards over the whitest table cloth you ever seed in your life, Brooks! Well! I felt the hot steam begin to gather about my cheeks and eyes. But I'm not a man to back out for trifles, so I makes another *e*-fort and the darned thing took a flight and lit right in Mrs. Lamar's lap! Well, you see, Brooks, then I was taken with a blindness, and the next thing I remember I was upon the *hath* a-kicking. Well, by this time I began to think of navigating. So I goes out and mounts Rasum, and cuts for North Carolina! Now, Brooks, you don't blame me! Do you?"

William Gilmore Simms (1806-1870)

A native of Charleston, South Carolina, William Gilmore Simms, along with his contemporaries Washington Irving, James Fenimore Cooper, and Edgar Allan Poe, was among the first American writers to dedicate their careers to making a living as professional authors. Wide-ranging in his intellectual and social interests, grounded in a strong sense of the history of his region, and supported by a community of writers that gathered at Russell's Bookstore to form the "Charleston School," during his lifetime Simms would edit at least ten periodicals and produce more than eighty volumes of history, poetry, criticism, biography, drama, essays, stories, and novels.

He made a bid for a major presence on the American literary scene through his nationally popular border romances about life on the frontier and historical romances about the American Revolution. *Guy Rivers* in 1834 and *The Yemassee* in 1835 were notable successes that put Simms in a good position to achieve a national reputation but with all the disadvantages of a southerner at a distance from the presses and publishing houses of New York City. Because of his self-conscious awareness of his regional position, and his devotion to exploring the southern experience in his writing, he was in a sense the founding father of southern literature.

Simms is not known as a humorist, although like most professional writers he would turn to it as occasion or assignment dictated. His deep familiarity with the frontier experience, and his appreciation for the eccentricities of backwoods existence, would lead him to write humorous pieces that reflected the rowdy, dangerous, and unreliable nature of life at the margins of civilization. In so doing, he demonstrated a command of the materials and techniques of the humor of the Old Southwest, just as they were being developed by Augustus Baldwin Longstreet and his followers in the pages of the New York *Spirit of the Times* and southern newspapers. His best comic tales include "How Sharp Snaffles Got His Capital and Wife" and "Bill Bauldy."

Text: "Ephraim Bartlett, the Edisto Raftsman" *Literary World* 10 (February 7, 1852) 107–10.

Ephraim Bartlett, the Edisto Raftsman

I resume my narrative. In my last, we had just hurried across the common road, once greatly travelled, leading along the Ashley, to the ancient village of Dorchester. Something was said of the fine old plantations along this river. It was the aristocratic region during the Revolution; and when the Virginians and Marylanders, at the close of the war, who had come to the succor of Carolina against the British, drew nigh to Charleston, their hearts were won and their eyes ravished, by the hospitalities and sweets of this neighborhood. Many brave fellows found their wives along this river, which was bordered by flourishing farms and plantations, and crowned by equal luxury and refinement. Here, too, dwelt many of those high-spirited and noble dames whose courage and patriotism contributed so largely to furnish that glorious chapter in Revolutionary history, which has been given to the women of that period. The scene is sadly changed at this season. The plantations along the Ashley are no longer flourishing as then. The land has fallen in value, not exhausted, but no longer fertile and populous. The health of the country is alleged to be no longer what it was. This I regard as all absurdity. The truth is that the cultivation was always inferior; and the first fertile freshness of the soil being exhausted, the opening of new lands in other regions naturally diverted a restless people from their old abodes. The river is still a broad and beautiful one, navigable for steamers and schooners up to Dorchester, which, by land, is twenty-one miles from Charleston. There is abundant means for restoring its fertility. Vast beds of marl, of the best quality, skirt the river all along the route, and there is still a forest growth sufficiently dense to afford the vegetable material necessary to the preparation of compost. As for the health of the neighborhood, I have no sort of question, that, with a dense population, addressed to farming, and adequate to a proper drainage, it would prove quite as salubrious as any portion of the country. Staple culture has always been the curse of Carolina. It has prevented thorough tillage, without which no country can ever ascertain its own resources, or be sure of its health at any time.

Cooper River, on the right, is at a greater distance from us. This, too, was a prosperous and well cultivated region in the Revolution. In a considerable degree it still remains so, and is distinguished by flourishing country seats, which their owners only occupy during spring and winter. The cultivation is chiefly rice, and the rice plantation is notoriously and fatally sickly, except among the negroes. They flourish in a climate which is death to the European. But of this river hereafter. I may persuade you, in future pages, to a special journey in this quarter, when our details and descriptions may be more specific. Between the two rivers the country is full of interest and full of game, to those who can delay to hunt for it. He who runs over the railroad only, sees nothing and can form no conception of it. A few miles further, on the right, there is a stately relic of the old British parochial establishment, a church edifice dedicated to St. James, which modern veneration has lately restored with becoming art, and reawakened with proper rituals. Built of brick, with a richly painted interior and tesselated aisles, surrounded by patriarchal oaks, and a numerous tentantry of dead in solemn tomb and ivy-mantled monument, you almost fancy yourself in the midst of an antiquity which mocks the finger of the historian. In this neighborhood flourished a goodly population. Large estates and great wealth were associated with equally large refinement and a liberal hospitality, and the land was marked by peculiar fertility. The fertility is not wanting now, but the population is gone—influenced by similar considerations with those which stripped the sister river of its thousands.

Until late years, the game was abundant in this region. The swamps which girdled the rivers afforded a sure refuge, and the deer stole forth to the ridges between, to browse at midnight, seeking refuge in the swamps by day. We have just darted through an extensive tract named Izard's Camp, which used to be famous hunting-ground for the city sportsmen. Twenty years ago I have cracked away at a group of deer, myself, in these forest pastures, and even now you may rouse the hunt profitably in the ancient ranges. There are a few sportsmen who still know where to seek with certainty for the buck at the proper season. The woods, though mostly pine, have large tracts of oak and hickory. The scrubby oak denotes a light sandy soil, of small tenacity, and, most usually, old fields which have been abandoned. Along the smaller water-coursers, the creeks and branches, long strips of fertile territory may be had; and the higher swamp lands only need drainage to afford tracts of inexhaustible fertility, equal to any Mississippi bottom. The introduction of farming culture will find these and reclaim them, and restore the poorer regions.

A thousand stories of the Revolution, peculiar to this country, would reward the seeker. Nor is it wanting in other sources of interest. Traditions are abundant which belong more to the spiritual nature of the people than their natural history. The poorer classes in the low country of the South were full of superstition. Poverty, for that matter, usually is so, but more particularly when it dwells in a region which is distinguished by any natural peculiarities. Thus the highlands of Scotland cherish a faith in spectral forms that rise in the mist and vapor of the mountain; and the Brownie is but the grim accompaniment of a life, that, lacking somewhat in human association, must seek its companions among the spiritual; and these must derive their aspects from the gloomy fortunes of the seeker. The Banshee of Ireland is but the finally speaking monitor of a fate that has always more or less threatened the fortunes of the declining family; and the Norwegian hunting demons are such as are equally evoked by the sports which he pursues and the necessities by which he is pursued himself. In the wild, deep, dark, and tangled masses of a Carolina swamp region, where, even by daylight, mystic shadows harbor and walk capriciously with every change of the always doubtful sunlight, the mind sees and seeks a spiritual presence, which, though it may sometimes oppress, always affords company. Here, solitude, which is the source of the spiritual and contemplative, is always to be found; and forces herself—certainly at one season of the year—upon the scattered forester and farmer. The man who lives by pursuit of the game, the deer or turkey, will be apt to conjure up, in the silent, dim avenues through which he wanders, some companion for his thought, which will, in time, become a presence to his eye; and, in the secluded toils of the farmer, on the borders of swamp and forest, he will occasionally find himself disturbed by a visitor or spectator which his own loneliness of life has extorted from his imagination, which has shaped it to a becoming aspect with the scene and climate under which he dwells. Many of these wild walkers of the wood are supposed to have been gods and spirits of the Indian tribes, who have also left startling memories behind them; and though reluctant to confess his superstitions—for the white hunter and forester dread ridicule more than anything beside—yet a proper investigation might find treasures of superstition and grim tradition among our people of this region, such as would not discredit any of the inventions of imagination.

One of these traditions occurs to me at this moment, the scene of which is at hand but a short distance from us, but not visible from the railroad. Here is not only a haunted house, but a haunted tract of forest. The tale was told me many years ago, as derived from the narrative of a raftsman of the Edisto. The Edisto, of which we may speak hereafter, is the great *lumber* river of South Carolina. Its extent is considerable, penetrating several distinct divisions of the State, and upon its two great arms or arteries, and its tributary creeks or branches, it owns perhaps no less than one hundred and fifty mills for sawing lumber. It supplies Charleston, by a sinuous route, almost wholly; and large shipments of its timber are made to the island of Cuba, to Virginia, and recently to New York, and other places. Its navigation is difficult, and, as it approaches the sea, somewhat perilous. Many of its rafts have been driven out to sea and lost, with all on board. It requires, accordingly, an experienced pilot to thread its intricacies, and such an one was Ephraim Bartlett, a worthy fellow, who has passed pretty much out of the memories of the present generation.

Ephraim was a good pilot of the Edisto, one of the best; but he had an unfortunate faith in whiskey, which greatly impaired his standing in society. It did not injure his reputation, however, as a pilot; since it was well known that Ephraim never drank on the voyage, but only on the return; and as this was invariably by land, no evil could accrue from his bad habit to anybody but himself. He rewarded himself for his abstinence on the river, by free indulgence when on shore. His intervals of leisure were given up wholly to his potations;

and between the sale of one fleet of rafts, and the preparation for the market of another, Ephraim, I am sorry to say, was a case which would have staggered the temperance societies. But the signal once given by his employers, he would shake himself free from the evil spirit, by a plunge into the river. Purification followed—his head was soon as clear for business as ever; and, wound about with a bandanna handkerchief of flaming spot in place of a hat, it would be seen conspicuous on the raft, making for the city. With cheerful song and cry he made his way down, pole in hand, to ward off the overhanging branches of the trees, or to force aside the obstructions. Accompanied by a single negro, still remembered by many as old 'Bram Geiger, his course was usually prosperous. His lumber usually found the best market, and Ephraim and 'Bram, laying in their little supplies in Charleston, with a sack over their shoulders, and staff or gun in hand, would set out from the city on their return to Lexington, the district of country from which they descended. On these occasions, Ephraim never forgot his jug. This was taken with him empty on the raft, but returned filled, upon his or 'Bram's shoulders. They took turns in carrying it, concealing it from too officious observers by securing it in one end of the sack. In the other might be found a few clothes, and a fair supply of tobacco.

On the particular occasion when Ephraim discovered for himself that the ancient house and tract were haunted, it happened that he left the city about midday. It was Saturday, at twelve or one o'clock, according to his account, when they set out, laden as usual. They reached the house, which was probably twelve or thirteen miles from town, long before sundown; and might have stretched away a few miles farther, but for a cramp in the stomach, which seized upon Old 'Bram. Ephraim at once had resort to his jug, and a strong noggin was prepared for the relief of the suffering negro. At the same time, as 'Bram swore that he must die, that nothing could possibly save him under such sufferings as he experienced, Ephraim concluded to take lodgings temporarily in the old house, which happened to be within a few hundred yards of the spot, and to lie by for the rest of the day. The building was of brick, two stories in height, but utterly out of repair—doors and windows gone, floors destroyed, and the entire fabric within quite dismantled. It was a long time before 'Bram was relieved from his suffering and fright. Repeated doses of the potent beverage were necessary to a cure; and, by the time this was effected, the old fellow was asleep. In the meantime, Ephraim had built a rousing fire in the old chimney; had gathered *lightwood* sufficient to keep up the fire all night; had covered the old negro with his own blanket, which he bore strapped beneath the sack upon his shoulders; and had opened his wallet of dried meat and city bread for his supper. Meanwhile, the fumes of the whiskey had ascended gratefully to his own nostrils; and it seemed only reasonable that he should indulge himself with a dram, having bestowed no less than three upon his companion. He drank accordingly, and as he had no coffee to his supper, he employed the whiskey, which he thought by no means a bad substitute. He may have swallowed three several doses in emulation of 'Bram, and in anticipation of a similar attack, before he had quite finished supper. He admits that he certainly drank again when his meal was ended, by way of washing down the fragments. 'Bram, meanwhile, with the blazing fire at his feet, continued to sleep on very comfortably. When Ephraim got to sleep is not so certain. He admits that he was kept awake till a late hour by the fumes of the whiskey, and by strange noises that reached him from the forest. He recalled to memory the bad character of the dwelling and neighborhood as haunted; and is not so sure, but thinks it possible that this recollection prompted him to take another draught, a stirrup cup, as it were, before yielding himself to sleep. But he denies that he was in any way affected by the whiskey. To use his own language, he had none of the "how-come-you-so" sensation upon him, but insists that he said his prayers, rationally, like any other Christian, put several fresh brands upon the fire, and sank into the most sober of all mortal slumbers.

I am the more particular in stating these details, since a question has been made in regard to them. 'Bram had his story also. He admits that he was sick, and physicked as described—that Ephraim had gathered the fuel, made the fire, and covered him with his blanket, while he slept—but he alleges that he awoke at midnight, when Ephraim himself was asleep, and being still a little distressed in the abdominal region, he proceeded to help himself out of the jug, without disturbing the repose of his comrade; and he affirms, on his honesty, that he then found the jug fully half emptied, which had been quite full when he had left the city; and he insisted that, in giving him his several doses, Ephraim had always been very careful not to make them over strong. 'Bram admits that, when he had occasion to help himself, as the attack was still threatening, he preferred to take an over dose rather than peril his safety by mincing the matter. It is very certain, from the united testimonies of the two, the whiskey had, one half of it, most unaccountably disappeared before the night was half over. I must suffer Ephraim to tell the rest of the story for himself, and assert his own argument.

"Well, now, you see, my friends," telling his story to a group, "as I said afore, it was mighty late that night afore I shut my eyes. I reckon twarn't far from day-peep when I slipped off into a hearty sleep, and then I slept like a cat after a supper. Don't you be thinking now 'twas owing to the whiskey that I was wakeful, or that I slept so sound at last. 'Bram's troubles in the stomach made me oneasy, and them strange noises in the woods helped the matter."

"But what were the noises like, Ephraim?"

"Oh! like a'most any thing and every thing. Horns a-blowing, horses a-snorting, cats a-crying, and then sich a rushing and a trampling of four-footed beasts, that I could 'a-swore it was a fox hunt for all the world. But it warn't that! No! 'Twas a hunt agin natur'. The hounds, and horses, and horns that made that racket, warn't belonging to this world. I felt suspicions about it then, and I reckon I knows it now, if such a matter ever is to be made known. Well, as I was a-saying, I got to sleep at last near upon day-light. How long I did sleep there's no telling. 'Twas mighty late when I waked, and then the noise was in my ears again. I raised myself on end, and sat up in my blanket. The fire was gone out clean, and I was a little coldish. 'Bram, the nigger, had scruged himself into the very ashes, and had quite kivered up his head in the blanket. How he drawed his breath there's no telling, since the tip of his nose warn't to be seen nowhere. Says I, "Bram, do you hear them noises?" But never a word did he answer. Says I, to myself, 'the nigger's smothered.' So I onwrapt him mighty quick, and heard him grunt. Then I know'd there was no harm done. The nigger was only drunk."

"Nebber been drunk dat time," was the usual interruption of 'Bram, whenever he was present at the narration.

"'Bram, you was most certainly drunk, sense I tried my best to waken you, and couldn't get you up."

"Ha! da's 'cause I bin want for sleep, so I nebber consent for ye'r (hear). I bin ye'r berry well all de time; but a man wha's bin trouble wid 'fliction in the stomach all night, mus' hab he sleep out in de morning. I bin ye'r well enough, I tell you."

"You old rascal, if I had thought so, I'd ha' chunk'd you with a lightwood knot!—but the nigger *was* asleep, my friends, in a regular drunk sleep, if ever he was; for when I hearn the noises coming nigh—the hounds and the horses—I drawed him away from the ashes by the legs, and laid him close up agin' the wall t'other side of the fire-place, and pretty much out of sight. I kivered him snug with the blanket, and let him take his sleep out, though I was beginning to be more and more jub'ous about them noises. You see, 'twas the regular noises of a deer-hunt. I could hear the drivers beating about in the thick; then the shout; then the dogs, yelping out whenever they struck upon the trail; I know'd when they nosed the cold trail, and when the scent got warm; and then I heerd the regular rush, when the deer was started, all the dogs in full blast, and making the merriest music. Then I heerd the crack of the gun—first one gun, then another, then another, and another, a matter of four shots—and I felt sure they must ha' got the meat. The horns sounded; the dogs were stopped, and, for a little while, nothing but silence. Oh! I felt awful all over, and monstrous jub'ous of something strange!"

"But why should you feel awful, and what should there be so strange about a deer-hunt near Izard's Camp—a place where you may start deer even at this day?"

"Why, 'twas Sunday, you see, and nobody now, in our times, hunts deer, or anything, a-Sundays; and it 'twan't till after midnight on Saturday that I heer'd the noises. That was enough to make me jub'ous. But when I remember'd how they used to tell me of the rich English gentleman, named Lumley, that once lived in the neighborhood, long afore the old Revolution; what a wicked man he was, and how he used to hunt a-Sundays; and how a judgment come upon him; and how he was lost, in one of his huntings, for a matter of six months or more; and when he was found, 'twas only his skeleton. Well I reckon, to think of all that, was enough to give me a bad scare—and it did. People reckoned he must have been snake-bit, for there were the bones of the snake beside him, with the rattles on, eleven and the button; he must have killed the snake after he was struck. But it didn't help him. He never got away from the spot till they found his skileton, and they know'd him by the ring upon his finger, and his knife, and horn, and gun; but all the iron was ruined, eaten up by the rust. Well, when I heer'd the horns a-Sunday, I recollected all about Squire Lumley, and his wickedness; and, before I seed anything, I was all over in a shiver. Well, presently I heerd the horns blowing merrily again, and the sounds come fresher than ever to my ears. I was oneasy enough, and I made another trial to wake up 'Bram, but 'twas of no use. He was sounder than ever."

"I 'speck I bin sleep den, for true," was the modest interruption of 'Bram, at this stage of the narrative. With a grave shake of the head, Ephraim continued—

"I went out then in front of the house, and the horns were coming nigher from behind it. I was a-thinking to run and hide in the bushes, but I was so beflustered that I was afeer'd I should run right into the jaws of the danger. Though, when I thought of the matter agin,' I got a little bolder, and I said to myself, 'what's the danger, I wonder. I'm in a free country. I'm troubling no man's property. I've let down no man's fence. I've left no man's gate open to let in the cattle. This old house nobody lives in, and I wouldn't ha' troubled it, ef so be 'Bram hadn't been taken sick in his bowels. What's the danger?' When I thought, in this way, to myself, I went in and took a sup of whiskey—a small sup—only a taste—by way of keeping my courage up. I tried to waken 'Bram again, for I said, 'two's always better than one, though one's nigger,' but 'twas no use; 'Bram's sleep was sounder than ever. It was pretty cl'ar that he had soak'd the whiskey mighty deep that night!"

"'Ki! Mas Ephraim! How you talk! Ef you nebber been drink more than me, dat night, you nebber been scare wid de hunters dat blessed Sunday morning."

"The nigger will talk!" said Ephraim, contemptuously, as he continued his narrative.

"Well, I felt stronger after I had taken that little sup, and went out again. Just then there came a blast of the horns almost in my very ears, and in the next minute I hear'd the trampling of horses. Soon a matter of twenty dogs burst out of the woods, and pushed directly for the house as if they knowed it; and then came the riders—five in all—four white men and one nigger. Ef I was scared at the sounds afore, the sight of these people didn't make me feel any easier. They well enough to look at in the face, but, lord bless you, they were dressed in sich an outlandish fashion! Why, even the nigger had on short breeches, reaching only to his knees, and then stockings blue and red streaked, fitting close to his legs;—and sich a leg, all the calf turned in front, and the long part of his foot pretty much where the heel ought to be. Then he had buckles at his knees, and buckles on his shoes, jest for all the world like his master. And he wore a cap like his master, though not quite so handsome, and a great coat of bright indigo blue, with the cuffs and collar trimmed with yellow. His breeches were of a coarse buff, the same color with the gentlemen, only theirs were made with a finer article—the real buff, I reckon. They had on red coats that were mighty pretty, and all their horns were silver mounted. Our Governor and his officers, nowadays, never had on prettier regimentals. Well, up they rode, never taking any more notice of me than ef I was a dog; and I saw the nigger throw down a fine buck from his saddle. There was only one, but he had a most powerful head of horns. While they were all getting off their horses, and the nigger was taking 'em, I turned quietly into the house ag'in to try if a kick or two could get 'Bram out of his blankets. But, lord have mercy, when I look in, what should I see but another nigger there spreading a table with a cloth as white as the driven snow, and a-setting plates, and knives, and forks, and spoons, and bottles, and salt, and pepper, and mustard, and horse-radish, all as ef he had a cupboard somewhere at his hand. I was amazed, and worse than amazed, when I seed my own jug among the other things. But I hadn't the heart to touch it. For that matter, the nigger that was setting out the things kept as sharp an eye upon me as ef I was a thief. But soon the dishes began to show upon the table. There were the pots upon the fire, the gridiron, the Dutch oven, and everything, and the most rousing fire, and 'Bram still asleep in the corner, and knowing nothing about it. I was all over in a sweat. Soon, the gentlemen began to come in, but they took no sort of notice of me; and I slipped out and looked at their horses; but as the nigger was standing by 'em, and looking so strange, I didn't go too nigh. But the deer was still a-lying where he first threw it, and I thought I'd turn the head over and see the critter fairly, when, as I'm a living man, the antlers slipped through my fingers jest as fast as I tried to take 'em,—like so much water or smoke. There was a feel to me as ef I had touched something, but I couldn't take hold no how, and while I was a-trying, the nigger holla'd, in a gruff voice, from the horses—'Don't you touch Maussa's meat!' I was getting desp'rate mighty fast, and I thought I'd push back, and try what good another sup of whiskey would do. Well, when I went into the house, the gentlemen were all a-setting round the table, and busy with knife and fork, jest as ef they were the commonest people. There was a mighty smart chance for feeding at the table. Ham and turkey, a pair of as fine wild ducks, English, as you ever seed; a beef tongue, potetters (potatoes), cabbage, eggs, and other matters, and all for jest five men and their servants. Jest then, one of the gentlemen set his eyes on me, and p'inted to one of the bottles—says he, jest as if I had been his own servant—

"'Hand the bottle.'

"And somehow, I felt as ef I couldn't help myself, but must hand it, sure enough. When he had poured out the liquor, which was a mighty deep red, yet clear as the sunshine, he gin me back the bottle, and I thought I'd take a taste of the stuff, jest to see what it was. I got a chance, and poured out a tolerable dram—supposing it was a sort of red bald face (whiskey)—into a cup and tossed it off in a twinkle. But it warn't bald face, nor brandy, nor wine, nor any liquor that I ever know'd before. It hadn't a strong taste, but was something like a cordial, with a flavor like fruit and essence. 'Twarn't strong, I say; so I tried it ag'in an' ag'in, whenever I could git a chance; for I rather liked the flavor; and I warn't mealy-mouthed at helping myself, as they had enough of the critter, and, by this time, they had begun upon my own old bald-face. They seemed to like it well enough. They tried it several times, as if 'twas something new to them, and they didn't find it hard to make the acquaintance. I didn't quarrel with them, you may be sure, for I never was begrudgeful of my liquor; and, besides, wasn't I trying their'n? Well, I can't tell you how long this lasted. 'Twas a good while; and they kept me busy; one after the other of 'em calling out to me to hand 'em this, and hand 'em that, and even the nigger motioning me to help him with this thing and the other. He didn't say much, and always spoke in a whisper. But, it so happened, that, when I was stretching out for one of the bottles, to try another taste of the cordial, one of the cursed dogs would come always in my way. At last, I gin the beast a kick; and, would you believe it, my foot went clean through him—through skin, and ribs, and body, jest the same as if I had kicked the wind or the water. I did not feel him with my foot. I was all over in a trimble; and the dog yelped, jest as if I had hurt him. Sure enough, at this, the great dark-favored man that sot at the head of the table, he fastened his eye upon me and said in a big threatening voice:

"'Who kick'd my dog?'

"By this time, my blood was up a little. What with the scare I had, and the stuff I'd been a-drinking, I felt a little desperate; and my eye was sot upon the man pretty bold as I said:

"'I was just reaching for my own liquor,'—(now, that warn't exactly true, I confess, for I was reaching for one of their own bottles)—'when the dog came in my way, and I just brushed him with my foot.'

"'Nobody shall kick my dog but myself,' said he, more fierce than ever; and looking as if he meant kicking! That made me a sort o' wolfish, and, just then, something put the old story of Lumley and the rattlesnake fresh into my head; and, I couldn't help myself—but I gin him for answer as nice an imitation of a snake's rattle—you know how well I kin do it, my friends—as ever he heerd in his born days.

"Lord! you should have seen the stir and heard the racket. Every fellow was on his feet in a minnit, and before I could dodge, the great dark-featured man, he rose up, and seized my jug by the handle, and whirled it furious about his head, and then he sent it at me, with such a curse, and such a cry, that I thought all the house a-tumbling to pieces. Like a great wind, they all rushed by me, men and dogs, and nigger, throwing me down in the door-way, and going over me as ef I was nothing in the way. Whether it was the jug that hit me, or them rushing over, and trampling me down, I can't say; but there I lay, pretty much stunned and stupefied; not knowing anything for a long time;—and when I opened my eyes, and could look around me, there I was with 'Bram stooping over me and trying to raise me from the ground."

"*Dat's* true!" said 'Bram, laying special emphasis on dat's and shaking his head significantly. Ephraim continued:

"The strangers were all gone in the twinkling of an eye,—they had swept the platters,—carried off every thing clean,—carried off tables and chairs, bottles and cups, plates and dishes, dinner and drink, pots and ovens, and had even put out the fire; sence, when 'Bram waked up, there was not a sign of it to be seen. My jug was broke all to pieces, and lying beside me at the door, and not a drop of liquor to be had. What they didn't drink, they wasted, the spiteful divels, when they broke the jug over my head."

Such was Ephraim's story, grown into a faith with many, of the Haunted Forest and House near Izard's Camp. In Ephraim's presence, 'Bram does not venture to deny a syllable of the story. He only professes to have seen nothing of it, except the full jug when they arrived at the house, and the broken and empty vessel when he awoke from his sleep. In Ephraim's absence, however, he does not scruple to express his doubts wholly of the ghostly visitors and the strange liquor. His notion is, that Ephraim got drunk upon the "*bald-face*" and dreamed the rest. His only subject of difficulty is that the jug should have been broken. He denies, for himself, that he took a drop too much—considering the state of his stomach.—We must resume our journey hereafter.

Joseph M. Field (1810-1856)

Actor, playwright, newspaper editor, theater manager, and humorist, Joseph M. Field, probably born in England, migrated to the United States sometime after the end of the War of 1812, and settled in New York City with his family. He began his acting career at the Tremont Theater in Boston in 1827, and then after an acting stint in New York, in 1833, joined Sol Smith's touring company, which played in St. Louis, Cincinnati, Mobile, Montgomery, and many towns in between. From 1835 to 1844, Field and his wife, Eliza Riddle, were mainstays in Noah Ludlow and Sol Smith's acting company, with Field's principal roles being comical ones. In addition, Field wrote plays of his own, mainly farces and burlesques, but none achieved popular success. Among these are *Tourists in America* (1835), a play satirizing English travelers in America, and *Oregon, or the Disputed Territory* (1846), which employs allegorical characters in treating the conflict between the United States and England over the Northwest Territory.

As a touring actor, Field spent periods of time both in New Orleans and St. Louis, two cities that would also figure prominently in his journalistic career. In 1839, Field, under the pseudonym "Straws," began contributing poems to the New Orleans *Picayune,* and a year later this newspaper sent him to Europe as their foreign correspondent. It seems likely that Field's experience as a writer and reporter for the *Picayune* played a part in his decision in 1844 to found, along with his brother Matthew and Charles Keemle, the St. Louis *Reveille,* a newspaper that would be a major regional outlet for Old Southwest humor. The *Reveille* featured comic sketches not only of the Field brothers but also of Sol Smith, John S. Robb ("Solitaire"), others with pseudonyms like Jo, Bird, Thunder, and Wing, and still others by anonymous contributors. Though Matthew died shortly after the newspaper was established, Joseph Field and Keemle continued to edit the *Reveille* until 1850. During his tenure as editor, Field, using the pseudonym "Everpoint," contributed frontier humor sketches, both to the *Reveille* and William T. Porter's *Spirit of the Times.* In fact, Porter included Field's "Kicking a Yankee" in his anthology of humorous pieces *A Quarter Race in Kentucky, and*

Other Sketches (1847), all previously published in the *Spirit*, and an indication of Porter's fondness for this sketch.

Among Joseph Field's other contributions to the genre of Old South humor were two pieces on Mike Fink. In "The Death of Mike Fink," published in the *Reveille* in 1844, Field sought to clear away the "mythic haze" regarding Fink's death. And in a longer work, "Mike Fink: 'The Last of the Boatmen," published in the *Reveille* in 1847, Field captures effectively the vernacular speech of keelboatmen as well as presents lively and sometimes crude comedy in his description of the collision between Mike's keelboat and a Mississippi steamboat and the subsequent sinking of both crafts. In 1847, Field collected some of his previously published humorous newspaper sketches in *The Drama of Pokerville; the Bench and Bar of Jurytown, and Other Stories*, which helped to give his work wider exposure. The sketches, all published between 1844 and 1846, cover many of the familiar subject areas of southwestern humor, including hunts, politics, riverboat activities, theater life, courtroom antics, roguery, drunkenness, pranks, and the experiences of a country bumpkin in the city.

While Field was the editor of the *Reveille*, he received a letter, dated June 15, 1846, from Edgar Allan Poe, whom he knew, soliciting his assistance (and hopefully through his influence that of the editors of the New Orleans *Picayune* as well) in disclaiming false allegations and impressions, spawned by the editor of the New York *Evening Mirror* and damaging to Poe's reputation. Field responded by issuing a defense of Poe in the June 30, 1846, *Reveille*.

When the *Reveille* was sold in 1850, Field returned to the theater, managing theaters in Mobile and St. Louis.

Texts: "A Lyncher's Own Story," St. Louis *Daily Reveille*, July 6, 1845. "Kicking a Yankee," St. Louis *Daily Reveille*, July 19, 1845.

A Lyncher's Own Story

"I never fight when angry, gentlemen."—Jas. Bowie

"I go in for reprisals, gentlemen—by the eternal heavens, reprisals! Seize on abolition property in New Orleans, Natchez—wherever found. Seize on the Yankee scoundrels, themselves, and exchange them for our own kidnapped slaves—nigger for nigger, by thunder!"

This violent speech, delivered with savage energy by a thin, wiry looking man—one of a group collected around the stove in the "social hall" of a Mississippi steam boat—was received with a shout of applause by all assembled.

"Good, by gracious!" "That's the talk!" "You're a horse, Judge!" &c., &c., followed the explosion, like a rattle of small thunder, till an enormous figure, in a white hat and blanket coat—yet, withal, a good looking man—arose slowly, stretched himself, and brushed back the thick hair from his broad forehead, and then, in quiet yet evidently pleased accents, said, with a smile:

"Yes, Judge, that's the talk, I believe! Gentle*m*en, we'll take a little something."

There was a general demonstration as if to rise, when the barkeeper, who made one of the crowd, and who appeared to be singularly impressed with the new doctrine of "reprisals," begged the "Colonel" would keep his seat, and the "drinks" should be brought.

"Sit down, Colonel," cried the *energetic* 'Judge,' emptying his mouth of a 'chew,' by way of preparation for 'one more drink,' and at the same time running his heels higher up the stove pipe—"sit down, this thing has got to be fixed between the North and the South, and a little talk about it won't be lost."

All resumed their seats, the "drinks" were brought, and, by the spirit with which fresh cigars were lighted, it was evident that the subject had only got fairly under headway in the assembly. It was in the fall of 18—. During the preceding summer, a couple of slaves had been seduced and finally wrested from their masters by the Boston Abolitionists, and the numerous southerners, then at the north, filled with violent indignation, gave vent to the most furious threats and denunciations. It is not intended, here, to argue, or even comment upon the vexatious question of slavery, but simply to sketch a few features and incidents of southwestern character and adventure.

It was a cold and rainy night, the steamer plunged along amid dense shadows, in which the unpracticed eye could not even distinguish an outline; the main cabin was spread with mattresses, and the persons around the stove, the last up, deserting some half hour previously a couple of card tables, and falling upon an exciting topic, now promised to make a night of it.

"Yes, gentlemen," resumed the fiery Judge, "it may seem like a desperate doctrine, but what except desperation is left us; the crisis *must* come! My slave is my property, guaranteed to me by the constitution; if Massachusetts sanctions the seizure of our niggers, who shall cry shame on Louisiana, should she retort upon their ships!"

Another cheer of approval, further stimulated the speaker, who rushed into a vehement relation of several other Abolition outrages, which led to certain stories of southern vengeance upon Abolition agents; a sort of vindictive phrenzy spread among the company; fresh drinks were called in; "lynching" was a theme upon which all were eloquent, and well known cases of punishment under that summary code, were repeated, commented and gloated on with a savage enjoyment which promised a rough fate for the next tract distributer who might be caught by any of the party.

During this time the "Colonel," though evidently of kindred sentiments with the company, had preserved his equanimity; he smoked his cigar deliberately, listened to the different speakers with an assenting smile, or, may be, a "just so, Doctor," or a "quite correct, gentlemen," but, finally, after the relation of a retaliating capture and execution under horribly exciting circumstances, he, in mild tones, and with an aspect that indicated any thing but ferocity, signified his intention to relate "a little circumstance," himself.

"I'm not a passionate man, gentlemen," said he, drawing up his legs slowly, and adjusting his vast bulk in the chair,—"I'm rather a calm man, and apt to bear putting upon, rather, but I go in for Lynch law, *some*, for all that. I had a little case of my own with one of these Abolition gentlemen, once, and I acted up to the law, fully—on my honor, I did, gentlemen. I am a family man, gentlemen, and a friend who comes to see me, or a stranger wishing to put up, if an honest looking white man, always finds my house a home while in it. I keep servants to wait on them, purposely, I do, gentlemen, and treachery under such circumstances is a mean thing—it's not a white man's act, gentlemen." An emphatic assent was expressed on all hands. "Well, I lost two boys, valuable servants, gentlemen, by entertaining wolves in sheep's clothing, and I *de*termined that the next one who called, should be punished, *some*, and I didn't wait long, for, somehow, they had got the hang of my house, gentlemen, and took advantage of my temper. A very polite stranger, with his *wife* and a 'dear-born,' came along; *he* had something, however, the matter with his eyes, *when I looked at him*, and so I put my own servant, Jake—a very good boy, gentlemen—a perfect *white man*, and whom I never said a cross word to, in my life—I put Jake to 'tend on them, and, sure enough, after I was in bed, back came the boy to say that the gentleman had offered to run him off! Well, I told Jake to go with him,—first leaving word which way he was to travel, and then I went to sleep. In the morning, Jake's wife—a decent wench, gentlemen—a perfect lady—came to tell me all about the arrangement, so taking my overseer with me, I started after them."

"I should *think* so!" "Wake snakes!" "Go ahead, Judge!" A dozen eager exclamations evinced the zest with which the climax of the story was expected. The narrator, however, proceeded with *a sang froid* that was inimitable.

"I hadn't gone but a few miles, when back comes Jake, meeting me. The fox, gentlemen, had smelt a trap and *put*, with his wife and wagon, leaving the boy to take care of himself. Of course, I didn't drop the matter, but followed up and soon got on the trail. I tracked him back a good many miles from the river, but missed him near a lake which was back of our plantations, and lost a good deal of time. Towards afternoon, returning by another road towards the river, between the *bayou* and Dr. Boll's new. clearing, I heard voices and in a minute, drove right up to a crowd of neighbors, who had got my visitor, his wife, and his 'dearborn' right in the middle of them! The fact is, gentle*men*, one or two of them had got notice that there were wolves about, and were on the look out for varmint, as my acquaintance drove in among them."

"Ha! ha! ha!" A general chuckle of delight was succeeded by a grin of anticipation.

"I found my friend, gentlemen, talking right and left, like a lawyer—making every thing straight and agreeable, when suddenly he caught sight of me, at the next moment of Jake; and, gentlemen, if ever man gave up the ghost before the breath was out of him, it was that fellow; his eyes glazed, a dark circle settled round them, while his lower lip, blue and quivering as the blood left it, after making an effort, as it were, to recall the relaxed jaw to its duty, finally fell with it; and there the man sat, staring at me—motionless, with the exception of his throat, which worked spasmodically in the effort to supply itself with moisture from the parched mouth. Gentlemen, he was the picture of a small rascal caught in a tall snap! I first blushed that he was a white man, and next that he was an American!"

"American h—ll!" interrupted one of the pilots of the boat, who, perched upon a pile of trunks, had hitherto said nothing—"he was a d—d *Yankee*, that's what he was!" This distinction was recognized with great applause, of course. The "Colonel" resumed:

"There was just about a tolerable court on the spot, gentlemen, and it was agreed to try the fellow right thar. There was evidence besides mine, for one man had followed him up along the plantations for twenty miles; but yet the woman kinder stood between him and his due, and I thought I'd question her, too. She was young, gentlemen, with a simple look—had evidently neither the heart nor the wit of a woman about her, and at my first question—something put it into my head—'Are you *married* to this man?' she burst into tears, and sobbed as if her heart would break. I had him taken away at once, and out it all came—with no thought of injuring her companion, though; it was the simple impulse to relieve a timid mind by confession. She was *not* his wife, gentlemen. She had taught school in Tennessee, where this man saw her, and first persuading her to aid him in the circulation of abolitionist tracts, finally seduced and carried her to New Orleans, where, growing more bold as he extended his acquaintance with the country, he had made another arrangement with the 'Society'— one of greater profit and of greater risk—namely to 'run off' negroes from the plantations along the coast. Gentlemen, this is a mighty long story, Barkeeper—"

"Oh, no, no!" go ahead, Colonel." "Drinks" at the moment were declined, but the shorter operation of taking a fresh "chew" was indulged in, by way of filling up the pause.

"I had another question to ask the woman. 'Do you love this man?' said I. The poor creature wept worse than ever, gentlemen; she said her only desire was to go to some friends in Illinois, where she hoped to be welcome and to get along more wisely. 'He abuses you then,' said I. 'Oh,' said she. 'I wouldn't mind that if I thought he wouldn't *kill me!*' In short, as I hope to live a mild and considerate citizen, gentlemen, that livid, cowardly scoundrel, had, during my pursuit of him, after threatening his victim—now his burthen—till she was nearly lifeless, actually attempted to *drown her in the swamp!* I needn't tell you, gentlemen, how unanimous the verdict was in this case; the woman, for whom we subsequently made up a subscription, was moved off towards the nearest house; the man—a mighty small figure any how—shrunk to half his natural size; discolored as if the last corrupting change had anticipated the grave; his arms bound behind his back—and shivering on the ground, too spent to exhibit a spasm,—with the rein which he had lately held in his hand, buckled round his neck for a halter—like a thing too abject, even to *hang*—awaited the selection of a crotch for him to swing from."

It may be supposed that the picture, the horrid features of which were thus in detail described, had gradually excited the phlegmatic limner,—not at all! His sentences swelled, not from the mere impetuous gathering of ideas, but, as it seemed, from a good natured desire to make the story as interesting as possible to his hearers; while in no respect exhibited nervelessness, therr was not a flash of *passion* during the whole relation. This was not the case with the hearers, though. The eyes of the "Judge" seemed bursting from his head in eager expectation, while the "chewing" operation on his part was a moment suspended; others were like him; a few again, by an eager but painful contraction of the brows, betrayed a softer nature,—at any rate, more sensitive nerves.

"Yes, gentlemen, there was a moment's delay in choosing a limb; in the mean time, by way of hanging the culprit with a little life in him, some one had given him a mouthful of whisky, when, recovering his tongue, he began to beg; from begging, gentlemen, he got to screaming; blood actually trickled from his straining eyes, and it was getting *unpleasant*,—no dignity about it! an *idea* struck me; I just climbed up, hand over hand, a pretty stout sapling close by me; I'm a heavy man, gentlemen, and, as I mounted, over the young tree came with me—bent like a fishing rod—"

There was a breathless silence in the company; an enormous "roach," peeping from a crack in the paneling, could hardly have crossed without being heard, while each eye was riveted horribly upon the speaker.

"The culprit, gentlemen, took the *idea* sooner than any of the others, and his shrieks and ravings were dreadful—really dreadful! Another climbed after me, and, with the added weight, down we both came, half hid amongst the light boughs of the top, and the loose end of the rein was made fast in a second. '*One instant, for God's sake! I've got children! for the sake of my soul*'—a half-uttered scream, gentlemen, mingled with the rush of the boughs, as *we* dropped to the ground, and the nigger thief, with a jerk that *snapped his neck,* flew into the air, describing a half-circle as spanned by his halter, and swinging back to us again from the other side!"

A long breath was drawn by the whole company. The "Judge" was the first to break the succeeding pause:

"Well, that *was* an idea! We'll drink on that, gentlemen, by thunder!"

All moved to the bar—some two or three silently, the others as to a mere change of *enjoyment.* "Colonel," cried the Judge, "name your liquor—that *was* an idea!"

"Yes!" exclaimed another, with no less enthusiasm, "a first rate idea!"

"A splendid idea!" "A glorious idea!" was the general chorus.

"Yes, gentle*men,*" complacently observed the giant, as he raised his glass—"I think, myself, that it *was a sweet* idea!"

Kicking a Yankee

A very handsome friend of ours, who a few weeks ago was *poked* out of a comfortable office up the river, has betaken himself to Bangor, for a time, to recover from the wound inflicted upon his feelings by our "unprincipled and immolating administration."

Change of air must have had an instant effect upon his spirits, for, from Galena, he writes us an amusing letter, which, among other things, tells us of a desperate quarrel that took place on board of the boat between a real live dandy tourist, and a real live yankee settler. The latter trod on the toes of the former; whereupon the former threatened to kick "out of the cabin" the latter.

"You'll kick *me* out of this cabing?"

"Yes, sir, I'll kick you out of this cabin!"

"You'll kick *me,* Mr. *Hitch*cock, out of this cabing?"

"Yes, sir, I'll kick *you,* Mr. Hitchcock!"

"Wal, I guess," said the Yankee, very coolly, after being perfectly satisfied that it was himself who stood in such imminent peril of assault—"I guess, since you talk of kicking, you've never heard me tell about old Bradly and my mare, there, to hum?"

"No, sir, nor do I wish—"

"Wal, guess it won't set you back much, any how, as kicking's generally best to be considered on. You see old Bradly, is one of these sanctimonious, long-faced hypocrites, who put on a religious suit every Sabbath morning, and with a good deal of screwing manage to keep it on till after sermon in the afternoon; and as I was a Universalist, he allers picked me out as a subject for religious conversation—and the darned hypocrite would talk about heaven, hell, and the devil—the crucifixion and prayer, without ever winking. Wal, he had an old roan mare that would jump over any fourteen rail fence in Illinois, and open any door in my barn that hadn't a padlock on it. Tu or three times I found her in my stable, and I told Bradly about it, and he was 'very sorry'—'an unruly animal'—'would watch her,' and a hull lot of such things, all said in a very serious manner, with a face twice as long as old Deacon Farrar's on Sacrament day. I knew all the time he was lying, and so I watched him and his old roan tu; and for three nights regular, old roan came to my stable about bed time, and just at daylight Bradly would come, bridle her, and ride off. I then just took my old mare down to a blacksmith's shop, and had some shoes made with 'corks' about four inches long, and had 'em nailed on to her hind feet. Your heels, mister, ain't nuthing tu 'em. I took her home, give her about ten feet halter, and tied her right in the centre of the stable, fed her well with oats about nine o'clock, and after taking a good smoke, went to bed, knowing that my old mare was a truth telling animal, and that she'd give a good report of herself in the morning. I hadn't got fairly to sleep before the old 'oman hunched me and wanted to know what on airth was the matter out at the stable. Says I, 'Go to sleep, Peggy, it is nothing but Kate—she is kicking off flies, I guess!' Putty soon she hunched me agin, and says she, Mr. Hitchcock, du git up and see what in the world is the matter with Kate, for she is kicking most powerfully.' 'Lay still, Peggy, Kate will take care of herself, I guess.' Wal, the next mornin', about daylight, Bradley, with bridle in hand, cum to the stable, and, as true as the book of Genesis; when he saw the old roan's sides, starn, and head, he cursed and swore worse than you did, mister, when I came down on your toes. Arter breakfast that mornin' Joe Davis cum to my house, and says he, 'Bradley's old roan is nearly dead—she's cut all to pieces and can scarcely move.' 'I want to know,' says I, 'how on airth did it happen?' Now Joe Davis was a member of the same church with Bradley, and whilst we were talking, up cum that everlastin' hypocrite, and says he, 'Mr. Hitchcock, my old roan is ruined!' 'Du tell,' says I. 'She is cut all to pieces,' says he; 'do you know whether she was in your stable, Mr. Hitchcock, last night?' Wal, mister, with this I let out: 'Do I *know* it?'—(the Yankee here, in illustration, made a sudden advance upon the dandy, who made way for him unconsciously, as it were)—'Do I know it, you no-souled, shad-bellied, squash-headed, old night-owl you!—you hay-hookin,' corn-cribbin,' fodder-fudgin,' centshavin,' whitlin'-of-nuthin' you!—Kate kicks like a mere dumb beast, but I've reduced the thing to *a science!*" The Yankee had not ceased to advance, or the dandy, in his astonishment, to retreat; and now, the motion of the latter being accelerated by an apparent demonstration on the part of the former to "suit the action to the word," he found himself in the "social hall," tumbling backwards over a pile of baggage, and tearing the knees of his pants as he scrambled up, a perfect scream of laughter stunning him from all sides. The defeat was total;—a few moments afterwards he was seen dragging his own trunk ashore, while Mr. *Hitch*cock finished his story on the boiler-deck.

Hardin E. Taliaferro (1811-1875)

Though a prominent Baptist minister on the Alabama frontier, where he moved in 1835, and senior editor of *Southwestern Baptist*, a periodical principally intended for Baptist preachers and laymen in the state, Taliaferro (pronounced Tolliver) was born in 1811 on a farm on the Little Fisher River in Surry County, North Carolina, a region bordering the Blue Ridge Mountains of Virginia. He is best known for a collection of humorous sketches and tales, *Fisher's River (North Carolina) Scenes and Characters, by "Skitt," "Who was Raised Thar,"* published by Harper and Brothers in 1859. His formative years in Surry County served as the chief inspiration for Taliaferro's humor.

In *Fisher's River* Taliaferro did what no other antebellum southern humorist had done before: he transcribed some of the tales, sketches, and sermons he remembered hearing local Surry County yarn spinners recount. Like his successor Joel Chandler Harris, the creator of Uncle Remus who would appropriate the animal folktales that he had heard slaves tell and would provide an authorial framework to introduce these humorous fables, Taliaferro also created a frame, using it to describe his local raconteurs such as Davy Lane, Oliver Stanley, Johnson Snow, Larkin Snow, and the Reverend Charles Gentry, the latter an African American slave and Baptist preacher and one of the few black characters featured in Old Southwestern humor. In Gentry, Taliaferro moved an African American character from the margins to the center. Using the frame device, Taliaferro set the stage for their oral accounts and anecdotes, with the first twenty-three chapters of *Fisher's River* focusing on scenes in the northwestern section of Surry County.

Following the publication of *Fisher's River*, Taliaferro, though very busy with his activities as a minister and editor and publisher of a Baptist periodical, continued to write humorous sketches. In the summer of 1860, he wrote George William Bagby, the editor of the *Southern Literary Messenger*, inquiring about contributing some humorous sketches. Between November 1860 and October 1863, Taliaferro, under the signature of "Skitt," the same pseudonym he had used in *Fisher's River*, wrote nine humorous pieces for the *Messenger*, most treating subjects and characters similar to those in his book, but with less vernacular voice. The best of the *Messenger* pieces—"Parson Squint, by Skitt, Who Has Seen Him," "Tasting Religion," "Sketch by Skitt: Johnson Snow and Uncle Davy Lane," and "Deacon Crow"—all treat religious subjects.

At the end of the Civil War, Taliaferro distinguished himself in yet another way from other southwestern humorists. In response to requests by some of the newly emancipated slaves, the American Baptist Home Mission of Society of Boston instigated a campaign in the South to establish African American churches and to provide ministerial training for interested black candidates. Taliaferro was one of the few white Baptist ministers in Alabama to volunteer, and between 1869 and 1872, he dutifully assisted in training blacks for the Baptist ministry in towns near Tuskegee. In addition, he promoted and helped to organize the first Baptist State Convention of African American Alabamian Baptists.

Taliaferro's contributions to the humor of the Old South in *Fisher's River*, featuring lively folk materials, some of which are tall tales, mock-sermons, and oral anecdotes of real-life storytellers, are largely sympathetic, and an indication that he genuinely liked and appreciated the characters and scenes he treated. In his assessment of *Fisher's River*, Cratis D. Williams observed that it "perhaps the most important book portraying the social life and customs of the Southern mountain people to appear before the Civil War."

Texts: "Ride in a Peach Tree," "The Pigeon Roost," "The Origin of Whites," and "Jonah and the Whale," *Fisher's River (North Carolina) Scenes and Characters, by "Skitt," "Who was Raised Thar"* (New York: Harper Brothers, 1859).

Uncle Davy Lane

I MUST not forget, in these random sketches, my old friend and neighbor Uncle Davy Lane. Some men make an early and decided impression upon you—features, actions, habits, all the entire man, real and artificial. "Uncle Davy" was that kind of man.

I will mention a few things that make me remember him. His looks were peculiar. He was tall, dark, and rough-skinned; lymphatic, dull, and don't-care-looking in his whole physiognomy. He had lazy looks and movements. Nothing could move him out of his slow, horse-mill gait but snakes, of which "creeturs he was monstrous 'fraid." The reader shall soon have abundant evidence of the truth of this admission in his numerous and rapid flights from "sarpunts."

Uncle Davy was a gunsmith, and, as an evidence of the fact, he carried about with him the last gun he ever made. His gun, a rifle, was characteristic of its maker and owner—rough and unfinished outside, but good within. It was put in an old worm-eaten half-stock which he had picked up somewhere, and the barrel had never been dressed nor ground outside. He would visit a neighbor early in the morning, sit down with his rifle across his knees, in "too great a hurry" to set it aside, would stay all day, would lay it by only at meals, which he seldom refused, but "never was a-hongry."

He had a great fund of long-winded stories and incidents, mostly manufactured by himself—some few he had "hearn"—and would bore you or edify you, as it might turn out, from sun to sun, interspersing them now and then with a dull, guttural, lazy laugh.

He became quite a proverb in the line of big story-telling. True, he had many obstinate competitors, but he distanced them all farther than lie did the numerous snakes that "run arter him." He had given his ambitious competitors fair warning thus:

"Ef any 'um beats me, I'll sell out my deadnin' and hustle off to other deadnin's."

In sheer justice to Uncle Davy, however, and with pleasure I record the fact, that he reformed his life, became a Christian, I hope, as well as a Baptist, and died a penitent man....

Ride in a Peach Tree

"Now when I got my shot-bag off uv the moon, I lost no time, which I'd lost a great deal arter that old buck, as jist norated. I moseyed home in a hurry, straightened old Bucksmasher, and piked off to Skull Camp* to smash up a few old bucks on that grit. Soon as I landed I seen a dozen old bucks and one old doe. I planted myself, fur they was comin' right smack to'ads me, and I waited tell they got in shootin' range, as it were. I knowed ef I smashed Mrs. Doe fust I'd be right apt to smash all the Mr. Bucks. That's the way with all creation—the males allers a-traipsin' arter the females.

"So I lammed away at her, fotched her to the yeth, and the bucks scampered off. Agin I got loadened up they come back to the doe, smellin' round, and I blazed away agin, and tripped up the heels uv one uv 'um. They'd run off a little ways uvry time, but agin I'd load up thar'd allers be one ready to be smashed, and I jist kep' smashin' away tell there were but one left, and he were a whopper.

"I felt in my shot-bag, and, pox take the luck! there warn't a bullit in it—nothin' but a peach-stone. I crammed it down, thort I'd salute him with that, and blazed away, aimin' to hit him right behind the wethers, and, by golly! ef he didn't slap down his tail and outrun creation, and give it two in the game. I run up, out with my butcher-knife, stuck uvry one on 'um afore you could cry' cavy. And sich a pile on' um, all lyin' cross and pile, you nuver seen in yer borned days.

"I moseyed home in a turkey-trot, got Jim and Sanders and the little waggin, went arter 'um, and, I tell you, we had nice livin' fur a fortnight. Some o' the old bucks would a cut four inches clare fat on the rump. Molly didn't hev to use any hog fat nur fry no bacon with 'um. We sopped both sides uv ur bread, and greased ur mouths from ear to ear. It made the childering as sassy as it does a sea-board feller when he gits his belly full uv herrin'. Thar was skins plenty to make me and all the boys britches, and to buy ammernition to keep old Bucksmasher a-talkin' fur a long time, fur he's a mighty gabby old critter to varmunts uv uvry kind, well as to old bucks, he is.

"Arter makin a desput smash among old bucks uvry whar else fur three very long years, I thort I'd try my luck in Skull Camp agin. I took plenty ammernition with me this time—didn't care about shootin' peach-stones any more out'n old Bucksmasher—and piked off full tilt.

"Soon as I got on good hunting yeth, I seen right by the side uv a clift uv rocks (I were on the upper side uv the clift) a fine young peach-tree, full uv master plum peaches. I were monstrous hongry and dry, and thanked my stars fur the good luck. I sot down old Bucksmasher, stepped from the top uv the clift inter the peach-tree—nuver looked down to see whar it were growin'—jerked out old Butch, and went to eatin' riproarin' fashion.

"I hadn't gulluped down more'n fifty master peaches afore, by golly! the tree started off, with me in it, faster nur you uver seen a scared wolf run. When it had run a mile ur so, I looked down to see what it mout mean. And what do you think? True as preachin,' the peach-tree was growin' out'n an old buck, right behind his shoulders.

"I thort my time had come, for on he moseyed over logs, rocks, clifts, and all sorts o' things, and me up in the tree. He went so fast, he did, that he split the wind, and made it roar in my head like a harricane. I tried to pray, but soon found I had no breath to spar in that way, fur he went so orful fast that my wind was sometimes clean gone. He run in that fashion fur fifteen mile, gin out, stopped to rest, when I got out'n my fast-runnin' stage mighty soon, and glad o' the chance.

"I left him pantin' away like he were mighty short o' wind, returned thanks fur once, tuck my foot in my hand, and walked all the way back to old Bucksmasher. I seen more old bucks on my way than I uver seen in the same length uv time in all my borned days. They knowed jist as well as I did that I had nothin' to smash 'um with. Thar they was a-kickin' up thar heels and snortin' at me fur fifteen long miles—miles measured with a 'coon-skin, and the tail throwed in fur good measure, fur sure. It were a mighty trial, but I grinned and endured it. I piked on and landed at the place whar I started in my peach-tree stage, found old Bucksmasher, shouldered him, and moseyed fur home, with my feathers cut, fur I'd made a water haul that time, fur sure and sartin'.

"To—be—shore, Mr. Lane?" said old Mr. Wilmoth, a good, credulous old man; "ef I didn't know you to be a man of truth, I couldn't believe you. How do you think that peach-tree come up in the back of that deer?"

"Bless you, man! it was from the peach-stone I shot in his back, as jist norated—nothin' plainer."

*A spur of the Blue Ridge, at the foot of which one or two human skeletons were found at the first settling of the country, where there were signs of an old hunters' camp; hence the name of the mountain.

The Pigeon Roost

"Now, do ye see, a man will git tired out on one kind o' meat, I don't care a drot what it is ('ceptin' Johnson Snow, who nuver gits tired o' hog's guillicks and turnup greens). So I got tireder of them thar turkeys, which thar was so many, than I uver did uv old buck meat. I hearn uv a mighty pigeon-roost down in the Little Mountings,* so I 'tarmined to make a smash uv some uv 'um, to hev a variety uv all sorts o' meat. I had got to turnin' up my nose whenuver Molly sot turkey on the table, which I hated to do, fur she's a mighty kind critter.

"So I just fixed up old Tower** and filled my shot-bag chug full uv drap-shot, mounted old Nip,*** and moseyed off fur the pigeon-roost. I 'ruv thar 'bout two hours by the sun, and frum that blessed hour till chock dark the heavens was dark with 'um comin' inter the roost. It is unconceivable to tell the number on 'um, which it were so great. Bein' a man that has a character fur truth, I won't say how many there was. Thar was a mighty heap uv saplins fur 'um to roost in, which they would allers light on the biggest trees fust, then pitch down on the little uns ter roost.

"Now jist at dark I thort I'd commence smashin' 'um; so I hitched old Nip to the limb uv a tree with a monstrous strong bridle—a good hitchin' place, I thort. I commenced blazin' away at the pigeons like thunder and lightinin'; which they'd light on big trees thick as bees, bend the trees to the yeth like they'd been lead. Uvry pop I'd spill about a pint uv drap-shot at 'um, throwed at 'um by Thompson's powder, which made a dreffel smash among 'um. By hokey! I shot so fast, and so long, and so often, I het old Tower so hot that I shot six inches off uv the muzzle uv the old slut. I seen it were no use to shoot the old critter clean away, which I mout have some use fur agin; so I just quit burnin' powder and flingin' shot arter I'd killed 'bout a thousand uv 'um, fur sure.

"Arter I'd picked up as many uv 'um as my wallets would hold, I looked fur old Nip right smack whar I'd hitched him, but he were, like King Saul's asses, nowhar to be found. I looked a consid'able spell next to the yeth, but, bless you, honey! I mout as well a sarched fur a needle in a haystack. At last I looked up inter a tree 'bout forty foot high, and thar he were swingin' to a limb, danglin' 'bout 'tween the heavens and the yeth like a rabbit on a snare-pole. I could hardly keep from burstin' open laughin' at the odd fix the old critter were in. The way he whickered were a fact, when I spoke to him—wusser nur ef I'd a had a stack uv fodder fur him ur a corn-crib to put him in."

"How come him up thar, Uncle Davy?" said Bill Holder, a great quiz.

"Why, I hitched him to the limb uv a big tree bent to the yeth with pigeons, you numskull, and when they riz the tree went up, and old Nip with it, fur sure."

"But how did you get him down?" said Bill again.

"That's nuther here nor thar; I got him down, and that's 'nuff fur sich pukes as you ter know. Soon as I got him down I piked fur home with my pigeons, and we made uvry pan and pot stink with 'um fur one whet, and they made us all as sassy as a Tar River feller when he gits his belly full uv fresh herrin.'"

*A range of mountains by that name, an offshoot from the Blue Ridge, in the "Hollows of the Yadkin."
**The name of his musket
***The name of his horse.

Rev. Charles Gentry

I MUST not entirely omit the negroes, as some of them were men of renown. I have made honorable mention of "Gingy-cake Josh Easley." What the people would have done for "gingy-cakes" at their musters and public gatherings I can not tell, had it not been for clever Josh. Josh was respected by all, white and black. His master moved to Missouri, and there Josh died. He used to keep us all alive singing corn songs at "corn-shuckings."

I could mention many good and clever negroes, but will only pay my respects to Rev. Charles Gentry. Charles was a Baptist preacher, and belonged to "Shelt Gentry." His master and mistress were Baptists, and Charles was quite a privileged character. Next to Rev. Pleasant Cocker, Charles stood highest in their estimation. He was not without "gifts," nor was he destitute of a proper amount of vanity. As to grammar, if he ever heard of it, he had no use for it, not he. His theology was not always sound, yet a good deal of it was quite original, as the two extracts from his sermons which I shall give the reader will abundantly prove. Rev. Charles had a *penchant* for controversy, and was often running up against established views, and upsetting them by the force of his cataract voice and rail-mauling gestures, if not by argument.

Naturalists have for ages been trying to account for the different forms and complexions of men. Some will have them to be of different races, not all descended from the same pair, Adam and Eve. Others contend that all have descended from the same pair, but climate and accidental causes have made the difference; hence Professor A and Professor B have their diverse theories and their disciples and admirers. When men leave the plain teachings of the Bible and go into vague speculations, one man's hypothesis is nearly as good as another's.

The Origin of Whites

I will now give my readers a new theory from the lips (for negroes do not write) of the Rev. Charles Gentry and commend it to the consideration of Professor Agassiz and Dr. Nott. The Rev. Charles Gentry was "explanifying" to his "bredderin ob color" how the first white man came into existence. He held forth on this wise:

"Beloved bredderin, de white folks ar clean out of it when dey 'firm dat de fust man was a white man. I'm not a-gwine to hab any sich doctering. De fact is, Adam, Cain, Abel, Seth, was all ob 'um black as jet. Now you 'quire how de white man cum. Why, dis a-way. Cain he kill his brudder Abel wid a great big club—he walkin-stick—and God he cum to Cain and say, 'Cain! where is dy brudder Abel?' Cain he pout out de lip, and say, 'I don't know; what ye axin' me fur? I ain't my brudder Abel's keeper.' De Lord he gits in airnest, and stomps on de ground, and say, 'Cain! you Cain! whar is dy brudder Abel? I say, Cain! whar is dy brudder?' Cain he turn white as bleach cambric in de face, and de whole race ob Cain dey bin white ebber since. De mark de Lord put on de face ob Cain was a white mark. He druv him inter de land ob Nod, and all de white folks hab cum frum de land ob Nod, jis' as you've hearn."

Jonah and the Whale

Some divines, to pacify infidels and skeptics, and make, as they suppose, the Bible more acceptable to them, have a knack of explaining the miraculous truths of the Bible on natural principles and according to the teachings of human wisdom, and their preaching and expositions are, to say the least of it, semi-infidelic. Rev. Charles Gentry had heard one of those preachers somewhere who explained all miracles according to natural sequences. Charles had any amount of ambition, and wished to show his "larnin'" in the same way. Accordingly, at his next appointment, he delivered a learned dissertation on Jonah and the whale. He held his audience "spellbound" for some time, but I can only give the *narrative* part of the able discourse. It was as follows:

"Dearly beloved brudderin, dar is much said about dis Jonah and de whale business; a heap a-spoutin' about it, tryin' to outspout de whale hisself; but one half o' 'um don't know what dey talkin' 'bout; dis chile does, howsomeber, 'bout de whole matter. Den listen, dat ye may hear. Well, Jonah he tries to git away from de Lord, and he gits in a ship—a big un, too—and tinks dat is de place fur him; but he miss him fur as ef he'd a burnt he shirt. Dar Jonah he lie snug in de ship as a flea under a nigger's shirt collar. But, bless you, brudderin! De Lord he raise a mighty whirlygust, and de ship rock to and fro like a drunkard man. De men dey guess what was de matter, and dey cum and take Jonah by de nap o' de neck and de hind part o' de britches, and swing him backuds and foruds; last dey pitch him head foremost, *co-souse,* inter de sea.

"De whirlygust he stop right smack. But, bless de Lord! whar Jonah? A great big fish cum up and lick him down like salt—hardly a bug mouful fur sich a big whoppin feller. Jonah, when he gits down inter de paunch o' de fish, he squawks out, 'O Lord, what hab I done?' De fish he say, 'Hush yer mouf!' And de fish he swim, swim, swim, and kep' a-swimmin,' and Jonah he bawls out de same ting. De fish he gits more in airnest, and say, 'Hush yer mouf, I tell yer' and on he swim, swim, swim, till he cum to de Luxine Sea, as de white folk call him, but I call him *Black Sea,* 'caze he's black as jet, like a nigger.

"But pardon dis 'gression.

"When de fish he gits inter de Persian Gulf, near de mouf ob de old Euphrates, Jonah he gits mighty restless, and cries out agin, 'O Lord, what hab I done?' De fish he tell him to hush agin. No use; Jonah he holler louder and louder. De fish no mind him. Now Jonah he hab mighty sharp finger-nails, and he use 'um good, I tell yer. He begin ter claw and scratch the fish's paunch, 'tarmined to git out'n dar. De fish he gits sick in de craw, and he swim, swim, swim right fur land, 'tarmined to throw him up to dry. And, sure nuff, he gin one great big hee-oh, and out cum Jonah right on de flat of he back on de bank.

"De Lord he say to him, 'Gwine to preach now, Jonah?' Jonah he say, 'Yes, Lord, dat I will!' and off he moseyed to Nineveh, and done some ob the biggest preachin' ye ubber hearn tell on. Dis, brudderin and sisterin, is de true varsion ob Jonah and de whale. All de rest is false, and rotten as mud."

John S. Robb (1813-1856)

The most prominent and prolific of the humorists who wrote for the St. Louis *Reveille*, John S. Robb (whose pseudonym was "Solitaire") like the best-known humorous contributors to this newspaper—Joseph M. Field, his brother Matt, and Sol Smith—moved to the Old Southwest from the North, seeking opportunities and new enterprises. Presumably born in Philadelphia, Robb, like his father, followed the printer's trade and worked on or wrote for newspapers in Philadelphia, Detroit, New Orleans, Sacramento, and most importantly St. Louis. In St. Louis, Robb edited the *Ledger* in 1842, then became printer for the *Missouri Republican*, and in 1845, served as printer for the recently established St. Louis *Reveille*, which, along with the New York *Spirit of the Times*, became a major regional venue for frontier humor. With the departure of George L. Curry, the assistant editor of the *Reveille*, Robb was promoted from the printing department to the editorial staff in April 1846.

Robb's journalistic responsibilities with the *Reveille* included serving as the newspaper's roving correspondent and writing feature articles. In June 1848, as one of his assignments, Robb took a steamboat excursion north to Fort Snelling, Minnesota, to tour and write about the post, the post commander Captain Seth Eastman and his wife, and various Indian tribes of the area. Robb's travelogue, which consisted of four letters, was published in the *Reveille* in late July 1848. At Fort Snelling, Robb met Henry Lewis, an artist who had drawn sketches of the upper Mississippi River, and who accompanied him on a sketching excursion from Fort Snelling, where he was able to observe and report in the *Reveille* Lewis's panorama of the Mississippi. In 1849, Robb, in the company of some other St. Louisans, departed from New Orleans for California to cover the gold rush in a series of letters for the *Reveille*, which were published in the paper between February 12 and October 29, 1849. Robb, however, did not return to St. Louis, electing to stay in California, editing the Stockton *Journal* and the *Sacramento Age*.

Robb's most significant journalistic contributions were his humorous sketches and dialect letters, focusing on the eccentricities and way of life on the Missouri frontier. His first humorous sketch, "Not a Drop More, Major, Unless It's Sweeten'd," published in the *Reveille* on October 21, 1844, and his second and arguably most popular sketch, "Swallowing an Oyster Alive," a narrative about an innocent Sucker from Illinois being the victim of a practical joke, appeared in the *Reveille* in December 1844; it was reprinted in William T. Porter's *Spirit of the Times* on January 18, 1845, and in Porter's anthology *The Big Bear of Arkansas, and Other Sketches* (1845). By the end of 1845, Robb had published more than eighteen additional sketches in the *Reveille*.

In 1847 as part of the Library of Humorous American Works, Carey and Hart of Philadelphia published Robb's only humor collection, *Streaks of Squatter Life and Far-West Scenes. A Series of Humorous Sketches Descriptive of Incidents and Character in the Wild West. To which are added Other Miscellaneous Pieces*. Consisting mostly of sketches he had published previously in the *Reveille* or the *Spirit*, *Streaks of Squatter Life*, Robb admitted, was the "production of the few short hours outside of *eight* in the morning and *ten* at night, the time between being occupied by arduous duties which almost forbid thought, save of themselves." The book is enhanced with eight wood engravings by F. O. C. Darley and treats many of the familiar subject categories of Southwest humor, including hunts, electioneering, courtship, frontier theater, practical jokes, drunkenness, tall tales, and mock-yokel letters, and one piece "The Pre-Emption Right," even makes overtures toward portraying an African American slave's humanity, thereby contesting the racial politics of the time.

"Settlement Fun," the only dialect letter in *Streaks of Squatter Life*, a missive from Bill Sapper to his cousin, illustrates Robb's effort to give a common man voice and dominance in controlling a narrative, both what is recounted and how it is recounted. Between April 26 and July 18, 1846, Robb would write eight more Bill Sapper letters, all of which appeared in the *Reveille*.

In assessing John S. Robb's literary achievement, Fritz Oehlschlaeger observes that he was "perhaps the most accomplished writer of the group of humorists associated with the *Reveille*."

Texts: "Nettle Bottom Ball" New York *Spirit of the Times* May 19, 1845 "Fun with a 'Bar.' A Night Adventure on the Missouri," St. Louis *Daily Reveille*, December 3, 1845.

Nettle Bottom Ball; or, Betsy Jones' Tumble in the Mush Pan

"WELL, it *are* a fact, boys," said Jim Sikes, "that I promised to tell you how I cum to git out in these Platte diggins, and I speculate you mout as well have it at onst, kase its bin troublin' my conscience amazin' to keep it kiver'd up. The afarr raised jessy in Nettle Bottom, and old Tom Jones' *yell*, when he swar he'd 'chaw me up,' gives my meat a slight sprinklin' of ager whenever I think on it.

"You see, thar war a small town called Equality, in Illin*ise*, that some speckelators started near Nettle Bottom, cos thar wur a spontaneos salt lick in the diggins, and no sooner did they git it agoin' and build some stores and groceries thar, than they wagon'd from Cincinnat*e* and other up-stream villages, a p*a*cel of fellers to attend the shops, that looked as nice, all'ays, as if they wur goin' to meetin' or on a courtin' frolic; and 'salt their picters,' they wur etarnally pokin' up their noses at us boys of the Bottom. Well, they got up a ball in the village, jest to interduce themselves to the gals round the neighborhood, and invited a few on us to make a contrary picter to themselves, and so shine us out of site by comparison. Arter that ball thur wan't any thin' talked on among the gals but what nice fellers the clerks in Equality wur, and how nice and slick they wore their *har,* and their shiny boots, and the way they stirrupp'd down their trowsers. You couldn't go to see one on 'em, that she wouldn't stick one of these fellers at you, and keep a talkin' how slick they looked. It got to be perfect pizen to hear of, or see the critters, and the boys got together at last to see what was to be done—the thing had grown perfectly alarmin'. At last a meetin' was agreed on, down to old Jake Bents'.

"On next Sunday night, instead of takin' the gals to meetin', whar they could see these fellers, we left 'em at home, and met at Jake's, and I am of the opinion thur was some congregated wrath thar—whew wan't they?

"'Oil and scissors!' says Mike Jelt, 'let's go down and lick the town, *rite strait!*'

"'No!' hollered Dick Butts, 'let's hitch these slick badgers comin' out of meetin,' and tare the hide, and feathers off on 'em !'

"' Why, darn 'em, what d'ye think, boys,' busted in old Jake, ' I swar if they ain't larnt our gals to wear *starn cushins;* only this mornin' I caught my darter Sally puttin' one on and tyin' it round her. She tho't I was asleep, but I seed her, and I made the jade *r*epudiate it, and *no* mistake—*quicker!'*

"The boys took a drink on the occasion, and Equality town was slumberin', for a short spell, over a *con*-tiguous yearthquake. At last one of the boys proposed, before we attacked the town, that we should git up a ball in the Bottom, and jest out-shine the town chaps, all to death, afore we swallowed 'em. It was hard to gin in to this proposition, but the boys cum to it at last, and every feller started to put the afarr agoin'.

"I had been a long spell hankerin' arter old Tom Jones' darter, on the branch below the Bottom, and she *was* a critter good for weak eyes—maybe she hadn't a pair of her own—well, if they warn't a brace of movin' light-houses, I wouldn't say it—there was no calculatin' the extent or handsomeness of the family that gal could bring up around her, with a feller like me to look arter 'em. Talk about gracefulness, did you ever see a maple saplin' movin' with a south wind?—It warn't a crooked stick to compar' to her, but her old dad was *awful*. He could jest lick anythin' that said *boo*, in them diggins, out swar Satan, and was cross as a she *bar*, with cubs. He had a little hankerin' in favor of the fellers in town, too, fur they gin him presents of powder to hunt with, and he was precious fond of usin' his shootin' iron. I detarmin'd, anyhow, to ask his darter Betsy to be my partner at the Nettle Bottom Ball.

"Well, my sister Marth made me a bran new pair of buckskin trowsers to go in, and rile my pictur, ef she didn't put stirrups to 'em to keep 'em down. She said *straps* wur the fashion, and I should ware 'em. I jest felt with 'em on, as ef I had somethin' pressin' on me down—all my joints wur sot tight together, but Marth insisted, and I knew I could soon dance 'em off, so I gin in, and started off to the branch for Betsy Jones.

"When I arriv, the old fellar wur sittin' smokin' arter his supper, and the younger Jones' wur sittin' round the table, takin' theirs. A whappin' big pan of *mush* stood rite in the centre, and a large pan of milk beside it, with lots of corn bread and butter, and Betsy was helpin' the youngsters, while old Mrs. Jones sot by. admirin' the family collection. Old Tom took a hard star' at me, and I kind a shook, but the *straps* stood it, and I recovered myself, and gin him as good as he sent, but I wur near the door, and ready to break if he show'd fight.

"'What the h—ll are you doin' in *disguise*,' says the old man—he swore dreadfully—'are you comin' down here to steal?'

"I riled up at that. Says I, if I wur comin' fur sich purpose, you'd be the last I'd hunt up to steal off on.'

"'You're right,' says he, 'I'd make a hole to light your innards, ef you did.' And the old savage chuckled. *I* meant because he had nothin' worth stealin,' but his darter, but he tho't 'twas cos I was afear'd on him.

"Well, purty soon I gether'd up and told him what I cum down fur, and invited him to come up and take a drink, and see that all went on rite. Betsy was in an awful way fur fear he wouldn't consent. The old 'oman here spoke in favour of the move, and old Tom thought of the licker, and gin in to the measure. Off bounced Betsy up a ladder into the second story, and one of the small gals with her, to help put on the fix-ups. I sot down in a cheer, and fell a talkin' at the old 'oman. While we wur chattin' away as nice as relations, I could hear Betsy makin' things stand round above. The floor was only loose boards kivered over wide joice, and every step made 'em shake and rattle like a small hurricane. Old Tom smoked away and the young ones at the table would hold a spoonful of mush to thur mouths and look at my straps, and then at each other and snigger; till at last the old man seed 'em.

"'Well, by gun flints,' says he, 'ef you ain't makin' a josey—'

"Jest at that moment, somethin' gin way above, and may I die, ef Betsy without any thin' on yearth on her but one of these *starn cushins,* didn't drop rite through the floor, and sot herself, *flat into the pan of mush!* I jest tho't fur a second, that heaven and yearth had kissed each other, and squeezed me between 'em. Betsy squealed like a 'scape pipe,—a spot of the mush had spattered on the old man's face, and burnt him, and he swore dreadful. I snatched up the pan of milk, and dashed it over Betsy to cool her off,—the old 'oman knocked me sprawlin' fur doing it, and away went my *straps.* The young ones let out a scream, as if the infarnal pit had broke loose, and I'd jest gin half of my hide to have bin out of the old man's reach. He did *reach* fur me, but I lent him 'one with my half-lows, on the smeller, that spread him, and maybe I didn't leave *sudden!* I didn't see the branch, but as I soused through it, I heerd Tom Jones swar he'd *'chaw me up,* ef an inch big of me was found in them diggins in the mornin'.

"I know fur a spell whar I was runnin', but hearing nuthin' behind me, I slacked up, and jest considered whether it was best to go home and git my traps strait, and leave, or go see the ball. Bein' as I was a manager, I tho't I'd go have a peep through the winder, to see ef it cum up to my expectations. While I was lookin' at the boys goin' it, one on 'em spied me, and they hauled me in, stood me afore the fire, to dry, and all hands got round, insistin' on knowin' what was the matter. I ups and tells all about it. I never heerd such laffin', hollerin', and screamin', in all my days.

"Jest then, my trowsers gin to feel the fire, and shrink up about an inch a minit, and the boys and gals kept it up so strong, laffin at my scrape, and the pickle I wur in, that I gin to git riley, when all at onst I seed one of these slick critters, from town, rite in among 'em, hollerin' wuss than the loudest.

"'Old Jones said he'd chaw you up, did he?' says the town feller, 'well, he *all'ays keeps his word.*'

"That minit I biled over. I grabbed his slick *har,* and may be I didn't gin him *scissors!* Jest as I was makin' him *a chawed specimen,* some feller holler'd out,—*'don't* let *old Jones* in with that ar *rifle!'* I didn't hear any more in that Bottom,— lightnin' could'nt a got near enough to singe my coat tail. I jumped through that winder as easy as a bar 'ud go through a cane brake; and cuss me if I hear the grit of old Jones' teeth, and smell his glazed powder, until I crossed old Mississippi."

Fun with a "Bar." A Night Adventure on the Missouri

AT the head of a ravine on the border of the river Platte, one bright night in June, was gathered a party of Missouri hunters, who were encamped after a day's chase for buffalo. The evening's repast was over, and as they stretched themselves in easy attitudes around their stack of rifles, each looked at the other with a kind of questioning expression, of whether it should be *sleep* or a *yarn?* The bright moon, with full round face, streamed down into their midst, and sprinkled her silvery sheen over shrub and flower, investing night in those vast solitudes with a strange charm which forbid sleep, and with common consent they raised themselves into a sitting posture and proposed a talk as the red skins say. Dan Elkhorn was the leader of the party, and all knew his store of adventure inexhaustible, so as unanimous call was made upon Dan for a story. "Come, Dan," cried a crony, "give us something to laugh at, and let us break this silence, which seems to breed a spirit of melancholy—stir us up, old fellow, do!"

Dan pulled his long knife out of his belt, and laying it before him, smoothed back his long grey hair. He was a genuine specimen of the hardy American mountaineer,—like the Indian, he dressed in deer skins and wore the moccason, while every seam in his iron countenance told of 'scapes and peril. Seeing that all were attention he commenced—

"Well, draw up closer, boys, so I shan't have to holler, 'cause breth is gittin' kind a short with me now, and I want to pacel it out to last pretty strong till the wind-up hunt. You, Mike, keep your eye skinned for Ingins, 'cause ef we git deep in a yarn here, without a top eye open, the cussed varmints pop on us unawars, and be stickin' some of thur quills in us—nothin' like havin' your eye open and insterments ready. I've a big idea to gin you an account of some fun I had with an old *bar,* on the Missouri, when I was a younker, and considerably more spry than I am jest now. I want to tell you fust, boys, that bars are knowin' animals, and they kin jest tell a younker of the human kind as easily as they kin a small pig from the old sow;—they don't fool with me now, for they've got to *know me!*

"Well, old Alic Dennison, a neighbour of mine on the Missouri, had bin about two years up in the mountains, and when he came home he gin a treat to all the fellars within thirty miles of him—that was jest seven families—and among 'em, in course, I got an invite. Alic and I had sot our cabins on opposite sides of the drink, near enough to see each other, and a red skin, ef he'd come on a scalp visit, would a bin diskivered by either. When Alic's frolic was to cum off, I was on hand, sartain. About evenin' I got my small dug-out, and fixin' my rifle carefully in the fore eend, and. stickin' my knife in the edge whar it would be handy, I jest paddled over the drink.

"A little above our location thar wur a bend in the stream which kind a turned the drift tother eend up, and planted them about the spot between our cabins—snags and sawyers, jest thar, wur dreadful plenty, and it took mity nice padlin' to git across without tiltin'; however, I slid atween 'em, sarpentine fashion, and got over clar as a pet coon. Thar wur considerable folks at Alic's, fur some of the families in them diggins had about twenty, in number, and the gals among 'em warn't any on your pigeon creaturs, that a fellar dassent tech fur fear of spilin' 'em, but raal scrougers—any on 'em over fourteen could lick a *bar,* easy. My decided opinion jest now is, that thur never was a grittyer crowd congregated before on that stream, and sich other dancin' and drinkin' and eatin' *bar* steaks, and corn dodger, and huggin' the gals, don't happen but once in a fellar's lifetime, and scarcely that often. Old Alic had a darter Molly, that war the most enticin,' gizzard-ticklin,' heart-distressin' *feline* creatur that ever made a fellar git owdacious, and I seed Tom Sellers cavortin' round her like a young buffalo—he was puttin' in the biggest kind a licks in the way of courtin,' and between her eyes and the sweetened whiskey he'd drank, you'd a thought the fellar would a bursted. Jest to make matters lively, I headed up alongside of Molly, and shyed a few soft things at her, sech as askin' how she liked bar steaks cooked, and if Jim Tarrant warn't equal in the elbow to a mad *panter's* tail, when he war fiddlin' that last reel, and sech amusin' light conversation. Well, boys, Tom started swellin' *instanter.* He tried to draw her attention from me; but I got to talkin' about some new improvements I war contemplatin' about my cabin, and the cow I expected up from St. Louis, 'sides lonely feelins I'd bin havin' lately, and Tom couldn't git in a show of talk, edgeways. Didn't he git mad?—wur you ever near enough to a panter when his *har* riz with wrath? Well, ef you have, you can create some idea of Tom's state of mind, and how electricity, from liquor and love, run out to the eends of his head kiverin.' It wur easy to see he wur a gittin' dangerous, so I slid off and left him alone with the gal. Arter I got a talkin' to another one of the settlers' young women, Molly kept lookin' at me, and every now and then sayin' somethin' pleasin' across to me, while she warn't payin' any attention to Tom at all. He spread himself into a stiff bow and left her; then movin' across the floor like a wounded deer, he steadied himself on the back of my seat, and lookin' me in the face, says:

"'Mister Elkhorn, I shud be strenuously obleeged to you ef you'll step down thar with me by the old persimmen tree."

"I nodded my head, and told him to trot outside and wait till I got the docyments, and as soon as he moved I sent his old *daddy* to accompany him. I jest informed the old fellar that Tom wanted a fight, and as he was too full of corn juice to cut carefully, I didn't want to take advantage of him. The old man said he was obleeged to me, and moved out. Tom, thinkin' it wur me, staggered ahead of the old man, and I concluded, as it war near mornin,' to leave; 'cause I knew when Tom found out his daddy was along with him instead of me, he'd have a fight any how. I acknowledge the corn, boys, that when I started my track warn't anythin' like a *bee-line;*—the sweeten'd whiskey had made me powerful thick-legged; but arter a fashion I got to my dug-out, with nothin' of weapon along in the world but the paddle. Thar war jest enough light to tell that snags wur plenty, and jest enough corn juice inside to make a fellar not care a cuss fur 'em. I felt strong as a hoss, too, and the dug-out hadn't more'n leaped six lengths from the bank afore—*zip—chug—co-souse* I went—the front eend jest lifted itself agin a sawyer and emptied me into the *element!* In about a second I came up bang agin a snag, and I guess I grabbed it sudden, while old Missouri curl'd and purl'd around me as ef she was in a hurry to git to the mouth, so she might muddy the Mississippi. I warn't much skeer'd, but still I didn't jest like to hang on thar till daylight, and I didn't want to make a fuss fur fear they'd say I war skary. I had sot myself on the eend of the snag, and was jest tryin' to cypher out some way of gittin' to shore, when I thought I diskiver'd a fellar sittin' on the bank. At fust, he looked so black in the coat I thought it war Tom Sellers, who'd sot himself down to wait fur a fight:—Tom had on at the frolic a black blanket coat with a velvet collar, and he thought it particularly nice. Arter lookin' at him move about and sit down on his hunkers once or twice, I thought I'd holler to him; but he appeared so dreadful drunk that I didn't expect much help from him.

"'Tom,' shouted I, 'come out here with a dug-out, and help a fellar off, will you?'

"He sot still, without sayin' a word. 'Well,' says I to him, 'you're meaner than an Ingin! and would bait a trap with your daddy's leggins.' He didn't move fur a spell; at last into the drink he popped, and now, thought I, he *is* mad and *no* dispute. I could see him paddlin' right fur me, and I holler'd to him that I had no insterments, but he didn't say a whisper, only shoved along the faster. At last up he come agin my snag, and the next minit he reached fur me, and then he tried to fix his teeth into my moccason; so guessin' it war time to do somethin,' I jest grabbed fur his muzzle, and I'm blessed, boys, ef it warn't a great *he bar!* The cussed varmint had watched me from the house and seed I had no weapons, and when I upsot he just counted me his'n, and was quietly calculatin' on the bank how he'd best git me out of the water. I had nothin' in the yearth but a small fancy pen knife, but I stuck that in him so quick that he let me go, and while he swam for one snag I reached for another. I never heerd a bar laugh out loud afore, but I'm a sucker ef he didn't snigger twice at the way he rolled me off my log.

"We sot lookin' at one another fur a spell, when I seed the varmint gittin' ready to call on me agin, and in about a second more off he dropped, and strait he took a shute for my location. As he came up close to me I slit his ear with the small blade, and he got mad; but jest as he was circling round me to git a good hold, I dropped on to his hinder eend and grabbed his har, and I guess I made him move fur shore a leetle faster than a steam boat—my little blade kept him dreadful *itchy*. Well, the fun of the thing wur, boys, as soon as the varmint teched shore, he turned right round on me, and I'm cussed if I hadn't to turn round, too, and scratch for the snag agin! with that consarned *bar* feelin' my legs with his paw every stroke I war makin' to git away from him! I got a little skary, now, and a good deal mad, fur thar the varmint war a waitin' for me, and whinin' as ef he had been ill-treated, and thar I wur perched up on a sawyer, bobbin' up and down in the water. At last I sot a hollerin' and kept on at it, and hollered louder, until I seed some one cum from the house, and singin' out agin they answered me. I asked who it war, and found that it war Molly, old Alic's darter; so I gin her a description of my siteaytion, and she war into a dug-out in a minit, and paddlin' towards me. I believe I said wonce, boys, that bars wur knowin' critters, but ef thar's anythin' true on this yearth, it's the fact, that this consarned animal had made up his mind to upsot that gal, and I'm blessed ef he didn't jest as cute as ef he'd bin human! Startin' from his snag he swam to the dug-out, put up both paws, and over it went—over went Molly into the stream, and off slid Mister *bar,* laffin' out *loud!* as I'm a white man.

"I seized Molly as she came floatin' towards me, and stuck her upon my sawyer, while I started for an adjinin' snag. I could hear Molly grittin' her teeth, she war so bilin' mad, and jest as soon as she could git breath, she hollered to me to be sure I never rested till I killed that varmint. I swore on that snag that I'd grow thin chasin' the critter, and she seemed to git pacified. Well, than we wur, in the stream, and it a leetle too rough to swim in easy, so we had to sing out for help, and I yelled till I war nigh onto hoarse, afore anythin' livin' stirred about the house; at last, nigger Jake came down to the edge of the river, jest as day was breakin,' and his hand over his eyes, he hollers—

"'Why, Massa Dan, is dat you wot's been hollowin' eber so long for somebody!'

"'You've jest took the notion to cum see, have you, you lazy nigger—now git a dug-out and come out here and git your missus and me off these snags, and do it quick, too, or I'll make *you* holler!'

"'What, Missus dar, *too!*' shouted the nigger, 'well, dat's funny—de Lor!' and off the cussed blueskin started fur the house, and in a few minits all that could gathered out to see us and laugh at our water locations.

"I had bin gittin' riled by degrees, and now was at a dangerous pint—the steam began to rise off on me till thar wur a small fog above my head, and as the half drunken varmints roared a laffin, and cracked their jokes about our courtin' in the middle of the drink, I got awful excited. 'I'll make ribbons of every man among you,' says I, 'when I git whar a chance to fight.' And then the cussed crew roared the louder. Tom Sellers yelled out that we'd bin tryin' to *elope,* and this made Molly mad,—her daddy got a little mad, too, and I bein' already mad, thar wur a wrathy trio on us, and the old fellow said, ef he thought I'd been playin' a two-faced game, and bitin' his friendship like a pizen varmint, he'd drop me off the log I wur on with a ball from his rifle. I jest told him to fire away and be d—d, for I wur wore out a patience. Some of the boys held him, while others got the dug-out and came to our assistance. I jest got them to drop me on my side of the river, and to send over my rifle, and as soon as it war on hand I onloosed my dog Yelp, and started to wipe out my disgrace.

"That infernal bar, as soon as he'd tossed Molly in the stream, started for the woods; but, as he had reasoned on the chances, the varmint came to the conclusion that he couldn't git away, and so got up into a crotch of a low tree, about a quarter of a mile from my cabin. Old Yelp smelled him, and as soon as I clapped peeper on him I let sliver, when the varmint dropped like a log,—I went to him and found he'd bin dead for an hour. My little blade couldn't a killed him, so it's my opinion, clearly entertained, that the owdacious varmint, knowin' I'd kill him for his trick, jest climbed up thar whar I could easy find him, and died to spite me!

"His hide, and hard swearin,' got me and Molly out of our elopin' scrape, and the lickin' I gin Tom Sellers that spring has made us good friends ever sence. He don't wonce ventur' to say anythin' about that *bar scrape,* without my permission!"

Christopher Mason Haile (1814–1849)

In the late 1830s, Christopher Mason Haile, a young adventurer from Rhode Island who had recently resigned from the United States Military Academy because of extended illness, migrated to the Gulf South and settled in the small Mississippi River town of Plaquemine, Louisiana, in Iberville Parish. In making the north-to-south migration, Haile followed the path of other young men, who, like him, would become professional journalists and amateur humorists, such as George Wilkins Kendall, Thomas Bangs Thorpe, Matt and Joseph Field, Johnson Jones Hooper, Sol Smith, and John S. Robb. Marrying into a prominent Cajun family, Haile established and edited a weekly bilingual newspaper, the *Planters' Gazette,* in late 1840, an enterprise he would continue for the next five years.

During this same period, Haile, under the pseudonym of Pardon Jones, began writing a series of dialect letters using the salutation "Pic," to George W. Kendall, the editor of the New Orleans *Picayune*. These letters were his principal contribution to the genre of southwestern humor, in the same epistolary tradition practiced by northeasterner Seba Smith in his letters from Jack Downing and southerners Charles F. M. Noland in his Pete Whetstone letters and William Tappan Thompson in his letters from Major Joseph Jones, and brought Haile local as well as some national exposure. Of the sixty-seven extant Pardon Jones letters, sixty-five were published initially in the *Picayune* between December 1840 and April 1848, and some of these were reprinted in Porter's *Spirit of the Times.*

Though Haile's fictional epistles generally fit the cultural profile of Old Southwest humor, they are unique in several ways. Unlike most other writers in this humorous tradition, Haile, in the letters from Pardon Jones, frequently reminds the reader of his northern origins, even in some of the letters he sets in Louisiana. In still other letters, Haile has Pardon Jones return to his old home in Massachusetts, sending letters from that locale that focus on the antics and scrapes involving Jones and local characters, many of whom are his friends and relatives, thus making Haile the only southwestern humorist to make the Northeast a prominent setting for his humor. In addition, in a more emphatic manner than most of his fellow southwestern humorists, Haile often alludes in his letters to national political issues—the tariff debate, boundary disputes between the U.S. and Canada, the controversy over a national bank, the conflict between states' rights and nationalism, the annexation of Texas, and the conflict with Mexico, which led to war.

During the Mexican War, the *Picayune* hired Haile as a special correspondent, and in that professional capacity he proved to be one of the best warfront reporters of several crucial battles, activities, and camp life. He wrote over one hundred detailed, engaging, and sometimes even humorous dispatches, which were published in this newspaper and some reprinted in northern papers as well. In April 1847, however, he resigned from his position at the *Picayune,* joined the regular army, and was appointed first lieutenant. While in Mexico, both as a professional correspondent and soldier, Haile continued to write his Pardon Jones letters, which, between 1846 and 1848, appeared sporadically in the *Picayune.* In their portrayal of Pardon Jones's rag-tag volunteers and some of their ludicrous noncombatant activities in their encounters with Mexican soldiers, the final missives in the Pardon Jones series are discernibly transnational in scope, giving Haile the distinction of being the most Southwest of the Southwest humorists, the only one to treat a culture south of the Old South.

Shortly after his discharge from the army, Haile returned to Louisiana and in 1849 was hired by the state's Department of Engineers as the captain of a Mississippi River snag boat. Suffering from yellow fever that he had contracted in Vera Cruz, Mexico, in 1847, during the war, Haile died at Indian Village on Bayou Plaquemine in Iberville Parish, Louisiana, on September 10, 1849. The obituary in the New Orleans *Daily Picayune* offered testament to Christopher M. Haile's achievement, acknowledging that he "was endowed with a fertile fancy, and was as remarkable for the vigor of his style as for his genuine humor."

Texts: "Dear Chase," New Orleans *Daily Picayune,* April 16, 1841. "Pardon Jones on the Rio Grande," New Orleans *Daily Picayune,* July 6, 1846.

Dear Chase.

UP THE COAST, April 10, 1841

My Dear Pic,—I'm eenamost tired tu death to-night. Sich a time as we've had to-day don't happen often, I can tell you! 'Bout a dozen on us has ben on a deer chase to-day, and I've rid myself near about to death. I feel's if I'd ben pounded in a mortar. There's a stranger just cum here from England, a "nobleman," he calls himself—he ain't a very noble lookin feller tho,' I can tell you—and he wanted to show the folks here how they hunted in his country; so we got together, 'bout a dozen on us, and rid off into the woods this morning, the nobleman in the gang. He is a leetle tenty feller, the nobleman is—not bigger than the gineral run of boys fourteen years old, and to-day he was dressed up in buckskin britches jest as tight as the skin, so that his legs didn't look much bigger than a pair of tongs, and they was dreadful crooked at that. Wall, he got on to a creowl hoss that never'd ben rid much, and was fiery as a rattlesnake, and he wore a big gold spur on both feet, and every time he tetched his hoss the critter would jump a rod, and then trot off, right up and down, as hard as a fullin-mill.—We all got along very wall, huntin till arternoon. We killed a whole passel of rabbits and squirrels, and so on, and then got together and took a bite of suthin to eat, and drinked full as much as we'd ought to, all round, and then started off agin.

Pooty soon the hounds started up a dear.—*Jehosaphat!* you'd ought to seen how the little nobleman dodged round among the trees with his little hoss, when he found out that a deer was afoot! He started off, full chisel, arter the dogs, and we all scattered about, and some of the old hunters went and took their *stands* and *waited* for the critter to come round. Wall, the nobleman he went streakin it through the bushes, jest, I 'spose, as he used to du in England, in the fields and groves, and tu or three long briar vines that had growd acrost the path raked their hull length acrost his nose, and peeled the skin all off. But what does a *nobleman* keer about briars! Jest nothing at all, for briars is beneath their dignity. We begun to get afeerd he would git into the swamp, and git miss't or lost, so we put on arter him, as fast as we dass tu.

The nobleman he heerd the dogs a howlin a little ways ahead, and he wanted to be the "fust at the death," so he stuck his spurs in the deeper, and went, I s'pect 'bout as fast as a railroad car. He see the dogs round a big briar patch, howlin and snarlin, and he gin one more punch with his spurs—but jest then a long grapevine that hung from one tree to another, and was 'bout as big round as your arm, ketched him round the middle. He was goin tu fast to stop, and as soon's the grapevine had stretched out as fur's 'twould it sprung back, and carried the nobleman with it—hangin on it jest like britches on a close-line, and it throwed him back, kinder sideways, 'bout twenty feet, right into a thick green-briar patch! He fell on his shoulders, and lay there with his heels stickin up, wedged down into the briars, and couldn't stir a hooter! His hoss run off and left him. Wall, puty soon three or four on us rid up, and seein the dogs round the briar patch, we didn't know but they'd got the dear in there, tangled up, and so we begun to peek round. "Sachry! munseer," says a frend, "I see him—look at his horns there!" and he pinted to where the nobleman lay with his tu little buckskin legs stickin up—and his back pinted right twards us. I'll be darned if that part on him we could see didn't look jest like a *dear's* head, through the leaves!

The dogs made sich a noise we couldn't hear nothin, hardly. "I'll pepper him!" says one feller. "No—hold on!" says another; "let me bore a hole into his head with my rifle." "I'll bet I can put five buck-shot right between his eyes," says I, and I raised up my gun, and was jest goin to let him have it, when I see suthin that looked like a *hand* stickin up, and I stopped. The nobleman he hollered then with all his might, and says he—"For God's sake, gentlemen, don't shute me; don't murder me in cold blood, if you please; or else you'll have to anser for it to the British Government. McCleod aint a succunistance to me," says he; "*he's* only a deputy sheriff and I'm a nobleman!"* Didn't we laff when we see what it was in the briar patch, and didn't he squirm and swear! Wall, we cut a path tu him, and got him out.

Instead of a *dear,* the dogs had ben running arter a wild cat, and he'd run into the briar patch and up a tree that growed out of the middle on't. Wall, the nobleman he swore away a spell about *conspiracies,* vulgar huntin grounds, poor dogs, and so on, till he got tired, and then he took a horn of brandy out of my canteen and cooled off, and we all come home good natur'd nuff—the nobleman ridin behind me, and telling me all the time to look out for grape vines.

Your frend,
PARDON JONES.

*Alexander McLeod, a Canadian and the deputy sheriff of the Niagara District, became notorious for his involvement as part of a loyal Canadian military contingent that seized the U. S. steamer *Caroline* in 1837. The *Caroline* had been carrying men and supplies to Canadian rebels who wanted a more democratic government. McLeod and his fellow Canadian loyalists set the *Caroline* on fire and let it drift over Niagara Falls. Many Americans who lived near the Canadian border were irate, and this incident created widespread anti-British sentiment. Violence was averted, however, when American forces under General Winfield Scott were dispatched to the area. Succunistance is possibly a corruption of succeedent, which seems suitable in this instance since the Englishman is begging the hunters not to shoot him, for if they do, he says, they "will have to answer for it to the British Government."

Pardon Jones on the Rio Grande

OUT TO THE RIO GRANDY, with Gineral Zachary Taylor, June the [there! dod rot my picter if Jim Folly, our drummer, hasn't lent my almynack to somebody.]

My Dear Pic—I know *you* aint 'stonished to hear that I've come out here to sarve my cuntry, and you won't open your eyes much when I tell you that Capting Potter is with me. Simon Spaldin is next tu me in command, and Capting Potter orders us all about, same's if he was Major Ginral. We've got ten privates, one drummer and one fifer, and considerable many commissioned officers.

Capting Potter is dressed up in the uniform he used tu wear in the last war, and I've got on my Curnel's uniform, that I used tu wear tu the Bay State. We come out through Bayou Pluckumin, in a fishin' smack, and coasted it along, till we got tu Santyaggo, and then put into Pint Izzybel. When Capting Potter see the U.S. flag flyin' over the Fort, his ebenezer got up so that he stamped and snorted like a tew year old colt. Nothin' would du but he must take and Dead Cow Brook Artillery company flag and stick it up on the mast—Jack Jones come near breakin' his neck tyin' it up—and fired both of his old troopers' pistols to salute the fort. One on 'em kicked clean of his head, and hit Simon Spaldin acrost the bridge of his nose, and knocked the skin off. Wall, we all landed, Jack Jones and Jim Folly played Yankee-Doodle, right up tu the nub, and we marched up tu the commander's tent. Arter we'd got threw with introducin' one another, the Majer axed us where we come from, how many there was on us, and what we wanted. Capting Potter told him that we used to live in the Bay State, but had sense become natives of Luzyanny, that we didn't want nothin' 'cept tu du a little missylaneous job of fightin,' on our own hook, and that there was jest twenty on us. "And yet," says the Majer, smilin' as perlite as could be, "you've got a Curnel, and all the rest of the regimental officers—it requires more'n twenty men to make a regiment." "Sir," says Capting Potter, drawin' his sword, "we're a *host* in ourselves; we didn't come here to obey nobody's rules and regulations, and articles of war—we come tu fite the battles of our free and enlitened country, and, sir, we'll *du* it, or perish in the 'tempt. We don't belong to nobody's corpse 'cept our own, and shan't jine the regular army of volunteers;—if we get tired of the sarvice, we'll go hum when we get reddy, and if Gineral Taylor won't let us stay long with him, we'll march back threw Texas and kill sum buffaloes!" "Hem!" says the gentlemanly old Majer, kinder tickled, "I beg your pardon—didn't mean to 'fend you—wusn't aware of the nature of your regiment nor of the nature of the service you had marked out—it's all right, no doubt, and I rather guess your country 'll hear from you—is there anything I can du fur you?" "Nothin 'cept tu keep an eye on our fishin' smack, out yonder; enny time you want to go out with your wife and children a sailin, you ken just take her, only keep an eye skinned that no harm happens tu her."

Wall, that arternoon we packed up and got reddy to march to Mattymorus. I'n the capting and Simon bought us a Mexican mule a piece, and each on us had an alfired big pack-saddle, stuffed full of things that Jerushy had fixed up for us. Capting Potter kerried the licker in his bags, and so on, all round. We sent the sogers on ahead, to reconnotter, and told 'em tu jest keep the wagon track and keep agoin on till we ketched up with 'em, and if they see enny Mexicans on the road, to make em prisoners of war. Wall, the old capting he tuckered 'bout the fort till arter dark, larnin about the cuntry, and so on, and finally said that he knowed the road like a book, and we might feel as safe as if we wus tu hum, 'cause *he* would guide us. The fust hill we went down arter we left the fort, the capting's mule begin to kick up, and wouldn't go ahead another step. Simon Spaldin rid up and stuck his sword intu the crittur's rump, and he started off full run. The old man couldn't stop him, and our mules wouldn't stay behind, so we went it over the prary, lickety switch, for as much as six mild, afore we could halt. "All right?" said the ole man, "nuthin lost? nobody hurt?" "No, capting, we're fust rate, barrin a little shook up." "Wall, feller sogers, let's take a small tetch of Monongyheely—it'll du us good, arter that ride," and he took a stout pull, and handed his canteen round. We rid on agin, a few milds furder, and the old man begin to complain of bein tired—"we'd better lay down an hour or tu in this high grass," says he, "and then go on, fresh." Simon concluded to keep on and ketch up with the sogers. His mule started off, arter a good deal of whippin, and a prick or tu from my sword, and run as hard as it could. When he ketched up with his friends, they see him commin at such a rate that they thought it was a Mexican chargin on 'em, and they all fired at him, but he was tu far off to be hit. Wall, I'n the Capting lay down awhile, and then got up and went on. We crossed a pond-hole, and the Capting took a wrong road, and we follered it off into the prary till there want no more road to be seen. We was lost! "Grashus Jemimy, Pardon!" says the Capting, kinder trubbled, "here we be, jist as helpless as the babes in the woods, with Mexicans, and wolves, and Tonky Injuns all round us. Wall, let's be sogers, and take everything jest as we happen tu ketch it." We tied our mules together, and went to sleep. When daylight broke, the darned critters was gone! We spied 'em, tho,' arter a while, feeding on a rise, 'bout a mild off, and went and ketched 'em. It didn't take long tu find the right road, but it was cloudy, and the Capting was turned round. He pretended that he knowed all 'bout it, tho' and we rid towards Mattymorus. Arter we'd rid a mild or tew, the old man said he 'bleeved he'd go back tu Fort Polk and scrape a better 'quaintance with that fine old Major. "I like that man," says he, "he's a true soger and true gentleman. I guess I'd better ride back and stay with him awhile, and larn a little 'bout modern tactics, eh, Parding?" I see't the old man was tired of this kind of sogerin, and wanted an excuse to go back tu where he could be comfortable, so I told him go by all means. "Parding," says he, shaking on me by the hand, "mind the pond-holes that I've described, and mind and take a good look at both fields of battle. There aint no danger of Mexicans—*I* wouldn't be the least afeard—if you *du* get into a fite, Parding, and get killed—[Here the old man's eyes begin tu fill up]—I'll be husband to Jerushy, and a father to the little gal." "No," says I, "Capting, I don't bleeve Jerushy would ever get married agin if I was killed, besides that, you're most tu old tu—" "Oh, you buster, you!" says the old man, smilin threw his tears, "you *will* have your jokes, even right here in the enemy's cuntry—you're like old Zachary and Twiggs, and the brave fellers round 'em, that fit and joked, eternately, the other day, up above here."

The Capting rid back, and I went on. 'Fore long I come in sight of some shippin and a camp. Jest then a feller rid up and I axed him what that was. "It's Pint Isabel," says he "you're sure on't?" says I. "No mistake," says he; and I rid back as hard as my mule would go, tu ketch up with the Capting. 'Twant long 'fore I got faint and thusty, and hed to set down on the grass and rest. Putty soon a hull lot of Mexicans come down the road, drivin ten ox carts, with sharpened sticks. Thinks I, "Curnel Joneses' time is come now," and I riz up. My face was pale, cause I'd been so faint afore. "Look here, old feller," says I to an old chap [on] hoss-back, I'll surrender at discretion, if you'll jest give me a drink of water 'fore you cut my throat!" Of course I made motions all the time I was talkin. One feller got on tu my mule, and another gave me a big dubble barreled gourd full of water, and another lifted me into a cart, and put a Mexican blanket up on sticks, to keep the sun off. Thinks I, "this looks like civilized warfare," and I lay down on my back, and drinked one barrel of gourd empty 'fore I stopped. I hadn't more'n dun it afore I see Capting Potter come streakin it along arter us with his sword drawn, hollerin "halt! You dam bloody rascals!—here's to the reskew!" And be pitched intu the Mexicans, right and left. Some jumped out of their carts and run off, others dodged round behind the wheels. "Rise, Pardon, and less put the rascals tu the sword!" hollered the old man. "No" says I, "'twont do—I've surrendered at discretion, and 'twouldn't be chivalrous to fite 'em now—less go down tu the Pint agin, and you ken get me exchanged, I guess, for a trifle." So we motioned the Mexicans back, and they took me tu the fort a prisoner of war. The old man had rid on and got an interpeter, and met us at the gate. "Ax that old cock what he wants me tu give him for Curnel Jones," says the old man. The interpeter axed, and says he: "they say they want a bottle of whiskey." "Tell 'em my frend shan't be exchanged for one bottle of whiskey—I'll give 'em a dimmyjohn full." So I got free agin by exchange. That night an officer come down and said he'd met Simon Spaldin's company, with a lot of Mexican cartmen, prisoners, and had had a good deal of fuss tu make him let 'em go. We've done a good deal sense then, but I hain't time tu say no more now. Capt. Potter sends love.

Your true frend, Pardon Jones.
Curnul, and so futh.

Adam Geiselhard Summer (1818-1866)

Journalist, planter, lawyer, naturalist, horticulturist, state printer, legislator, humorist, and publisher of antebellum humorous writers, Adam G. Summer was born in the Dutch Fork section in central South Carolina on the family plantation in Pomaria. He was the principal promoter of the Dutch Fork School of amateur humorists, including his kinsman and longtime friend Dr. Orlando Benedict Mayer and others who were also his friends and neighbors. The Dutch Fork had been settled in the mid-eighteenth century by German and Swiss Protestants, and when Summer was growing up there the German language, customs, and folklore were widely prevalent.

Between 1845 and 1848, Summer edited the Columbia *South Carolinian*, a weekly agricultural paper, except during legislative sessions when it was issued semi-weekly. Along with agricultural news and political events in the state legislature, the *South Carolinian* also regularly published backwoods humor during Summer's tenure as editor. Aptly acclaimed by James E. Kibler, Jr., as a "kind of Southern William Trotter Porter," Summer published not only sketches and tales of some of the well-known southern humorists of the 1840s—Hooper, Thompson, Thorpe, George Washington Harris, Sol Smith, Joseph Field, and John S. Robb—but also those of local humorists such as Mayer and others from Upcountry South Carolina who wrote under pseudonymous bylines but who have not been identified—"Pea Ridger," "Nat Slocum," "Phil Gilder," "Some Punkins," and "Capting Luke Snuzeby." Several of these humorists also published in Porter's *Spirit of the Times*.

Summer, too, under the pseudonym Vesper Brackett, contributed to the *South Carolinian* both backwoods humorous tales, such as "Natural Angling, or Riding a Sturgeon," which appeared there on May 8, 1845, and sentimental autobiographical tales such as "Winter Green, A Tale of My School Master," which was published on February 18, 1848. "Natural Angling" was reprinted in the *Spirit* on May 24, 1845, and "The Vegetable Shirt-Tail; or, An Excuse for Backing Out" appeared originally in the *Spirit* on September 5, 1846.

> At the age of thirty, Summer left Columbia, giving up the editorship of the *South Carolinian* to return to Ravenscroft, his plantation in Lexington County, where he pursued his interests in ornamental plants and gardening, livestock and breeding, and agricultural chemistry. With his brother William he founded the State Agricultural Society. He and his brother also established Pomaria Nurseries, one of the first major nurseries in the lower South. Summer's agricultural interests led him back to journalism; from 1853 to 1856, he edited the *Southern Agriculturalist* and the *South Carolina Agriculturalist*. Along with his many other pursuits, in 1850 Summer served in the South Carolina Legislature.
>
> A man of many talents, Adam G. Summer was the major impetus in promoting the humorous writing of the South Carolina Dutch Fork. In describing Summer, fellow humorist O. B. Mayer called him a "rustic humorist who could hold his own with the roughest joker."
>
> Text: "Natural Angling, or Riding a Sturgeon," Columbia *South Carolinian* May 8, 1845.

Natural Angling, or Riding a Sturgeon

Fishing is not the same wild and exciting sport it was, when our rivers were untamed, and instead of the subdued and present worn appearance, their banks were pictures of nature in her most romantic and captivating garb; and when the chief charms of *divine divertissement* consisted of the break-neck adventures and real peril of the pursuit. Now-a-days, woe to them! anglers must fish with quaint bait, recommended by that venerable piscatorial saint, great Izaak; and though they submit to the modern innovation of a generous Limerick hook—the remainder of the tackle must be arranged by the book—and taciturn demeanor is always to be observed, even though they angle under a Niagara; for the sage hath said, that silence in the fisherman is conducive to great success. This fastidiousness has, in my opinion, driven the most princely fish from our waters; at least, I can in no wise, account for their disappearance, unless *these patent draw our Conroy's*, with their thousand yards of gossamer gut, have caused the surprising immigration. Where now can we snare the vigorous rock-fish, or the tasty and gentlemanly trout of a dozen pounds weight?—All gone! and it has really come to pass, that fifty pounds of small-fry, taken in one ramble at some breeding place, is a capture astonishing to boys, and talked of for a week at least.

Belton Tinkerbottom was the last fisherman of the old sort whom I knew, and he was a hook well tied on. I saw him, in our last excursion, draw in a thirteen pounder with "a love of a reed" cut by my own hands—selected from a million on Hampton's Island, and a line twisted by his own skill, with a grace that would have taught a nibble or two, to the patent spring-pole gentry of the present times. He did it in native American style, which was of course original, and methought when his line whistled in the eddying circles of Cohees' dashing currents, that the river-gods, who dwelt thereabouts, must have been in trepidation, lest their peculiar divinity should not entirely protect them from the skill of the sturdy angler.

There are many angling stories told about Tink, but the best came under my own observation. Even at the risk of prolixity I must favor you with it:—We were just ready to leap into our little dug out, with lines all properly measured and tied on, when, after admiring the first Limerick hook he had ever beheld, it was transferred to his mouth for safe keeping until we should reach "*trout pond,*" a beautiful eddy between two sluices in Cohees, which, good reader, is a romantic shoal in Broad River, South Carolina. Tink stumbled, his foot pressed the rod, and before he could gain an upright position he was hooked most endearingly through his right cheek. *The Trouticide* had tied in *that hook* and he would not permit me to cut it loose from the line, for he was determined to fish *with that hook;* and, of course as there was no chance of further sport in his being both bait and angler, I was forced at his request to cut it out of his cheek, which operation I performed with my old jack-knife, and with such surgical grace that we made a glorious day's sport, and though he was the largest fish caught by *that hook,* it carried the *take-in* deep amongst the finny patriarchs on that occasion—and it contributed but little to lessen his beauty, for Tinkerbottom's mouth was the best natured feature in the world, and never was known to object to dilation in any manner whatever. Soon after this occurrence he was hooked by Father Time, who once in a while hunts up even anglers, and is now I sincerely hope, reveling amid the wonders of the strange waters to which he has been translated, or perhaps is discussing with the aforesaid St. Izaak the comparative merits of *natural* and *artificial* fishing.

The immediate predecessor of Tinkerbottom was Honyucle Hallman, who was still more natural in his warfare on the finny tribe. Catting was his great *forte,* and the needle fins saw perfect sights the days he thought proper to invade their domains. He caught cats to please his wife, and extenuated the awful crime in those days by saying, "Sally loves cat-fish, but I love shad," and always insisted that "a man who wished all his fellow-warmints well would only eat fish in the shad season," and as for perch, brim and *sich like,* Honyucle would as soon have been caught eating mud-suckers or pond-roaches. He would condescend to fish for rock and trout, as he said they had a gentlemanly flutter; and tried honestly to save their lives. He lived for the shad season and angled for sport alone, and to see him hook a magnificent rock-fish with his long float-line—to mark his varying countenance, and to judge of his excitement by the velocity with which he rolled the quid in his cheek, was enough of the sport for an observer. You might have noted a thousand attitudes before he finished his capture. Honyucle never went on the principle of satiety; one rock-fish was enough, and when that one was secured, like "old Washington," (the sobriquet of an aged eagle who frequented this part of the river) he retired from Cohees. Another favorite diversion of Honyucle's was spearing sturgeon as they lay in their pebble beds among the shallows, during the warm days in the month of May; in fact, this was whale fishing in miniature, with all its excitement attended with some peril, for frequently the pierced fish would dart off with such velocity that his canoe would be upset; and amongst the rapids of Cohees, with a boat fastened to a sturgeon, that circumstance is not altogether as funny as some might suppose. But in time sturgeon grew shy or wise, or perhaps the water was not sufficiently clear in the proper season for him to see them, and Honyucle pined away; he grew morose, and waited for the next season with hope anticipating that some change would manifest itself in the realm of sturgeon-*dom*. February, March and April, glorious season of shad flew by, and each day found him with his nets among the shoals, wind or rain, as regularly insinuating his skill amongst the salt water visiters as "old Washington" and his white headed partner went to the raft of drift-wood in the middle of the river, from whence they generally picked up their daily rations of dead fish and terrapins.

Though moderate success always attended his efforts he grew moodier as the spring tide brightened, and frequent spells of the "blue dipper" gave his wonted communicativeness a singular feature of interest. Speaking of success, Honyucle was no "*water-haul*" man,—he was a perfect seducer of fish, and it was the belief of the honest Dutch in that neighborhood that he could charm them, owing to certain secret powers by him alone possessed. If the "green-haired maiden of the sea" could wile the Spanish mariner to—

"Isles that lie,
In farthest depths of Ocean; girt with all
Of natural wealth and splendor—jeweled isles,
Boundless in unimaginable spoils
That earth is stranger to." (*Simms' Atalantis.*)

with a voice "like the winds among a bed of reed" Honyucle in his turn enchanted the water divinities, and his achievements with rod and line always scattered grief in the realms below, even if it was not agreeable to the scaly captives. Settled melancholy begets peevishness in meditative minds; and Sally's ingenious inquiries failed to extract the cause of his gloom. The clack of his mill seemed to knock this unusual feature deeper into his soul every day, and he scored and tolled a thoughtful man.

May-day, in the South, you have enjoyed, my dear P***er, but as you have never seen Cohees, with its sparkling sluices flashing in the warm and mellow sunlight—the ancient wave-worn rocks, on which the heron race in light-blue and snow-white garbs delight to rest 'mid their aquatic wanderings, the green islands with clustering vines bending to the water's edge, and casting shadows of fairylike greeting on the tide beneath, with cliffs rising abruptly from the shore, crowned with the flax-colored shoots of the late-springing hickory, a green pine-forest standing like sentinels in the rear; and below this, on a level almost with the water, is a little kingdom, yet another realm of nature, comprising the beautiful river Laurel, the dwarf cedar, the stinted river-ivy, and the thorny leaved holly with its red berries still unshed, and contrasting with beautiful effect its green foliage, forming a sheltering covert, and letting in just enough sunshine to keep the prickly cactus, the creeping perriwinkle, and other modest daughters of the floral kingdom—from languishing. As you have never enjoyed this scene of enchantment, you will pardon my asserting its kindred to magic, because it was the first impression which invaded the "bad humor" of Honyucle. All this was *goose-grease* to his discontented soul, and it

"Called up sweet fancies from his pliant hope,
And stirr'd the languid spirit into life,
Surveying the blue waters and his home." *Atalantis.*

He saw the fish leaping from the bright river, the skimming swallows fluttering o'er its shining surface; he looked up at the blue sky, "old Washington's" savage scream arrested his attention, and high up, poised upon the air, with his bald pate glittering like a jeweled crown, and the grey down of his pinions reflecting the beams of the morning sun in brilliant effulgence, he marked with admiration the rapid whirl of the old patriarch of Cohees, who darting downwards like a stream of light headlong into the foaming surf beneath, vanished for a moment; then emerging, rose heavily from the bed of the river, and flapping his wet wings, with a glittering prize in his talons, sailed slowly towards his time-honored and uninvaded eyry.

Honyucle's groom relaxed—there was no straining for contentment visible in his countenance, and he sallied forth, trout rod in hand, once more to enjoy his accustomed sport. On foot he entered the river and picking his path among the rapids, now wading a rapid sluice to the depth of his waist, now leaping from rock to rock; and anon peering into the crystal waters, as was his custom when on a piscatorial scout, he suddenly seemed transfixed, his body became motionless, and he stood as firm as if his brawn had been moulded from the enduring granite on which his form rested. Beneath him in the waves lay a large sturgeon, unconscious that the foe of his race was so near; but the deadly sturgeon-spearer was unarmed, and his usually eager excitement was tempered into admiration. There lay the fresh water monster, and the more Honyucle looked at him the ruddier grew the crimson glow of the scales on his sides in the sunny water. In the red gills, opening with the regular breathing of the fish, he saw proper reins to hold by,

"And a thought, for a deed,
Cast his on the water steed!"

Slapping his hands into the gills of the sturgeon, who, not relishing this obstruction to his respiration *by poking straws* into his *side nostrils,* instantly contracted them, and having thus secured his rider, darted with the rapidity of fright down the rocky and jagged sluice. A few flights and the shallows were passed; at one time Honyucle's head might have been seen, and then he was quickly drawn below the water, and thus alternately hope and despair agonized or cheered his wife, who stood sole witness of the scene on the distant shore. After traversing with the rapidity of lightning the downward course of the river, several hundred yards, one hand of the drowning man was released, and the water was violently lashed by the tail of the infuriated sturgeon, who now, instead of keeping a straight course, circled round several times, still dragging Honyucle by his side. His left hand had become entangled in the throat or gills of the powerful fish, and the sturgeon became incommoded by the broad hand of Honyucle; round and round they went, the prisoner having only a chance now and then to gasp for breath, he was tremendously thumped by the lashing of the sturgeon's tail. At this period of the *melee* the blood from the torn cartilage of the throat of the fish was ejected with great force, and the red tide of life mingled with the agitated water; another struggle and conqueror and victim floated side by side on the surface of the river. One more ineffectual attempt to free himself and the last flutter of the dying sturgeon, faint and weak as he was, threw them on a low rock, and he was thus providentially rescued from the death which so imminently threatened him. His wife leaped into a canoe and rowed hastily to him, to give whatever succour was in her power, and when he was released from the dead fish it was ascertained that his wrist was severed to the bone; his body was covered with contusions, and his legs were terribly lacerated by the tail of the bruiser.

This adventure cured Honyucle of grieving after the scarcity of sturgeon, and though he continued a devotee of the rod to his dying day, he always avoided the scene of his ride.

Orlando Benedict Mayer (1818-1891)

One of the South Carolina Dutch Fork humorists, like his close friend and kinsman Adam G. Summer, Orlando Benedict Mayer was born and raised in Pomaria, an area between the Broad and Saluda Rivers in central South Carolina, and spent most of his adult life as a country doctor in the town of Newberry. Many members of the Dutch Fork group published humorous tales and sketches in the Columbia *South Carolinian,* a weekly newspaper specializing in agriculture and state politics and edited by Summer. Familiar with the genre of Old Southwest humor, Mayer wrote some of the most entertaining and best-crafted works featuring Dutch Fork settings, culture, and characters.

A graduate of South Carolina College and the Medical College at Charleston, Mayer, spent the early 1840s in Europe, studying culture, language, and medicine, and returned to his home in Pomaria in 1847 to resume his medical practice and then moved to nearby Newberry. His first known story, though not of a humorous kind, is a travel sketch entitled "A Sunday Evening in Germany," which was published in the *South Carolinian* on November 5, 1847. There followed other sketches based on his European travels and in the popular Gothic mode reminiscent of works of Washington Irving and Edgar Allan Poe.

It is Mayer's humorous work, however, upon which his reputation rests, tales with Dutch Fork settings and featuring customs, folkways, and characters reflective of the Teutonic culture which first settled the region. Mayer published his best comic sketches under the pseudonym "Haggis" in the *South Carolinian.* The first of these, "The Innocent Cause, Or How Snoring Broke Off a Match," employs the epistolary form of the yokel letter to the editor, a familiar staple of Southwest humor, and features a comic rogue of the same fabric as George Washington Harris's Sut Lovingood. "Snip—A Tale," a sympathetic piece on courtship, focusing on a rural Dutch Fork wedding and customs, showcases instances of physical and congenial comedy. Two Dutch Fork courtship sketches followed. "The Easter Eggs," featuring vernacular dialect, employs a performative boast between two competitive suitors and "The Corn Cob Pipe," inspired by Irving's "The Legend of Sleepy Hollow," examines a power conflict between a spirited Dutch Fork farm girl and her parents concerning the man whom she should marry.

In addition to his *South Carolinian* sketches and tales, all of which Mayer published in 1848, he also wrote fiction for *Russell's Magazine* and the *Southern Bivouac,* the best of which is "Aberhot Koselhantz, the Wizard Gunsmith," a tale published in *Russell's* in May 1857 that effectively combines humor and Dutch Fork folklore. Mayer also wrote a novel, *John Punterick,* a fragment which he probably penned in 1860, but which was not published until 1981. *John Punterick* employs a framework with friends swapping tales about the Dutch Fork days of old, some of which are farcical and employ motifs common to Old Southwest humor.

In helping to popularize a pocket of traditional culture known as the Dutch Fork, which was passing into history, and treating it with sympathetic levity and understanding, O. B. Mayer helped to open up new territory for humor. In describing Mayer's achievement as a humorist, Edwin T. Arnold, who regards Mayer as one who had a knack for reconciling opposites, writes that "his combination of propriety and absurdity, of melancholy and merriment, of commiseration and comedy sets him apart from most his fellow humorists in a manner that is much to be admired."

Text: "The Innocent Cause, or How Snoring Broke Off a Match," Columbia *South Carolinian,* January 25, 1848

The Innocent Cause, or How Snoring Broke Off a Match

A TALE OF HOG KILLING TIME

Dear Colonel.—Here is a letter written to me long ago by my esteemed friend, Belt. Seebub, or Belzebub, as he was more generally known. What he records may be true, or it my not: my opinion is, that there is something in it.

My Dear Sir:—After spendin an agreeable time among you down there, jest as I was mountin my hoss to bid you adiew, you requested me to write to you a long letter narratin some adventure of my own personal occurrunce. It seems that fate was aware many centuries ago, that you was goin to make sech a request, for I had'nt been home here more then two weeks when the very thing, the all-firedest, cussedest thing tuk place as ever yet had tukken place in relation to me. I'll write it down jest as it all happened.

You know Micheal Ann Hull, the cousin of Liza Paul what you kissed so much in playin Sister Phebe when you was up here? Well I tuk a likin to her, becase we was raised together, and her mother has been, next to my own, the kindest soul ever sense I can recollect myself and before I could, if what folks ses is true. I have been in love with Micheal Ann now more than a year, and it is amusin' to trace the imperceptabilities of the rise and progress of my affections and hern. She first begun by puttin young kittens in my coat pocket, but she soon quit that, for one night when I wasn't aware of any thing bein in my coat pocket, I set down in the arm cheer and mashed the little innocent so ded that it hadn't time to squawl nor scratch.—She cried a good deal about it, but it was'nt two months before she commenced poking straws up my nose while I'd be pertendin to be asleep by the fire; and once Liza Paul told her if she was in her place she'd kiss me, and Micheal Ann exclaimed "La, Liza Paul, aint you ashamed of yourself." Well things went on so ontel I and Micheal Ann got to kissin one another when we was both as wide awake as old Wilks when he is affected with the delirius tremendus. This fetches me perty nigh up to the matters what are goin to interest you.

You know my name is Belton Seebub, or Belt. Seebub, as the boys hereabouts call me; but Mr. Dukes, the Universalist preacher, calls me Belzebub, becase, ses he, I am the only devil the existence of which he is convinced of. If the galls had'nt to laughed at it as a good thing, I'd have licked him for sayin of it. It is true, as you very well know, that I am a devilish fellow, fond of fun, and that I am often sorry, as most terrestrial devils are, for the pranks I perpetrate.

Now old Mrs. Hull got to hear of some of my scrapes, and she give it to me in a sperit of wrath that was dredful. I reconciled her in a few days, however, and got a regular bloodsuckin kiss of reconciliation with me at the same time and on account of the same circumstances. Well, a week afterwards Mrs. Hull give me an invitation to cum down to her house to superintend the butcherin of twenty hogs. Good! that was jest what I wanted. Thinks I to myself I'll do things so nice, and be so industrious that the old woman cant find in her hart to defer mine and Micheal Ann's weddin day any longer. So down I goes with my oldest breeches on and a red flannel shirt with the sleeves rolled up over my elbows. I was on the place by three o'clock, and all the fires kindled, water made hot, hogs killed, scraped and gutted, before Micheal Ann got up, and I give her a lecture on laziness right before her mother. By twelve o'clock I was so greasy all over that neither Lizy Paul nor Micheal Ann would let me git nigh 'em. In the course of the day I made myself useful in a thousand different ways, sech as seperatin the fat from the intustynes, choppin sawsudge meat and saltin away poke.

Night come on, and we all sot round a big poplar tray filled with sawsudges meat and intustynes, and we commenced stuffin sawsudges and makin merry. I was up to the bizziness of stuffin; so with my broad thumb and goard handle stuffer, I beat Micheal Ann and Liza Paul all to pieces. Old Mrs. Hull got down a musheene made out of tin and sed she was goin to beat us all, but she busted the intustynes so frightfully that she flung the thing at Ranger, (one of the savudgest dogs I ever saw,) jest as he was stickin his nose inte the sawsudge meat. The old woman cum mighty nigh bustin out in wrath, but I told a funny joke, and jest then a traveller hollered at the gate—

That was the eend of my happiness. I have often sence more than a hundred times wished that the Kentucky hog driver what hollered at the gate that night, had been the driver of the lot of hogs what are sed in the days of the Apossels to have taken the devil in their heds and run into the Yeuxyne see. But he couldn't help it. He was only the innosent cause of my truble. It is my opinion ser, that these fellers who are the innocent causes of misfortune, are the most detestebul of all fellers; becase there is no possibility of gittin any revenge out of 'em. A moralist would tell you that you might as well skin your knuckles agnst a stump over which you stumbled, as to chestize a man what has innosently injured you.

As soon as the Kentuckian hollered, Liza Paul, Micheal Ann and her mother all jumped up, and run into the house to entertain him. I got all-fired mad. There was no more use of Micheal Ann's going into the house than there was on me goin, and there was no use of that, as you will see in the sequil. Well I got to bustin intestynes myself, and Liza Paul's mammy had to reprove me for it. That made me hot. Jest then Ranger come into the kitchen, and I kicked him clean out the door into a barrel of feathers, where he yelped most piteously. I herd the winder sash in the house go up, and out cum Mrs. Hull's voice—she is a terribul woman when she is inraged. "Who on yearth is that abusin that poor dog?" ses she. "He is hollerin mam, from the effects of the blow you give him with the sawsudge stuffer," ses I. Down goes the sash, open come the door, and out springs the old lady into the Piazzer. "You're a lier," ses she, "an unmannerly, good-for-nothin lier, for I missed him. Look here Belt you've been a good feller all day, now don't go kickin up any shines in there sens I aint there." —I coiled up my fingers into the knottiest sort of a fist, fotch it down against the edge of the old tray, and knocked out a smart sized little rollin target. At the same time I got up, and sed I'd be durned to durnnation if I'd stuff any more sawsudges that night. "You'll cetch it tomorrow mornin, my cherip," sed Liza Paul's mammy, as I went out of the kitchen.

When I got into the house, the old woman was by herself, the Kaintuckian havin gone out to see about his hoss. "Now Belt, why will you do so, you know I love you as I do my own son," sed she, with tears in her eyes. I threw myself into her arms, and sheddin an abundance of tears, exclaimed "my dear mother forgive me and I will never do any thing again to offend you."— "That's a good boy," ses she, pressin me to her bussum. "You shall have Micheal Ann as soon as you like." My extussy was more that I can describe. Just then the Kaintuckian cum in, and I caught sight of Liza Paul becconin to me to go there. She and Micheal Ann had been all the time in the little shed room fryin sawsudges.—I rushed into the room, and told Liza that her mammy was goin to injure me in the estimation of Mrs. Hull, and that she should go to the kitchin, and remunstrate with her, and Liza Paul was gone in an instant.

"Why did'nt you foller me out of the kitchen Belt? You might have known that I cum out on purpus for you to foller me," sed Micheal Ann, settin down on my nee.

"Becase," ses I, "it was predestyned from infinity that at times I should make a fool of myself: and it seems to me that tonight I am so full of the devil that it chokes me."

Micheal Ann put her mouth right on mine to prevent me, as she sed, from blasphemin. I squeezed the dear gall to my buzzum, and we both busted into tears.

"Micheal Ann," ses I, "you cant begin to conceive how much I love you. It's jest as far above your comprehension as the doctryne of the Trinity."

"And yet Belt, I believe in the Holy Trinity notwithstandin I cant see into it."

Here Micheal Ann put one eend of a sawsudge into her mouth, and turning her face towards me, I bit off the sawsudge even with her teeth.

"You'l quit all your devilment won't you?"

"Yes, honey, after we are married. And speakin of marryin, your mammy ses we may git married whenever we like."

"Now Belt, when did you ax mammy?"

"Never you mind," I responded, "you jest say when you are willin to become mine, wholly mine, and nothin but mine so help you God."

"Belt aint you ashamed of yourself?"

"I never was ashamed of any thing in all my life," ses I.

Here she commenced enumeratin a great many biergrafickal purtickularities concernin myself, which she sed I ought to be ashamed of, if I wasn't. She laid sum stress upon that scrape you herd talk of when you was up here about me and Betsy Hardwick. I call God to witness that I am as innocent of it as the child itself. —But all I could say would'nt convince Micheal Ann, and now I suppose I never can convince her.

"You jest hush Belt," ses she, "mammy ses it's jest as much like you when you was a baby as any two pattridge eggs—"

"All babies are as much alike as all the pattridge eggs as ever was laid," I answered. "But settin all that aside let's get married before Chrismus, and then you know you'll prevent me from frolickin the Christmas hollerdays."

"Well, Belt, whenever you want to," ses the charmin gall.

"Next, Thursday a week we'll get married then—, eh?"

"Well."

I and Micheal Ann drew nearer to the fire and eat sawsudges out of one another's mouth until two o'clock, when I axed her where I was to sleep.

"In the garret room where the Kaintuckian is."

"Good!" ses I, and I kissed her, tuk up a candle, and went up stairs.

If ever I git to be as happy agin as I was while I was goin up them stairs, I will appint a day of thanksgivin and keep it as strictly as a preacher keeps Sunday. Ah, little did I think that the next mornin I would see Micheal Ann pleadin for me on her nees before her inraged mother. And that durned Kaintuckian was the innosent cause of it all.

When I reached the door of the garret room, I herd the hog driver snorin most dredfully. He did'nt wake when I went in, and I walked right up to him with the candle in my hand, jest to see how a man did look while he was snorin, for out of all the folks ever herd snore, I never yet had seen one.

His face wore a terrubul expression. He lay flat upon his back, with his hed berried in the piller, his eyes sot and half open, and his under jaw hung down tel his tung could be seen as dry as a swinged pig tail. In fact, his mouth looked like a steel trap set for a otter and baited with a piece of dried beef. The diffikulty of respuration under which he labered made my flesh crawl. There was a little stove at the hed of his bed. And the stove pipe was about three feet over his face out through a hole in the wall. It was an old stove, and had not been used for a long time. I sot the candle down upon it, pulled off my clothes, and hopped into bed. I wanted to go to sleep as soon as possabul, so that I might dream about Micheal Ann, but it was onpossabul, for the Kaintuckian snored so loud that the candlestick rattled upon the stove as it would have done from the jar of distant thunder.

I stuck my thumbs into my ears, but it did no good, for I do not think there is a man living who can go to sleep with his thumbs stickin in his ears. I lay I recken an hour waitin for the hog driver to quit snorin, until at last the devil in me got of such a consistence that I was forced to cast it out. The stove pipe came into my mind—quick as a thought I leaped out of bed, and runnin up to the stove, raised the eend of the stove pipe from the stove and clapt it right over his mouth, includin his nostruls, his eyes, and his chin. In the same moment I hopped back into my bed. The snorin instantly stopped, and I was beginning to place the pillow so that I could easily get hold of it in case I should need it to hug while dreamin about Micheal Ann, when lookin through the window by the light of the full moon, I saw issuin out of the mouth of the stove pipe, out side of the house, an awful torrunt of sut. Thinks I, he has remarkabul strong powers of respurration to create such a purterbition in the sut, I wonder, thinks I, if he draws as much sut into his lungs out of one eend of the stove pipe as he forces out at the other. It amused me very much, but that was the very beginnin of trubulation; for all at once a sound accumpined the sut out of the stove pipe, that made the very hairs in my nostruls move like the legs of a sentipede. It was the most unyearthly noise that ever yet was hearn on yearth or ever will again be hearn this side of the general resserrection day. If I would attempt to describe it, I would say it was sumthin between the howl of lettin off steam and the scream of a circular saw cuttin through a hard pine-knot.

It is no use for me to tell you that it was the Kaintuckian snorin though the stove pipe, and before I could jump up and take it from his mouth he had effected the following important results upon the plantation, that is to say, the hosses in the stable tuk fright at the second sound and commenced kickin and whickerin most dreadfully.—Ranger barked purty savrdgely at the first sound but at the second he changed the tone of his barkin so that it was easy for a child to tell that his tail was stuck between his legs. He tuck a strait course for the creek swamp and Liza Paul told me yesterday that he had not been hearn of since. The old muscofy drake that was made a present to Micheal Ann before she commenced sheddin teeth, tuk alarm at the third sound, and fluttered across the yard like a whole flock. He got tangled amung some boards, as well as I could judge from the noise and his flutterin grew weeker and weeker tel it ceased altogether. At the fourth sound Mrs. Hull gave a shriek and hoppin out of bed, I heard her scream out "you Bill, you Alford, I say, some of you out there in the kitchen, what on yearth is that noise?" There was considerable disturbence down stairs but after half an hour every thing became quiet. I tell you the cold pusperation busted from every pore in my body when I heard Mrs. Hull, but at length I went to sleep myself.

The next morning I was waked up about day light by the voice of Mrs. Hull, she was abusin somebody most dreadfully, and I thought I heard Eliza Paul and Micheal Ann crying. Thinks I, what has the gals been doin.

"Jest go up stairs and wake up the retch," exclaimed Mrs. Hull down stairs, and I knew from the emfussis of her voice that she was tearin mad. I thought it was the Kaintuckian she alluded to, and that he had been doin somethin he ought'nt to. I hops up and runs to his bed with the dutiful intention of suffocatin him, but he was gone. I put on my clothes and went down stairs.

"You infernal rascal." Screamed my mother-in-law apparent, "clear out, leave this place, you triflin scoundrul."

"Oh, mammy mammy," exclaimed Micheal Ann, "there's no great harm dun, we can wash 'em again this very day."

I looked about and begun to see what was the matter. There was a nice white diepper towel hanging on the piazzer, with the great biggest ugliest blackest spot in the middle of it immadgunabul. It was where the Kaintuckian had wiped his face before he went away. The wind had blowed the sut in little drifts all about the yard and there was all Micheal Ann's perty white stiff starched petty coats on the clothes line ruinationed by the cussed sut. The old woman was becommin appeased when Liza Paul's little brother cum in draggin the old muscofy drake—. He was completely ded and covered over with hog's fat.

"Where did you get that, you little imp."—Asked Mrs. Hull in a terribul voice, that set the little feller cryin.

"In the fat pot mam out side the smoke house door."

There was a mistery explained. The old drake in his flight had flew up against the boards coverin the big pot filled with melted lard that had been left out to cool, and fallin into the fat, had died in laudibul exertions to extricate hiself. As soon as I saw it, I sprang out of the piazzer and run for my life, but I wasn't swift enough to escape the vituperatin expressions she sent after me, for she looked upon my flight as an acknowledgement of guilt.

"Begone you scape gallus, clear out—never do you put your foot on this place again, you vagabone you, what jest runs from one place to another in hog killin time jist to eat the nabers' back bones and spare ribs!— A-i-n-t you ashamed of yourself?— Jist think of it now.—Oh you good for nothing stinkin villian, to treat me so—me who suckled you for three months when your mammy couldn't give enuff of milk to keep you from starvin, and the marks is on my breast yet where you bit me, you good for nothin impertinunt rascul you."

The pleadins of Micheal Ann rose up in this storm of rage like a rainbow in a tempist. I run for a quarter of mile and laid down on the ground and rolled over and kicked and snorted in my unsupportabul despair. I wish you would write to me and give me some advice, for advice from a friend is comfort, and God knows I need it.

Yours every inch.
Belton Seebub.

N.B. Liza Paul ses she would take a hankerin after you if you wasn't so cussed proud.

B.S.

I am happy to add, that the difficulties under which my friend Seebub found himself at the close of his letter have since been happily removed and that Mrs. Hull was proud of him as a son in law to her last day. I have several letters from Belt: relating the circumstances of the reconciliation, and describing his wedding, but they are unfortunately mislaid. If I should ever find them they shall be at your service.—If in twenty years my friend Belt be not the patriarchal centre of a thriving family circle, appearances are deceitful, for I and Liza Paul were sponsors last Sunday three weeks to the last twins Micheal Ann presented him.

William C. Hall (c. 1819–1865)

Little is known about the life of William C. Hall. Though his family was originally from Tennessee, Hall, born in Yazoo County, Mississippi, attended Transylvania University in Kentucky, and became a newspaperman in New Orleans. His fame rests principally on five humorous sketches, the "Yazoo Sketches," published initially in the New Orleans *Daily Delta* and *Weekly Delta* in 1849 and 1850, under the signature of "H." These "Yazoo Sketches" all focus on Mike Hooter, based on real-life Yazoo County resident Michael Hooter, a mild-mannered, devoutly religious, civic-minded, and prosperous cotton planter, whom Hall, according to John Q. Anderson, helped to transform into a mythic frontier icon.

While not as well known as Davy Crockett or Mike Fink—both widely popular real-life heroes whose exploits were also mythologized—Mike Hooter was, in his fictional form, a character of a similar ilk. A rough-and-tumble, tall-talking backwoodsman and lay preacher, Hooter was reputed to be a great bear hunter, largely the result of his own boasting and self-promotion. In fact, as the sketches about Mike Hooter attest, his principal passions were bear hunting, drinking, preaching, and tale-telling. Because Mike demonstrated in three letters published in the New Orleans *Delta* in 1856 and 1857 that he could deliver loud and lively sermons, he also came to be known as "Mike Shouter." In one of the sketches, "How Mike Hooter Came Very Near 'Wollopin' Arch Coony," Arch refers to Mike's preaching as "nuthin' but loud hollerin.'"

The first of the "Yazoo Sketches," "Mike Hooter's Fight with the 'Bar,'" a frame tale, establishes Mike's fascination for bear hunting, showcasing his backwoods vernacular and oral yarn-spinning. The second sketch, "Mike Hooter's Bar Story," told almost entirely in Mike's voice, exaggerates in tall-talish fashion the intelligence and spectacular human-like skills of Yazoo County bears. Henry Clay Lewis, the author of *Odd Leaves in the Life of a Louisiana Swamp Doctor* (1850) who lived for a while in Yazoo County, also wrote one sketch that clearly draws on materials associated with the Mike Hooter myth in his portrayal of the hunter Mik-hoo-tah, whose name means "the grave for bears," in "The Indefatigable Bear Hunter."

The most graphic, amusing, and engaging of the "Yazoo Sketches," however, is "How Sally Hooter Got Snake-Bit." In it, Mike Hooter relates an embarrassing incident involving his daughter Sally, who defies his wishes by creating a makeshift bustle from a large sausage that her mother prepared so she would be fashionably dressed for a camp meeting. But when the sausage, which Sally mistakes for a snake, slips loose and falls about her ankles, Mike saves her from the serpent. The earthy humor of this sketch, like that of Thorpe's "The Big Bear of Arkansas" and of Harris's "Parson John Bullen's Lizards," is built around suggestively risqué subject matter.

James H. Justus describes Hall's loud-talking braggart as a "skilled manipulator of delaying tactics and fruitful evasion," a character who "dramatizes a shift from the heroic mold to the modern one, constructing himself as a witty, wry, and resilient personality unafraid of self-mockery."

While his work is not widely known today, William C. Hall is notable for creating a likeable, entertaining character in Mike Hooter, though Hooter is somewhat of an antihero. Moreover, Hall achieved some national exposure when three of his "Yazoo Sketches" were reprinted in Porter's the *Spirit of the Times* soon after they appeared in the *Delta*. In the 1850s, several of Hall's Mike Hooter sketches were even anthologized in T. A. Burke's *Polly Peablossoms's Wedding; and Other Tales* and W. E. Burton's *Cyclopedia of Wit and Humor*.

Texts: "Mike Hooter's Bar Story," New Orleans *Delta* January 6, 1850; "How Sally Hooter Got Snake-Bit," New Orleans *Delta* March 24, 1850.

Mike Hooter's Bar Story: A Yazoo Sketch—No. II

Showing how the Bear outwitted Ike Hamberlin.

"It's no use talkin,'" said Mike, "'bout your Polar Bar, and your Grisly Bar, and all that sorter varmont what you read about. They ain't no whar, for the big black customer that circumlocutes down in our neck o' woods, beats 'em all hollow. I've heard of some monsus explites kicked up by the brown bars, sich as totein off a yoke o' oxen, and eatin' humans raw, and all that kind o' thing; and Capten Parry tells us a yarn 'bout a big white bar, what 'muses hisself cumin' up the North Pole and slides down to keep his hide warm; but all that ain't a circumstance to what I've saw.

"You see," continued Mike, "there's no countin' on them varmonts as I's been usened to, for they comes as nigh bein' human critters as any thing I ever see what doesn't talk. Why, if you was to hear any body else tell 'bout the bar-fights

I've had, you wouldn't b'leeve 'em, and if I wasn't a preacher, and could not lie none, I'd keep my fly-trap* shot 'tell the day of judgment.

"I've heard folks say as how bars cant think like other human critters, and that they does all the tricks what they does, from instink. Golly! what a lie! You tell *me* one of 'em don't know when you've got a gun, and when you aint? Just wait a minit, an my privit 'pinion is, when you've hearn me through, you'll talk tother side of your mouth.

"You see, one day, long time ago, 'fore britches come in fashion, I made a 'pointement with Ike Hamberlin, the steam doctor, to go out next Sunday to see whether we couldn't kill a Bar, for you know bacon was skace, and so was money, and them fellers down in Mechanicsburg wouldn't sell on "tick," so we had to 'pend on the varmints for a livin.'

"Speakin' of Mechanicsburg, the people down in that ar mud-hole ain't to be beat nowhere this side o' Christmas. I've hearn o' mean folks in my time, an' I've preached 'bout 'em a few; but ever sense that fellow Bonnel sold me a pint of red-eye whisky—an half ov it backer juice—for a coon-skin, an' then guv me a brass pickayune fur change, I've stoped talkin.' Why, that chap was closer than the bark on a hickory tree; an' ef I hadn't hearn Parson Dilly say so, I'd ov swor it wasn't er fac, he was cotch one day stealin' acorns from a blind hog. Did you ever hear how that hoss-fly died? Well, never mind. It was too bad to talk 'bout, but a heap too good for him.

"But that ain't what I was spoutin' 'bout. As I was sayin' afore, we had to 'pend on the varmints fur a livin'. Well. Ike Hamberlin, you see, was always sorter jubious o' me, kase I kilt more bar nor he did; an,' as I was sayin,' I made a 'pinement with Ike to go out huntin.' Then Ike, he thought he'd be kinder smart, and beat 'Old Preach' (as them Cole boys usen to call me;) so, as soon as day crack, he hollered up his puppies, an' *put!* I spied what he was 'bout fur I hearn him larfin' to one o' his niggers 'bout it the night afore—so, I told my gal Sal to fill my privit tickler full a the old "raw," and then fixed up an' tramped on arter him, but didn't take none o' my dogs. Ike had n't got fur into the cane, 'fore the dogs they 'gin to whine an' turn up the har on ther backs; an,' bime by, they all tucked tail, an' sorter sidled back to whar he was stanin.' "Sick him!" says Ike, but the cussed critters wouldn't hunt a lick. I soon diskivered what was the matter, for I kalki- lated them curs o' hisn was n't worth shucks in a bar fight—so, I know'd that was bar 'bout, if I *didn't* see no *sine.*

"Well, Ike he coaxed the dogs, an' the more he coaxed, the more they wouldn't go, an' when he found coaxin' wouldn't do, then he scolded and called 'em some of the hardest names ever you hearn, (sich as "son-of-er-bitch" an sich like,) but the tarnation critters would n't budge a peg. When he found they wouldn't hunt no how he could fix it, he begin a cussin.' He didn't know I was thar. If he had er suspicioned it, he'd no more swore than he'd dar'd to kiss my

Sal on er washin' day; for you see both on us belonged to the same church, and Ike was class-leader. I thought I 'should er flummuxed! The dogs they sidled back, an' Ike he cussed; an' I lay down an' rolled an' laughed sorter easy to myself, 'till I was so full I thought I should er bust my biler! I never *see* enny thing so funny in all my life! There was I layin' down behind er log, fit to split, an' there was the dogs with their tails the wrong eend down, an' there was Ike a rarin' an' er pitchln'—er rippin' an' er tarrin'—an' er cussin' wus nor a steamboat cap'n! I tell you it fairly made my har' stan' on eend! I never see er customer so riled afore in all my born days! yes I did too, once—only once. It was that feller Arch Coony, what usen to oversee for old Ben Roach. Didn't you know that ar hossfly? He's a few! well, *he* is. Jewhilliken, how he could whip er nigger! and swar! whew! Didn't you ever hear him swar? I tell you, all the sailors an' French parrots in Orleans ain't a patchin' to him. I hearn him let hisself out one day, an' I pledge my word he cussed 'nuff to send twenty preachers like old Joe Slater an' Parson Holcom an' them kind er Jewdases, right kerplumpus into h—, an' what was wus, it was all 'bout nothin,' for he warn't mad a wrinkle. But all that aint neither here nor thar. But, as I was sayin' afore, the dogs they smelt bar sine, an' wouldn't budge a peg, an' arter Ike had almost cussed the bark off'n a dogwood saplin' he was stanin' by, he le'nt his old flint lock rifle up agin it, and then he peeled off his old blanket an' laid her down, too. I diskivered mischief was er cumin,' fur I never see a critter show wrathy like Ike did. Torecly I see him walk down to the creek bottom, 'bout fifty yards where his gun was, and then he 'gin pickin' up rocks an' slingin' 'um at the dogs like bringer! Cracky! Didn't he link it into 'um? It minded me o' David whalin' Goliah, it did! If you'd er seed him, and hearn them puppies holler, you'd er thought he'd er knocked the hine sites off'n every bitch's son of em! But that aint the fun yet. While Ike was er lammin' the dogs, I hearn the alfiredest crackin' in the cane, an' looked up, and thar was one of the eternalest whollopin bars cumin' crack, *crack,* through the cane an' kerslosh over the creek, an' stoped right plumb slap up whar Ike's gun was. Torecly he tuk hold er the old shooter, an' I thought I see him tinkerin' 'bout the lock, an' kinder whislin,' and blowin' into it. I was 'stonished, I tell you, but I wanted to see Ike outdone so bad that I lay low an' kep' dark, an' in about a minit Ike got done lickin' the dogs, an' went to git his gun. Jeemeny, criminy! if you'd only bin whar I was! I *do* think Ike was the madest man that ever stuck an ax into a tree, and his eyes glar'd like two dogwood blossoms! But the bar didn't seem to care shucks for him, for he jis sot the old rifle rite back agin the saplin,' and walked on his hine legs jist like any human. Then, you see, I gin to get sorter jealous, an' sez to myself, Mister Bar, sez I, the place whar you's er stanin' aint perzacly healthy, an' if you don't wabble off from thar purty soon, Misses Bar will be a wider, by gum! With that, Ike grabbed up old Misses Rifle, and tuk most pertickler aim at him, and by hokey, she snapped! Now sez I,

Mister Bar, go it, or he'll make bacon of you! But the varmint didn't wink, but stood still as a post, with the thumb of his right paw on the eend of his smeller, and wiglin' his tother finger thus:—and Mike went through with the gyration. All this time, Ike he stood thar like a fool, er snappin and er snappin, an' the bar he look in' kinder quare like, out er the corner o' his eye, an' sorter larfin at him. Torecly I see Ike take down the ole shooter, and kinder eksamine the lock, an' when he done that, he laid her on his shoulder, an' shook his fist at the bar, and walked towards home, an' the bar he shuk his fist, an' went into the cane brake, and then I cum off.

Here all the Yazoo boys expressed great anxiety to know the reason why Ike's gun didn't fire. Let's licker fust, said Mike, an' if you don't caterpillar, you can shoot me. Why, you see, concluded he, the long and short of it is this, that the bar in our neck o' woods has a little human in um, an' this feller know'd as much about a gun as I do 'bout preachin'; so when Ike was lickin' the dogs, he jest blowed all the powder outen the pan, an' to make it all safe, he tuk the flint out too, and that's the way he warn't skeered when Ike was snappin' at him.

*By "fly-trap," Mike probably meant to indicate his "mouth."

How Sally Hooter Got Snake-Bit
A Yazoo Sketch—NO. IV

Our old acquaintance, Mike Hooter, made another visit to town last week, and being, as he supposed, beyond the hearing of his brethren in the church, (for be it remembered, that Mike is of pious inclining, and a ruling elder in the denomination of Methodists), concluded that he would go on a "bust." Having sold his crop of cotton and fobbed the "tin," forth sallied Mike with a "pocket full of rocks," and bent on a bit of a spree. After patronizing all the groceries, and getting rather mellow, he grew garrulous in the extreme, and forthwith began to expatiate on his wonderful exploits. After running through with a number of "Pant'er and Bar fights," and several "wolf disputes," he finally subsided into the recital of events more nearly appertaining to members of his family. "That Yazoo," said Mike, "is the durndest hole that ever came along. If it ain't the next place to no whar, you can take my head for er drinkin gourd—you can, an' as for that ar devil's camp ground, what they calls Satartia, if this world was er kitchen, it would be the slop hole, an' er mighty stinkin one at that! I pledge you my word, it comes closer bein' the jumpin off place than any I ever hearn tell on. Talk about Texas. It ain't nothin' to them Yazoo hills. The etarnalest out-of-the-way place for bar, an' panters, an' wolfs, an' possums, an' coons, an' skeeters, an' nats, an' hoss flies, an' cheegers, an' lizzards, an' frogs, an' mean fellers, an' drinkin' whiskey, an' stealin' one-anothers' hogs, an' gittin' corned, an' swappin' hosses, an' playin' h—ll generally, that ever you did see! Pledge you my word, 'nuff to sink it. An' as for snakes! whew! don't talk! I've hearn tell of the Boa Constructor, an' the Annagander, an' all that kind er ruptile what swollers er he-goat whole, an' don't care er switch uv his tail for his horns; an' I see the preacher tell 'bout Aaron's walkin' stick what turned itself into er sarpent, an' swoller'd up ever-so many other sticks, an' rods, an' bean poles, an' chunks o' wood, an' was hungry yet—an' all that kinder hellerbelloo, but that's all moonshine. Jist wait er minit till you've hearn 'bout the snakes what flourishes up 'bout my stompin' ground, an' how one uv 'um come precious nigh chawin' up my datter Sal, an' if you don't forgit evrything you ever know'd, then Mike Hooter's the durndest liar that ever straddled a fence rail. Jeeminy, criminy! Jest to see him, one uv them ar great big, rusty rattlesnakes, an' hear him shake that ar tale uv hizzen! I tell you what, if you didn't think all the peas in my corn field was er spillin in the floor, thar ain't no 'simmons! Talk about the clouds burstin an' the hail rattling down in er tin pan! Why 'taint er patchin to it! Cracky! its worse nor er young earthquake—beats h—ll!

"Now, I don't valley er snake no more nor er she bar in suckin time—'specially er rattlesnake, cause you see it's er vurmin what always rattles his tail 'fore he strikes, an' gives you time to scoot out'n the way, but the *wimmin* folks an' my gal Sally is always, in generally, the skeerdest in the world uv' em. I never seed but one woman what wouldn't cut up when er snake was 'bout, an' that was ole Misses Le May, an' she didn't care er dog on bit for all the sarpints that ever cum er 'long. That old gal was er hoss! Pledge you my word I b'leeve she was pizen!—couldn't be no other way. Didn't never hear how that ole petticoat bit the snake? Well, I'll tell you.

"She went out one day an' was er squattin' down, pickin' up chips, an' the first thing she know'd she got onto the whappinest, biggest, rustiest yaller moccasin that ever you shuck er stick at, an' bein' as how she was kinder deaf, she didn't hear him when he 'gin to puff an' blow, and hiss like. The fust thing she knowed he bit her, *slap*—the all-firedest, biggest kinder lick! You orter seen that old gal, how she fell down, an' rolled, an' waller'd, an' tumbled 'bout and holler'd nuff, an' screamed, an' prayed, an' tried to sing er sam, and played h—ll generally! You'd er thought the very yearth was er cummin to an eend! Then she begin hollerin' for help. Sez she, Misses Hooter, cum here an' kill this here snake! Well, my wife run out and fetch the old 'oman in the house an' gin her some whiskey, an' she tuk it like milk. Torectly she sorter cum to herself, and sez my wife to her—sez she to Misses Le May, sez she—'Misses Le May, what hurts you?'

"'Snake-bit!' sez she.

"'Whar'bouts?' sez I.

"'Never mind,' sez she—'snake bit!'

"'But Misses Le May!' sez I, 'tell me whar he bit you, so as we may put somethin' to it.'

"Sez she, lookin' kinder glum, and turnin' red in the face—sez she to me, 'It don't want nuthin' to it: I'm snake-bit, an' taint none er your bizziness whar!'

"With that I smelt a mice, and commenced larfin. You orter hear me holler! If I didn't think I'd er bust my biler, I wish I may never see Christmas! I ain't larfed so much since the time John Potter got on the bar's back without no knife, an' rode him 'round, like er hoss, and was skeer'd to get off! I give you my word I farly rolled!

"Soon as the ole 'oman 'gin to open her eyes, an' I see thar warnt nuthin' much the matter with her, my wife she grabbed up the tongs an' went out to kill the snake, an' I follered. When I see the reptile, sez I to my wife, 'jest wait er minit,' sez I. ''Taint no use killin' him—he's past prayin' for!' I pledge you my word he was as dead as Billy-be-d—d! 'What made him die?' sez my wife to me. 'Don't know,' sez I—'spose he couldn't stand it.' Toreckly Mat Read he cum up, an, when he hears what had been goin' on, he was so full er larf his face turned wrong side out'ards, and sez he—'Poisoned, by golly!'

"That ole 'oman ain't been skeer'd uv er snake sense, an' goes out huntin 'em reglar. I told her one day, sez I, 'Misses Le May,' sez I, 'I'll give you the best bunch of hog's bristles I've got to brush your teeth with, if you'll tell me how not to git skeer'd uv er snake!' She didn't say nare a word, but she turned 'round an' took me kerbim right 'tween the eyes! I tell you what, it made me see stars. I ain't sed snake to her since.

"Howsever, that ain't tellin' you how the sarpint kinder chawed up my darter Sal. I'll tell you how 'twas. You see there was gwine to be a mity big camp meetin' down at Hickory Grove, an' we all fixed up to go down an' stay er week, an' my wife, she looked up everything 'bout the house, an' all sorts of good things—bacon, an' possum fat, an' ash cake, an' a great big sausenger, 'bout as big as your arm, an' long enuff to eat er week—'cause, she said Parson Dilly loved sausengers the best in the world. Well, when we got there, I went to the basket what had the vittals in it, to git somethin' to eat, but the sausenger wasn't thar, an' sez I to my darter, sez I, 'Sally, gal, what's 'come er that ar sausenger?' Then she turned red in the face, an' sez she, 'Never mind—it's all right.' I smelt that thar war somethin' gwine on wrong—for you see the wimmin folks 'bout where I lives, is h—ll fur new fashions, an' one day one uv them ar all-fired yankee pedlars come er long with er outlandish kind uv er jigamaree to make the wimmin's coat sorter stick out in the t'other eend, an' the she's, they all put on one, case they 'sposed the he's would love to see it. Well, my Sal, she got monsous stuck up 'bout it, an' axed me to giv her one; but I told her she had no more use for one, nor er sittin' hen had for a midwife, an' I wouldn't do no such er thing, case how she was big enough thar at first.

"Well, as I was er sayin,' camp meetin' day it came, an' we was all thar, an' the she-folks they was fixed up in er inch uv their lives, an' thar she was er fijjittin, an' er twistin' an' er wriglin about with er new calico coat on, all stuck up at the hind eend, an' as proud as er lizzard with two tails! Tell you what—she made more fuss nor er settin' hen with one chicken! I was 'stonished what to make uv that whoppin big lump on behind. Howsever, it was 'simmon time, an' she'd bin eatin er powerful sight uv um, an' I 'sposed she was gittin fat—so I shut up my fly trap, an' lay low an' kep dark! Toreckly the preachin' it begin, an' Parson James, he was up on er log er preachin,' an' er goin' it 'hark from the tomb!' I tell you what Brother James was loud that day! Thar he was, with the Bible on er board—stickin 'twene two saplins, an' he was er *cummin'* down on it with his two fists worse nor maulin rails; an' er stompin his feet, an' er slobberin' at the mouth, an' er cuttin up shines worse nor er bob-tail bull in fly time! I tell you what, ef he *didn't* go it boots that time, I don't know! Torectly I spy the heatherns they commence takin' on, and the sperit it begin to move um, for true—for brother Sturtevant's ole nigger Cain, an' all uv um, they 'gin to kinder groan an' whine, an' feel erbout like er corn stalk in er storm, an brother Gridle, he begin er rubbin his hands an slappin' um together, an' scramblin' about on his knees, an' er cuttin' up like mad! In about er minit, I hearn the all-firedst to do, down 'mongst the wimmin, that ever cum along, and when I kinder cast my eye over that way, I spy my Sal er rarein' and er pitchin,' er rippen' an' er tarein' and er shoutin' like flinders! When brother James see that, he thought she'd done got good, an' he cum down off the log, an' sez he, 'Pray on sister!'—an' the she's they all got round her, an' cotch hold uv her, and tried to make her hold still. But 'twarnt no use. The more they told her to 'don't' the more she hollered. Toreckly I diskiver she'd done got 'ligious, an' I was so glad, it kinder lift me off'n the ground—an' sez I, 'go it Sal!—them's the licks!—blessed am them what seeks, for them's 'um what shall find!' Then the wimmin they all cotch holt of her by the har, an' commence wollerin' her 'bout in the straw, an' sez I, 'that's right, sisters—beat the Devil out'n her.' And they *did* too! I tell you what—the way they did hustle her about mongst the straw and shucks was forked! In about er minit I 'gin to get tired and disgustified, an' tried to make her shet up, but she wouldn't, but kep a hollerin worser and worser, an' she kinder keeled up like a possum when he makes 'ten he's dead! Toreckly she sorter cum to herself so she could talk, an' sez I, 'Sal, what ails you, gal?' The fust word she sed, sez she, 'Snake!'

"'Whar 'bouts?' sez I.

"'Snake,' says she agin—'sarpent! take it off, or he'll chow me up be g—d!'

"'Well!' sez my wife; 'that's cussin!'

"'Whar's enny snake?' sez I.

"'Snake!' sez she; 'snake! snake!!' an' then she put her han' on the outside of her coat, an' cotch hold uv somethin, and squeezed it tight as er vice!

"When I seed that, I knowed it was er snake sure nuff, what had crawled up under her coat; an' I see she'd put her hand on the outside uv her clothes, an' cotch it by the head. Soon as I see'd that, I knowed he couldn't bite her, for she helt onto him like grim death to a dead nigger; and I 'cluded 'twarn't no use bein' in too big er hurry; so I told John Potter not to be skeer'd an' go an' grab the sarpent by the tail, and sling him h—llwards! Well, Potter he went and sorter felt uv him on the outside uv her coat, an' I pledge you my word, he was the whappiness biggest reptile that ever scooted across er road!—I tell *you* if he warn't as big as my arm, Mike Hooter is as big er liar as ole Dave Le May—and you know he's a few in that line! Well, when Potter diskiver that she helt the snake fast, he begin feelin' up for the reptile's tail, sorter like he didn't like to do it at fust, an' then sorter like he did. When it come to that, Sal she kinder turned red in the face and squirmed er bit, but 'twarn' no time for puttin' on quality airs then, and she stood it like er hoss! Well, Potter he kep er feelin' up, an' feelin' an' er feelin' up, sorter easy like, an' toreckly he felt somethin' in his han.' 'I've got him,' sez Potter, 'well I have, by jingo!' 'Hole on to him, Sal,' sez I, 'and don't you do nothin, Mr. Potter, till I give the word, and when I say "go!" then, Sal, you let go uv the varmint's head; and Potter—you give the all-firedest kind an er jerk, and sling him to h—ll and gone!'

"I tell you what, them was squally times! and I vise you, the next time you go up to Yazoo, jest ax enny body, and if they don't say the snakes up in them parts beats creation, then Mike Hooter'll knock under."

At this point of the narration we ventured to ask Mike what became of the snake.

"As I was er sayin,'" continued he, "thar was my Sal er holein the sarpent by the head, and John Potter he had him by the tail, and Sal she was er hollerin' and er screamin,' an' the wimmin, they was all stannin' round, skeered into er fit, and the durndest row you ever hearn—'hole on to him, Sal,' sez I; 'and you, John Potter, don't you move er peg till I give the word; and when I say "jerk!" then you sling him into the middle of next week.' I tell you what, we had the orfullest time that ever I see! Let's liquor!

"That's the best red eye I've swallered in er coon's age," said the speaker, after bolting a caulker. "But, how did you manage at last?" asked a listener.

"Well, you see," said he, "thar was my Sal, an' thar was all the folks, and thar was the snake, an' John Potter holein' him by the tail, skeer'd out'n his senses, and h—ll to pay! I was gettin' sorter weak in the knees, I tell you, an' brother James' eyes looked like they'd pop out'n his head, an' sez I to John Potter, sez I to him, sez I, 'John Potter, don't you budge tell I say go! and when I gives the word, then you give him er jerk, and send him kerslap up agin that tree, and perhaps you'll gin him er headache. Now John Potter,' sez I, 'is you ready?' sez

I. 'I is,' sez he 'Now look at me,' sez I, 'and when I drap this handkercher,' sez I, 'then you jerk like flujuns,' sez I. 'Yes,' sez he. Then I turned round to Miss Lester, and sez I, 'Miss Lester, bein' as how I haint got no handkercher, 'spose you let me have that koonskin cape uv yourn'. Sez she, 'Uncle Mike, you can have enny thing I is got.' "Bliged to you,' sez I, 'and now John Potter,' sez I, 'when I drops this koon-skin cape, then you pull!' 'Yes,' sez he. 'Now,' sez I, 'keep your eye skinned, and look me right plum in the face, and when you see me drap this, then you wallum the sarpent out. Is you ready?' sez I. 'Yes,' sez he. 'Good,' sez I, 'jerk!' an' when I said jerk, he gin the *whoppinest* pull, and sent him ker-whop! about er mile an er feet! I pledge you my word, I thought he'd er pulled the tail of the varmint clean off!"

Here Mike took a quid of tobacco, and proceeded—"I've bin in er heap er scrapes, and seen some of the all-firedest cantakerous snakes that ever cum erlong, but that time beats all!"

"What kind of a snake was it," asked a listener. "I'll tell you," said he "'twarnt nuthin more'n I 'spected. Sal thought she'd look big like, an' when she was shoutin' and dancin' er 'bout, that sausenger what she'd put on for er bustle, got loose round her ankle, and she thought 'twas er snake crawlin' up her clothes!"

Mike left in a hurry.

Francis James Robinson (1820-1872)

Born in Georgia in 1820, Francis James Robinson, using the pseudonym Kauphy, published in Athens, Georgia, a collection of seven humorous sketches, *Kups of Kauphy: A Georgia Book in Warp and Woof* in 1853. Robinson acknowledges in his preface that two of the "kups"—"Snipe Pie" and the "Fright'd Serenaders, or the B'hoys in a Fix," the latter a sketch featuring rural youthful pranksters possibly inspired by Washington Irving's "The Legend of Sleepy Hollow"—had been published previously in newspapers. His book published "at the solicitation of many kind friends," Robinson paid homage to fellow Georgians Augustus Baldwin Longstreet and William Tappan Thompson, who preceded him in the field of antebellum southern humor and who achieved popularity in the genre. In explaining the intended purpose of his book, Robinson writes, half whimsically, that it is his "fond hope . . . that the Kauphy will exhilarate, without intoxication—amuse, while it may instruct, and convey a pleasure, if no more than momentary, upon those who may imbibe." If one is willing to "imbibe," Robinson further notes, "either at the *concoction* or the *concoctor*—no matter which, so you *laugh* at something; a hearty *cachinnation* being far better for your health and happiness than a whole "*box of pills*" or a quart bottle of "*Schnapps.*"

"Old Jack C—," one of the sketches in *Kups of Kauphy,* features an African American slave as the central character who was based on a real-life waiter in Madison, Georgia. In the tale, Jack serves as a vehicle to initiate situations that function so readers can experience the therapeutic effects of laughter. Though seemingly a stereotype, Jack shows that he is much more, actually transgressive in his display of ingenuity in duping white men, thereby proving himself to be more clever and more capable than they are. Moreover, Robinson gives Jack a dominant voice, allowing the slave the freedom to speak in his own vernacular tongue, saying openly what seems to be on his mind. As a staunch advocate of slavery, critic of abolitionists, and owner of slaves, Robinson, despite intrusive editorial commentary espousing traditional southern views of African American inferiority, actually shows that Jack, as a prankster, has found a way to get along in a racist society without seriously having to compromise his personal individuality.

Robinson's observation about the therapeutic benefits of humor is appropriate because he was a dentist, practicing in Lexington, Georgia, and he may have found laughter relieved his patients' pain. At various times in the 1860s and early 1870s, Robinson also served Oglethorpe County in several public capacities as clerk of inferior court, clerk of superior court, ordinary, school commissioner, and justice of the peace. In addition, like many other Old Southwest humorists, he wrote for several newspapers in his native state, such as the *Southern Banner* in Athens and the Augusta *National Republican* in the 1860s. While he was clerk of superior court in 1863 in Oglethorpe County, he wrote a patriotic notice for the *Southern Banner*, urging the county's women to support the appeal by General Foster, the quartermaster general of Georgia, to knit winter socks for local Confederate soldiers. In 1868, for several months, Robinson served as local editor of the *National Republican*, which helped to elect Rufus B. Bullock as the governor of Georgia. Soon after, in a letter to Bullock, dated June 29, 1868, concerning the presidential campaign, Robinson, who wanted to be the editor of the *National Republican*, became disenchanted because Bullock apparently would not endorse him for this position. Expressing his displeasure with the newspaper, Robinson announced that he was resigning from the staff.

While as a whole the sketches in *Kups of Kauphy* do not compare with the best in Longstreet's *Georgia Scenes* or the vernacular epistles that comprise Thompson's *Major Jones's Courtship*, Robinson's handling of scene, plot conventions, dialect, and stylistics shows his keen familiarity with the genre of Old Southwest humor and his ability to employ these materials so that his most memorable characters, such as Old Jack, can speak in their own voices, "us[ing] their own language in portraying their *individuality*."

Texts: "Lije Benadix," and "Old Jack C—," in *Kups of Kauphy: A Georgia Book, in Warp and Woof, Containing Tales, Incidents, etc. of the "Empire State of the South"* (Athens, GA: Christy & Chelsea, 1853).

Lije Benadix

In the year 18— there vegetated a specimen of the *genus homo,* in the county of K—in the glorious old junior State of the original thirteen, about whom we propose to say a few words, and as a description of his *tout ensemble,* manners, etc. will the better elucidate our tale, we will proceed to give our readers a pen and ink sketch of our friend and hero, *Mr. Lije Benadix*. He was, we suppose, some forty years of age—married, and, as a natural consequence, his table was surrounded with many "olive branches." To feed all these mouths, required from *Lije,* pretty hard scratching; though the principal *feeder* seemed to be Lije himself. He was, withal, incorrigibly *lazy*—now with plenty to satisfy the appetite—again without a dust of meal in his larder. In fruit season, he could manage to get his fill of fruits; and when plums and cherries became ripe in May, then Lije, cormorant-like, would gulp them down in large quantities, bolting then *en masse!* It is fair to presume that with his lazy habits, enormous appetite and a generous diet, Lije would have soon become a second Falstaff, but as he did not have the good fortune to possess the last named very important accompaniment, he was gaunt as a grey hound, his skin yellow and wrinkled, features shrunken and extremities diminutive! Upon the whole, an observer would at once pronounce him to be a man unused to a diet sufficiently healthy and nutritive: for upon *ordinary* occasions, with his "copperas mixed" clothes hanging upon him as upon a drying line, the conclusion would also be pretty certainly arrived at, that Lije was either "drying" up, preparatory to flying away, or had his garments made amply large for *extra-ordinary* occasions too. As often as he became possessed of a bushel of meal, in pay for "splitting rails," (the only species of work of any kind he seemed to fancy,) he would lie at home, and himself and family would cook and eat continuously until the last "hoe cake was baked" and eaten; then, perhaps, he would stir around for another job of work. Sometimes the opportunity was afforded him to "provision his ship," as for instance when called to the county seat during the session of the Superior Court. On these occasions "landlord, cook and waiters" suffered; for his usual allowance, to give a specimen, *was thirteen cups of coffee* and other provisions in the same proportion. Once he ventured to call for the *"fourteenth"* cup, when his host could stand it no longer, and ordered him peremptorily to leave the house, telling him he was welcome to what he had eaten.

"Why, Landlord, do let a fellow finish eatin—I aint nigh done yit!" protested Lije.

"Get out of my house, I tell you; for I'd as soon undertake to feed a caravan of animals, with a circus thrown in!"

And poor Lije, *still hungry,* as he protested, and ready to pay for all he ate, was obliged to *vamoose.*

At one time Lije became possessed, by some means, of a large turkey, which he took to a neighboring county seat during the session of the Court there.— This bird he *sold* to the hotel keeper, and as we shall see, also *sold* the purchaser. Lije received, in cash, one dollar, and was to have his dinner in the bargain! The fowl was duly spitted, *secundem artem,* and our host congratulated himself upon this accession to his ordinary supplied table, and thus being able to give his boarders a treat. In the meantime, Lije hung around the hotel, noticing from time to time, the clock, and peering into the dining room to make his observations. Just before the dinner hour he slipped into the dining hall, called a waiter, told him he was in a hurry to go home, and as his master had promised him his dinner, he wanted some of the "Old Gobler." It was set before him, and he attacked it bravely. Not a long while after Court adjourned, and the landlord took occasion to announce a fine fat turkey for dinner, setting all who heard him on the *qui vive*. As soon as the bell rung all rushed to the table; anxious eyes wandered up and down it—while every one called for *turkey!* The landlord, hearing a report of "there's none, massa, lef," pricked up his ears and called out,

"Waiter! what does this mean? Where's that turkey?"

"Him eat up, sir, all but de bone!"

"The d—l! Who done it, you rascal? Tell me, or I'll break every bone in your skin!"

"Dat man you bot um from, sir, I spec, for he come a little while ago and tell me you promise 'im his dinner—he was in hurry—and wanted de *turkey!* Dat all I know 'bout um, massa."

"Bring me the dish, sir!"

The dish was brought, and upon it reposed as nice a skeleton as one would wish to see; not a particle left upon the bones that was eatable. At this "visible explanation," the whole table was set in a roar, and the joke being so good a one, each one good-humoredly forgot his disappointment and made the most of the "common doins" before them.

With these specimens of "Lije's" prowess in the eating line, we shall again introduce him to you in another, as the cap-stone of all. There poor Lije lies, stretched on his back, swollen to three times his natural size and laboring under not only indigestion, but the most desperate state of constipation, perhaps, ever attempted to be removed by the medical faculty. It was in the midst of plum and cherry time, and in default of more digestible food, Lije had supplied his larder with a quantity, and had attacked them with his usual voracity and disregard of consequences. Hence his situation; for, like the Anaconda, who upon bolting his occasional meal becomes inert, so Lije had gorged himself until he had become helpless. Contrary to his expectations, his digestive apparatus was insufficient to accomplish the Herculean task thus imposed, and he was placed thereby, completely *hors du combat*, exhibiting a kind of inanimate existence, only. At this particular stage of his case he called in a physician, who, after exerting his skill for some time, gave him up, with the conviction that there was not yet made known in the Pharmacopiae of Medicine any *emetic or purgative* sufficiently powerful to be brought to bear successfully upon the truly appalling case under his care. He, therefore, retreated from the field, leaving poor Lije in the hands of his Creator and to his own natural powers, satisfied that all human means having failed, nothing short of a miraculous intervention would ever restore poor Lije to active life and to the helpless and dependant family around him. His condition was noised abroad and many of Lije's neighbors had called to see him, and among them was, a *"Yerb Dokter,"* as he called himself, named *Lobelia,* with the prefix, of course, of "Dockter." This professional gentleman had, however, no idea of trying his skill, not he! but proposed that a messenger should be sent some fifteen miles to an adjoining county to procure the services of a practitioner of extensive practice and long experience in medicine; who, by the way, was well known in that region, his practice even extending there usually. As Dr. Lobelia made the proposition, he was selected as the messenger to Dr. W———, and there might have been seen the very unusual sight of a "yerb" doctor's going for an allopathic physician! However, we must charitably suppose that Dr. L—was actuated by sympathy for suffering humanity, and for once laid aside all his professional prejudice and antipathy so notoriously known to exist between the one and the other. He found Dr. W—worn down with fatigue and unable to return with him that evening, but received the prescription of a dose of *calomel* and the promise of a visit next morning. Now, it is very well known that a mad-dog has no greater antipathy to water than has a "yerb" doctor to *calomel,* the medicine prescribed; and Dr. Lobelia took occasion to express his disbelief in its use, and a want of confidence in it any way!

"Give it to him, sir, as I direct," said Dr. W—, "and it will do him as much *good* as if *you* had every confidence in it!"

Dr. L— returned to Lije's that evening, but remaining in the "same opinion still" in regard to the calomel, did *not* administer the dose as directed.

The next morning (Monday) by 10 A.M. Dr. W—. arrived at the place. There he found a large number of Lije's neighbors, men and women, collected in the house and about the yard, discussing his case pro and con; for it had excited the curiosity of every one, besides interesting many who had kind feelings for him and his family. Dr. W. entered the house, a small, contracted affair, built of round logs and covered with oak boards. In *the* room, for we believe the house contained but a single apartment, on a bed Lije was stretched on his back, an uninterested witness of all that might be said and done. The doctor approached his bedside and made the inquiry,

"How do you feel to-day, Mr. Benadix?"

"V-e-r-y p-o-o-r-l-y, d-o-c-t-o-r," replied Lije.

The doctor then proceeded to examine him, and found his symptoms to be these: "pulse slow and rather feeble, without fever, skin rather cooler than natural, vomiting about every half hour, ejecting a half pint of a morbid secretion accumulated between the intervals of vomiting, abdomen enormously distended and as tight as a drumhead, and tongue but slightly coated." After this examination of the case was concluded he asked,

"Well, Mr. Benadix, how many plums and cherries have you eaten?"

"Not—very—many—doctor!" replied Lije, in a slow and drawling tone of voice.

"Yes, you did," spoke up his wife quickly, "you eat nearly or quite two pecks, and you eat hulls, stones and all—you did."

"Ah! indeed," remarked Dr. W., "it is very strange that a man of your age, Mr. Benadix, should eat such a quantity of plums and cherries, stones and all!—Now, sir, if you had been an old turkey gobler, you might, with some show of reason, have ate those articles, because, then you would have had a *gizzard* with which to have *ground up* such an indigestible mass!"

His wife hearing this and thinking it necessary that "the truth, the whole truth" of the affair should be made known to the doctor, again spoke up and said,

"Yes, an' you eat a pan full of honey-comb on top of 'em too—you did."

"I-n-d-e-e-d!" remarked the doctor, somewhat tartly, "if you had only ate the pan full of *rich soil* instead of the *honey-comb*, you might very soon have had an orchard and nursery very convenient!"

The doctor was somewhat vexed at the unprecedented imprudence of his patient, and in anticipation of the trouble he would have in consequence; but having received all the information he could, he at once determined to attempt to relieve him if possible. Before leaving home, he had provided himself with all the emetic and purgative medicines, from the simplest to the most powerful known; and, on his way, passing a store, procured a pound or so of tobacco (for enemas) as a *corps de reserve*. He asked and obtained the gratuitous services of a gentleman present as assistant, and to work they both went, commencing with purgatives, they gave him during the day, Castor Oil, Salts and Senna, Salts and Magnesia, Jalap and C. Tartar, Rhubarb and Aloes, Gamboge and Scammony, and Calomel to no purpose, for the stomach would not retain any of them longer than from a half to one hour. *Croton Oil* and a very strong *infusion of Tobacco*, were reserved until towards evening. Continually embarrased by the ejection of the medicines, but determining not to be backed out, as fast as one dose was ejected another was given, with little regard to quantity, varying the matter occasionally by a simple *enema*. After the day was well nigh spent, and the patient being, (as he very frequently and invariably would say, when asked how he felt) *"about as usual,"* the doctor determined to "charge the enemy" with the "advance guard" of his "reserve forces" in the shape of *Croton Oil*—informing his assistant before he did so, "that it was a powerful drug, and if it could be retained in the stomach one hour he would be hopeful of giving his patient relief, and he would be able to tell in that time what it was capable of accomplishing." So Lije swallowed *two drops!* and the doctor, watch in hand, sat by his bedside to count the moments as they flew, asking his patient at intervals how he felt, and receiving the same unsatisfactory answer of *"about as usual."*

"Do you not feel any effect from the last medicine you have taken?" asked the doctor, Lije being unaware of its name or quality.

"It—burnt—my——throat—a—little!" answered Lije.

The hour passed—an additional half hour—no effect was produced by the Croton Oil—the patient seeming to be *"about as usual!"* Finding the enemy so well fortified, the doctor informed his assistant "that the potent and all powerful 'reserve' must now be resorted to—that tobacco enemas must be used—that the remedy seldom failed to overcome the most obstinate constipation; that at the same time it produced such a relaxation of the system as to give one the appearance of being about to die, and that he (the assistant) must not get alarmed if this should prove to be the fact in Lije's case!" The tobacco had been infused for six hours, and was necessarily very strong; but upon using the *enema* even longer than usual in such cases, the disheartening result was the same as with all the other remedies. For Lije remained still *"about as usual!"* Baffled at all points, the doctor rested awhile from his labors, only, however, to continue the onset with renewed vigor! The sun was now nearly set, and the doctor, before leaving for home, put up a large number of powders, consisting wholly of calomel, about three grains in each, with directions for one to be administered every three hours, day and night, until he saw the case again on the following Wednesday. Before taking his departure, the doctor went to the bedside of his patient to bid him "good-bye," and to speak a few words of hope and encouragement. As he turned towards the door and before reaching it, Lije drawled out the question of

"D-o-c-t-o-r, w-h-a-t s-h-a-1-1 I e-a-t?"

Now this was a little more than human nature could put up with, and the doctor turned towards him instinctively and replied,

"Eat! Eat, the d—l! Get what's in you out first, then it will be time enough for you to eat more, sir!" and left him.

Wednesday came and found the doctor, according to promise, at Lije's bedside, who, he found, upon making inquiry, *"about as usual"*—no better and no worse. He had regularly taken the powders day and night. They were continued, and in addition about the same routine was pursued as on the Monday previous; and after a day's labor with the same result, sundown again finding Lije "about as usual," a large supply of the powders were then made and the same directions given. On this visit the doctor found several of the neighbors at the house, and they were very inquisitive as to the situation of the patient as well as to the kind of "physic" given him. To all the questions put, the doctor cheerfully responded, and was very much amused at the commentaries made. Those who swore at all, swore "he would die in the fix he was in any how, and that if the disease did not *kill* him, the doctor would with all that *calomel!*" Said they:

"Why, dod-rot it, he'll be salivated so badly, all his teeth will *drap* out and his jaws be eat off, so ef he does git over it, he never kin eat nothin.' He'd e'nyrnost be dead, for if Lije loves ennything at all, it's eatin."

"Oh! there's no danger," replied the doctor, "the secretions are all suspended, and he cannot be salivated in the situation he is now in!"

"Dun know so well about that nuther, for Dr. Lobelia sez there's many a man's leg bones full of *quicksilver!*"

"Pooh! pooh! what nonsense—all stuff!" answered the doctor, as he turned away to prepare for his departure.

But they continued the discussion, and one might hear an exclamation occasionally of, "Poor fellow! ef the plums don't kill him, the *doctor* and his *calomy* will!" Upon the doctor asking Lije again how he felt, he gave the invariable reply of *"about as usual."* He left him, and did not repeat his visits, though he heard from time to time how his patient was progressing. The calomel powders were continued regularly up to the *following Saturday evening.*

Four weeks after exactly, the doctor, being on a professional visit in the same region of country, observed in the road ahead of him, not very far from a mill and near the stream upon which it was situated, a thin, tall, gaunt man, who at the distance was not a familiar form to him. The man bore some resemblance to "Lije," but the portly aldermanic rotundity he possessed when lying on his back a few weeks before had all disappeared, and instead, he had become shrivelled and shrunken, lank and lean as usual. On a nearer approach, however, the doctor at once recognized his old patient, and accosted him with,

"How are you, to-day, Mr. Benadix?"

"A-b-o-u-t a-s u-s-u-a-1, d-o-c-t-o-r," replied Lije.

"I am very glad, indeed, sir, to see you about, Mr. Benadix, for at one time, we all thought you were not long for this world, sir! I presume after all our labor and pains, the medicine was effective and relieved you at last, sir?" continued the doctor.

"O, yes, doctor, it commenced about sundown on Saturday evening arter you was thar, and it 'taint done till yit!" answered Lije, as the doctor, unable to contain himself, he was so full of laughter, made off. His resurrected patient lived many years after, and though he still retained the same *"love of eatin,"* he was careful not to try again the powers of his *digestive* apparatus by bolting such another lot of plums and cherries, "seeds, hulls and all!"

Old Jack C—

We will imagine the reader just seated at the well-spread tea table, for the first time in his life, at one of the best Hotels, in all its appointments, to be found in the interior of Georgia, or of perhaps any other State; and having, like a dependant creature as he is, returned thanks to the Giver of the bounties before him, is quietly approached by a neat and tidy "colored gemman" on the wrong side of fifty, who asks in the blandest of voices, whether "master will have tea or coffee?" Now, we will suppose you to answer *tea;* you will be asked by the same smiling darky, "if you'll have *black* or *green, sage* or *sassafac?*" This question rather startles your propriety, and you turn upon the questioner, evidently intending to exhibit some sort of resentment, but you observe the polite "gentleman from Africa" with a perfectly innocent countenance, awaiting your orders; then you lose the intent and reply, *Hyson,* determined to watch the movements of your attentive servitor. Off he flies and in a trice, presents you with a delicious cup of tea, then hands you *"de clarified"* to "sweeten um" and *"de cream to qualify de strength wid,"* following up in quick succession with *"de hen fruit," "de burkshur ham," "de durham beef," "de virgin pullet," "de flannel as substitoot for de buckwheat cakes,"* and so with all the variety of fish, flesh and fowl that may be upon the table! By this time you will have regained your good humor, and with a pleasant smile, return answers to all his questions; at the same time wondering who this eccentric specimen can be, dark as ebony, old, yet active as a boy. So respectful with all his apparent impudence, in fact, we shouldn't wonder at all if you had not already become so much interested in the character, as to wish to learn his name. Don't then be surprised when we tell you that, that waiter is the veritable and inapproachable "*Old Jack C—,*" and as he would say himself, were you to ask him who he was, "*it ain't nobody else, sir!*" Possessed of quick perceptive faculties, a love of the ridiculous, cunning and smart, we have known many of greater pretensions, who were glad enough to retreat from a match with him, in a contest of wit and repartee.

We propose to give a meager sketch of his life, or rather to string together a few of the many laughable incidents in his life, in the way of anecdotes told by those who had acquaintance with him during the last quarter of a century. We shall not pretend to gather up a tithe of the *riches* a full history of his life would contain; for many of these have passed from the memories of the living; while few remain who knew *Jack*.

"When his *old head* was heavy."

Those incidents we have here gathered together have been told us, or have occurred under our own observation, and we shall endeavor to relate them as near as possible as they happened.

No one should wonder that Jack has become so *sharp-witted;* for with his natural powers to be brought into daily contact, as they have been for years, with all kinds of men and all sorts of manners, from the highest dignitary to the lowest civilian in the land, he has had every opportunity of becoming well versed in human nature. Nor do we believe that many can be found in any station of life, who are better enabled than Jack to judge of the characters of the men he meets. To the superficial observer, Jack has the appearance of being too impudent for a *slave,* but those who know him best, and who can thus better appreciate his eccentricities by this knowledge, know him to be an obedient and industrious servant; contented in his station in life, and with not the shadow of a wish to change it. Attached to his master's family, and always acting—not as a mere servant, but as a person deeply interested in all that concerns them—none can be more gay and lively when pleasure is the order of the day; and should sorrow bring clouds, none evince more disinterested grief than *Jack*—thus ready "to laugh with those who laugh, and weep with those who weep"—though, no doubt, like all of his race, he'd rather "be merry than sad." Who would not? Placed in the same situation with the slaves at the South? Without a care for to-morrow, who but a fool, would sigh and cry to-day? With food and raiment, and comforts of all other kinds necessary, regular hours to work, to eat, to sleep and to play, there is not on the broad earth a happier set of mortals than the Uncle Tom's and Aunt Philis's of the South—the lies and slanders of the fanatics of New and Old England to the contrary notwithstanding! Mawkish sensibility—Infidelity—Socialism—and all other incentives that have actuated the fanatics of the world in its onslaught against the institution of slavery, so far from loosening the chains (as they call it) have only served the purpose of riveting each link still firmer; for however much disposed slave-owners may be to have the chains stricken off, that the descendants of *Ham* may return to that portion of the earth set apart for them after the flood, they know too well the hypocrisy of those pretended friends, by their treatment of those they have enticed or stolen from a Southern clime, the few slaves who have had the temerity of putting faith in their protestations and deserted their homes and protestors. And it is a strong evidence of the humanity of slave-owners, that they everyday become more and more rigorous in the exercise of their rights over the person of the slave. Thus endeavoring, by retaining him in the position God designed him to occupy, to prevent the certain degradation and often total destruction of the human beings intrusted to his keeping by an all-wise Providence, should they once pass Mason and Dixon's line. "Old Jack" would laugh to scorn a proposition from one of these fanatical compounds, yeleped abolitionists. Indeed would he: and with a few exceptions, so would nearly every slave at the *South!* But we are away from our subject.

Our older readers will recollect that during the administration of George M. Troup as Governor of Georgia, there was a misunderstanding between the Executive and the General Government, in relation to the Indian Territory between the Ocmulgee and Flint Rivers. This land was purchased from the Indians by the United States, and made over to the State of Georgia in lieu of her claim to the *lands* embodied in the *Yazoo Fraud*—and the United States were bound to remove the Indians and extinguish all the title they held. Be this as it may, about the time when Governor Troupe was having it surveyed, preparatory to his having it divided by lottery, *Jack* committed some offence, and the punishment awarded was deferred for future execution. When the time arrived, *Jack was non est inventus,* and for three months nothing was heard of him, although advertised extensively. At the end of this time his master, as usual, was pacing to and fro in his backyard one afternoon, when he observed approaching him through the garden, a dirty, ragged, negro. When he came up lo and behold, through his rags and dirt he beheld Jack, and accosted him with,

"Hallo! Jack, is that you?"

"Yes master," replied Jack.

"Where have you have you been, you black rascal, for the last three months or more, sir?"

"Well, master, to sebral places, but de las' place, sir, was down in de low country, sir."

"Down in the low country! Why, what upon earth took you there, sir?"

"Well, master, you know Gov'nr Troop an de Gineral Government hab a quarrel 'bout some land we got from de Indians?"

"Yes—I know all that!"

Well, master, you know de Gov'nr' send his surveyors to lay off de land?"

"Yes—I know that too! But what has all that to do with your running away, you rascal?"

"Well, master, *Gov'nr' Troup giv' me an appintment an' I bin down tendin to de bizness, sir!* Provisions got nearly all out and my clothes give out too—so I cum back to git some more, sir—dat all, master!"

"Clear yourself out of my sight, you incorrigible scamp!"

"Yes, master," replied Jack, as he trotted off to the kitchen, chuckling at the *invention* which had enabled him to escape a trouncing.

This, we believe, was *Jack's* last attempt at running away, as he found better rations at home and concluded very wisely, to take whatever might come in the future; although we believe his ingenuity at evading correction saved him many a sound thrashing. One of his methods was to get to someplace and get on his knees, *praying* so loudly that his master could hear him. In his petitions he would acknowledge his many sins and short comings—promise amendment, not forgetting to ask a blessing upon his master and family. Of course, after this he was forgiven, or his sins were passed over and he escaped scot-free.

Some twenty or more years ago, there emigrated to Georgia from the "Old Keystone State" a young man—a descendant of some one of the numerous Dutch families who settled the States of New York and Pennsylvania. This young man was a *deutcher* and no mistake; and a fine representative of those stolid and solid citizens of our Repubic, who have done so much towards settling up our western wilds. He came to the town of——and was engaged as a barkeeper and general superintendent by Jack's master. He was, as a matter of course, ignorant of the duties devolving upon him—but a willing student. It was *Jack's* province to instruct him in many matters appertaining to his position, and it afforded Jack considerable pleasure to induct and initiate *master Wills* into his office—never losing an opportunity of playing off a joke upon him, and never compromising himself so as to lose the confidence of *Wills* in any of his pranks, he, or others by his instigation and abetment, so often found it convenient to practice upon the confiding *young* Dutchman. A few days after his induction into office, orders were issued to *Wills* and *Yack* (as he called him) to the effect that a young beef should be killed and dressed in the afternoon for supplying the table. This was an unusual and strange manner of doing business, *Wills* thought, and as soon as opportunity offered, he counseled with *Jack* in this wise:

"Mine Got, Yack, how de *tyful* we kills de beef?"

"We shoot 'em, mas Wills, in de head wid a gun—cut de trote, sir, and den take off de hide, sir!"

"Yaw—but den Yack, who shoots mit de gun?"

"Why, you, ob course, mas Wills!"

"Mine Got, Yack, I knows nothing 'bout guns—never shoot wid one in mine life!"

"Neber mine, mas Wills—I load 'em for you, all you hab to do is, point de gun and pull the trigger!" And so saying Jack left *poor Wills* uttering muttered exclamations to himself, such as "mine Got, what a people dis! Got in Heimeul! but I'se never in mine life heard of de ting in Old Pennsylvania!" When Jack left *Wills* he slipped a musket from the room of a member of the —— "Blues," and knowing a gentleman in town, a boarder in the house, as fond of a joke as himself, to him he took the gun and made known his business. The two proceeded to load the musket, and when they finished, the load measured "ten fingers," consisting of *powder, buck and duck shot!* A most terrible load, one would suppose, for the unsophisticated Dutchman to stand behind.

The trio repaired to the lot, the beef was selected, the musket handed to *Wills,* with the proper instructions how to *"take sight,"* and to point the gun when the head of their victim was fairly presented. Jack occupied *Wills'* rear, some few paces off, while H. was on one side, rather behind. When all was ready, *Wills* raised the gun, pointed it and took aim—but not being satisfied that he had a good one, turned his head back and asked,

"Yack, ish de gun straight now?'

"Yes, you got *beed sight* on im, mas Wills," answered Jack, as he glanced along the gun, "pull de trigger!"

At the word *off went the load,* missing the beef at least ten feet! and *back went the musket, knocking poor Wills down,* and passing on to Jack, *sprawled him out upon the ground,* while H— *took to his heels,* fully persuaded, from the report and the result he beheld, that *both had been killed!* The musket was uninjured, but it had *pirouetted* through the air in imitation of a *French danseuse,* as it passed from *Wills* to *Jack.* The latter soon picked himself up, more scared than hurt, and assisted poor *Wills* to the house, taking *good care as he went along to attribute the catastrophe to Wills' awkwardness in holding the gun!* never once alluding to the outrageous load he had placed in it. Whether or not *Wills* ascertained the true facts of the case, we are unapprised, but we do know that he remained for some length of time in his situation, and still continued to look upon Jack as his friend.

There was a time in the history of our State, before Rail Roads were so plenty, that all lawyers, above the "saddle-bags degree," traveled as a general thing around their circuits in a vehicle upon two wheels—very appropriately termed a *sulky.* A certain member of the legal profession, and at the time also an M. C., on leave of absence, possessed of very agreeable manners indeed, and ever ready to smooth over rough places with oily compliments, as well as to try to gain the good will of everybody with the same cheap expenditures, was on his way to attend a Court in a County beyond, and passing through —— stopped at the — Hotel over night, of which establishment the aforesaid *Jack* was chief waiter. In preparing on the next morning after breakfast to leave, sulky and horse at the door, and Jack securing the luggage upon it, a company of gentlemen were gathered to hear the news and ask after the health of our M. C. After a short and pleasant gossip with his friends, he bade them adieu, and on turning to step into his vehicle, he was arrested in his movements by observing *Jack. Now,* the Colonel thought it would never do to pass so notable a "color'd gemman," without bestowing upon him a few compliments, and accordingly he remarked,

"Well, Jack, how are you? I had no idea you were so celebrated a character—known so well over the country! I find you have acquaintances in all the cities where I have been, in New York Washington, etc. *You certainly must be the greatest man in Georgia !"*

Jack, in imitation of the suavity *of* manners of the Colonel, and making an humble bow, with his hat off, replied,

"*Except you, Col. Z—.*"

With one bound into his sulky and a crack of his whip the Colonel left, as the shout of merriment resounded long and loud, while Jack, with a sly wink, as much as to say, "*I got him dat time,*" departed into the house.

As we have before intimated, Jack has come in his lifetime, in contact with men of all classes, and we will now give one of his tilts with a clerical gentleman, which came under our own observation. A preacher observing him one day with a suspicious-looking long-necked black bottle under his arm, and in a store where "blue ruin" was sold too, concluded, as conceived himself duty-bound so to do, to reprove the old fellow for his *habits*, believing that common report would sustain him in his surmises that *Jack* was a toper. He commenced his onslaught by saying,

"Why, Jack! old fellow! is that whisky in your bottle? Ah! Jack, you are getting old, you should set a better example to the young! Come now, you ought to quit such things; it won't do!"

" Well, mas John, de fact is, I been thinking ober de matter, an' weighing ob de subject myself, sir; an' hab come to dis conclusion whisky serves my friends very badly, makes 'em fight an' quarrel, lie an' steal, makes man an' wife quarrel and fight, an' I'm gittin old as you say ; *darfore, sir, I b'lieves it to be duty to distroy as much ob it as I kin while I lib !*"

This was *a settler;* and our parson turned away, while *Jack*, with his peculiar wink and smirk of the face, chuckled over his success in flooring his antagonist.

We well recollect a visit of the "Razor Strop man" as he is familiarly called, to the town of —. Few persons who ever saw and heard him, as he recounted the wonders of his "magical, tragical razor strops," will ever forget the author of the following lines upon "Cold water drinking,"

> "He that drinks water—Adam's own *ale*.
> Will be hearty and health—rugged and hale;
> Will *live*, till his head's as white as a sheep!
> And *die*, like a baby going to sleep!"

Or become oblivious to the deep bass voice with which he awakened attention and curiosity, as he perambulated the streets of a town, announcing *"a few more left of the same sort?"* He stopped at the — Hotel, as a matter of course, whereof "Old Jack" was generalissimo. Nov, it is not to be supposed that Jack had not had information of character of S—, but he kept his own counsel, and S— could not have learned anything of Jack in the short time elapsing before supper was announced. When the *gong* sounded S—, with a large number of others, made his way to the table, and quietly took his seat— not unobserved or unknown, as he may have supposed, for Jack's eyes were upon him, and in the performance of his duty he gave S— assiduous attention. Presented him with "*mocha coffee*" "*goshen butter,*" "*canawl flower biskits,*" "*berkshire ham*" etc.and lastly picked up a plate upon which reposed a lone, and solitary *warfle*—saying as be handed it to S—

"Master, have a square-toe'd warfle, sir? Dont be scared, sir, there's *a "few more left in the kitchen of the same sort!"*

This was enough, and dropping "knife and fork," with a mouthful of coffee, he let out, and for some moments fairly yelled with laughter, kicking and clapping his hands, to the utter astonishment of all at the table, except those in his own vicinity! while old Jack, with the gravity of a Spaniard, was standing behind his chair, looking on with perfect equanimity. Even after order was somewhat restored, S— would occasionally *break out* with a fit of uncontrollable laughter. He acknowledged himself fairly beat, and declared that in all his peregrinations over the land, nothing had occurred to him so appositely ridiculous. This did not end the acquaintance between the two, for during his stay many *"passages at tongues(?)"* was held between them; Jack holding his own, and claiming the victory, while S— would be often compelled to acknowledge himself fairly beaten. On the second evening when S— sat down again at the tea-table, he found a "cambric needle" lying upon his plate.

"Jack," he called out, "what does this mean?"

Well, master, I thought you needed *sharpening up,* and ef you would eat, de needle, perhaps in de morning you hab more *pint* about you, for I notice you gitting bery *dull!*" Another "guffaw" from and an acknowledgment that Jack "*had him* " was the consequence. S— *gulled* a good many "*white folks*" throughout the country with his "wonderful, magical, tragical razor strops," but be couldn't quite make *Jack* swallow the *bait* and lose his *half dollar,* with an almost certainty of ruining his *razor—not* he; and when asked his reasons for declining a purchase, by S— himself, he answered,

"Dat de strop make *everything so sharp, even to the man who sold* 'em! he was 'fraid ob de consequences to himself !" " De fact is;" continued Jack, " dem *strops* makes heap o' people "cut dere eye-teeth" jis by lying' on a table in de rooms dey sleeps in, an' I'm 'fraid dey'd make me *cut* a whole new sett!"

Still triumphant, Jack's antagonist let him alone, tho' he expressed his admiration to others before he *left town.*

Would-be-wits, find, in "running against" Jack, that they have "awoke the wrong passenger," for to such characters he allows no "quarters." We have now in our mind's eye one of these tournaments where one of these characters attempted a display of his metal, but found to his dismay that the old fellow drew all the "temper from his steel." Soon after the completion of the —— Rail Road, at its terminus, an embryo city was just being fledged, which, it was rumored all about, was making wonderful strides towards attaining a growth and importance second to no other in the State. In fact, we ourselves, heard a report down the Road, that efforts were being made to create a seaport (at least three hundred miles from salt-water!) among the black jack ridges of the county of —— at the aforesaid point. "Sich" another place, the unsophisticated natives had never seen, heard or dreamed of. Of course a person occupying Jack's position in a public hotel would have his curiosity excited! This is natural—and the next thing to be done, as he thought, was to know the truth by inquiry and ocular demonstration. As soon then as leave of absence cold be obtained, he took a seat in the "train," and by the time the sun gilded the top of Rock Mountain he had been set down in the city(?) of —. On alighting, he proceeded with the rest of the passengers to the Hotel, and breakfast being soon after announced, while the rest sat down at the table, he took up his old business and "flew around" the table, dispensing the *feed* thereon to the sharpened appetites of his former fellow-travellers. Between this and dinner, ample time was allowed him to "take observations" and visit the "lions " "tigers(?)" and their "dens," which occupied so large a portion of the city(?). This he did, no doubt, to his satisfaction, for although he kept his own counsel as to his private opinion, he publicly expressed his doubts of the possibility of its being anything more than common! Again at dinner he assumed his usual position; and commencing with *"de hen fruit"* he proceeded with *"de stewed chicken," "de bake fowl," "de fried virgin pullet,"* on up, in all the various modes of preparing *"de sheeken"*—(for about that time fears were expressed by those of us who boarded in the house, that we should *eat chicken* until we would be "feathered over" and learn "to crow") it being a standing dish! We were rather late to dinner on that day, and while sitting at the table with several others—in stepped Jack, valise and hat in hand, to bid adieu to our host before departing on the train soon to leave. As the latter observed Jack thus prepared, be accosted him with,

"Hallo, Jack! about to be off, eh? without settling your bill! Come, let's have the money."

"I'm not prepared to settle *now—jis' charge 'im an your books,* sir."

"O, no Jack! you cant get off that easy! How did you ride on the Rail Road without money?"

"Well, I ride, on de rode like oder folks, but I'm a stockholder an' ride free gratis, for nothing, Sir." "Good bye, sir." So saying he went out at one door, as the discomfited publican slipped out at the other, glad enough to escape our laughter. This was neither the first last time that "our host" "caught it" from Jack—but like the most of his *genus,* they are never satisfied; because of an inordinate self-esteem, which as a class, they possess to an astonishing degree.

Coupled with Jack's humor is a good deal of eccentricity in actions and manners. Besides his position as waiter, he has also the important office to fill, of *purveyor* for the larder of the hotel; and in all the region of country, extending for twenty miles or more, even to the surrounding counties, does he extend his researches for "fish, flesh and fowl, butter, eggs," etc.

To see him armed and equipped for his travels, one would suppose him overloaded with useless articles; not so, however, for he has a present use for all. *A tin bugle* is one of the articles he finds very necessary to him, for it saves him time, by informing the farmer's wives, long before he can be seen, that he is not far off; the notes he blows upon it being peculiar to himself, and they knowing very well that no one but Jack made the sounds. He does not forget to provide himself also with an "antifogmatic" in case of sickness of self or horse—for he is often absent on these forays a week or more. In "sunshine and in storm" he holds his way. "Many a time and oft" have we seen him enter, as the rays of a mid-day August sun were pouring down upon the parched earth, holding a *wilted bush* over his head as a protection, while lying by his side was *a closed umbrella!* He possesses an innate antipathy to any exhibition of "high life below stairs," "swell headedness" or "Codfish aristocracy," and suffers no favorable opportunity to pass unimproved, by which be can "take off" the actor or actors. We recollect once of witnessing his encounter with a country *swell,* who, dressed very well—came to town, and endeavored "to show off" himself and "feathers" to the greatest advantage ; but unfortunately *indulged* in *spiritual* refreshment to such an extent that by the afternoon he was at least "three sheets in the wind." Being thus unable to *navigate,* he had *"brought to,"* and "anchored" on a dry goods box in front of a store. Here he remained not very *drunk,* but oh ! *how sick!* Just as Jack was passing along, he was "casting up accounts," and soiling his "fine feathers," Jack stopped, took a good look at him, and than remarked to those standing close by,

"Ha! my fine feathers gittin spilte—'spec I better stay at home arter dis, till I learn how to 'have myself—I know you nebber ketch dis chile comin' to town 'agin dressed up so fine, an' takin' on board so many groceries, I hab to git on a box in de street to "lighten de kargo!" Yes, an' dat not all; ef I did git so, and hab so far to go home, I tink I *start* fore' dar night, for *blacking* mighty plenty in dis town!" and so saying, he departed on his way. Now, whether the last hint about *blacking* or the lightening of ship by throwing overboard part of the cargo, enabled the Captain to "up anchor and away"—we know not, but certain it is, many moments did not elapse, before he sailed off towards home.

Visiting A—, as Jack often does, especially on "big occasions," he has the *"freedom of the city,"* so far as the Hotels are concerned—all making him welcome as long as he pleases to stay. At no one of them, however, does he locate himself permanently; preferring, as he says himself, to *"try 'em all."* Hence he will sup with one, lodge at another, breakfast at a third, and dine at a fourth; and the reason he gives for doing so is, that he wishes to know which is the best from personal experience—that when called on by his particular friends for a recommendation, he may be enabled, by thus being "posted up," to give them correct information! He has too, the *entre* to those "seething caldrons"—hotel kitchens, reeking with all sorts of "fish, flesh and fowl," baked, broiled and stewed, and from whence issue at stated intervals supplies for those "who eat to live and live to eat," daily surrounding the tables of public houses.

Here it is, that "ignorance is bliss!" nor perhaps would it be other than folly, for any of our appetites, that we should *be wise in kitchen matters* any where! We doubt not but that Jack *takes notes of* his observations, made during these friendly visits, and as an apt scholar, learns lessons for future improvement!

Jack sometimes acts as a luggage porter from *hotel* to depot, often carrying a large trunk upon his head or shoulders, and expecting a fee, of course. It happens occasionally that a traveller, either from thoughtlessness or a desire to save his dimes, does not respond unless a gentle hint be given him. It is now that Jack finds his ingenuity called into play, for desiring his fee, he must so frame the application for it, as to produce compliance, and at the same time be free from giving offence. He will step up to the delinquent, remove his hat, make a low obeisance and say,

"Master, I had de honor, sir, oh bringin' your trunk down, sir; I hab put it in de right car for Union Point, sir, an' master, I'd merely remark dat I takes *dimes* for *sevenpences,* dat is at *par,* sir; de merchants and oder folks here dont do so sir, but Jack does!"

This appeal is certain to be heard, and often Jack gets a large fee, given to him with a cheerful smile and perhaps an apology for the seeming neglect.

We are not aware that Jack is a member of any church, but he attends service; and to see him dressed in "sober black," promenading the streets, no one would suppose him past the prime of life, while he is really far beyond in years, if not in feeling and action. Old time has indeed, dealt kindly with his physical man; for his locks are not white, hardly sprinkled o'er with the frosts of years"—while his bodily vigor is remarkable, and his spirits still exhibit a wonderful effervescing power. In truth, old Jack is one of a thousand, a specimen of the African race rarely seen. We have remarked that he attends on occasion a rather ludicrous conclusion was had to a meeting where some excitement was going on, under the harangue of a white preacher. An invitation at the close was given to all who wished, to approach the altar. Jack sat unmoved, though serious;—the preacher having descended from the pulpit, and traversing the isle, approached him. Addressing him in a loud voice, he exclaimed,

"My color'd friend, YOU MUST BE BORN AGAIN!"

Old Jack, thus accosted so vehemently, looked up and replied,

"Master, I'm 'fraid, sir!'

"Afraid!" shouted the preacher, "afraid to be born again! Of what are you afraid?"

"Dis nigger might BE BORN'D A GAL, sir!" answered Jack, while the discomfited preacher made tracks for the pulpit— "Pooh-ing"—as he went, as the suppressed tittering of the colored population was heard from all the surrounding seats. At once all seriousness departed and the meeting came to a close.

In this connexion we may as well relate that in his younger days, Jack would sometimes conceive it to be his duty to attempt to preach to his color'd friends; then he would invariably take as his text, the words, "No blind man shall see de Lord" —announcing it as to be found in the "Third Book of Maccabees, Saint

Paul and Saint Peter." As we were not fortunate enough to live in those days, when we might have heard his elucidation of the subject, we cannot do otherwise, than leave it to the imagination of our readers, merely suggesting that no doubt *"spiritual"* and not *"physical" blindness* was what was meant in his text.

Having thus given a few of the many incidents of old Jack's life, and touched lightly upon his position as a slave, we cannot dismiss the subject, without as a Southern man, giving expression to some of our own views and opinions upon the position of the slave and his owner in the Southern States. While we do this, we shall endeavor to be as concise as possible. Speaking the truth without fear, affection or favor, and regardless of consequences. Our position is, that nine-tenths of the foes to slavery; patriarchal slavery—as it exists in the Southern States, are made so without the least thought or consideration of *their own:* suffering themselves to be wiled into the ranks by the idle tales, falsehoods and false witness of a few leaders! Taking upon *trust* the vilest slanders—they join the crusade, and madly rave at the upholders of our institution—whose workings, social position, and general character are as unknown to them as the "manners and customs" of the savages in the wilds of Africa! Never seeming to think once, that this state of things was first introduced and lastly forced upon us *by their own ancestors;* and never recollecting that the *riches* many of them *possess, first come directly or indirectly through the means of the slave-trade!* Ignorance *of facts is the foundation stone,* and *Infidelity* is the *cap-stone*—while the intermediate portion of this monument of folly and fanaticism is composed of all the *"isms"*—*"known* and *unknown"*—on "earth or beneath the earth"—and even reaching into the "spirit world" (if we may believe *them.*) It is passing strange, that, with the facilities of travel and inter-communications now existing between the free and the slave States of this Confederacy, so very few of the professed abolitionists ever endeavor to inform themselves of the *true* state of the case.

Can we at the South hope for a better feeling, so long as this is the fact? These fanatics forget that *self-interest*—the pocket-nerve—upon which point Yankydom is so tenderly sensitive—*would restrain us,* if they will not yield us the possession of higher and better motives—and not only restrain us, from the perpetuation of cruel acts of inhumanity to our slaves, but would the more urgently commend to us, and urge upon us, the exercise of every effort by which we might enhance the value of our slave property? Or, in other words, while we exacted their time and labor, would we not also be subserving our own interests greatly, to *feed* and *clothe,* and thereby strengthen them for the performance of their duties? as well as preserve them in health by proper attention to their physical wants and necessities? For if we failed thus to act, from whence would flow remuneration for the capital invested in them? Besides these "pocket-nerve" considerations—there is an identity of interest, a family tie created between master and slave, a bond which death does not even always dissolve! This extends from generation to generation—from father to son—from mother to daughter! We have often witnessed the exultation of an aged slave at the good fortune of "young massa," who in his infancy may have slept in her bosom and drawn the nourishment that sustained his infantile existence from the same fountain as did her own child, or again weep over the misfortunes of a young mistress, whose footsteps as she "toddled about" were directed by the same kind and faithful hand! Do these facts make slavery a curse? God forbid. While we may admit isolated cases of inhumanity and ill-treatment of the master to his slave, they are but reprehensible exceptions which no one views with greater detestation and abhorrence than those around such an one, slaveholders themselves! With these facts—for they are stubborn facts—how comes that these slanderous falsehoods obtain credit? With the single one of SELF-INTEREST, urging upon slave-owners the necessity of good treatment and the preservation of such property, we are surprised, we must acknowledge that we of the South cannot escape the vituperation and abuse heaped upon our devoted heads, by *yankydom;* a section of our country so amenable to the charge *of never losing sight of* NUMBER ONE! And when we consider the subject in a moral and religious point of view, then most surely do we find it to be our *duty* to *care for* the negro race in every way; and it is a *duty,* too, that no right thinking slaveholder fails to perform to the best of his ability. With either the motive of *self-interest* or *duty* actuating slaveholders, can any candid man conceive of a reason for the *starvation* and *maltreatment,* as charged upon us collectively, of this species of property, the most valuable of any other we may possess? Surely not. Then are we not justified in saying that *ignorance of facts*—it may be in many cases pre-determined and therefore immovable, is a main ingredient in the abuse and vituperation, we of the South, receive at the hands of our northern fellow-citizens? We think so; and while we may grant them the prejudices of education and all that, WE CLAIM AS A RIGHT, guaranteed by the Constitution, TO BE LET ALONE! We desire no compromises not also guaranteed in that instrument, not immunities not clearly and indisputably our due.

Give us these, and the sunny South, in her characteristic generous spirit, will again affiliate in kindly brotherhood with her Northern fellow-citizens, while each in union and in strength may together perpetuate and preserve intact the glorious liberties we now enjoy.

Marcus Lafayette Byrn (1826-1903)

Medical doctor, real-estate investor, evangelist, book printer, author of medical pamphlets and booklets imparting useful information, publisher of a newspaper, the *United States Gazette,* and a medical journal, the *New York Medical Journal,* and humorist, Marcus L. Byrn was born in Statesville, Tennessee, on September 4, 1826. But Byrn is the only Old Southwest humorist to have resided most of his adult life in the North. Beginning the study of medicine in the office of a doctor near his home, Byrn subsequently received more formal training at the medical department at the University of Louisville in 1848 and 1849, completing his medical training at New York University and receiving his M.D. in March 1851. He then returned to the South, practicing medicine as a frontier doctor in Tennessee and Mississippi for the next two years, an experience that provided the inspiration and subject matter for his books of frontier humor.

Though Byrn practiced medicine in New York City for the remainder of his life, from 1853 to 1903, he seemed to be a man of multiple interests and talents. A prolific and versatile writer, some of his most popular books were medical pamphlets, which he printed and marketed himself. His first published medical work, *Detection of Fraud and Protection of Health. A Treatise on the Adulteration of Food and Drink: With Plain and Simple Directions for Detecting Them* (1852), later advertised under the title *Poisons in Our Food,* examines the debasement of various foods—flour, salt, tea, coffee, beer, whiskey, starch, and others. He also wrote a pamphlet, *The Effect of Tobacco on the Human System Mentally, Morally, and Physically,* leveling an indictment on the potential hazardous consequences of using tobacco, citing cancer, tuberculosis, dyspepsia, and an inclination to drunkenness and suicide as some of the likely outcomes. As one who sought to incite popular taste, Byrn also wrote a pamphlet on love and sex and an essay, "Solitary Vice. Of the Secret Habits of Youth, Known as Masturbation, Onanism, or Self–Pollution," Byrn's most frequently reprinted medical writing and one that describes the consequences of this "solitary vice" on males as well as females.

Besides popular medical pamphlets, Dr. Byrn wrote utilitarian and evangelical books, such as *The Complete Practical Brewer* (1852), *The Handbook of Science*

(1867), *Twenty Ways to Make Money* (1869), and *The Singing Evangelist* (1883), the latter consisting of thirty-three religious hymns, relating to Byrn's own personal evangelical experiences.

Yet Byrn's humorous books represent his most important contribution as a writer, particularly important are those recounting the misadventures of David Rattlehead, a physician who narrates his mishaps and scrapes in the first person and who seems a thinly disguised portrait of the author. *The Life and Adventures of an Arkansaw Doctor* (1851), Byrn's first and most entertaining book, seems strikingly similar to Henry Clay Lewis's *Odd Leaves of a Louisiana Swamp Doctor* (1850), a collection of first-person humorous sketches on antebellum frontier medical practices as told by Dr. Madison Tensas, Dr. Lewis's alter ego. Presented in a picaresque form, Rattlehead's adventures provide a mirthful window to the life, society, and folkways of the Arkansas frontier. Byrn uses the conventions of the southwestern humor genre in presenting David's sometime tall-talish escapades. A young man, David has a natural proclivity for springing pranks on persons with whom he comes into contact. One of his more memorable pranks—involving releasing hornets at a wedding under the door of a church—is an adaptation of a familiar script from frontier humor employing stinging insects to create humor and painful chaos for others. In another episode, David is captured by Indians but successfully effects his escape by putting morphia, laudanum, and paregoric in their whiskey. Two more Rattlehead books would soon follow: *Rattlehead's Travels: or, The Recollections of a Backwoodsman* (1852), which continues David's adventures as he leaves Arkansas, travels to New York to further his medical studies, and then returns to the South to mock and dupe quack doctors; and *Rattlehead's Chronicles* (1852), which focuses on David's further adventures after leaving the South.

While Byrn's humorous work does not exhibit the level of artistry of that of fellow physician-writers Henry Clay Lewis and Orlando Benedict Mayer, *The Life and Adventures of an Arkansaw Doctor* is one of only a few books in Old Southwest humor featuring a single character around which a writer weaves a sustained narrative that has the vitality to engage the interest of contemporary readers. In assessing his achievement, Michael J. Pettengell astutely observes that Marcus Lafayette Byrn was an "overly health-conscious evangelist, idealist, and con-man . . . , [who] raised on self-made philosophy . . . [,]used human ingenuity and Yankee know-how in attempting to reform the world, with an eye always on the profit motive."

Texts: "Spontaneous Ebullition in a Drunkard," and "The Resurrection, or How to Take Up a Negro," in *The Life and Adventures of an Arkansaw Doctor,* ed. W. K. McNeil (Fayetteville: University of Arkansas Press, 1989).

Spontaneous Ebullition in a Drunkard

Air—Open the gate and let him out.
The drunkard with his thirst unquenched
Came knocking at my door—
"I come to be, and will be drenched
As I have been before."
I told him no; 'twas all in vain,
But soon I did knock under;
Poor man, you will not come again
To see a student's wonder.
FRUNTAS.

After making such an extraordinary start in medicine I felt rather careful, and thought I would use more precaution in the future. The next morning being appointed by my preceptor for me to make a formal commencement of studying the healing art, I went according to promise quite early to the office. He was waiting for me, lest I might commit some deed equally as desirable as I had done the day previous. He commenced by telling me the different medicines that were poisonous, and those that I must not touch until I became acquainted with them. He then told me what book to commence reading, and advised me to be a close student and learn as fast as I could. I listened with eager attention to all he said, like it had been law or gospel; told him I would do the best I could, laid off my beaver and went at it.

I had been diving into the hidden mysteries of the science I suppose for an hour or more, when I was interrupted by a sound at the door. I looked up and saw a noted old drunkard, whom I had known for a long time. I knew he was the greatest old pest in the country, and concluded that I was in for a long do-nothing spell, unless I cut his head or his acquaintance at once. He walked in with as much authority as a negro at a corn-shucking and said to me,

"Uh, ah! yes, you look like making a doctor, don't you; I knew you before you was born, and you were no 'count then, nor never will be. Where is the old Doc?"

Says I, "What do you want with him?"

"I want some soda; when I comes in here he gives me some good bilin' stuff."

I told him I knew nothing about his boiling stuff or soda either, and told him to go off and not trouble me, I wanted to read. This only made him worse. I found I had as well try and get rid of him as soon as possible, on any reasonable terms, and got up to see if I could find the soda he was speaking of. I had heard of soda water and seen it used, but knew nothing about preparing it.

I was deeply interested in the book I was reading, and wanted to get him off to resume my studies. I commenced looking, and was not long in finding the soda, and near it was the tartaric acid. I put the two jars on the counter, procured two glass tumblers, and soon all things were ready for taking a cooling beverage. Here I was somewhat at a loss to know how to mix them. I did not know which was to be taken first, the soda or the acid; neither did I know how much water or how much soda and acid. I was not to be foiled in my attempts in this way, and thought guesswork was as good as any other when it hit right. I poured each glass about two-thirds full of water. I then put into one glass one table-spoonful of soda, and the same quantity of the acid into the other. I gave him the soda, and told him to drink it. I then gave him the acid.

I had read of explosions by gunpowder, and bursting up of steamboats, railroad accidents, and hailstorms; but that laid everything in the shade, and Bill Measles besides. The old fellow made for the door, put one hand on each side, threw his mouth open, stretched out his neck about a foot, shut his eyes, and then, if ever you saw water boil, it boiled out of him in a stream as big as your arm. For near five minutes his mouth was a living fountain. I thought the man would certainly burst open. His stomach roared like distant thunder; his eyes, starting from their sockets, looked like the full moon rising in midsummer, and his nostrils, distended to the size of a dog's mouth, looked like one side of creation. In his pouting he threw off more bread than would kill an Irishman, more beef than would fatten a dead negro, more oysters than would choke a turkey-gobbler, more mackerel than would make a nice supper at a boarding-house, and more gas than would make lies enough for a political demagogue in two speeches. He continued his upturning of gastric forbearance for about five minutes without being able to open the door of his respiratory prolongation. I saw him begin to turn as black as a sheet; his frame trembled, his hands lost their hold, and down he came like a log of wood in winter at the door of the office.

> Fire and water,
> Mud and mortar,
> Beef and hogs! what a slaughter.
> Old man, may I have your daughter?

What a scrape I am in again; the most unfortunate man in the world; never went to do anything in my life but I was making some mistake; but I'm in for it again, and must get out the best way I can. Here came the whole village again, bellowing like so many calves in a farmyard. In less than fifteen minutes I had a crowd at the office large enough to storm a fort, and fools sufficient to kill any man with as much sense as would go round your hat. One smart old gentleman wanted to know what I had done to the man. I told him of the old drunkard wanting soda, and that I had given him some to get him to go off.

"*Pisen'd pisen'd!*" was the cry raised instanter, and off some one went to find my preceptor, or some other physician, that could tell what to do. In the excitement some person mistook *pisen'd* for *fire,* and then the tune was changed to *fire! fire!* Everybody broke like doctors from a graveyard, as they knew I always kept a little "powder" about, that was hard to put out when once it took fire. Out they ran, and in a little less time than a merchant can tell the truth, we had a deluge of water pouring into the office. Such a rattling of buckets, washbowls, slop tubs, and salt barrels, has not been heard since Job killed the "fat turkey."

I have often heard persons blamed for raising a false alarm of fire, but this was one time it did good. The poor old drunkard lying there in a state of suspended animation from his long spouting spell, was aroused by the cold water. He bawled out, and wanted to know if the "second floor" was coming: being informed by many voices "no," he raised himself up about six feet high, sprung out of the door like a blue streak of lightning or "Moffat's pills" was after him, and ran home to his wife, promised her never again to trouble a medical student, signed the pledge, and has never been known to touch a drop of the "critter" since.

The Resurrection, or How to Take Up a Negro

Tune—You dig and I'll watch.

If doctors go to seek a prize
Among their patients dead,
They must be bold, they must be wise
To save them from an aching head;
And if when they have once began
To dig and raise the sod
They must not stop though dog and man
Should come all in a squad.
GOURDHEAD.

After the trouble with the drunkard, things went as well as I could expect for several days, considering that I was never known to be out of some sort of scrape for more than a few days at a time. As I was the first student the old doctor had been troubled with for some time, he was out of a skeleton. This desideratum had to be met as soon as circumstances would *assist.* We were not long left in want of an opportunity to obtain one. My preceptor had a patient, a negro, that had been sick for some time with a chronic disease, and who was destined to fall a prey to its influence very soon. The patient died, and amid the heartfelt sorrow of the owner for his loss, and the numerous explanations of the old doctor why the disease had terminated fatally in spite of all remedial agents, he was interred in the silent grave with as little ceremony as is usual on such occasions. My preceptor returned home after staying with the patient until his *last expiring moment,* and told me that as I had just commenced the study of medicine, and would have many trying scenes to pass through before I made a doctor of myself—he wanted to see whether I would do to "tie to" or not, and said, that on the next night I must be ready to go with him to take up the negro that had died the night previous. I told him I was in, and he might depend on me as being as good as ever fluttered, and said to him, "If I grunt, make an ugly face, or turn up my smeller for the first time you may kick me out of the office to-morrow morning, and drive me twenty feet in an ash pile, never said again to rise until old 'Pidey's' horn goes off."

He remarked very calmly that as for him he was an old hand at the business, and never thought of being armed about trifles, any more than a Yankee does of selling goods under first cost, or a tin peddler of passing a farm without his share of the gatherings of the longneck squallers.

There was one part of the "undertaking" that rather puzzled us: the old doctor and I were both small, and not able to do much more hard work than a dozen Irishmen, and therefore would need some assistance. He would have to employ a man, and the difficulty was of getting a man that would not become alarmed when we most needed his assistance.

My preceptor, like every doctor, had many debts owing him by the poorer class, that he knew could never pay him and thought that would be the best chance to get a man to assist. He put off in the "hollows" to see a man that was owing him a bill of some size, and finding him in the woods mauling rails, all in a crowd by himself, he told him if he would go and help us, he would credit his account for five dollars. The fellow was glad of a chance to pay up, and agreed to be with us on occasion. The hour and the place were named for us to meet.

My preceptor told me of the arrangement, and said we must not go off together, or something might grow out of it of a serious nature; and told me at the same time of the dreadful responsibility, and that should we be caught and the law enforced, we would both go to "Jack's house" for the term of three years.

This news played thunder with my bravery. I felt like I was fifty feet in the air and nothing to hold to; thought how the doctor and myself would employ our time in the State prison; would they let him follow his profession and practice among the convicts, and would I roll pills for him as usual? How sorry my old mother would feel—and worse than all, I could not get to see my angel sweetheart any more, for she would never have me after I had been in prison. Oh! horrid thought—why did I ever commence such a profession? why was it I had not thought of these things before commencing? what was I to do? do like they do over the river? do without saying any more, or thinking of it in any way? I eventually reconciled myself to go through it at all hazards. The night appointed arrived; eleven o'clock and everything was still as death in that little village. I waited the moment; I turned the key of the office and started. Going round a little string of fence at a certain post, I might have been seen, if it was daylight, but it wasn't, moping my way in the dark, hunting for a spade and an old bag. The bag was intended to put the negro in. I found them, went and saddled my horse, mounted, and soon was on my mission of grave-robbing for the first time. I went on until I arrived at the place appointed for us to meet. I then whistled, and was answered by my preceptor and his assistant. It was in a dark skirt of woods, where we could not distinguish a man from a hornet's nest only by the "feel." We met, and then for the grave-yard; it was near the woods. In a short time we reached it; and it was then a time to talk about gravery over a dead negro. We all went walking as easy as a cat on straw, round and round the grave. I kept waiting to hear what the old doctor was going to say. I waited for some time in the greatest agony, and not a word was spoken. His bravery he had showed more before reaching the field of glory, and he had forgotten to bring it in his saddle-bags, and there he was without any. Getting tired of waiting, and finding I was more composed than he was, I said to him, "Doctor."

"Don't call my name, you fool you."

"Well, doctor," said I, "if you have come here to get up the negro, let us be at it right off."

"Well," said the doctor, "you and Dick work awhile and I will watch."

I told him to go a piece from us and listen for the approach of danger; that he must be very alarmed about taking up an old negro, and him dead as a forty year old trout.

I tried to appear very bold to the old doctor, but I can tell you I felt a little of the awfulest I ever had, up to that time, and had it not been I thought my preceptor was trying to scare me, I would have felt worse than a sheep in the forest at midnight. He went off a piece from us, and Dick and I commenced operations in earnest; he digging, and me giving directions and feeding him occasionally on old whiskey to keep up his strength and spirits. We were working away at a great rate when we were interrupted by the sudden approach of my preceptor, puffing and blowing worse than a steamboat in a fog on the Mississippi. He came up, and said that they were after us. Dick dropped the spade as quick as though it was hot; I dropped the bottle of whisky as slick as if it were an oyster or the white of an egg, and off we all went, faster than a rabbit with forty dogs after him in an old field. We went until we reached the thick woods, and there stopped to await the result. Very soon we found it was a false alarm.

I rebuked the old doctor sharply for his chicken-heartedness, notwithstanding I felt myself as though I was not larger than a pound of soap after a hard day's washing. I told him he need not watch for us any more, as he would do more harm than good. My *apparent* boldness gave him a little self confidence, and he concluded he would stay with Dick and me the rest of the time. We commenced again, and were getting on as well as a sinner at a camp-meeting, not fearing anything or anybody. The night was fast wasting away, and we had much to do before the approach of bright morning. As our "deeds were evil," we sought darkness rather than light, and must finish before daylight. We worked rapidly and gave little attention to surrounding objects. We had nearly secured our prize, and the doctor was getting brave again. Dick was doing his cleanest, best, and—bim—

"Halloo! what is the matter, Dick?"

"I have got to the coffin," says he.

Here we were in a nice fix; we had come off from home without anything with which we could open the coffin. The doctor became very much enraged at his own negligence, talked really *loud* and plain, and said he would not be disappointed in any such way. There was a rail fence about one hundred yards from where we were. He went to that and got a big rail and brought it to the grave.

"Let me get there a moment, Dick."

He took the rail, turned one end down, and in a short time he had the top of the coffin knocked in, sure enough. Then came the trial, who would go down and lay hands on the *subject*. The doctor said he thought he had done his part, and proposed to Dick to go down. Dick did not say much, but, grunted worse than a man with the toothache going for a load of wood, turned up his nose a little like he smelt something, and thought he had worked harder than either of us. I began to get tired of hearing so much talk about a small matter, threw off my coat and went down. I was in the act of fastening a rope round the negro's neck, by which he could be pulled out, and was congratulating myself that I should have the praise next day for my daring and fearless conduct. I fancied the skeleton hanging up in my own office; I thought of the pleasant times the doctor and I would have in the big cave we were going to take him to; I considered the danger all over, thinking everybody was asleep at that late hour; and now for a—hush! hush! what has happened? I heard a noise in the upper world like the heaving up of a volcano. I heard the dogs barking, chickens flying from their roosts, geese running and flapping their wings equal to knocking the two ends of creation together; the cows lowing, and the sound was like the last sad sound of the hunter's horn; bushes cracking, sheep bleating, and, to cap the climax, an old owl as big as a whisky barrel, hollowing loud enough to raise tadpoles out of water. I had not time to think what was the matter before I heard my preceptor cry out, "Good God!" and away he went as fast as legs would carry him. Dick bawled louder than a two year old calf turned loose in a hailstorm, and that was the last of him too, for he was so scared that he would not have known an ox-cart from an elephant. Well, if ever I was in a real "quandary" I was then: there I was, left in the grave with none to keep me company but the dead negro, and not so much as a stick to assist me out of the grave, which was very deep. I thought I was doing my last job on earth, or rather *in* the earth, and that not a very desirable one, considering the consequences.

I was not long in thinking what to do. I knew if any persons were after us, that unless I got out of that place my time was up. I squatted down like a dog going to jump a fence, made one powerful exertion, and out I came slick as butter out of a hot skillet. I took to my heels as hard as I could go, not looking to see what the noise and confusion was all about. Dick and the doctor were not far ahead of me, and I soon got up with them. We all run for life, not stopping even to see what sort of rails were on the fence, but, jumping over, or trying to, we knocked down two hundred panels of it, making as much noise as an earthquake. The noise of the fence falling alarmed our horses, which were tied out in the woods nearby, and they commenced pulling harder than a woman that wears the breeches hold of her dear husband's nose. Their pulling, like the candy-maker's, was not in vain, and soon they broke loose, and away they went like buffaloes from a prairie on fire.

Of all the fixes that *Tom Knowling* and *Bill Chumny* ever got into since *Blithersdorf* had the neuralgia, we were in it then. Our horses were gone; the grave open, a hole knocked in the top of the coffin; my coat, Dick's hat, and the doctor's old saddle-bags, being close around I thought—and I thought I had not time to think any thing about it—and about the time I got to thinking, I thought the dogs were after us, and they were. We had got off some few hundred yards from the grave-yard when I heard the loudest, the longest, the keenest yelling of greyhounds, little fierce bob-tail curs, and bull-pups, that ever screamed this side of the Rocky Mountains. On they came, making more noise than a thousand old women at a quilting, after us. I felt most awful, but could not help laughing at Dick and the doctor. They kept trying to swallow each other to get out of the way of our pursuers, and had it not been that they commenced at the wrong end, they would have accomplished it. While they were at this, the dogs kept coming with all the speed of their feet, heads and tails.

I saw something had to be done about as quick and as slick as swallowing an oyster, and told them to hold their horns a moment and I would tell them how to do. I went a few steps and found a bending tree that I thought we could climb. I heard a loud shrill halloo in the distance, and the dogs commenced worse than ever. I just expected they would have us all for breakfast next morning. (Thought if they did, they would have as tough a pulling at Dick's carcass as medical students on bull-beef at a boarding house at three dollars a week.) I spoke to my two companions and told them of the bending tree; they were as glad to hear it as a negro is at the sound of the dinner horn in cotton picking time, and came to me as soon as I named it. We all hurried up the tree, and had barely time enough to get comfortably located before the dogs came up and said good night to us, stopped, and seated themselves at the root of the tree. We looked down on them with contempt, until we thought probably their backers were not far off. I thought of a great many things in a short time; among other things, thought what a fool I was that I did not get sick before leaving home and stay there. This thinking then, did about as much good as rubbing your nose with a cow's horn.

Very soon we discovered the source from which this human bellowing proceeded, as we could distinctly hear persons talking and encouraging the dogs. I had often heard of persons being tree'd, but this was the first time I ever saw people in good earnest "tree'd." Well, how could the persons at the house tell we were all at the grave-yard taking up the negro? Somebody betrayed us; can't help it now: we'll be shot out of here when daylight comes.

The owners of the dogs came up (the owners of the dead negro they were), and looked all round to see what tree the dogs were at. The dogs commenced barking at the root of the tree we were in. There was another tree standing two or three feet from the one we were in. After looking a few moments, I heard one of the men say,

"Boys, we'll cut it down."

My old straw hat and Jack Cooper! how I felt when I heard that. I could not have felt worse on a bar of iron in the Atlantic Ocean. I now saw and soon would feel what it was to learn to be a doctor. They commenced cutting, the tree was small and it must soon fall, and then we will—will—all get knocked into eternity. What now was to be done? If we hallooed it would only make it worse; they would kill us anyhow: we must all die when the tree falls. I heard Dick making his last compliments to his Maker. He said:—

"My old providence in heaven and earth, I am come to it now; have mercy on me, for you know I stole Gills' meat, and he starved. I won't do so no more if I die. Take care of Polly and the children, and don't let them work old Paddy in the slide agin. And oh! how sorry I am I didn't stay at home, and—and—farewell—oh! here I go—oh!"

And down came the tree, but it was the one standing near to us. As the tree struck the ground they set up an unmerciful yelling, dogs, men, and all together—and what do you think it was about? It was an old fool coon that happened to be in the tree resting himself. The dogs bounced on him like a duck on a Junebug, and used him up in a short while. The men boasted of their dogs for a short time, how they went out at night without anybody with them, and tree'd a big old coon worth two bits in old whisky the next "muster" they had in town, and put off home. How good we all felt. After they got out of hearing, Dick let off his breath like he hadn't breathed for two hours, and said he felt very thankful to me for naming to them of the tree. We all slid off that tree like terrapins of a hot day, and it was only two hours today. I told them, when we commenced anything we must go through with it. We went back to our work, and without much more trouble we got up the negro and carried him to a cave, a short distance off in the side of a hill, covered him up safe, and started home to see what had become of our horses. We found them safe at home, and by the time we got all things to rights it was day. My preceptor never boasted any more about his spunk. Dick said he wouldn't be a doctor for the world, and I said but little, knowing I had rather slashed the old doctor on the first heat.

Hold on—hand me a fly with a little wanillifidity on it; hush your gab and take that worm out of your mouth! Here we will go to dinner.

Southern Frontier Humor
A Selected Bibliography

The following bibliography lists only the most essential secondary materials about the genre of southern frontier humor. Organized into two sections, this bibliography includes general studies: books, selected unpublished dissertations and Web sites and general studies: articles. For a more comprehensive bibliography of and ongoing scholarship on frontier humor and on individual authors, both those featured in this anthology as well other antebellum southern humorists, readers should consult *The Humor of the Old South*, edited by M. Thomas Inge and Edward Piacentino, University Press of Kentucky, 2001; the SSSL Bibliography: A Checklist of Scholarship On Southern Literature, http://www.missq.msstate.edu/sss, "The Year's Work in Humor Studies" in *Studies in American Humor*; *American Literary Scholarship: An Annual*; and the online *MLA International Bibliography of Books and Articles on Modern Languages and Literatures*.

General Studies:
Books, and Sections or Chapters from Books, Web Sites

Arac, Jonathan. "Southwestern Humor." In *The Cambridge History of American Literature*, Vol. 2, edited by Sacvan Bercovitch, 630–41, New York: Cambridge University Press, 1995.

Austin, James C. *American Humor in France: Two Centuries of French Criticism of the Comic Spirit in American Literature*. Ames: Iowa State University Press, 1978.

Beidler, Philip D., ed. *The Art of Fiction in the Heart of Dixie*. Tuscaloosa: University of Alabama Press, 1986.

Bier, Jesse. *The Rise and Fall of American Humor*. New York: Holt, Rinehart, and Winston, 1968.

Blair, Walter. "A German Connection: Raspe's Baron Munchausen" *Critical Essays on American Humor*, edited by William B. Clark and W. Craig Turner, 123–39. Boston: G. K Hall, 1984.

———. *Native American Humor*. New York: American Book Co., 1937.

———, and Hamlin Hill. *America's Humor: From Poor Richard to Doonesbury*, 23–30 and *passim*. New York: Oxford University Press, 1978.

Bridgmann, Richard. *The Colloquial Style in America*. New York: Oxford University Press, 1966.

Brown, Carolyn S. *The Tall Tale in American Folklore and Literature*. Knoxville: University of Tennessee Press, 1987.

Carr, Duane. *A Question of Class: The Redneck Stereotype in Southern Fiction*. Bowling Green, OH: Popular Press, 1996.

Cohen, Hennig and William B. Dillingham. Introduction. *Humor of the Old Southwest*, edited by Cohen and Dillingham. Athens: University of Georgia Press, 1994.

Cohen, Sandy. "South and Southwest." *American Humorists, 1800–1950*, edited by Stanley Trachtenberg. Vol. 11 of *Dictionary of Literary Biography*. Detroit: Gale, 1982.

Covici, Pascal, Jr. *Mark Twain's Humor: The Image of a World*, 3–91. Dallas: SMU Press, 1962.

Cox, James. M. "Humor of the Old Southwest." *The Comic Imagination in American Literature*, edited by Louis D. Rubin, Jr., 101–12. New Brunswick: Rutgers University Press, 1973.

Cox, Rosemary D. "The Old Southwest: Humor, Tall Tales, and the Grotesque." *A Companion to American Regional Literature*, edited by Charles L. Crow, 247–65. Oxford, UK: Blackwell, 2003.

Current-Garcia, Eugene. *The American Short Story Before 1850: A Critical History*, 99–118. Boston: Twayne, 1985.

Flanagan, John T. "Western Sportsmen Travelers in the New York *Spirit of the Times*." *Travelers on the Western Frontier*, edited by John Francis McDermott, 168–86. Urbana: University of Illinois Press, 1970.

Flautz, John T. "The Dialect Sermon in American Literature." *Popular Literature in America: A Symposium in Honor of Lyon N. Richardson*, edited by James C. Austin and Donald A. Koch, 129–45. Bowling Green, OH: Bowling Green University Popular Press, 1972.

Grammer, John M. "Southwestern Humor." *A Companion to the Literature and Culture of the American South*, edited by Richard Gray and Owen Robinson, 370–87. Oxford, UK: Blackwell Publishing, 2004.

Gretlund, Jan Nordby. "1835: The *Annus Mirabilis* of Southern Fiction." *Rewriting the South: History and Fiction*, edited by Lothar Honnighausen and Valeria Gennaro Lerda, 121–30. Tubingen: Francke Verlag, 1993.

Griffith, Nancy Snell. *Humor of the Old Southwest: An Annotated Bibliography of Primary and Secondary Sources.* New York: Greenwood, 1989.

Hauck, Richard Boyd. *A Cheerful Nihilism: Confidence and "the Absurd" in American Humorous Fiction.* Bloomington: Indiana University Press, 1971.

Hill, Hamlin. *Essays on American Humor: Blair Through the Ages.* Madison: University of Wisconsin Press, 1993.

Hubbell, Jay B. *The South in American Literature, 1607–1900,* 658–86. Durham: Duke University Press, 1954.

Inge, M. Thomas, ed. *The Frontier Humorists: Critical Views.* Hamden, CT: Archon Books, 1975.

———, and Edward J. Piacentino, eds. *The Humor of the Old South.* Lexington: University Press of Kentucky, 2001.

Joost, Nicholas. "Reveille in the West: Western Travelers in the St. Louis *Weekly Reveille.*" *Travelers on the Western Frontier,* edited by John Francis McDermott, 203–40 Urbana: University of Illinois Press, 1970.

Justus, James H. *Fetching the Old Southwest: Humorous Writing from Longstreet to Twain.* Columbia: University of Missouri Press, 2004

———. "The Lower South: Space and Place in Antebellum Writing." *Southern Landscapes,* edited by Tony Badger, Walter Edgar, and Jan Nordby Gretlund, 3–13. Tubingen: Stauffenburg-Verlag, 1996.

Kuhlmann, Susan. *Knave, Fool and Genius: The Confidence Man as He Appears in Nineteenth-Century American Fiction* Chapel Hill: University of North Carolina Press, 1973.

Lenz, William E. *Fast Talk and Flush Times: The Confidence Man as a Literary Convention* Columbia: University of Missouri Press, 1985.

Lofaro, Michael. "Riproarious Shemales: Legendary Women in the Tall Tale World of the Davy Crockett Almanacs." *Crockett at Two Hundred: New Perspectives on the Man and the Myth,* edited by Michael A. Lofaro and Joe Cummings, 114–52. Knoxville: University of Tennessee Press, 1989.

Lynn, Kenneth S. *Mark Twain and Southwestern Humor.* Boston: Little, Brown, 1959.

McKee, Kathryn. "Writing in a Different Direction: Women Authors and the Tradition of Southwestern Humor, 1875–1910." PhD diss. University of North Carolina at Chapel Hill, 1996.

Martin, Gretchen. *The Frontier Roots of American Realism.* New York: Peter Lang, 2007.

Masterson, James R. *Tall Tales of Arkansas.* Boston: Chapman and Grimes, 1943.

Mayfield, John. *Counterfeit Gentlemen: Manhood and Humor in the Old South.* Gainesville: University Press of Florida, 2009.

Meine, Franklin J. *Tall Tales of the Southwest: An Anthology of Southern and Southwestern Humor, 1830–1860* New York: Alfred A. Knopf, 1930.

Messenger, Christian K. *Sport and the Spirit of Play in American Fiction: Hawthorne to Faulkner.* New York: Columbia University Press, 1981. *The Mississippi Writers Page.* http://www.olemiss.edu/depts/english/ms-writers/ (accessed May 14, 2007).

Moliano, John. *Southwestern Humor: Criticism and Defense of an American Character* http://xroads.virginia.edu/~HYPER/DETOC/sw/front.html (accessed January 31, 2009).

Morgan, Winifred. "The African American Trickster and the Humor of the Old Southwest." In *The Enduring Legacy of Old Southwest Humor,* edited by Ed Piacentino, 210–26. Baton Rouge: Louisiana State University Press, 2006.

Morris, Christopher. "What's So Funny? Southern Humorists and the Market Revolution." *Southern Writers and Their Worlds.* College Station: Texas A & M University Press, 1996. Baton Rouge: Louisiana State University Press, 1998.

Piacentino, Ed., ed. *The Enduring Legacy of Old Southwest Humor.* Baton Rouge: Louisiana State University Press, 2006

———. "Humor." *The New Encyclopedia of Southern Culture* Vol. 9. edited by M. Thomas Inge, 85–92. Chapel Hill: University of North Carolina Press, 2008.

———. "Intersecting Paths: The Humor of the Old Southwest as Intertext." *The Enduring Legacy of Old Southwest Humor,* edited by Ed Piacentino, 1–35. Baton Rouge: Louisiana State University Press, 2006.

Railton, Stephen. "The Democratic Nonesuch: Southwestern Humor." *Authorship and Audience: Literary Performance in the American Renaissance,* 90–106. Princeton: Princeton University Press, 1991.

Rickels, Milton. "The Grotesque Body of Southwestern Humor." *Critical Essays on American Humor,* edited by William Bedford Clark and W. Craig Turner, 155–66. Boston: G. K. Hall, 1984.

Romine, Scott. "Southwestern Humor." *The Companion to Southern Literature: Themes, Genres, Places, People, Movements, and Motifs,* edited by Joseph M. Flora and Lucinda H. MacKethan, 844–50. Baton Rouge: Louisiana State University Press, 2002.

Rose, Alan Henry. "Blackness in the Fantastic World of Southwestern Humor." *Demonic Vision: Racial Fantasy in Southern Fiction* 19–38. Hamden, CT: Archon Books, 1977.

Rourke, Constance. "The Gamecock in the Wilderness." *American Humor: A Study of the National Character* 33–76. New York: Harcourt Brace, 1931.

Rubin, Louis D. Jr., "The Great American Joke." *The Comic Imagination in American Literature,* edited by Louis D. Rubin, Jr., 3–15. New Brunswick, NJ: Rutgers University Press, 1973.

Schmitz. Neil. "Forms of Regional Humor." *Columbia Literary History of the United States*, edited by Emory Elliott, 306–23. New York: Columbia University Press, 1988.

Silver, Andrew. *Minstrelsy and Murder: The Crisis of Southern Humor, 1835–1925.* Baton Rouge: Louisiana State University Press, 2006.

Skaggs, Merrill Maguire. *The Folk in Southern Fiction,* Athens: University of Georgia Press, 1972.

Smith, Henry Nash. "Origins of a Native American Literary Tradition." *The American Writer and the European Tradition,* edited by Margaret Denny 63–77. Minneapolis: University of Minnesota Press, 1950.

Smith, Thomas Ruys. *River of Dreams: Imagining the Mississippi before Mark Twain* Baton Rouge: Louisiana State University Press, 2007.

Spirit of the Southern Frontier An Archive of Antebellum Humor, Journalism, andFolkways. http://writing2.richmond.edu/spirit/about.html (accessed March 15, 2008).

Watson, Ritchie Devon, Jr. "Southwest Humor, Plantation Fiction, and the Generic *Cordon Sanitaire.*" *Yeoman Versus Cavalier: The Old Southwest's Fictional Road to Rebellion* 56–69. Baton Rouge: Louisiana State University Press, 1993.

Wimsatt, Mary Ann, and Robert L. Phillips. "Antebellum Humor." *The History of Southern Literature,* edited by Louis D. Rubin et al., 136–56. Baton Rouge: Louisiana State University Press, 1985.

Yates, Norris W. *William T. Porter and the "Spirit of the Times": A Study of the Big Bear School of Humor.* Baton Rouge: Louisiana State University Press, 1957.

General Studies: Articles

Allen, Michael. "'Sired by a Hurricane': Mike Fink. Western Boatman and the Myth of the Alligator Horse." *Arizona and the West* 2 (1985): 237–52.

Arpad, Joseph J. "The Fight Story: Quotation and Originality in Native American Humor." *Journal of the Folklore Institute* (1973): 141–72.

Beidler, Philip D. "'The First Production of the Kind, in the South': A Backwoods Literary Incognito and His Attempt at the Great American Novel." *Southern Literary Journal* 24 (1992): 106–24.

Betts, John R. "Sporting Journalism in Nineteenth Century America." *American Quarterly* 5 (1953): 39–56.

Blair, Walter. "Americanized Comic Braggarts." *Critical Inquiry* 4 (1977): 331 49.

Boatright, Mody C. "The Art of Tall Lying." *Southwest Review* 34 (1949): 357–63.

Budd, Louis J. "Gentlemen Humorists of the Old South." *Southern Folklore Quarterly* 17 (1955): 232–40.

Cardwell, Guy A. "The Duel in the Old South: Crux of a Concept." *South Atlantic Quarterly* 66 (1967): 50–69.
Caron, James E. "The Violence and Language of Swapping Lies: Towards a Definition of the American Tall Tale." *Studies in American Humor* 5 n.s. (1986): 27–57.
Clark, Thomas D. "The American Backwoodsman in Popular Portraiture." *Indiana Magazine of History* 42 (1946): 1–28.
Cox, James E. "Humor and America: The Southwestern Bear Hunt, Mrs. Stowe, and Mark Twain." *Sewanee Review* 85 (1975): 573–601.
Current-Garcia, Eugene. "Alabama Writers in the *Spirit*." *Alabama Review* 10 (1957): 243–69.
———. "Mr. Spirit and *The Big Bear of Arkansas:* A Note on the Genesis of Southwestern Sporting and Humor Literature." *American Literature* 27 (1955): 332–46.
———. "Newspaper Humor in the Old South, 1835–1855." *Alabama Review* 2 (1949): 102—21.
Curry, Jane. "The Ring-Tailed Roarers Rarely Sang Soprano." *Frontiers* 2 (1977): 129–40.
Dondore, Dorothy A. "Big Talk! The Flyting, the Gabe, and the Frontier Boast." *American Speech* 6 (1930): 45–55.
Fellman, Michael. "Alligator Men and Cardsharpers in Deadly Southwestern Humor." *Huntington Library Quarterly* 49 (1986): 307–23.
Fienberg, Lorne. "Laughter as a Strategy of Containment in Southwestern Humor." *Studies in American Humor* 3 n.s. (1984): 107–22.
Gernes, Sonia. "Artists of Community: The Role of Storytellers in the Tales of the Southwest Humorists." *Journal of Popular Culture* 15 (1982): 114–28.
Gorn, Elliott J. "'Gouge and Bite, Pull Hair and Scratch': The Social Significance of Fighting in the Southern Backcountry." *American Historical Review* 90 (1985): 18–43.
Hauck, Richard Boyd. "'Let's Licker' Yarnspinning as Community Ritual." *American Humor: An Interdisciplinary Newsletter* 5 (1978): 5–10.
———. "Predicting a Native Literature: William T. Porter's First Issue of *The Spirit of the Times.*" *Mississippi Quarterly* 22 (1968–69): 77–84.
Inge, M. Thomas. "Literary Humor of the Old Southwest: A Brief Overview." *Louisiana Studies* 7 (1968): 132–43.
Ives, Sumner. "A Theory of Literary Dialect." *Tulane Studies in Literature* 2 (1950): 137–82.
MacKethan, Lucinda. "Southwestern Humor: The Beginning of Grit Lit." *Southern Spaces* March 1, 2004. http://www.southernspaces.org/contents/2004/mackethan/4a.htm

Oehlschlaeger, Fritz. "A Bibliography of Frontier Humor in the St. Louis *Daily Reveille,* 1844–1846." *Studies in American Humor* 3 (1984–1985): 267–89.

———. "A Bibliography of Frontier Humor in the St. Louis *Daily Reveille,* 1847–1850." *Studies in American Humor* 4 (1985–1986): 262–76.

Oriard, Michael. "Shifty in a New Country: Games in Southwestern Humor." *Southern Literary Journal* 12.1 (1980): 3–28.

Pearson, Michael. "Pig Eaters, Whores, and Cowophiles: The Comic Image in Southern Literature." *Studies in Popular Culture* 9 (1986): 1–10.

Penrod, James H. "The Folk Hero as Prankster in the Old Southwestern Yarns." *Kentucky Folklore Record* 2 (1956): 5–12.

———. "The Folk Mind in Early Southwestern Humor." *Tennessee Folklore Society Bulletin* 18 (1952): 49–54

———. "Folk Motifs in Old Southwestern Humor." *Southern Folklore Quarterly* 19 (1955): 117–24.

———. "Minority Groups in Old Southern Humor." *Southern Folklore Quarterly* 22 (1958): 121–28.

———. Women in Old Southwestern Yarns." *Kentucky Folklore Record* 1 (1955): 41–47.

Rickels, Milton. "Elements of Folk Humor in the Literature of the Old Southwest." *Thalia: Studies in Literary Humor* 4 (1981): 5–9.

———. "Inexpressibles in Southwestern Humor." *Studies in American Humor* 3 (1976): 76–83.

Schmitz, Neil. "Tall Tale, Tall Talk: Pursuing the Lie in Jacksonian Literature." *American Literature* 48 (1977): 471–91.

Shields, Johanna Nichol. "A Social History of Antebellum Alabama Writers." *Alabama Review* 42 (1989): 165–91.

Tilford, John E. "Literary Traditions in Southwest Humor: 1830–1860." *Emory University Quarterly* 4 (1948): 239–45.

Turner, Arlin. "Seeds of Literary Revolt in the Humor of the Old Southwest." *Louisiana Historical Quarterly* 39 (1956): 143–51.

Wonham, Henry. "Character Development of the Ring-Tailed Roarer in American Literature." *Southern Folklore* 46 (1989): 265–79

———. "In the Name of Wonder: The Emergence of Tall Narrative in American Writing." *American Quarterly* 41 (1989): 284–307.

Yates, Norris W. "Antebellum Southern Humor as a Vehicle of Class Expression." *Bulletin of the Central Mississippi Valley American Studies Association* 1 (1958): 1–6.

———. "'The Spirit of the Times': Its Early History and Some of Its Contributors." *Papers of the Bibliographical Society of America* 48 (1954): 117–48.

About the Editors

M. Thomas Inge (left) is Blackwell Professor of the Humanities, Randolph–Macon College, whose most recent books are *The Incredible Mr. Poe: Comic Book Adaptations of the Works of Edgar Allan Poe, 1943–2007* and *The New Encyclopedia of Southern Culture, Volume 9: Literature*. Ed Piacentino (right) is Professor of English, High Point University, and editor of *The Enduring Legacy of Old Southwest Humor* and *C. M. Haile's "Pardon Jones" Letters: Old Southwest Humor from Antebellum Louisiana*.

Photo by Jessica Robertson